THE ETHNIC CULTURES OF AMERICA

OTHER PUBLICATIONS BY P.R. FISCHETTI AND EDUCATIONAL EXTENSION SYSTEMS:

The World Calendar *

The Ethnic Cultures of America Calendar *

The Cultural and Festival Days of the World Poster *

The World Business Advisory and Calendar *

The Citizen Handbook

Religion and Ethnicity (Religion and Education; Religion and the Workplace)

* Revised and published annually.

THE ETHNIC CULTURES
OF AMERICA

A REFERENCE SOURCE FOR TEACHERS, LIBRARIANS,

ADMINISTRATORS AND HUMAN

RESOURCE DIRECTORS

P.R. FISCHETTI

EDUCATIONAL EXTENSION SYSTEMS
WASHINGTON, D.C.-WAYNESBORO, PENNSYLVANIA

Library of Congress Catalog Card Number 97-90005

ISBN 0-8108-4253-X

Printed in the United States of America

Edited by Debra Durocher

...MY DAUGHTERS, DAWN AND GAY, AND MY WIFE, JOAN.

TITLE CHANGE FROM

DATE 5/20/02   INITIALS

The ethnic cultures of America "reference book", reference source for all Americans"

TABLE OF CONTENTS

*   - See page 81-87
** - See page 218-224
*** - See page 135-137

ACKNOWLEDGMENTS

In compiling this book I relied on many different sources of information, and I wish to acknowledge each of them. My sources included the publications in 1980 and 1990 from the Bureau of the Census, not only for their statistical and graphical data but also for narratives the bureau published. I also would like to acknowledge my use of the publication *We the People* (Macmillan, 1988), compiled by James Paul Allen and Eugene James Turner, which derived much of its data from the 1980 Census. It contains much historical and introductory data on ethnic groups. *The Harvard Encyclopedia of American Ethnic Groups* (Harvard University Press, 1980) was most helpful in many topics, most importantly in supplying definitions concerning ethnicity and in offering historical data on the origins of certain ethnic groups. *Gale's Encyclopedia of Multicultural America* was also helpful in providing much needed information on small ethnic groups about which very little has been written. In addition, the two volumes helped enormously in verifying information on traditions and customs.

Because I wanted this book to come from a contemporary rather than historical perspective, much of the research over a seven-year period used news reports on ethnic groups. These valuable sources included articles in newspapers such as the *New York Times*, the *Washington Post* and others that have covered from time to time the activities of the United States' ethnic groups.

I also wish to acknowledge the Shap Working Party on World Religions in Education, a report on religious festivals published in August 1989 in London, England. Their statements and definitions should be valuable to educators or human resource directors when dealing with or teaching members of different religions or ethnic groups, as I hope this book will be.

I have tried to be accurate; I have also attempted not to be excessively detailed—or not detailed enough—on any particular ethnic group or religion. However, the data available on some topics precluded me from writing about all the groups to the same extent. A lack of information on some groups prevented me from being overly detailed about them; with other groups an abundance of information forced me to consolidate.

I am also thankful to the Balch Institute of Philadelphia for its many reference sources, one of which was its exhibition and booklet titled *Something Old, Something New: Ethnic Weddings in America*. The booklet was useful in compiling about different wedding customs. Other useful Balch sources included its booklets on crafts and communities. Also, my thanks go to the Association of Bridal Consultants in New Milford, Connecticut, for its information on the renewal and continuance of many ethnic wedding customs.

This reference book and its information should help teachers or professors at all levels; librarians, who might require ready sources of such information; administrators in all parts of the U.S. educational system; and human resource directors in corporate and government organizations.

I have tried to follow a systematic format in discussing each ethnic group, but for some groups certain data were unavailable. As in other studies on this subject many ethnic and religious groups in the United States are so obvious and pronounced that very little research was necessary. Some, however, came from nation-states unrelated to their ethnicity but are unquestionably distinctive in language and religious customs—groups such as Assyrians, Basques, Gypsies and Jews. In its report on this subject *The Harvard Encyclopedia* made some important statements about several groups and gave some definitions of them. For example, it referred to several groups as "Made in America," e.g. the Mormons, who originated entirely in the United States, and the Amish and Hutterites, who also have an American distinctiveness and cohesiveness that justifies such a classification. It also identified American regional groups such as Appalachians as "Made in America." Therefore, to equate "ethnic" with "foreign" can be a mistake. Some ethnic groups that were initially small have grown in recent years. Readers may wish to give them more attention and further inquiry.

The book does not include a category titled "American"; yet in the 1980 and 1990 Census many respondents to the question on ancestry responded "American." The figures for such a response in the 1980 Census were minimal—about 1 million. But the figures in the 1990 Census rose to about 12.4 million. What accounts for this? Some of this might be attributed to those who in 1980 responded "English" (more than 49.5 million). In 1990 only 32.6 million people responded as having "English" ancestry. The difference might be reflected in the figures representing "Americans." Most of the differences occurred in data from the Southern region of the United States. Most Americans (except in the case of American Indians, Eskimos and Aleuts, who came thousands of years ago) who are not immigrants have ancestors who came from outside the United States. Despite all our diversity, coming from other places is something Americans have in common.

This book is not about how to teach ethnic studies. It is a reference guide for those in education and industry who may be called upon from time to time to improve understanding of the cultures, customs, religions and traditions of those students and personnel in their charge. This book also is not a history of ethnic groups. It attempts to provide a base for a working knowledge of the many ancestral groups that make up the American mosaic. Do not expect a long discourse on each ethnic group. The book should serve as a resource in everyday working and teaching life. The book does not present one particular ethnic perspective but rather, if at all possible, tries to present an American viewpoint, as intrinsically diverse as that might be. Finally, this is not a book about theology, but by necessity the book addresses religion because of its close ties to the culture of many ethnic groups. Despite the various challenges in information gathering about such a wide array of ethnic groups, I tried to examine and obtain enough information on each of them to give various users some basic and pertinent information to use in everyday activities to better understand, teach or supervise Americans with different ethnic and cultural backgrounds.

A FEW INTRODUCTORY NOTES

This book, *The Ethnic Cultures of America,* compiles information about ethnic diversity, the people of the United States, more than 100 different ethnic groups, something about their cultures, traditions and religions, and more. It explains cultural practices that continue today and, for the most part, are respected by those who know about them. It will not answer all the intellectual questions posed on the subject. However, there are enough interesting data, stories and facts so that each teacher or director of human resources, for example, will have the knowledge and awareness of diverse ethnicities to use in his or her classroom or to address in training sessions. The book encompasses a large volume of information in a small package and in a practical way because teachers and human resource directors need a ready reference that enables them to impart lessons on these subjects celebrating the various differences among Americans as they together shape the country's cultural landscape in a way that makes sense.

In compiling, developing, researching and writing this book, I hope to bring about a new motivation for all Americans to learn and understand more about their own ancestral roots and about those of their neighbors, both near and far. The book can be used and displayed in classrooms, in offices, in libraries and in the homes of schoolchildren to inspire them to learn about the cultures of their parents, grandparents and great-grandparents, as well as of their friends and neighbors. I hope educators and human resource professionals will find the publication an easy-to-use educational aid to help students and employees develop an awareness of America's multicultural heritage.

SOME IMPORTANT POINTS TO BE AWARE OF WHEN USING THIS BOOK

A.) The dates given for Muslim holy days are only approximate because the precise time can be fixed only a few days before the actual event.

B.) All Jewish holy days commence at dusk on the evening before the dates given.

C.) Some religious traditions include observances and restrictions on holy days that may prohibit children from attending school and adults from working if they wish to adhere strictly to the customs.

D.) Sikhs and Buddhists are sometimes prepared to defer the celebration of significant feasts to the weekend closest to the actual event.

E.) Festivals and religious dates of some Asian festivals vary in date and custom. This might be attributed to the vastness of the Indian sub-continent. In particular, Buddhist festivals and holy days are difficult to summarize since in different countries in which large Buddhist communities are found, different traditions and festivals are observed.

F.) Because the U.S. Congress in 1980 decided that questions pertaining to religion could not be asked in the decennial Census, no exact data can be provided on the Jewish population in the United States. However, Jews are an ethnic group, as well as a religious group, and clearly have a sense of shared identity as a special people.

At times this book includes the phrase "movable date or dates" to describe religious and ethnic holidays of an ethnic group or religion, meaning that the holiday or festival date is not fixed on the Gregorian calendar, with which Americans are most familiar. The dates do not move, but the calendars upon which they are fixed are not calculated the same way as the Gregorian calendar. Remember, the Gregorian calendar, while used in the U.S., marks time's passage only in a small portion of the world's religions and cultures. Islamic, Buddhist and some African areas, for example, use other calendars.

Also notable is the fact that in many religions and cultures a month does not have to be thirty-one, thirty or, in February's case, twenty-eight or twenty-nine days—a month can mean as few as nineteen days. And some days do not start at midnight but rather at the sightings of new or full moons. Further, in many cultures and religions we are not in the twentieth century; according to the Islamic calendar we are in the fifteenth century, in the Chinese calendar we are in the forty-seventh and in the Byzantine calendar we are in the seventy-sixth.

ETHNIC TERMINOLOGY

Out of political necessity and for practical usage, terms to describe groups of people have been forced upon Americans that may change over time. And some already have. Though broad and generalizing terms such as Hispanic, Asian-American and Native American can be confusing, I have started certain sections of the book with them as umbrella groups. However, I do not condone their overuse, as they mask distinctions between separate and distinct groups. For example, if you equate the culture of a Filipino and a Japanese as the same under the Asian-American umbrella, you do a disservice to both. These cultures are not the same. Their customs and religions are different. Ninety percent of Filipinos are Catholic; less than 1 percent of Japanese are Catholic (91 percent are Buddhists). So, despite the broad categorical names sprinkled throughout the book, remember that those umbrellas are held up by diverse hands.

WHAT IS AN AMERICAN?

Ever since Europeans (and later Africans, Asians and Latin and South Americans) began to settle North America, the question of "What is an American?" has intrigued both native and foreign observers. As Mark Stolanik, former president of the Balch Institute, remarked in his group's newsletter in 1990, "Because so many ethnic groups have either come here, or have evolved in our midst, our society reflects the cultures of the rest of the world. On the other hand, the various ethnic cultures that exist in the United States are no longer the same as they were in their country of origin. Every ethnic group that has come here has abandoned certain cultural characteristics, borrowed others already found here, and preserved others that it considers to be vital to its identity." Although this book does not fully answer the question "What is an American?" it makes an attempt to do so, if only in part, because as long as newcomers continue to arrive at our shores, our culture will keep evolving. Perhaps this is what is so unique about the United States.

In a speech in the U.S. Senate, former Senator George J. Mitchell described this uniqueness[1] in a brief but elegant way: "Most nations derive from a single tribe or a single race. They practice a single religion. Common racial, ethnic and religious heritages are the glue of nationhood for many. The United States is different. We have all races, all religions, a limited common heritage. The glue of nationhood for us is the American ideal of individual liberty and equal justice. The rule of law is critical in our society. The law is the great equalizer, because in America everybody is equal before the law."

We can describe the United States and its people in many ways and try to explain their difference from other nations and people. I have tried to encapsulate what would be helpful to know when discussing this subject.

First we will take up the question "Who came to America?" The easiest answer is everyone, because every part of the world contributed someone to the United States. Writer Heidi Benson put it this way: "In a country of sometimes overwhelming diversity, there is one thing that most Americans have in common: A few generations ago, their families lived somewhere else."

Historians find it difficult to determine where people in the United States came from prior to 1820 because no accurate records exist from before that time. According to *The Harvard Encyclopedia of American Ethnic Groups*, records of immigration to the various colonies, to the extent that they exist at all, are uneven and spotty, and have yet to be systematically assembled and studied. The available estimates sometimes have been based on fragmentary sources or have been inferred retrospectively from later data. But, since around 1820, the U.S. has good records for the 50 million or so newcomers to the United States. Later we will discuss each of these groups.

Next we will address the question of why emigrants from near and far chose to come to the United States. In *The Ethnic Almanac* Stephanie Bernardo explained why by using the Italian proverb *"Chi sta bene non si munove"* ("He who is well off, doesn't move"). The three principal reasons why people came and continue to come to the United States are economic hardship, religious persecution and political oppression, according to Bernardo. She went on to explain that, for the most part, those who immigrated had survival on their minds.

Emma Lazarus, a poet, wrote the words that are engraved on a plaque inside the pedestal on the Statue of Liberty: "Give me your tired, your poor, your huddled masses yearning to breathe free. The wretched refuse of your teeming shore, send these, the homeless, tempest tossed to me; I lift my lamp beside the golden door." These words from Lazarus' sonnet "The Colossus" probably best describe the people who came or were sent to America. The immigrants were not likely professionals, nor the most literate or best-educated from the homelands, but rather those Lazarus described. This seems also to be true of the more recent immigrants of the 1970s through the 1990s. Despite the generally poor state of people wishing to emigrate from their homelands, most migration theories agree that although most early immigrants were poor, they were not hopeless, nor were they all unskilled. But all shared a common desire to get to a new land and the willingness to take huge risks once they got there.

The first impression and view of America for most immigrants at the turn of the century was the one they got at Ellis Island in New York Harbor. Between 1892 and 1924, more than 12 million people entered the United States through that gateway. On April 17, 1907, according to the *History of Ellis Island*, the day with the most immigrants ever processed there, 11,747 immigrants passed through Ellis Island. At one time it had thirty-three piers where immigrants disembarked from the boats that carried them across the Atlantic. One immigrant described arrival at Ellis Island as "the nearest likeness to the final day of judgment when we have to prove our fitness to enter heaven." For it was at Ellis Island that strangers decided the newcomers' fate, and decided who was entitled to stay and who would be barred or sent home to an uncertain fate.

Most immigrants came to the United States to find work and decent wages. Their labor fueled a booming economy, and, by 1910, three-quarters of the populations of New York, Chicago, Detroit, Cleveland and Boston were immigrants or children of immigrants. What did they find when they first set foot on American soil? "I came to America because I heard the streets were paved with gold," one Italian immigrant said. "When I got here I found out three things: first, the streets weren't paved with gold; second, they weren't paved at all; and third, I was expected to pave them." In 1995 more than 100 million Americans—40 percent of the population—were the ancestors of those who came through Ellis Island during those peak years.[2] They were different from those who had come many years before: They had the means to pay for the journey and the stamina to withstand it. Many manufacturers, mining companies and railroads employed various foreign nationals to recruit immigrants. Some received subsidies for their passage, and the transatlantic crossing cost as little as $15. Before 1780 many of the white immigrants who settled in New England (and elsewhere) were indentured servants, and almost all blacks were imported as slaves. In the first decade of the 20th century about four emigrants left the United States for every ten people who arrived; in the 1980s there were fewer than two emigrants leaving for every ten immigrants who arrived. The availability of benefits—economic, religious or psychological—may help to explain why the rates of migrants back to their countries are much lower than in decades past. Immigrants may not be coming to the United States for social welfare benefits, but they may be staying here because of them.[3]

WHAT IS AN ETHNIC GROUP?

Ethnicity, as outlined by *The Harvard Encyclopedia of American Ethnic Groups*, is an immensely complex phenomenon. All of the groups the encyclopedia describes are characterized by some of the following features, in varying combinations: (a) common geographic origin; (b) race; (c) language or dialect; (d) religious faith or faiths; (e) shared traditions, values or symbols; (f) literature, folklore or music; (g) an internal sense of distinctiveness; and (h) an external perception of distinctiveness. The degree to which each of these features characterizes any group varies considerably with the size and specific history of the group, especially according to the length of time its members have been in the United States. Ethnic groups persist over long periods, but they also change, merge and dissolve because of assimilation, intermarriage and the length of time away from their homeland.

ETHNIC IDENTIFICATION

Ethnic identification, even when ethnic heritage is unmixed or fully understood, is a matter of individual choice, from passive acquiescence to active participation, from denial to mild curiosity to passionate commitment. The fluid and situational nature of ethnicity makes precise estimates of the number of individuals with ancestry other than American Indian impossible.

New elements of diversity are constantly being added. The capacity of the United States to absorb so many different peoples and to forge binding ties among them is no less pervasive. The complex interplay between assimilation and pluralism is one of the central themes of American history, and it will continue to be long into the future. It is estimated that representatives from more than 150 ethnic groups live in the United States, according to 1990 Census data.

A NOTE ON RELIGION

The mingling of religion with ethnicity has been common, particularly in groups with a history of social competition and conflict with others. People such as Irish Catholics, French Canadians, Poles, Amish, Armenians and Greeks are ethno-religious groups. The Italian *festa* for a patron saint, the Jewish *bar mitzvah*, the Irish wake, the Methodist church supper, black gospel music, and peyotism of American Indians are only a few of the better-known examples of religion with a specifically ethnic cast. The promise of religious freedom in the United States accounts for many groups' ability to retain their customs and religions, many of which were closely interlinked. Religious freedom in the U.S. served as a magnet for groups who were persecuted in their homelands because of their religious beliefs—in fact, religious freedom was a big reason why the original thirteen colonies came to exist.

A WORD ABOUT PREJUDICE

No book on American ethnic groups should go without a section on the subject of prejudice. *Webster's Dictionary* defines "prejudice" as "an irrational attitude of hostility directed against an individual, a group, a race or their supposed characteristics, or injury or damage resulting from some judgment or action of another in disregard of one's rights." Prejudice is intangible: you can't see it, touch it, smell it, or find it in a package on a shelf or buy it in a store. But you can be sure you will recognize it or feel it when it is directed toward you. Because it is intangible, teachers have long been concerned with the difficulties and dilemmas they face trying to teach about the evils of prejudice and about human values, human relations, ethnic studies and cultural diversity. These are difficult subjects to teach, because a student's progress is difficult to measure and because there are so many variables. After all, teachers can't open up the hearts of students to see if 10 percent, or whatever percent, of their prejudices have been reduced since the last time they checked. Teachers don't know immediately if their teaching or instruction has been effective or absorbed. The results may not appear for a long time afterward, perhaps not even until students are well into their careers or vocations and have reached adulthood.

Compounding the problem and discussion is the fact that those who were born in the 1930s, raised in the '40s, educated in public schools and who then attended public universities in the '50s find it difficult to understand how Americans, as a people, have regressed to the point where the evils of prejudice must be taught. They are asking, "What happened to the generations that followed us?" Remember: those Americans who are in their twilight years survived the turmoil of World War II and saw all America's immigrants, first, second, third and fourth generations, grouped together to fight common enemies, at least one of which believed in a master race. Many felt that the victory over Adolf Hitler in World War II ended once and for all the theory that one nationality was better than another. We now know that for some the victory did not end this kind of shallow thinking.

Even American politicians—and presidents—have shown signs of their prejudices. One of the largest and biggest expressions of bigotry ever expressed by an American president occurred in 1930 when President Herbert Hoover responded to a criticism from Italian-born U.S. Representative Fiorello La Guardia of New York, who later became mayor, by telling him, "You should go back to where you belong and advise Mussolini on how to make good honest citizens in Italy. The Italians are predominantly our murderers and bootleggers ... like a lot of foreign spawn, you do not appreciate the country which supports and tolerates you."[4] It was an outrageous expression of bigotry against a man who, in addition to becoming a distinguished mayor of the largest and one of the most important cities in the country, had flown in the U.S. Air Force in World War I and who in World War II would play a major role in directing the national war effort. Did Hoover make La Guardia feel like an outsider? Probably not. Like many other talented immigrants from Eastern and Southern Europe, he found it easy to claim membership in the American civic culture because its ideals, symbols and principles did not require him to stop feeling Italian, something that Hoover forgot or did not recognize.

Some immigrants claimed an American identity even though they were fresh off the boat. They did not have to wait to be thoroughly assimilated before laying claim to their new homeland. Jerry Eastland and William Bennett in *Counting by Race: Equality From the Founding Fathers to Bakke and Weber*[5] quoted Lincoln when they asked what accounted for the fact that foreign-speaking and -acting newcomers felt a direct link to the Founding Fathers. Lincoln had already given the answer in 1860 when he pointed out that though immigrants could not claim ancestors who won the Revolution or founded the Republic, they "felt a part of us" because those who wrote the ideals expressed in the Declaration of Independence meant for what they wrote to apply to all people of all time. That is why the newcomers had the right to claim the men as forefathers "as though they were the blood of the blood and the flesh of the flesh of the men who wrote the Declaration."

Anyone could claim the universal American ideals and principles, as they could the symbols, rituals and heroes connected to those ideals.

The attachment immigrants feel both to their heritage and to their new home is sometimes manifest in the hyphenation of their ethnicities, whether they consider themselves Italian-American, Mexican-American or Swedish-American. Lawrence H. Fuchs, writing in *The American Kaleidoscope*, said that the hyphen and its use unite an old identity with a new one. An example he cited was of a Slovenian-born journalist, Louis Adamic, who said that the chemistry of the hyphen intensified affinity toward both identities. In his autobiography, *My America*, Adamic told of returning to the village in which he was born and being asked, "Do you consider yourself an American or a Slovenian?" Adamic answered swiftly that he considered himself to be an American, "not only legally and technically but actually." He added, "I sometimes think I am more American than a great many of them." He must have confused many of the villagers when he then remarked, "I am also a Slovenian ... and I would say I am an American of Slovenian birth; but, if you would like it better, you can consider me a Slovenian who went to America when he was not quite 15 and became an American. There is no conflict between my original Slovenian blood or background and my being an American." The hyphen triumphed not in defiance of Americanism but as an expression of it.

Of all the European groups, the Jews provided the sharpest refutation of those who argued that American identity was based on one kind of religion or culture. In the United States, Jews would build hospitals, orphanages, cemeteries, schools, fraternal societies and commercial institutions just as they had in Poland, Russia and other European countries. But there was a difference. For the first time in the history of their diaspora they experienced not mere toleration as a group but protection of equal rights as individuals.

Most African-Americans share an ethnic identity, forged almost entirely by their experience in the U.S. and nourished by the church, food, habit, black English, folk tales, music, gospel and blues singers and the common memory of survival in white America. For many years neither whites nor African-Americans acknowledged the ethnic character of the African-American experience. Both thought of blacks only in terms of race. Ethnicity seemed to imply continuing cultural history linked to pre-

American ancestors. It also usually implied positive, triumphant ancestral memories. Consequently, African-Americans had to forge their ethnic identity almost entirely out of their experience in the United States.[6]

In his book, *On Toleration*, Michael Walzer, a contemporary political philosopher, said: "'Toleration'" sounds minimalist—you 'tolerate' what you can't stand." That's its strength. Historically, its extraordinary to achieve, as Walzer puts it, "the peaceful coexistence of groups of people with different histories, cultures and identities." We forget what a big deal this is. "Toleration," he writes, "sustains life itself because persecution is often to the death." Toleration "also sustains common lives, the different communities in which we live." Walzer then offers this brilliant definition: "Toleration makes difference possible; difference makes toleration necessary."

Yet, by 1998 an ignorant bigotry seemed to some to be routinely practiced against evangelical Christians and Catholics at "polite" dinner parties, and "leading" universities and establishment drawing rooms." So wrote Michael Horowitz, in the *Washington Post* (May 10, 1998). This seems to me to be especially true among those older Americans who grew up in a culture and at a time when every important part of the social and economic fabric of our society revolved around them and their beliefs and prejudices. It is disconcerting to say that all the reeducation dealing with such thoughts hasn't changed all, especially older males who are now in the twilight of their lives. They continue to think life will be the same if they can belong to a club or organization that continues to practice these old "values." These "organizations," however, have continued to dwindle in our society, and the overwhelming majority of the children and grandchildren of these older citizens have found themselves feeling ashamed of the bigotry practiced by their parents and grandparents. Many of this older generation find themselves in a defensive posture and also the objects of ridicule. I would venture to say that many are now the victims of prejudice thought by the descendants of those who were offended by such people. I don't condone this practice because two *wrongs* do not make a *right*.

Many third-generation children of the ethnic immigrants, who are now well-educated, seem never to pass up an opportunity to remind some young Americans who may have come into money, inheritance or social position only by virtue of just simply "being there." The task of holding on to those possessions, however, is not an easy one. Banking, Wall Street, publishing, entertainment, athletics and sports management are just a few of the professions and occupations in which ethnic names, versus the traditional WASP names abound.

Another example is in politics. In 1999 the U.S. Senate had 11 members of Jewish ancestry when only 20 years earlier, in 1979, it would have been difficult to find more than 2 or 3. At one point in 1999, the Clinton administration's national security advisor, secretary of state, secretary of defense, secretary of the treasury, and administrator of the federal reserve system all could boast of Jewish ancestry. This was unheard of 20 years before when these positions were traditionally held by bastions of the old WASP aristocracy.

Sometimes, people never learn. In May of 1997, *The Washington Post* reported a story concerning a board of education in the state of South Carolina. A state board of education member talked about displaying the Ten Commandments in public schools. The member, Henry Jordan, a surgeon, had a ready suggestion for groups that might object to the proposal. He displayed the type of prejudice many of our citizens had thought extinguished, but it reared its ugly head when he said: "Screw the Buddhists and kill the Muslims." He made his remark during the board's finance and legislative committee meeting, and he finished by saying, "And put that in the minutes."

Later, the remarks were expunged from the written minutes but were recorded on tape. This board member wasn't finished yet, however, because he wanted to allow students to vote to display the commandments at their schools and he wanted to pay for it with private money. "What I want to do is promote Christianity as the only true religion," Jordan said. "This nation was founded to worship, honor and glorify Jesus Christ, not Mohammed, not Buddha."

This is the type of prejudice that must be identified, rooted out and eliminated in our national school system. Teachers and administrators must be on the alert for this bigotry and make immediate corrections.

SUBTLE RACISM—AN EXPLANATION OF BEHAVIOR

The Orlando, Florida, *Sentinel,* in a copyrighted story in 1996, told of Valerie Batts, a psychologist in Cambridge, Massachusetts, who gave a talk about "modern racist behavior"—the subtle racism of people who don't believe they harbor prejudices. She breaks down these behaviors into five categories:

- The myth of color blindness—denying the significance of cultural difference. Asserting that the issue is as simple as skin color ("We are all God's people, whether white, brown, yellow. . .).

- The "Chinese food" factor—minimizing the importance of political, economic and other distinctions in status. An example: Summing up your empathy for a group of people by saying, "I love Chinese food" or "I'm really into Latin music."

- Avoiding contact—having only friends who are your same race. This is a particular problem for whites, Batts says, because they may encounter few blacks in daily life, whereas blacks encounter whites constantly.

- Blaming victims of racism instead of the perpetrators. An example: an employer who blames the company's first minority employees for doing poorly instead of examining problems that caused the failures.

- Dysfunctional helping—offering "help" that's not needed or appropriate. An example: a teacher who shouts to make herself understood when speaking to Hispanic students.

While racism still existed in the late 1990s, it had declined dramatically. James Glassman of the *Washington Post,* commenting concerning changes in the last 40 years, said: "Americans should feel pride not shame." A Gallop poll in 1997 had the following to say about racism.

- In 1958 just 35 percent of whites said they "would be willing to vote for a black candidate for president. In 1997, 93 percent would. Amazingly, more whites than blacks (91 percent) say they would vote for a black.

- In 1958 some 44 percent of whites said they "would move if blacks moved next door." By 1997 it was 1 percent.

- In 1972 only 25 percent of whites said they "approved of marriage between blacks and whites." In 1997 the proportion was 61 percent.

- Also, Gallop concluded: "A majority of whites indicate a preference for living, working and sending their children to school in a mixed racial environment."

Society in the United States has been referred to as the American mosaic. As American columnist Thomas Sowell has noted, "the mixture of unity and diversity runs through American history as it runs through American society today. No ethnic group has been wholly unique, and yet no two are completely alike. So, like a piece of mosaic artwork, each person is considered an essential part of society." Somehow, we all fit together.

Immigrants to the United States have been people of courage, endurance and determination. They have faced ethnic, cultural, financial, educational, linguistic and social challenges when settling in their new country. Their belief in faith, freedom, family, work and country has strengthened life and culture in the United States.

In a 1986 speech to the American Jewish Committee, then-Secretary of Education William Bennett said that our diverse society functions because we share core values. Foremost is our belief in human dignity, that every person is entitled to be treated with equal respect. We believe in equality, that each person has the same rights and obligations. We believe in freedom of thought, of movement and of choice. We believe in justice, the right to be treated fairly under the law. Our core values are the glue that keeps our society together. It is the duty of each citizen to uphold these values.

As a result, Bennett said, there is a durable and resilient common culture to which most American men and women of all races, religions and backgrounds subscribe. And this American common culture is composed of three central elements.

First, there is the democratic ethic, which has its roots in the Declaration of Independence. It recognizes human equality and that all people are endowed by their Creator with unalienable rights. The democratic ethic emphasizes freedom, tolerance and respect for the rights of all. It also encourages everyone to develop to his or her potential.

The second component of our common culture is the work ethic, which emphasizes the virtues of industry and diligence, the passion for excellence and respect for personal effort, individual enterprise and plain old hard work. Professional and economic success in the United States tends to elicit respect rather than resentment and envy, and this has surely contributed to a healthy spirit of enterprise, and to politics focused on individual opportunities rather than on group conflict.

The third element of the United States' common culture is the Judeo-Christian ethic. This ethic provides the fundamental ideals that underlie our entire political and social system ... ideals such as respect for individual standards for individual behavior and a commitment to decency and to service to others. These ideals help to make the United States and its people a genuine community—and not merely a collection of self-centered individualists "looking out for Number 1."

This common culture is distinctive because it has not been manufactured by the upper stratum of society. It embodies truths that all Americans can recognize and examine for themselves. These truths are passed from generation to generation, transmitted in the family, in the classroom and in churches and synagogues. This common culture expresses itself in the attitudes, states of mind and the rarely articulated premises that influence our conduct as a people. The American literary critic Lionel Trilling

15

once wrote about the "moral imagination" of the United States. This moral imagination penetrates all aspects of our lives: politics, social affairs and our personal conduct. Trilling went on to say: "The moral imagination of most Americans is tolerant, but increasingly hostile to all manifestations of religious and racial bigotry."[7]

Two hundred years after the Founding Fathers ratified the Constitution, our common culture remains strong and healthy. It will remain so as long as its fundamental premises are passed on to succeeding generations. One of the vital instruments for the transmission of the common culture is our educational system. It is through our educational system that we sharpen our children's understanding of America, its history, and the opportunities and responsibilities of citizenship in a free and diverse society.

SOME OTHER THOUGHTS ABOUT COMMON CULTURE

Americans do not share a common ancestry or a common blood. What they have in common is a system of laws and beliefs that shaped the establishment of the United States.[8] American society will not survive without tolerance, and cultural tolerance comes to nothing without cultural understanding. But for a society to thrive, its members must not only tolerate one another, they must understand one another. The challenge facing America will be the shaping of a truly common public culture, one responsive to the long-silenced cultures of color and intolerance. To give up the idea of the United States as a plural nation would be to abandon the experiment that America represents, which is too high a price to pay.[9] Our country is far from over in its development. It is a society that is forever evolving, and changes occur in rapid succession. Alexander Hamilton said it best, perhaps, when he wrote: "Let us remember: America is an experiment, which the whole world is watching, to see whether a society can be based on the principle of freedom rather than fear."

According to historian and politician Daniel Patrick Moynihan,[10] there were just eight nation-states that existed between 1914 and 1995 that did not have their form of government changed by violence during that time. These countries are the United Kingdom, four present or former members of the Commonwealth, Sweden, Switzerland and the United States. For the majority of the remainder of nation-states "the most frequent factor" explaining violent change, Moynihan said, was ethnic conflict.

In 1993, for example, ethnic wars, violence and conflict were ongoing in forty-eight nations around the globe, according to *The New York Times*.[11] The United States, notably, was not part of that group.

A powerful cohesive force makes the United States a "nation of nations" that restores luster to the motto on the seal of the United States: "*E Pluribus Unum*." In 1792, when the motto was adopted, it referred to the union built up from thirteen separate colonies; subsequently, it has come to suggest the ties that bind the remarkable array of diverse peoples who have settled here. Historian Philip Gleason of Notre Dame, in an essay on American identity in the *Harvard Encyclopedia* about American identity and Americanization, stated:

> An American nationality does in fact exist.... To affirm the existence of American nationality does not mean that all Americans are exactly alike or must become uniform in order to be real Americans. It simply means that a genuine national community does exist and that it has its own distinctive principle of unity, its own history, and its own appropriate sense of belonging.

Milton Gorden of the University of Massachusetts has further defined ethnicity as "a sense of peoplehood." All tendencies to underscore Americanism and national unity were massively reinforced by the entry of the United States in World War II. It is noteworthy to repeat an earlier statement—we were still a nation of immigrants, most of whom arrived here voluntarily. "In a country of sometimes overwhelming diversity, there is one thing most Americans have in common: A few generations ago, their families lived somewhere else," said writer Heidi Benson.

MULTICULTURALISM

Your school system may have adopted a multicultural curriculum. "Multiculturalism" has many shades of meaning. Sometimes terms such as "Eurocentric" or "Afrocentric" are used within the context of a multicultural curriculum. How people organize multiculturalism is up to them, depending on where they live, where they are from, and who they are. But what matters most is that what they teach is based upon accurate data and sound research. The United States has always been a multicultural society with a variety of public, private and religious school systems. The key question is: How are schools dealing with the fact that the United States is becoming more aware of its ethnic, cultural and linguistic diversity, and how, then, do you teach students to respect and honor those of different beliefs, customs and experiences?

In schools, at work and at home, advances in technology have changed the world and made neighbors of us all. Some of the changes have caused Americans to think and rethink some of the images and opinions they held of various people of the world. We are now making discoveries about our global neighbors. But besides keeping up with technological change, Americans need to keep pace with religious, social, economic and cultural evolution. One means of making the U.S., and the world, more affable to the idea of unity is education. And that education must not be only in schools—individuals must take it upon themselves to familiarize themselves with the differences that should enhance society, rather than split it.

Yes, the United States does have some lingering ethnic and racial prejudice, but tolerance for such prejudice is rapidly disappearing neighbor by neighbor, handshake by handshake, smile by smile. It is the job of all of us to work to eradicate the last residue of it in our society for the harmony amid diversity for generations to come.

IMMIGRATION

Stanley Karnow, writing in the *New York Times,* summarized the issue of immigrants in the United States in the following statement:

For a nation of immigrants, America throughout its history has been peculiarly schizoid on the question of immigration. Ben Franklin fulminated against the German influx in Pennsylvania, the Know-Nothing Party accused the Irish of promoting papist plots, and the Chinese Exclusion Act of 1882 sparked a series of egregiously racist statutes designed to keep Asians out of the country. By 1999, in contrast, the Poles who worked in the Pittsburgh steel mills are exalted as industrial heroes, the Jewish scientists responsible for nuclear energy have been deified, and a renovated Ellis Island is currently a shrine to the "huddled masses."

As the millennium approached, this debate continues. Some people (the restrictionists) seek to scrap the key provisions of the 1965 Immigration Reform Act, which drastically liberalized earlier statutes and over the past three decades has opened the door to hundreds of thousands—most of them Hispanics, Africans, Caribbeans and Asians. Some chauvinists maintained that immigrants were stealing jobs from native-born labor, clogging the welfare rolls and inflicting costly bilingual classes on schools.

In the book, *The Other Americans; How Immigrants Renew Our Country, Our Economy, and Our Values,* Joel Millman, a reporter by trade, illustrates how the case against immigrants is flimsy. He points out, and I agree, that by nature the overwhelming majority of immigrants are a superior breed. Knowing they face adjustment problems in a strange and frequently hostile environment, they are nevertheless ready to leave their homelands in hopes of improving their lives. And, while they often encounter difficulties, on the whole they contribute significantly to the American economy as entrepreneurs, technicians, craftsmen, farmers and unskilled workers. Their crime rate is remarkably low, and, contrary to allegations that they are a fiscal burden, they generate more tax revenues than they take in services. New York City, for example, owes a good portion of its revival in the 1990s to their presence. Going into derelict ghettos, they refurbished crumbling buildings and created middle-class neighborhoods. Millman points out that their achievements hinge on a trait ideally prized by Americans: devotion to family.

At the end of the twentieth century, New York City was soaking up immigrants at nearly the same torrid pace as at the beginning of the century. And the city is and was thriving, in large measure because hundreds of thousands of these new New Yorkers were reenacting grandpa's elbow-grease story. Instead of Italians, it is Dominicans. Instead of Irish it is Mexicans. Instead of Russians and Poles, it is a new generation of Russians and Poles. Each year in the decade of the 90s, the city absorbed 113,000 or so newcomers, many of them with both education and drive.

In 1920, just after the crest of America's greatest wave of immigration, 40 percent of New Yorkers were foreign born. That fell to 18 percent in the 1970s, a decade in which the city lost 10 percent of its population as it skidded into a bleak era of near-bankruptcy, crime and abandoned housing. By the end of the 1990s decade, about a third of New Yorkers were foreign born, with another 20 percent the offspring of new immigrants. Also by that time, the population was holding steady; there was hardly an empty apartment; and the economy was stronger than it had been in 10 decades.

It was felt that immigrants, quite literally, saved the homes of those who fled the city. A Dominican immigrant put it quite well when he said: "We come here with a focus. We didn't have a welfare system where we were born. Some New Yorkers knew the system and how to use it. Since we don't know, we have to work."

SOME NOTABLE VIEWS AND THOUGHTS ABOUT IMMIGRANTS

Ken Rangle, *Washington Post,* October 23, 1997, wrote:

The G.I. Bill of Rights of World War II gave us the resulting democratization of education which broke down the traditional walls that had separated the nation's huge pool of urban immigrants and their children from the mainstream of American society. Italians could be more than restauranteurs and sanitation workers, Irish more than policemen and politicians, Jews more than clerks and garment workers and blacks would receive their first massive and truly educational opportunity.

George Will, noted American writer, wrote in 1997:

> One argument against a welcoming immigration policy is this: That such a policy was fine a century ago, but it is incompatible with today's welfare state, which acts as a magnet for persons immigrating in search of comfortable dependency. A second argument is that in the 1990's, unlike the 1890's, a significant portion of American intelligentsia does not much like America. This portion's ambivalence about America is expressed in the ideology of multiculturalism. It is the doctrine that a common culture is "oppressive" and that Americans should be disaggregated into groups, each cultivating its cultural distinctives, resisting assimilation in the name of "diversity."
>
> The weakness of the first argument is that there is scant evidence of a "magnet effect" of the welfare state. The vast majority of immigrants are motivated by a desire to participate in, not be parasites on, the American economy. And they believe that the sooner their children learn English, the better the children will be at participating. Regarding the second argument, the support of Latinos for an initiative to halt compulsory bilingual education is a powerful refutation of the fear that immigrants accept the diversity argument by which anti-American Americans advance their agenda of Balkinization.

We are a nation of immigrants. Except for American Indians, all of our families came from some other country. We came for a variety of reasons: religious and political persecution, famine, economic hardship, the lure of the American dream. The American dream did not materialize instantly for those who came before us. Some of our families experienced deep animosity and prejudice as they tried to settle down in a new country. "Irish need not apply" signs were common. Italians and other southern and eastern Europeans were unwanted. Many of our families started at the lowest socio-economic rung and climbed their way upward slowly and painfully.

But today we seem to have forgotten all that. As a nation, we're behaving a lot like the so-called "nativists" who made many of our ancestors feel so unwelcome. Regrettably, the anti-immigrant wave sweeping the country in the late 1990s has found expression in the provisions of the new federal immigration law now beginning to take effect.

In an era when many people talk about family values, the new immigration laws in the 1990s threatened to separate families. Under that law, there could be cases when one spouse will be allowed to stay in this country while the other will be forced to return to an uncertain future in his or her country of origin. Their children, born in this country, could thus be deprived of the most important social benefit of all: an intact family.

James Cardinal Hickey, Archbishop of Washington, DC, in April 1997, writing in the *Catholic Standard,* stated: "Many of those targeted by that new law are Catholics. I wish I could report that every member of the Catholic community is free of the anti-immigrant prejudices so common in this era of political correctness. But I can't make that report. Far too many Catholics, forgetful of their own past, blindly assume that our newly arrived immigrants are lazy, incompetent, unwilling to learn, and are a drain on our booming economy. They've never seen men and women struggling to learn English in adult education centers. They've never talked to the many immigrants who work long hours, often under difficult circumstances, just to secure the bare essentials. They've never listened to the anxious young couples worried about their own future and that of their children. If they did, they'd know better."

GREGORY RODRIGUEZ, A fellow at the New American Foundation has made a detailed study on immigrant assimilation. He reported the following:

That today's immigrants are embracing U.S. life much the same way previous newcomers have always done. Throughout U.S. history, each new wave of immigrants has inspired debate. Although earlier immigrants were ultimately absorbed into the mainstream, each new generation of nativists found some characteristic or other that they claimed would prevent the contemporary newcomers from ever fully fitting in.

In the eighteenth century, Ben Franklin had misgivings about German clannishness and unwillingness to mix with outsiders. A century later, some worried that Irish Catholics would not only resent becoming part of a predominantly Protestant society, but also would serve as agents for the papacy. In the late nineteenth and early twentieth centuries, the presumed "racial" foreignness of eastern and southern European immigrants, as well as newcomers from East Asia, heightened concerns about their prospects for integrating into American life. With their severe disadvantages of limited education and high levels of poverty, they seemed destined to become permanent denizens of ethnically separated communities.

Contemporary arguments about today's immigrants tend to be a motley blend of these assertions and misconceptions. The ugliest brand comes from racialists who argue that nonwhite immigrants can never assimilate in what is at core a "white country." The more common complaint, though, focuses on the tendency of many immigrants to congregate with each other after arriving in the United States.

Latin American immigrants, who have forged sizeable enclaves in several U.S. cities, are of particular concern to modern-day nativists also because of their continued use of the Spanish language.

Throughout American history, newly arrived immigrants have clustered in specific cities and states. During the first two decades of the twentieth century, immigrants composed absolute majorities of the country's urban population. Italian and Irish immigrants clustered in the northeastern corridor. Norwegians, Finns, Danes and Germans created their own enclaves in the Midwest. Polish immigrants transformed Chicago into the second largest Polish city in the world. Japanese gathered in Los Angeles and Honolulu, while Jewish immigrants were once overwhelmingly located in New York.

The newcomers who settled together rarely discarded the language, symbols and tastes of their countries of birth upon arriving in the United States. Now, as then, these communities help immigrants adapt by mitigating the cultural shock of migration and providing crucial networks of jobs and information. Rather than being a harbinger of permanent self-segregation, these enclaves represent way stations where newcomers can gain a foothold in their new country.

Immigrants often retain some characteristics and loyalties from the old country-whether in the form of worship, food, or holidays-for generations to come. Indeed, even as they enter the mainstream, larger immigrant groups have always put their imprints on American culture. U.S. culture is constantly changing and adapting to immigrants just as immigrants adapt to it. Customs or foods that were once foreign became part and parcel of local tradition—bagels and Yiddish phrases in New York, bratwurst and beer in Milwaukee, and everything green in Boston, Italian pizza throughout American has become part of every child's diet and eating habits. Immigration patterns are also what make the typical Minnesotan (of Swedish origin) look and speak differently from the typical Pennsylvanian (whose roots are German). In places like California, Texas and Florida, today's immigrants are weaving many of their customs into the mainstream.

Assimilation is a long-term process, sometimes taking several generations.

Indeed, census data continue to prove unequivocally what common sense dictates: that the longer immigrants remain in the United States, the more likely they are to acquire English.

The idea that non-English-speaking clusters remain over generations is simply untrue. In 1990, more than 90 percent of second-generation Asian and Latino children reported speaking English proficiently or exclusively. Indeed by the third generation, 85 percent of Asian children spoke only English. In most families, after three generations in the United States, Spanish begins to disappear altogether. In 1990, fully two-thirds of third generation U.S. Latino children spoke no Spanish at all.

The majority of immigrants do become U.S. citizens within *25* years of residence in the United States. And those who are here the same number of years *(25)* actually buy their own homes at a higher rate than the native-born population.

For all the symbolic value that citizenship carries, there is no more profound indicator of social integration than intermarriage. It is not only a sign that a person has transcended the ethnic self-segregation of the first years of immigration, it illustrates the extent to which ethnicity no longer serves to separate one American from another.

After a generation or two of living in the United States, both Asians and Latinos, the two ethnic groups that make up the lion's share of contemporary immigrants, choose spouses of other ethnicities at extraordinary high rates. As the census data show, fully one-third of third-generation Hispanic women marry non-Hispanics and the rate is even higher (42%) for Asian-American women.

In addition to how immigrants affect the United States, particularly in economic terms, they are also a collection of uprooted individuals trying to adjust to what are often radically different conditions in their new country. They are drawn by the promise of the economically most dominant nation in history, whose culture and influence permeate the globe.

WHAT IT TAKES TO REMAIN THE INDISPENSABLE NATION

Excerpts from 2nd inaugural address by William Jefferson Clinton, January 20, 1997.

In the end, more than anything else, our world leadership grows out of the power of our example here at home, out of our ability to remain strong as one America.

All over the world, people are being torn asunder by racial, ethnic and religious conflicts that fuel fanaticism and terror. And the world looks to us to show that it is possible to live and advance together across those kinds of differences.

America has always been a nation of immigrants. From the start, a steady stream of people, in search of freedom and opportunity, have left their own lands to make this land their home. We started as an experiment in democracy fueled by Europeans. We have grown into an experiment in democratic diversity fueled by openness and promise.

My fellow Americans, we must never believe that diversity is a weakness—it is our greatest strength. Americans speak every language, know every country. People on every continent can look to us and see the reflection of their own greatness, as long as we give all of our citizens, whatever their background, an opportunity to achieve their greatness.

We are not there yet. We still see evidence of abiding bigotry and intolerance, in ugly words and awful violence, in burned churches and bombed buildings. We must fight against this, in our country and in our hearts. For no matter what our differences—in our faiths, our backgrounds, our politics—we must all be repairers of any breach. We may not share a common past, but surely we share a common future.

America is more than a place. It is an idea, the most powerful idea in the history of nations.

Nathan Glazer, professor emeritus in sociology at Harvard University, wrote in April 1995:

It is true that Irish Catholics were looked upon as unassimilable 150 years ago, Jews and Italians and Slavic peoples were considered so in the 1910s and all are now indistinguishable in their integration into a common American society and culture from the oldest settlers. What then do we have to fear from an immigration that is indeed 90 percent or more non-European, but of peoples no more different or foreign in culture, language, religion or hopes than earlier streams of immigrants?

In the debate on immigration, we will all have to keep our heads and remember we all came from someplace else.

In 1958 immigration was at historically low levels, and the vast majority of immigrants were white Europeans. By 1998, 40 years later, we had record high immigration, and the vast majority of immigrants were "of color." The top six sending countries in 1999 were Mexico, the Philippines, Vietnam, the Dominican Republic, China and India, with immigrants from these countries accounting for more than a third of the flow.

Immigration history shows that racial categories are not fixed and unchangeable. Groups once considered "nonwhite"—the Irish in the nineteenth century and southern and eastern Europeans in the twentieth—later crossed the color line. Other diverse immigrant groups such as Chinese, Filipinos and Indians are fitted into a racial category labeled Asian. These complications only underscore the fact that the concept of "race" in America is not, and can no longer be, a black and white discussion.

A statement by the Joint National Committee of Languages sums up these thoughts best: The United States is a nation to whose shores have come peoples from every continent, and history records their priceless contributions. From the beginning, the quality of life has been ennobled and enriched by them, and city and village streets have resounded with the music of many languages. It is a rich heritage, one to be nurtured, encouraged, cherished.

- *Beyond the Melting Pot: The Negroes, Puerto Ricans, Jews, Italians and Irish of New York City* by Nathan Glazer and Daniel Patrick Moynihan. (MIT Press, 1963) is a classic study that refutes the old myth that Americans will assimilate so thoroughly that they will eventually be indistinguishable from each other.

- Related works include *The Rise of the Unmeltable Ethnics* by Michael Novak (Macmillan, 1972) and *On Becoming American* by Ted Morgan (Houghton Mifflin, 1978).

- *Coming to America: A History of Immigration and Ethnicity in American Life* by Roger Daniels (Harper and Row, 1990) provides a useful and unemotional overview of immigration and how it has evolved. Also useful: *A Nation of Strangers: Prejudice, Politics and the Populating of America* by Ellis Cose (Moscow, 1992) .

- *Structuring Diversity: Ethnographic Perspectives on the New Immigration* edited by Louise Lamphere (University of Chicago Press, 1992) offers compelling, if somewhat detached, case studies of several of the new immigrant groups.

- *The Immigration Time-Bomb: The Fragmenting of America* by Richard Lamm and Gary Imhoff (Dutton, 1985) is one of several restrictionist books stating that increased immigration is creating a new underclass and threatening a population explosion.

- *Fresh Blood: The New American Immigrants* by Sanford Unger (American University, 1996).

- *Americans No More* by Georgie Ann Geyer (Atlantic Monthly Press, 1996). Geyer's central argument is that present-day immigrants are often unassimilatable and that demagogic leaders might use them to shred American society.

- *The Coming White Minority: California's Eruptions and the Nation's Future* (Time Books, 1996).

- *Immigrants Out: The New Nativism and the Anti-Immigrant Impulse in the United States* edited by Juan F. Perea (New York University Press, 1996).

- *.Assimilation, American Style* by Peter D. Salins (Basic Books, 1997) is hostile to both centrifugal multiculturalism and sour nativism. Salins suggests that immigration has worked in our past because immigrants have willingly conformed to American norms. These have included the acceptance of English, the "American Idea" of civic participation and personal freedom, and the Protestant ethic of individualistic self-responsibility. These are the characteristics of "assimilation, American style" that he feels are failing.

* This listing of books and commentaries is taken from the book reviews of Edward Countryman, professor in the Clements Department of History at Southern Methodist University and author of *Americans: A Collision of Histories,* and Sanford J. Unger, Dean of the School of Communication at American University.]

[1] The speech was given July 13, 1989.

[2] *The History of Ellis Island*

[3] Peter Skerry, Brookings Institute Fellow in Governmental Studies, the *Washington Post*, October 1996

[4] E.D. Baltzell, *The Protestant Establishment: Aristocracy and Caste in America* , New York Vintage Books

[5] New York Basic Books, 1979

[6] Laurence H. Fuchs, *The American Kaleidoscope: Race, Ethnicity, and the Civic Culture*

[7] William Bennett

[8] Donald Kagan of Yale University

[9] Henry Louis Gates of Harvard University

[10] *Pandaemonium*

[11] February 7, 1993

CHAPTER I:

FROM NORTHWESTERN EUROPE CAME AMERICANS OF BELGIAN, DUTCH, FRENCH, FRENCH HUGUENOT AND GERMAN ANCESTRY

As of the 1990 Census, 380,000 people in the United States were of Belgian ancestry. The people who came to the United States from Belgium represented both ethnic groups from their homelands: the Flemings in north Belgium, who spoke Flemish (related to Dutch and German), and the Walloons from southern Belgium, who spoke French. In the United States, as in Belgium, they lived in separate areas, but, as time passed, most called themselves Belgian rather than Flemish or Walloon.

Those who came to the United States tended to settle in the Midwest, particularly in Wisconsin and Illinois. They were predominantly Catholic.

The early nineteenth-century Belgian immigrants were farmers. After both world wars the Belgians emigrating to the United States were mostly middle class and urban professionals. As many groups before them, they came for economic opportunities and in hope of improving their lives. Between 1820 and 1970 about 200,000 people emigrated to the United States from Belgium.

HOLIDAYS AND CUSTOMS

Most Belgians celebrate traditional **Christian** holidays:

St. Nicholas Day—December 6—This marks the beginning of the Christmas season.

Rogation Day ("rogation" from the Latin verb meaning to ask)—May 31—the tradition calls for people to gather and to ask the Virgin Mary for her blessing on their plants and gardens. In the Catholic Church calendar, it is celebrated to commemorate Mary's visit to her cousin Elizabeth.

The 1990 Census showed 6,227,000 people in the United States of Dutch ancestry. The Dutch appeared in the United States in the early 1600s as they established a settlement called New Netherlands, which included New York City and the lower Hudson River Valley. Later, many of them moved slightly south to New Jersey. Others moved to the Midwest to farm or to become manufacturers; in fact, in 1995, Michigan had more people of Dutch ancestry than any other state.

Just a couple of hours from Chicago is Holland, Michigan. Back in 1847, a group of Dutch immigrants seeking religious freedom settled in the western part of the state. In 1997, the descendants of these immigrants in Holland and other local communities celebrated the town's sesquicentennial. The summer was filled with special events which were highlighted by the royal visit of HRH Princess Margriet of The Netherlands.

The residents have created many Dutch customs such as a replica of a Dutch village on an island filled with canals and tulip gardens. There is also a 200-year-old operating windmill, which is the last windmill Dutch officials allowed to move out of their country.

The 1990 Census reported that the Michigan counties of Allegan, Kent and Ottawa had the largest concentration of Americans of Dutch ancestry. Ottawa County, for example, had one-third of its population calling themselves Dutch.

Dutch immigration during the twentieth century was much slower.

World War I was the turning point in the acculturation of Dutch-Americans. Immigrant leaders encouraged the Americanization movement in their churches and schools. As a result, between World War I and World War II the Dutch-language preaching virtually disappeared, as did most Dutch newspapers and periodicals.

Some early Dutch immigrants may have been prompted to come to the United States for religious reasons, but economic reasons were the motivating factors for most of those heading for America. The great majority of Dutch immigrants were members of the Dutch Reformed Church.[1]

The Dutch immigrants who arrived later (in the mid nineteenth century) settled as most immigrants do—where members of the colonial Dutch community were still living. In the Dutch case that meant near Eastern cities. Many went to upstate New York, near and around Rochester and over into New Jersey into the factory towns of Paterson and Passaic. In 1880 it was reported[2] that Paterson had more Dutch-born people than any other American city. A hundred years later there remained over 10,000 people of Dutch ancestry in Passaic County. Counties along the shores of the Hudson River probably include people of Dutch ancestry who in the latter part of the twentieth century still had roots going back to the colonial era.[3]

Although the religion of the Netherlands was approximately one-third Catholic, only about 20 percent of the Dutch who emigrated to the United States were Catholic; most were Protestant, either Dutch Calvinist, Dutch Reformed or Christian Reformed; and some were Dutch Jews. But the largest group was the Calvinists.

Many of the people of Dutch ancestry in the United States who have left their original regions have assimilated so much they can no longer flourish nationally on ethnic exclusivity.

One thing to keep in mind is that Dutch immigrants are not the same as the "Pennsylvania Dutch." Americans of Dutch ancestry came from the Netherlands, while Pennsylvania Dutch are of *Deutsche*, or German, ancestry. The words "Dutch" and *"Deutsche"* sound so similar that they became mistakenly interchanged.

In an article on July 16, 1995, Peter Kilborn wrote in the *New York Times:* "More than three centuries after the Dutch settled the city that became New York, and a century after the peak of European immigration, scores of Dutch men have fled the crowded green pastures of the Netherlands for the oak-dappled ranges of North Central Texas and a land that for them can still open doors to riches and opportunity. These Dutch men have reinvented the state of the Texas dairy industry."

Since the late 1970s, Dutch immigrant dairymen—along with second-generation Dutch-American dairymen whose parents settled in California and Washington State—have been moving into a 100-square mile area around Stephenville, little more than an hour's drive southwest of Fort Worth. Other Dutch immigrants have settled east of Dallas around Sulphur Springs. These Dutch now own most of the newest, most efficient and biggest farms. They have brought Texas from next to nowhere in milk production to sixth in the nation.

As with immigrants in the past, the influx of Dutch dairy farmers has stirred some uneasiness among local folks. Merchants call them tightwads who invest freely in milking and processing gear but little in homes and good living. However, for the most part, the Dutch have been accepted.

Few of these recent Dutch immigrants are impoverished huddled masses yearning for freedom. They grew up on farms in the lowlands of the Netherlands and yearned to follow their fathers into the dairy business. But surpluses of milk in Europe have led to quotas to reduce production. The cost of land in the Netherlands is also substantial, leading to a stifling of initiative and opportunity. Getting started in Texas strikes the Dutch as a good deal.

The Dutch immigrants seem to acclimate easily to the local culture, donning boots and cowboy hats, buying second-hand pickups, drinking American beer and insisting that their children speak English at home. Still, some work in wooden shoes, and the single men—the majority of newcomers—tend to marry the second-generation daughters of Dutch dairymen. Most belong to the Christian Reformed Church, a conservative cousin of the Dutch Reformed Church.

HOLIDAYS AND CUSTOMS

Dutch-Americans generally celebrate the holidays that are associated with their respective religions or affiliations (**Christian and Jewish**). See section on religious holidays.

Other days of note for the Dutch include:

St. Nicholas Day—December 6—for exchanging gifts.

Tulip Festival—in mid-May—celebrated in Holland, Michigan with big parades and a festival.

The total number of Americans of French ancestry in 1990 was 12,550,000. Less than 40 percent of this ancestry emigrated from France, with the majority having come from French-speaking Canada. There were several groups that identified themselves as French. The largest of these groups are of French-Canadian origin rather than direct immigrants from France. People in the U.S. of French ancestry continue to be predominantly Roman Catholic but were originally of different cultural groups and have had different approaches for assimilation into English-speaking society. The immigrants and their descendants from France assimilated more rapidly into American society than those from French Canada.

The French people, in the United States mostly from Canada, were the earliest white settlers in what is today the central United States. They first came as soldiers and fur traders and priests. By 1790 the largest French settlements had moved farther south, into New Orleans. Those who are sometimes called French and other times referred to as Cajuns came from an area in Maritime Canada called Acadia (today the province of Nova Scotia). They were different from the large and main French settlements in Quebec in that, although they had French origins, they wished to remain independent— they claimed allegiance neither to French nor to Great Britain.[4] In 1735 a small group of Acadian Cajuns arrived in Louisiana. They became small farmers along the levees and bayous of the Gulf Coastal Plain in Louisiana. (See section on Cajuns.)

Another immigrant group associated with French ancestry and the French language is the Creoles. Originally from the French colony of St. Dominique and other Caribbean islands, they were often descendants of white plantation owners, their slaves and free blacks. Creole whites migrated mostly to New Orleans, and racially mixed or black Creoles moved to smaller counties in Louisiana. (See section on Creoles.) There is also what some refer to as French Louisiana, which is made up of Franco-Americans whose culture is partly but distinctively derived from France. The area that's considered to be French Louisiana, outside New Orleans and other cities, is the predominantly French part of the state and is composed of "societies," most of whose cultures were partially but distantly derived from France. This was further pointed out in the 1980 Census, when only an estimated 7,700 people in Louisiana listed either Acadian or Cajun as "single ancestry." This was less than 2 percent of the number identifying as French. This makes for some confusion in the understanding of French ancestry in the United States.[5]

In the United States' 1980 Census, the largest group to identify themselves as of French ancestry were French Canadians, who migrated to the United States from Quebec and Nova Scotia. Although many went to the Midwest, large concentrations of French-Canadians settled in New England, northern New York and, in particular, Vermont, Maine and New Hampshire because of the states' proximity to their homelands of Quebec and Nova Scotia. It has been estimated that as much as 18 percent of the population of New Hampshire speaks French as a first language.[6]

The term "Franco-American" generally described Americans of French-Canadian ancestry and, to a small degree, Americans of French ancestry. French-Canadian emigration to the United States occurred mostly from Quebec and the Maritime Provinces. The people of these two different immigrations came from different cultural traditions, not to identify with each other.

Franco-Americans are found in every state. The largest concentration and the highest density, though, is found in the Northeast, where 22 percent of the United States' Franco-Americans live.

According to Census data, the states with the highest percentage of Franco-Americans as compared to the total state population are:

Vermont-37.6 percent

New Hampshire-35 percent

Maine-31.1 percent

Louisiana-28.9 percent

Rhode Island-24.1 percent

Massachusetts-18.9 percent

Connecticut-13.4 percent

Michigan-11.7 percent

In 1775, British forces started the deportation of the Acadians from Nova Scotia, scattering the "French neutrals" all over the East Coast and beyond. While joining millions of immigrants from throughout the world in this new land of opportunity, the French-Canadians were also returning to a land either discovered or first explored by their forefathers. Unlike most immigrant groups, the French-Canadians have no ocean to cross to get to the United States, and most Franco-American communities are less than a day's journey from their mother country.

By the turn of the century, Franco-American communities, with their institutions and independent cultural life, have developed into large enclaves in almost every manufacturing city in New England. In 1900, for example, Fall River, Massachusetts, had become the third-largest French-speaking city in North America, after Montreal and Quebec. By 1930, New England's Franco-Americans had built and were maintaining close to 250 private institutions of learning, from kindergarten to college, that were attended by 90,000 young Franco-Americans.

In 1937, to renew ties with their roots, 4,000 Franco-Americans traveled to Quebec City to take part in the Second Congress on the French language. This event led to the establishment of permanent ties among all of the French-speaking communities on the continent, and, to this day, Franco-Americans are included in a number of international organizations dealing with the French presence in North America.

From the start, Franco-Americans have provided the labor backbone in key sectors of the economy of New England: farming, lumbering, textile, shoe and other light manufacturing. They have also generously contributed their sons and daughters to the religious life and to the professions.

Many French and French-Canadian traditions were revived in the 1970s and 1980s. The religion of French-Canadian immigrants to the U.S. is staunchly **Roman Catholic**. See section on Catholic holidays.

Bastille Day—July 14—Celebrated with many festivities especially in Washington, D.C. with Bastille Day races.

Mardi Gras—Celebrated the Tuesday before Ash Wednesday.

St. John the Baptist Day—June 24—Patron saint of the French Canadians.

St. Catherine's Day—November 25—French-Canadians celebrate by pulling taffy.

Fete des Rois—Epiphany—January 6—Both French and French-Canadians celebrate this holiday, which translates into "the Cake of Kings."

Candlemas—February 2.

Formal French wedding meals start with hor d'oeuvres (paté, caviar, various remoulades) and proceed to soup, a fish course, the entree and then the salad, followed by a cheese board with fruits and then the sweets.

French Protestants fled France after King Louis XIV revoked the Edict of Nantes in 1685, and incessant religious persecution ensued. There was not much room in Europe for a substantial group of well-educated Protestants, so they came to the United States for refuge. The United States was overwhelmingly Protestant, but not very tolerant of the French tongue. Therefore, the immigrants quickly changed their names to English pronunciations or translations, learned the English language and tried hard to forget their "Frenchness." So complete was their acculturation that today traces of Huguenot culture in America are rare.

What follows, therefore, is a partial list of people of unsuspected French Huguenot ancestry or of French Catholic ancestry who have helped shaped the United States.

Appolos Rivoire, father of Paul Revere

Pierre Beaudoin, grandfather of James Bowdoin, founder of Bowdoin College in Brunswick, Maine, and governor of Massachusetts in 1785

Priscilla Mullins, made famous in the love story about herself, Miles Standish and John Alden, was born Molines

John Jay, who signed the Treaty of Paris and was the first chief justice of the United States, was the son of Augustes Jay, who was from LaRochelle

Peter Faneuil, for whom Boston's Faneuil Hall—the "Cradle of Liberty—is named

Betsy Ross, who sewed the Star Spangled Banner, was a descendant of people from the French province of Alsace

George Washington, the first U.S. president, who is commonly known as the father of the United States, was a maternal descendant of the French Huguenot Nicholas Martiay.

The total U.S. population of German ancestry, according to the 1990 Census, was 57,945,000. Germans started migrating to Colonial America before the American Revolution and by 1790 made up approximately 9 percent of the U.S. population. Most of the German immigrants settled in Pennsylvania. The largest migration came between 1820 and 1900. People of German ancestry comprise the largest group (1990 Census) in the United States.

In terms of religion, German migrants were as divided as they were in Germany. About one-third were Roman Catholic; the remainder were Lutheran, Reformed and Evangelical Protestants.

Before World War I, most of the German immigrants came directly from Germany; others first migrated to other areas of Europe and then to the United States. Some, for example, were identified as German-Russians who fled Russia because they could not find religious and cultural freedom in either Germany or Russia. Most of these were Evangelical Protestants. Volga Germans settled in parts of Colorado, Minnesota, Montana, Nebraska and Wyoming. Black Sea Germans settled in the Dakotas.

In 1980, Pennsylvania was the state with the largest population of people of German ancestry. Many German immigrants tended to live in large cities. In the Midwest, for example, Chicago and Milwaukee had large German populations. In the East, Germans lived primarily in Philadelphia, Baltimore and New York.

Germans began immigrating to Maryland in the 1660s, and in the post-colonial period more immigrants came from Germany than from any other country, including England. Three Germans—F. Unger, H. Keffer and F. Volday—were among the followers of Captain John Smith, who founded the settlement of Jamestown, Virginia, in 1607. Germans participated on both sides of the Revolutionary War and the Civil War. They were among the first to respond to Lincoln's call for volunteers.

Between 1850 and 1900 Germans were never less than a quarter of all foreign-born people in the United States; between 1880 and 1920 they constituted the largest single group of first-generation immigrants in the nation.

Take Baltimore, for example, in the last decades of the 1800s, where a third of the populations spoke German. So prevalent was the language, according to the *Baltimore Sun*,[7] "a stranger could travel from one end of town to the other without the benefit of the English language."

Many immigrants, including Germans, became "redemptioners" to get to the United States. As redemptioners, they were allowed either to pay for their voyage within a certain time—usually two weeks after arrival—or be sold into servitude for a fixed period—four years was common—to cover the cost of their passage. About half of the Germans who made their way to the United States in the 1700s and the early 1800s found their way as redemptioners.

Strong ties to families in Germany made German-Americans targets of suspicion during both world wars. History points out, however, that the sons of German immigrants fought as members of the United States Armed Services in both world wars against their relatives in Germany.

Prior to World War I, German immigrants maintained their language and culture for three generations through their churches and schools.

A language report by James Brook in the *New York Times*[8] stated that half of the 640,000 residents of North Dakota in 1996 descended from German immigrants, and many kept up with the German language. In fact, as recently as 1990, one quarter of the households in the state included a German speaker. Although almost one-sixth of the U.S. population is of German origin, three generations of forced assimilation has reduced the use of the German language to a few pockets in the United States, and even in those areas some say the language is further endangered.

Because of continued forced assimilation, according to Michael M. Miller, who teaches a course on German immigration at North Dakota State University, twenty years from 1996 you are going to hear very little German spoken in North Dakota.

The two world wars sharply inhibited the use of the German language in all parts of the United States, and many local ordinances banned the use of German in churches, shops and telephone conversations. The federal government at one time went so far as to impose restrictions on German-language newspapers.

World War II and the stigma it caused people to attach to things German gave German-Americans a renewed stimulus to drop their accents, cancel their festivals, shut down their radio programs and anglicize their names.

"Well into the 1950s, there was a stigma against people of German background—that German equaled Nazi," said Don Heinrich Tolzman, director of German-American studies at the University of Cincinnati.

More recently, and specifically in 1996, there were scattered attempts to revive teaching German in Midwestern schools in Iowa, Minnesota, Nebraska, North Dakota, South Dakota and Wisconsin, where German descendants accounted for about half of the population. This has been the core U.S. area of German heritage, according to Edward Reichmann of the German-American center at Indiana University.

Despite their large numbers, Germans are among the least visible of ethnic groups because, like other immigrant groups, they have assimilated into American life. Of course, one can get good German food at a restaurant. But Germans have so infused American life with their folkways that their traditions have become one and the same with things considered "American." Christmas gift-giving and Santa Claus, for example, are German traditions, and Germans brought to the United States their *liederkrans* (choral singing), their *scheutzenfest* (rifle-shooting contests), and their *volkfests* (the grandfather of the modern picnic). They began the tradition of kindergarten (in German, literally, "a garden of children"). They brought delicatessens, beer, sausage, sauerkraut, cole slaw and German *schmierkese* (a yellow, spreadable cheese). More important than food, kindergarten and even Santa, though, is the spirit of industry and vast know-how that Germans brought to the U.S.

Germans always enjoyed a reputation as industrious, frugal, highly skilled farmers who "cared more for their land and livestock than for their own comfort," according to Ian Hancock, who teaches German-American history at the University of Texas.[9] Their discipline and aid to their families and communities brought them greater-than-average prosperity in the United States.

Many traditions associated with Christmas have been carried on through the years by people of German ancestry. First comes the **Feast of St. Nicholas** (from whom Santa Claus gets his name) on December 6. St. Nicholas was a fourth-century bishop in Asia Minor known for his generosity and caring nature. Children of German ancestry looked forward to a visit from the benevolent bishop but dreaded his sidekick, Knecht Ruprecht, also known as Krampus. Ruprecht, according to legend, would be there with a switch to swat any boy or girl who was naughty and to remind him or her to be good.

Children usually leave a boot, shoe or stocking so St. Nicholas can fill it with sweet treats. The traditional German Christmas tree was decorated with candles as well as edible treats like cookies, nuts, apples and oranges. On New Year's Day, children are allowed to eat the goodies. It is called "**Big Raid Day**."

In Germany they say "*frohe liche Weihnachten*" ("Merry Christmas"). Germany is a country where many traditional Christmas songs have been written. Among them are "*Stille Nacht, Heilege Nacht*" ("Silent Night, Holy Night"), "*Ihn Kindenlein Kommet*" ("Come, Little Children"), and "*O Tannenbaum*" ("Oh Christmas Tree").

The Christmas tree has its roots, so to speak, in Germany, where early Germanic tribes venerated the evergreen tree. Christians later adopted this rite and moved the tree indoors. Candles on the tree were lit for a short time on Christmas Eve. A feast on Christmas Eve included twelve different items for the twelve apostles, and German-Americans bought fish and cheeses for the evening meal. On Christmas Day, German-Americans often eat cooked goose, red cabbage and dumplings or mashed potatoes.

The **New Year's** meal traditionally features pork and sauerkraut. Gingerbread cookies and gingerbread houses are baked for the holidays. Poppy seed bread and Christ *stollen* (a cake with raisins, nuts, candied lemon and orange peel) are among the holiday foods, as well.

The **Feast of Corpus Christi**, a Catholic feast day celebrating the body and blood of Jesus Christ, is commemorated in some German-American communities by visits to cemeteries. According to the Church calendar, the feast is celebrated in spring, depending on the date of Easter Sunday.

Steuben Day—September 17—This holiday is named after the German General Friedrich von Steuben, who fought with General George Washington during the Revolutionary War. It is commemorated with parades in New York and Chicago.

German-American Day—October 6

Oktoberfest—October—An autumn festival that emphasizes merrymaking and the consumption of beer. Probably the most famous of German-American traditions, these festivities are patterned after the German tradition of celebrating the harvesting of crops. It is celebrated in various regions of the United States.

German Day festivals held around the country feature Bavarian dance and clothing such as *Lederhosen* (men's shorts with suspenders) and the *Dirndl* (women's full skirts). Replicas of German cities in the United States invariably assume an air of Alpine Bavaria during these festivities.

[1] *The Harvard Encyclopedia of Ethnic Groups*

[2] *We the People*

[3] *We the People*

[4] *The Franco-Americans of New England* by Robert B. Perrault, 1976

[5] *We the People*

[6] *The Great American Mosaic of Franco-American New England* by Robert Perrault

[7] Rita McWilliams, "Germans," *Maryland* Magazine

[8] March 2, 1996

[9] *The Harvard Encyclopedia of American Ethnic Groups*

CHAPTER II:
FROM THE BRITISH ISLES CAME AMERICANS OF ENGLISH, IRISH, SCOTCH-IRISH, SCOTTISH AND WELSH ANCESTRY

People of English ancestry in the United States are the third-largest of all ethnic groups counted in the 1990 Census, behind those of German and Irish descent.

Sometimes the term "British" is used to mean English. The term "British" includes not only the English, but Scots and the Welsh, though not the Irish. For the purposes of this chapter, "English" refers to people whose ancestors came solely from England.

The first period of immigration from England to what was to become the United States was in the early 1600s. By 1790 the English made up half of the total population of the United States and 60 percent of the white population. Although the English first came for religious reasons, the vast majority later came to the United States for economic opportunities.

Through the years, the English language and some other aspects of England's culture became dominant in the United States, so that many Americans have long recognized a cultural affinity to the English people.

The early English immigrants had rural roots, but by the 1830s experienced miners had migrated to the United States. Many people of English ancestry remained in their original settlements in the United States and became managers of the new immigrant groups—both English and others—that followed. This was only natural since English was the dominant language of the United States and the English, as a group, had the experience necessary to manage other people.

English migration to the United States began in 1607. By 1776, the time of the American Revolution, the English constituted half the population of the thirteen colonies. English immigrants were welcome in the United States, and upon arrival they fit nicely into the culture: they found familiar institutions, English Common Law, the written and spoken language, representative government and the Christian religion divided into numerous Protestant denominations, foremost of which was Episcopalian, an offshoot of the Church of England. Consequently, relative to other ethnic groups, the English met few obstacles to participation in the prevailing social and institutional life in the United States.

Emigration from England did not begin to decline until the first half of the twentieth century, but those who continued to emigrate tended to be skilled workers or professionals.

In 1620, "indentured service," based upon the English system, was introduced in the United States, and it became the principal means by which the colonies south of New England obtained their British and Irish farm labor, domestic servants and skilled artisans. Prospective emigrants covered the cost of their passage by an agreement, or indenture, to enter into service for a period of years during which time they received board and lodging but normally no wages. By the close of the seventeenth century, one-half to two-thirds of all the English and Irish migrants to the colonial United States south of New England arrived as unfree and unpaid labor. Indentured service continued to be the chief means of emigration to the Southern colonies, at least until the 1680s, when the importation of black slaves gave planters a more profitable source of labor.

The immigrants who came to New England rather than the Southern colonies, on the other hand, consisted chiefly of families and religious congregations and included far more women and children. For example, the Massachusetts Bay colony attracted clergymen, lawyers and merchants but few indentured servants.

The English found work and employment in all phases of the U.S. economy. Many were skilled workers and farmers who settled in all parts of the United States. They worked in textiles, mining, agriculture and in all other forms of industry.

By 1690, 90 percent of the mainland colonists were of English birth or descent. They retained their dominance in New England throughout the colonial period. After the American Revolution, and for many years thereafter, English immigrants could not express affection for England without increasing considerable hostility from those around them. After the War of 1812, an unprecedented period of immigration from England began, mostly due to economic problems in England. By 1850 it was estimated that more than 400,000 people had come to the United States from England and Wales. These immigrants were almost entirely self-financed. The largest movement of English immigrants ever to enter the United States began in 1879, and 82,000 or more arrived annually through 1893 as economic woes in England continued.

English immigration in the twentieth century was spotlighted by the number of people coming to the United States from England with professional qualifications, and the pattern persisted. For example, from 1957 to 1964, as health care in England was nationalized, it sent more physicians and surgeons to the United States than did any other country.

Charlotte Erickson, in *The Harvard Encyclopedia of American Ethnic Groups*, notes the following about people of English ancestry in the last decade of the twentieth century: "Americans of English descent today, insofar as they are conscious of their heritage, are perhaps less likely to proclaim it in the face of the upsurge of ethnic pride and loyalties by blacks, Mexicans, and other ethnic groups. Indeed, after centuries of intermarriage and internal geographic mobility, many are unable to determine a specific English origin. For these reasons, perhaps no other part of the pluralist American society is so difficult to describe as a separate entity as the English."

In the past decades, the label "WASP," or White Anglo Saxon Protestant, has been used to refer to people of dominantly English ancestry who have been the shapers and controllers of much of the United States' destiny. For many in the past few years, the tag "WASP" has been deemed derogatory. It has been used in some cases to express the resentment of members of non-British ethnic groups at the sometimes exaggerated influence of people of English ancestry. But "WASP" hasn't been the only label to describe the English ethnic group— "Yankee" is another, but this tag has been used mostly in New England.

Benjamin Schwarz, writing in the May 1995 *Atlantic Monthly*, said that in 1790 about 60 percent of the white U.S. population was of English origin, yet the United States was culturally quite homogeneous because most of the non-English people had lost much of their cultural distinctiveness to the unsparing dominance of the English language, customs and institutions. The non-English also lost their original genetic character to English numerical superiority. "In the late 1700s," Schwarz wrote, "the American nationality was not a blending as it is today of all the people that populated the United States, or even an amalgam of the white Europeans living in the country—an American was a modified Englishman."

In 1916, more than a century later, after wave upon wave of immigrants had inundated the United States, the liberal critic Randolph Bourne, in calling for a cosmopolitan, heterogeneous American culture, described an American that bewailed a "melting pot" under one aegis: "English snobberies, English religion, English literary styles, English literary reverences and canons, English ethics, English superiorities." He said that the United States' upper crust was an elite composed of Americans of Anglo-Saxon descent, which was "guilty of just what every dominant race is guilty of in every European country: The imposition of its own culture upon the minority peoples."

The Anglo elite was able up until around the 1960s to stamp its image on other peoples coming to the United States. This included its English religious and political principles, its customs and social relations and its standards of taste and morality, which were for 300 years the United States' and in some basic ways still are. Yet, as Schwarz wrote in the *Atlantic*, a single group, the English, whose proportion of the population has declined continuously throughout U.S. history, could so dominate American cultural and political life for three centuries—could define what it meant to be an American—and that is a remarkable achievement.

This is further exemplified by the decline in the number of people who identified themselves as English between 1980 and 1990. When asked their ancestry in 1990 more than 13 million who had answered English in 1980 answered American: 49,598,000 responded English in 1980 versus 32,650,000 in 1990.

HOLIDAYS AND CUSTOMS

Though the number of incoming English immigrants decreased after the start of the twentieth century, approximately 100,000 came after World War II. They differed from the earlier immigrants from England because they were of the middle and upper classes.

Because English immigrants gained easy acceptance into American life, they founded new organizations that were dedicated to the preservation of the English traditions of their homeland. They had a tendency to adapt and integrate into the larger American society and were absorbed into the mainstream of American life. For example, the **St. George's Society** and the **Odd Fellows Lodges** were among the first fraternal groups founded by English immigrants.

The Church of England became the **Episcopal Church** in the United States. This religious group, along with the **Methodists**, has remained an important segment of American Protestantism. The descendants of the English immigrants make up a significant and influential part of the Episcopal and Methodist Church memberships.

Very few holidays other than the traditional American and **Christian** ones are celebrated by English-Americans.

The English Speaking Union is probably the best-known, most active and most organized cultural group that celebrates English culture in the United States.

The 1990 Census listed almost 39,500,000 people in the United States of Irish ancestry. The people who first arrived in the United States from the island of Ireland in the 1700s were predominantly Protestant (Presbyterian), and most were of Scottish heritage, that is, they had migrated earlier to Ulster (Northern Ireland) from Scotland. These people have been referred to as the Scotch-Irish by Americans. It is thought that 2 million Scotch-Irish people have migrated to the United States since the 1700s. By 1790, they represented 10 percent of the population. The Scotch-Irish first settled in large numbers in Pennsylvania (please see the section on the Scotch-Irish).

The 1820s saw the beginning of what was the massive Irish migration, much of it caused by the famine in Ireland. By the 1840s Irish tenant farmers had become almost totally dependent on the potato for subsistence. When a fungus caused Ireland's potato crop to rot with unprecedented speed, disaster struck immediately. In 1845, a third of the crop rotted. Over the next two years, three-quarters was destroyed, while a third of the crop rotted in 1848.

Starving farmers couldn't pay their rent and were evicted. They faced death, emigration, or "taking the soup," in which Irish Catholics were forced to convert to Protestantism to receive food from church-based soup kitchens.

For most Irish, the choices were stark: stay put and face almost certain death, or board one of the rickety "coffin ships" that were sailing for North America. Between 1845 and 1855, some 2 million—a quarter of Ireland's population—chose to leave. By June 1847 Boston was teaming with refugees.

Being Catholic, poor, and uneducated, the Irish became the immigrant group most scorned in Yankee Protestant Boston. "No Irish Need Apply" was a common sign in the windows of shops and factories. Thomas O'Connor, a Boston College historian and author of *The Boston Irish,* says the experience of the Irish in Boston was unique because in other cities they were as new as most other residents, or their numbers, as in New York, didn't pose as much of a threat to the established order.

But the Irish sought strength in numbers, and by the end of the nineteenth century, with large families bursting from the city's signature three-decker tenements, they began flexing the political muscle that would take down the discriminatory signs and open doors to opportunity.[6]

Boston is the only major U.S. city with an Irish-American population of more than 20 percent (22%). Philadelphia is a distant second with 16 percent. Chicago and New York, which in the nineteenth century were teaming with famine refugees, now have Irish-American populations of just 8 and 7 percent, respectively. (All figures are according to U.S. Census figures 1990–1995.)

Census figures also show that, with 28 percent of its population claiming Irish ancestry, Massachusetts has the greatest concentration of Irish-Americans of any state. New Hampshire is second with 23.5 percent. New England, meanwhile, has the greatest regional concentration, with Rhode Island at 22.7 percent, Maine at 21 percent, and Connecticut and Vermont at 20 percent.

Of the nation's zip codes with the greatest concentration of Irish-Americans, 18 of the top 30 are in Massachusetts with as much as 57 percent in South Boston.

When the Irish Catholics started to arrive in the 1840s, the term Scotch-Irish was used to refer to Protestant Irish. The Scotch-Irish continued to be very common in areas of the United States where few Irish Catholics lived—in the South, for example.

The Irish Catholic settlers came primarily to Boston and New York. These Irish were different from other Irish immigrants in that they arrived with no money at all and were more concerned with the flight from Ireland and the English than with any choice of destination. They arrived with no special farming or industrial skills, and the men soon found that they were needed only for manual labor. Girls and women worked as servants in the homes of upper-class Bostonians and New Yorkers and also sewed garments at home in order to make a living. When the men were employed at various factories, they were often assigned to the most difficult and dangerous jobs. Irish women, who after the famine in Ireland migrated as single women in search of jobs, took the jobs that women of other ethnicities shunned. The Irish dug most of the canals and laid most of the railroad tracks in the East before the 1880s. They also worked in the coal mines in the anthracite region of Pennsylvania, and many people of Irish ancestry still reside in the northeastern part of the state, according to Census data. The California Gold Rush in 1849 attracted the Irish, and a western movement began.

By 1980, only 5 percent of the United States' Irish-ancestry population lived in the South, and a great percentage of those were Protestant. The religion of the Irish is predominantly Roman Catholic.

The Irish were the first ethnic group to immigrate in large numbers into the United States, and it probably complicated the neat world the British and Dutch had made for themselves in the New York area, according to a *New York Times* article.[1] The Irish were also the first to struggle as a group with the issues of discrimination and assimilation that still define the immigrant experience today—stereotypes with regard to employment and education, for example. Hundreds of thousands of Irish immigrants settled in New York from the mid-nineteenth century to the early twentieth century, and they became everything from ditch diggers to political powerhouses. Great numbers of Irish laborers built the subways of New York and much of its transportation infrastructure.

For three-quarters of a century after the heavy wave of immigration began in the mid-1800s, the Irish were generally treated as a low, and sometimes even untouchable, class. This followed the tragic discrimination the poor Irish Catholics faced in Ireland, a discrimination that may have played as large a role as the potato famine in encouraging the Irish to cross the Atlantic.

Once the Irish were in the United States, they tended to use established institutions—the police, the political parties, the church—as a means of enculturation in their new nation.

The Irish also showed other ethnic groups how to demonstrate that they occupied an important place in American life. One of the ways the Irish did this was to start and continue the St. Patrick's Day parade and celebrations on March 17 (or around that date). These parades gave the Irish a starring role in the cities and towns in which they became citizens.

HOLIDAYS AND CUSTOMS

In the United States, **St. Patrick's Day** is the quintessential ethnic celebration, highlighting Irish-American identity as non-British, non-Protestant, non-Italian or Polish (though Roman Catholic like these), not black nor Jewish, and in some quarters, not homosexual. St. Patrick belongs somewhat exclusively to the Irish, as Martin Luther King Day does to African-Americans and Columbus Day to Italians.

The St. Patrick's Day parades are witnessed by millions of non-Irish Americans, and as people stand by the roadside cheering, they do so knowing that, whatever ethnic group they are, their moment will also arrive in the calendar of ethnic glory days that define ethnic diversity in the United States. The parade in New York City, dating back to 1762, is the oldest public festivity in the United States.

Many Irish customs were discarded by the time the Irish started coming to the United States in large droves in the mid-1840s. British colonialism had suppressed or outlawed many Irish traditions, including their faith, and consequently most outward signs of faith were disguised or abandoned. Once the Irish were free to practice their religion in the United States, the Catholic Mass was the magnet on religious holidays. In addition, the Irish adopted many holiday traditions from their American neighbors.

Religious traditions are very much a part of holiday observance. **Christmas Eve** for the Irish is traditionally a day of fast and abstinence, and many families continue the ritual of having oyster stew. A candle, which in the past was lit on a table, was moved to a front window. It is placed there to help Mary and Joseph, the parents of Jesus, to find their way. Besides the candles, Irish homes are not elaborately decorated for Christmas, except with some holly and a nativity scene. The modern Irish are descendants of the ancient Celts, one of whose beliefs held that mistletoe and some trees are sacred. Some of the lack of decoration and the reverence for fauna is explained by the fact that only 4 percent of Ireland is forested.

Some people explain the candle tradition, which is still widely practiced in Irish homes, as a signal to passing clergy that they are welcome to stop in. The Irish also would traditionally keep their doors unlatched and leave some soda bread and milk on the table for the weary travelers who might be passing by and see the light.

On **Christmas Day** there is usually a very rich Christmas cake or pudding, usually made with Guinness Stout or Irish whiskey.

In many of the rural areas of Ireland, **Wren Day**, or "Feeding of the Wren," is practiced the day after Christmas, which is called **St. Stephen's Day**. In the original custom, boys paraded through the streets, singing or begging for money or candy. This tradition was picked up in the Irish neighborhoods of Philadelphia on **New Year's Day**, when people dress up in colorful and bizarre costumes and parade through the streets. This was the start of the famous **Mummer's parade** of Philadelphia in which various clubs parade in colorful costumes and perform all kinds of fun antics.

The Irish writer James Joyce, in his short story "The Dead," portrayed the annual gathering of family and friends as the focal point of the Christmas season. Christmas Day and the week afterwards are for family gatherings and hospitality. For the Irish, hospitality, family and their Catholic faith are the hallmarks of Christmas.

The Irish folk dance, i.e. the Jig and Reels, as well as the symbolic Irish leprechaun have been maintained by Americans of Irish ancestry.

WEDDING CUSTOMS

Many Irish weddings strike up an Irish toast with Meade, Ireland's legendary honey-based drink that dates back to the Middle Ages.

The Scotch-Irish are different in some respects from the Scots in their ancestral roots. The Scotch-Irish trace their ancestry to Scotland but through the six counties of Northern Ireland, which also was part of the British Empire (now the United Kingdom). The Scotch-Irish descend from the 200,000 Lowland Presbyterians who migrated to Ulster in the seventeenth century. The English encouraged this movement to strengthen their control of Ireland and to establish a Protestant population there.

Economic pressures that surfaced in the eighteenth century caused many of the Scotch-Irish to leave for the United States, and it is estimated that as many as 2 million descendants of the Scotch-Irish eventually migrated to the U.S. colonies. Also, many joined the mass migration brought on by the Great Potato Famine of the 1840s. Once they arrived in the U.S., many of the Scotch-Irish found their greatest opportunities in the Southern colonies.

In the 1990 Census, Scotch-Irish was counted as a distinct single group rather than as a multiple group. Those having Scotch-Irish ancestry numbered close to 6 million and made up the eleventh most-populous group in the U.S. (more than those of single Scot ancestry). A significant number of African-Americans and American Indians also claim Scotch-Irish ancestry.

The states with the highest concentrations of people of Scotch-Irish ancestry in 1990 were California, Texas, North Carolina, Florida and Pennsylvania, according to the Census. It should also be pointed out that many Appalachians are of Scotch-Irish descent. Please see the section on Appalachians.

HOLIDAYS AND CUSTOMS

The Scotch-Irish customs are similar to the Scots' and include the participation in the Highland Games, although their ancestry is in the Lowlands (please see section on the Scottish). Bagpipe music is also part of the Scotch-Irish tradition. Many Scotch-Irish families participate in the "gatherings of the clans" each year.

The Scotch-Irish are almost all **Protestants** (Presbyterians), and this plays a significant role in their American life.

Many Scotch-Irish celebrate:

Robbie Burns Day—June 25—See Scottish section.

St. Andrew's Day—November 30—See Scottish section.

Orangeman's Day—July 12—Celebrates the anniversary of William of Orange's victory over Catholics in the Battle of Boyne in 1690.

The 1990 Census counted slightly more than 11 million Americans of Scotch ancestry, a high number considering that in 1994 the population of Scotland was estimated at 5,130,000. Forty percent of the people reporting Scottish ancestry in 1980 came to the United States after first immigrating to Canada.[2]

Scots began to arrive in the United States in the 1680s and settled first in New Jersey. At that time in Scotland, there were two distinct groups of Scots: Highlanders and Lowlanders. Highlanders lived in the north and west and were mostly poor farmers, spoke Gaelic and were grouped into clans. Lowlanders, however, came from the southern and eastern regions and spoke a dialect English. The first of the two groups to come to the United States was the Highlanders, but after the early nineteenth century, differences between the two groups were of little concern as they settled into their new country—the United States. The religion of the Scots was Protestant, and many were of the Presbyterian denomination. Because Scots usually came to the United States as individuals to small family groups in the U.S., they felt no strong need to live near other Scots; they rarely clustered in urban areas.[3]

Early occupations of the Scots included mining (mostly bituminous coal mining), engineering, ship building and paper making. Also, some were clerks, managers and other professionals.

HOLIDAYS AND CUSTOMS

Each year on January 25, Scots all over the world celebrate the birth of **Robert Burns**, the plowman poet born in 1759 who immortalized the Scottish national dish and whiskey in his poems "To a Haggis" and "Scotch Drink." In the United States, it is no different, and Scottish-Americans in most major cities of the U.S. gather to celebrate the day. Burns started the Tarbolton Bachelor Club with a group of friends, and after his death they celebrated his memory on his birthday. "Whenever you have two or more Scots, they will form a club and celebrate Robert Burns' birthday," said Grace-Ellen McCrann of *North America Scottish World* magazine.

Scottish clubs abound in the United States. These include: **St. Andrew's Societies, Caledonian Clubs, Scottish-American Clubs** and, of course, **Robert Burns Clubs**. They are united in the tradition of Burns Night. The ritual seems to appeal to anyone who has a drop of Scottish blood in his or her veins. From the swirl of the tartan kilts to the skirling of bagpipes to the pole-length Lochaben Axes that form part of the haggis procession, it is an evening of formality and Scottish glory.

During the evening a member of one of the clubs is selected to give the official address, the reading of the poem "To a Haggis." With pomp and ceremony the speaker will carry the "haggis," a mixture of chopped mutton or lamb, sheep liver, suet, onions and seasonings in a sheep's stomach, into the dining room on a silver platter. He then will recite the poem, and when he is finished he will use a dirk or dagger to cut into the steaming haggis.

The first piece is given to the president of the club or society, along with a dram of Scotch served in a two-handled cup. According to the *New York Times*, after sipping, he will announce, "The haggis is fitting; the whiskey is fitting. Let the piper be paid."[4]

Another part of Scottish-American culture is the holding of the **Scottish Games**, or Highland Games, which feature musicians, clan societies, world-class athletes, dancers, animal exhibitions and vendors. Highland dancing is a stylized, disciplined art form and is one of the most colorful events at the games. The city of Alexandria, Virginia, was founded by Scottish merchants, and each year it stages one of the largest games over a period of two days of summer, usually in July.

Among the most popular attractions of the games is the series of professional and amateur athletic events, highlighted by the Caber toss. During this contest, competitors heave a 140-pound pole in the air with hopes that it will flip end over end, then land with precision. The athletic events trace their origins to the ancient Highland games of northern Scotland, where military chiefs demonstrated their strengths at annual gatherings. In modern times, the athletic events, such as the sheaf toss, have evolved into tests of the same skills needed in farming.

"*Hogmanay*" is what Scots call **New Year's Eve**. *Hogmanay*—the derivation of the word is hazy— is celebrated in a variety of ways. One tradition is called first-footing, in which the first person to enter a house after midnight is considered a portent for the coming year. The best omen is when the first person is a dark-haired man. In some parts of the United States bonfires or, in an ancient tradition to ward off evil spirits, torchlight processionals led by bands take place. When the clock strikes midnight there is much hugging and kissing and sharing of New Year's wishes and drinks.

In many states, Scottish-Americans partake in "gatherings of the clan," in which families and those of similar Scottish names mingle. The gatherings celebrate Scottish heritage.

The prestigious National Scottish Fiddling Championship—always held in Alexandria, Virginia— brings top fiddlers and judges from as far away as Scotland. The competitors in adult and junior classes play strathspeys, reels, marches and laments. Throughout the games, bagpipe music is heard during individual and band competitions and as an accompaniment to the Highland dance championships. (Bagpipe music is closely associated with Scottish-Americans.)

Other features include the popular heavyweight athletic events, a British automobile show, an exhibition and events featuring Scottish-breed dogs, sheep-herding demonstrations, Scottish concessions, a church service and a grand parade of Scottish clans and tartans. Visitors also can see Highland choreographed dance and team broadsword competitions.[5]

The Kirkin' of the Tartans—This is a special Scottish service which some call "a celebration of Scottish Presbyterian heritage." The service includes a re-enactment of the posting of soldiers called Cameron Guards. The guards were necessary during the seventeenth century to protect Scottish worshipers in the Presbyterian church from the soldiers of Charles I, the king of England. During the re-enactment, hymns are sung and bagpipe music is played that is similar to those played in the ancient Scottish churches.

The 1990 Census claimed 2,035,000 people in the United States of Welsh ancestry. Welsh immigrants first came to the United States in the 1680s from Wales and settled in areas around Philadelphia, Pennsylvania, in towns that still bear Welsh names such as Bryn Mawr, Merion and Gwynedd. Compared to Scottish and English immigrants, the Welsh tended to live in close proximity to each other. The early immigrants were from the rural areas of Wales, and they came to the United States looking to become farmers. The Welsh were predominantly Protestant, and many were Baptist and Methodist; but about 25,000 Welsh immigrants converted to the Mormon faith in the years after 1848, when they left the East Coast and migrated west to Utah and its farming areas.

The principal occupations of the later Welsh immigrants were mining and quarrying. The Welsh played a major role in the development of the coal, iron and steel industries. Many Welsh migrated to the anthracite fields of Pennsylvania, particularly in the northeastern part of the state. By 1880 there were more immigrants from Wales in Scranton, Pennsylvania, than in any other American city, or in any city worldwide outside England and Wales. As the jobs in mining started to dissolve, the Welsh began to move westward, and today the Los Angeles metropolitan area has more people of Welsh ancestry than any other area in the United States.

HOLIDAYS AND CUSTOMS

Many Welsh today have a hard time recalling the traditions the first generations brought to the United States, including the Christmas traditions of *"Lianfaipwllycrochon."* This shortened version of a village name means "St. Mary's Church in the hollow of the white hazel near a rapid whirlpool and the Church of St. Tysilio near the red cave." In modern America the Welsh language has almost disappeared. However, Welsh pride has not vanished. This is evidenced by the **St. David's**, **Cambrian** and **Red Dragon** societies that are alive and well in any town that boasts Welsh ancestry. Because the Welsh assimilated rapidly into American society, like many other immigrant groups, they wanted to leave much of the past behind, but chose to keep some traditions alive.

One of the great traditions brought to the United States by the Welsh was their religious (**Protestant**) faith and their love of song. The Welsh churches pioneered Sunday school for adults and children. Many churches whose congregations have members of Welsh ancestry continue to sponsor annual events known as **Gymanfa Ganu** (a hymn-singing festival) and **eistedd fod** (a music poetry competition). *Gymanfa Ganu* began in the little chapels and churches of Wales, particularly in the hills and valleys of Cambria. The *Gymanfa Ganu* expresses the skill and custom of the Welsh in their love for vocal music, particularly the choir. The tradition, less than a century old, is an expression of the soul of Cymry, or Welsh, since it provided outlets for deep feelings through voices blended in harmony. *Gymanfa Ganu* reflects the strong historical importance of the Welsh and their heritage. The program centerpiece is the choir, composed of members of regional churches.

St. David Day—March 1—This commemorates the death of St. David, the patron saint of the Welsh, with large dinners and choral concerts in churches.

Labor Day—First Monday of September—A National *Gymanfa Ganu* of the United States is held in key American cities and Canada.

[1] Paul Goldberger, March 15, 1996

[2] *We the People*

[3] *We the People*

[4] Olwen Woodier, the *New York Times*, January 24, 1990

[5] Alexandria, Virginia, Tourist Council

[6] Kevin Cullin, *The Boston Globe*

CHAPTER III:
FROM NORTHERN EUROPE
CAME AMERICANS OF DANISH,
FINNISH, NORWEGIAN AND
SWEDISH ANCESTRY

Scandinavia was the ancient name of the country of the Norsemen. Old Norse was spoken in Norway, Sweden, Denmark and Finland. Today, "Scandinavian" refers to a linguistic group of related languages. (Note that Finns are closer linguistically to Hungarians than to Scandinavians.) Although Norwegians, Swedes and Danes have often been grouped together as Scandinavians because of their geographical proximity as well as their closeness in religion, language and culture, the 1980 and 1990 Censuses found very few people in the United States who identified themselves as such. Rather, they identified themselves with the adjectives describing their particular countries—as Norwegian, Swedish or Danish.

The 1990 Census listed the total Danish ancestry population in the United States as 1,634,699. The migration from Denmark to the United States occurred primarily in the last half of the nineteenth century. An interesting aspect of the migration of some of the Danes was that it followed a religious conversion in Denmark. Most Danes, however, came for economic reasons rather than political or religious reasons. In the religious conversion cases, the Danes were mostly converted to Latter-Day Saints, or Mormons, and in somewhat smaller numbers to Baptists. Mormon missionaries arrived in Denmark in 1850, and they brought to Utah more Danes than any other immigrant group except the British. By 1980, nearly 9 percent of the total population of people in the United States of Danish ancestry lived in Utah.

Those who came not as followers of a religious group settled in many places besides Utah and took a wide range of jobs. They were mostly Lutheran.[1] In fact, though Salt Lake City is a large Danish center, the largest area of Danish-ancestry population is in Southern California, and the largest rural Danish population is in southern Wisconsin.

HOLIDAYS AND CUSTOMS

The Danes in the United States continue their tradition of being avid readers and having a great love of music. **Hans Christian Anderson Day** (April 2) is a hallmark of Danish culture, which celebrates the famous Danish writer known for his fairy tales such as *The Ugly Duckling*.

New Year's Day is a special day for celebration that Danes commemorate with festivities including food and drink designed to bring good luck in the new year.

So is **Prayer Day**, which is the fourth Friday after Easter, which is noted as a day of prayer and reflection similar to other Christian holidays but brought to the United States from Denmark. The usual **Christian** holidays are the others that are often celebrated in the Danish-American community.

Fastelavns Day is celebrated on the Monday before the start of Lent. This is when people use up the fats and sugars for baking in their homes before the beginning of the holy season.

On **Christmas Eve** "*culminaty*" is celebrated: families attend church in the afternoon, which is followed by a dinner of roast goose and rice pudding that has a whole almond in it. The person who gets the almond, according to the tradition, will have good luck in the coming year.

The Danes take note of **Mid-Summer Eve**, known to the Danish as St. John's Eve, on June 22. It is sometimes marked with bonfires to note the advent of longer days. They also commemorate **St. Martin's Eve** on November 16. These days aren't necessarily celebrated, but they are days of traditional Danish life for those who have come to the United States.

Many Danes celebrate Constitution Day, or **Grund Lowdog Day**, on June 5; the day marks the birthday of the modern Danish state in 1849.

On July 4, many Danish-Americans go to Denmark to celebrate American independence—it is the largest celebration of American independence outside the U.S.[2]

One of the traditions that has stayed with people of Danish ancestry is their politeness, which has always been of great value to them. For example, they have maintained a custom of shaking hands when entering or leaving a group, and, usually, only close friends use first names.

The 1990 Census showed 658,000 people in the United States of Finnish ancestry. Two distinct groups of Finns came to the United States—those who spoke Finnish and those who spoke Swedish. In the 1980 Census, these people identified themselves as either Swedes of Finns (the Swedish-speaking Finns lived near the southern coast of Finland). Most of them were Protestant, primarily Lutheran.

A great portion of the Finnish-American population settled in Minnesota and Michigan, and nearly all of the Finnish immigrants came from rural areas and settled on farms in the United States. Some of the settlers who went to Michigan worked in the copper mines. Many returned to Finland later to retire. Like the Swedes and Norwegians, Finns were easily accepted into established communities. By the 1990s Finns essentially became indistinguishable, and fit into the mass culture. Many do not visibly identify with any part of their heritage. Recent generations continue to move away from their culture. Finnish-Americans were themselves a multicultural society, being a part of the Laestadian, Finnish, Swede and Sami minorities. Finland once had, after all, been a part of Sweden; some Finns spoke Swedish, some spoke Sami (Lappish) from Lapland, and some were Gypsies.

HOLIDAYS AND CUSTOMS

Christmas Eve, not Christmas Day, is the highlight of the year in Finnish-American households. Families get together for the occasion, and children who have grown up and moved away from home try to return to their parents' home for the holiday. However, Christmas Eve is still a working day in most parts of the United States, at least until midday. At precisely noon, the "Peace of Christmas" is proclaimed by many. At sunset on Christmas Eve, families make their way to the churchyard, where a service is often held at around 5 o'clock. Candles are placed on the graves of loved ones, sometimes along with a wreath. A Finnish graveyard is a breathtaking sight on Christmas Eve. Countless candles shining out across the snow make for an unforgettable sight. Usually a hymn or two is sung, including Luther's religiously significant "*Ein' feste Burg*." For many Finns this is the most serious moment of the entire holiday.

The next day, **Christmas**, marks the turning point of the year. It is time to celebrate.

The Christmas season begins with the first Sunday in Advent, but long before this, as early as October, Finnish associations have already set about getting into the holiday spirit. Beginning preparations first are generally the women's organizations, planning their Christmas bazaars. Members get together in the old Finnish tradition, most often having Christmas parties that they call the delightful name "*Pikkujoulu*," meaning "Little Christmas." The "*Pikkujoulu*" has been part of the Finnish tradition in the United States since the 1920s.

On December 13 those Finns of Swedish-speaking ancestry celebrate **St. Lucia's Day**, a practice that spread from Sweden in the early 1920s.[3]

Kalevala Day—February 28—celebrates Finland as the "Land of Heroes" and the written folklore of the country. Kalevala Day, which is named after a 20,000-verse epic poem, is hailed as a great holiday with concerts and parades in Finland. Some communities in the United States hold programs in honor of poems.

Finnish Independence Day—December 6—Commemorated in some communities with Finnish residents, this day marks the anniversary of Finnish independence from Russia.

Mid-Summer Eve—June 21 and June 22—This is a tradition that dates back to the old country, which notes the arrival of longer days.[4] Remember, most Finns' settlements were in rural areas and on farms. In fact, more than half live in the Midwest and a quarter in the far west. Norwegians and Swedes also celebrate this with picnics and parades. Since all three ethnic groups come from the same region, there is solidarity among them in celebrating the time of the year with the most daylight.

In the United States, Finns have not lost their lore of the sauna. The sauna is a Finnish custom—a sweat bath without steam. Even in winter, Finns traditionally take these baths in outdoor bath sheds.

St. Urho's Day—March 16—a Finnish-American invention as a take-off on St. Patrick's Day that celebrates the saint's success in driving the grasshoppers out of Finland.

The 1990 Census listed the Norwegian-ancestry population in the U.S. at 3,869,395. The first Norwegians to come to the United States settled in and around New York City and formed a colony, which later failed. This (along with the attraction of new land) started a movement toward the Midwest, first to Chicago and southeastern Wisconsin. Norwegians, who were primarily farmers, were attracted to the possibilities of homesteading large areas of level and rolling grasslands. By the early 1900s, people of Norwegian ancestry occupied large portions of Minnesota and North Dakota. In some parts of Minnesota up to 60 percent, and in North Dakota more than 20 percent, of the population was Norwegian. Some migrated west to Washington and California, where the Norwegian settlers worked on the docks and in the shipyards, following the traditions of their seafaring homeland.

As of 1920 in the United States, of all the immigrant groups, Norwegians were the most likely to be engaged in agriculture, and 53 percent of them lived in rural areas, more than any other European immigrant group. By the 1980 Census, 20 percent of all people of Norwegian ancestry lived in Minnesota, twice as many as in any other state.

The religion of Norwegians was and continues to be mostly Protestant Lutheran.

HOLIDAYS AND CUSTOMS

Norwegian-Americans celebrate many of the traditional **Christian** holidays.

Norwegian Constitution Day—May 17—This is an important symbol of Norwegians' ethnicity. They celebrate with a parade, flags, music, and speeches in Norwegian-American centers in the U.S.

Mid-Summer Eve and Day—June 21 and June 22 (sometimes June 23, too)—This coincides with the Summer Solstice. Considering the high latitude of Scandinavia, the Summer Solstice has long been celebrated—with bonfires and light displays, for instance—because of the limited amount of sunlight these areas receive from November through March—they get as little as two to three hours in December! People of Norwegian ancestry in the United States have continued the tradition of Nordic and Alpine skiing. [5]

St. Olaf's Day—July 29—In honor of the patron saint of Norway, this day is celebrated in parts of Iowa and the upper Midwest of the United States. The Nordic festivals celebrating Norwegian culture take place in the latter part of July to coincide with the patron saint's day.

Leif Eriksson Day—October 9—This is celebrated in honor of the Norwegian explorer. Leif Eriksson was a Viking, the icon of Viking heritage, in fact. He explored the New World, and to commemorate his voyages, this day is sometimes followed by **Norsk Host Fest**, a festival featuring a program highlighting Norwegian-American heritage in parts of the upper Midwest including Idaho and North Dakota.

The 1990 Census showed 4,680,863 people of Swedish ancestry in the United States, 40 percent of whom lived in the Midwest and 30 percent of whom lived in the West. Swedes first arrived in the United States sometime between 1638 and 1655 in what is now northern Delaware. Only a few hundred Swedes settled there. For a period of about 200 years, very few Swedes came. In the 1840s, though, landowners and craftspeople by the thousands began to immigrate with their families. Most arriving before 1880 came primarily to buy cheaper land than was available in Sweden. Their destinations were typically the nearest region of good land that was still unoccupied, which was the upper Midwest. They also arrived looking for religious freedom because many were rebelling against the state-controlled Lutheran Church in Sweden. They hoped to found a Swedish Utopian Colony in Illinois, but when this did not last, they began to migrate to Minnesota. They bought land from earlier American settlers in the Chisago area, northeast of Minneapolis, which developed into the largest rural Swedish area in the United States.

By 1980 Hennipen County, in which Minneapolis is located, had the largest single Swedish-ancestry population of any county in the United States, followed by Cook County, Illinois, and specifically the area around Chicago. In 1900 Chicago had more Swedes than any other city in the world except Stockholm[6] and was home to about 10 percent of all Swedish immigrants. In 1920 Chicago had twice the Swedish-born population of either New York City or Minneapolis. Swedes also established communities in other parts of the United States, such as the Austin, Texas, area, where they became ranch hands and contract laborers. Some went to Maine and to the northwestern part of Pennsylvania, and others to Buffalo, New York.

The primary religion of most Swedes has remained Lutheran, the same as it was in Sweden.

Swedes in the United States have always interacted with other Nordic groups, especially Finns, because they were Swedish-speaking. In general, however, the Swedish made a fast and smooth transition to mainstream America.[7]

HOLIDAYS AND CUSTOMS

The Swedes celebrate midsummer as a major holiday on June 21 and June 22. The maypole, which does not derive its name from the month, with its traditional loops and decorations of flowers and leaves, is the center of all festivities. Young and old dance around it with both organized "action" dances and general "long dances" where everyone weaves in and out and in wide circles. Around this time, girls are supposed to find at least seven different flowers and make a crown for their head or sleep with them under their pillows to dream of their future mate.

St. Lucia's Day—December 13— In Sweden, Christmas comes as a welcome break in the long winter. It is the best-loved and most traditionally celebrated of all holidays, beginning with the festival of light, the celebration of Saint Lucia.

For the people of Swedish ancestry Lucia was a medieval saint who carried food and drink to the hungry folk of Varmland. According to custom, Santa Lucia appeared during the shortest and darkest day of the year. She was seen crossing a lake clothed in white with a crown of light encircling her head.

At dawn on December 13th, Lucia Day begins the traditional Swedish Christmas festivities. Families are awakened by Lucia, usually their eldest daughter, dressed in a white robe with a crimson sash, wearing a crown of lighted candles. She carries a tray with saffron buns to each of the members of the family as she sings the Sicilian song "Santa Lucia."

Her coming begins the feasting, merry-making, singing and spirit of friendliness and good will that lasts throughout the holidays. Though originally a family celebration, in recent years the Lucia tradition has developed into a community festival observed in many types of public places in the United States. A procession led by Lucia, dressed in a white gown, balancing a crown of lighted candles, she carries a copper tray set with a coffee pot, creamer and sugar bowl. She is followed by her maidens, also in white, and other children dressed as star boys, baker lads and totem, elf-like creations of Scandinavian folklore. Past Lucias also join the parade, each carrying candles used to light other candles held by people in the audience, until the room is filled with light.

On this day traditionally the eldest girl in the family assumes the role of St. Lucia, the "Light Queen," and she dresses in white with a crown of candles in her hair. She then wakes her parents with morning coffee. Her costume is reminiscent of the virgin martyr of Sicily, St. Lucy: the white dress, her innocence, the red belt, her martyrdom, and the crown—a halo—a symbol of her holiness. This crown is usually decorated with lingon sprigs and threaded with a red ribbon. St. Lucia's Day used to coincide with the shortest day of the year, which is why Lucia, the queen of lights, has gained such popularity.

On **Christmas Eve**, the "*Jultomtar*" (Christmas elves) bring gifts and entertain family members. The Christmas season is celebrated through January 13.

Swedish National Day—June 6—

WEDDING CUSTOMS

The Swedish wedding crown[8] has been a part of traditional weddings for centuries in Sweden. The crowns were loaned to brides by the church, which often owned them. Some families owned their own crown, heirlooms passed from generation to generation. In the United States, most wedding crowns are family-owned and are passed on from family member to family member. Each wedding crown is made from a basic design with suggestions from the bride and her family. They are made on a commission basis. On many, there is an open area on the front where an heirloom locket or pendant, or a custom-made pendant, can be temporarily attached for the wedding and detached later to be worn by the bride. Swedish weddings aren't complete without an elaborate smorgasbord, featuring various fish courses, cold meats, salads, hot dishes and aquavit (water of life).

[1] *We the People*

[2] John Mark Nelson and Peter L. Peterson of Dana College and West Texas A&M University

[3] See description in section about Swedish traditions.

[4] See description in section about Norwegian traditions.

[5] *Gale's Encyclopedia*

[6] *We the People, Gale's Encyclopedia of Multicultural America, Harvard Encyclopedia of American Ethnic Groups*

[7] Mark A. Granquist of St. Olaf's College, writing in *Gale's*

[8] Montgomery County, Maryland, Ethnic Festival

CHAPTER IV:
FROM SOUTHERN EUROPE CAME AMERICANS OF ALBANIAN, BASQUE, FORMER YUGOSLAVIAN (CROATIAN, SERBIAN AND SLOVENIAN), GREEK, ITALIAN, PORTUGUESE AND SPANISH ANCESTRY

Only small numbers of people of Albanian ancestry have migrated to the United States, mainly because Albania is such a small country. As of 1996, Albania's population was less than 3.5 million people; the 1990 Census showed less than 50,000 people in the United States of Albanian ancestry. The Albanian population in the United States in 1980 showed only 21,687 of single ancestry and 16,971 people of multiple ancestry. Most of the immigrants came from southern Albania, many from rural backgrounds.

Albanians are mostly Orthodox in religion, although some are Islamic and others Roman Catholic. When Albanians came to the United States, most arrived in Boston, where there were many restaurants owned by Greeks.[1] Because of the similarity between the Greek and Albanian Orthodox religions, many Albanians became cooks and other restaurant workers in establishments owned by Greeks. Also, many Albanians worked in textile mills. After 1950, those who arrived were primarily political exiles and settled in the New York City area. Many of these Albanians spoke Italian and settled around the Bronx, where many Italians lived.

Albanian-Americans hold fast to the cultural traditions threatened in their homeland because they affirm their cultural identity and uphold their community. The code of *Kanun*, which is an ancient set of laws that provide criminal, civil and family guidance for behavior, still has an influence on the lives of Albanian-Americans. It sets forth rights and obligations regarding church, family and marriage.

HOLIDAYS AND CUSTOMS

Many of the holidays celebrated are based on those of the **Albanian Orthodox Church**, the **Catholic Church** and **Islam**.

Albanian Independence Day—November 28—This festive occasion is commemorated with dinners among members of the Albanian-American community.

Albanians also celebrate **Orthodox** religious holidays.

WEDDING CUSTOMS

An interesting Albanian wedding tradition that continues in the United States is, just prior to the bride meeting the bridegroom, her youngest brother has the honor of putting on her shoes—a farewell tradition.

By the 1980 Census 23,213 people claimed single Basque ancestry and 19,927 multiple ancestry. The immigration of Basques from their obscure region in the western Pyrenees on the Bay of Biscay has been distinctive in its close relationship to the sheep industry. It was in South America, rather than the Basque country of Europe, that the early Basque immigrants to the United States learned the large-scale sheep management skills they needed to adapt for living in the western United States. Basques first left for California and Nevada as early as 1848, and by the 1860s the Basques began to develop their specialty of sheep management.

The division that pulled apart the Yugoslav union after decades of ethnic, religious, linguistic, economic and political tension was played out by their relatives in the United States. Croatia and Slovenia issued a Declaration of Independence from Yugoslavia in June 1991. In April 1992 the member states of the European Union recognized their independence, as well as that of Bosnia-Herzegovina. The United States followed this recognition later that month.

Early on, Serbian-American groups expressed opposition to the breakaway movement and expressed fear that the United States would officially recognize Croatian and Slovenian sovereignty, which the U.S. did.

Hundreds of thousands of people from the former Yugoslavia live in the United States. And many thousands more claim ancestry from there. A governor of Ohio, for example, George Voinovich, is the son of a Serbian-born father and a Slovenian-born mother.

The Croats, Slovenes and Serbs were part of the European migration to the United States between 1890 and 1910. The immigrants came to work in the coal and steel regions of Pennsylvania, Ohio and Illinois. More specifically, they came to Chicago, where the biggest Yugoslavian concentration in the United States, some 150,000 Croats and Slovenes and an equal number of Serbs, reside, according to Census data. Another popular city for those from the former Yugoslavia is Cleveland, Ohio, which in the early 1990s had a total of about 200,000 residents from the three groups.[2]

As of the 1990 Census, there were 540,000 people of Croatian ancestry in the United States. After World War I Croatia became part of Yugoslavia and remained so until 1991, when, after a civil war, Croatia again became an independent country. Croats are predominantly Roman Catholic and use a different alphabet than other groups from the former Yugoslavia, who use a version of the Cyrillic alphabet.

Islam is a minor religion of the Croats, which is important when considering the religious conflict (and its specific Muslim aspect) in Croatian-Americans' homeland.

Since 1880 about 60 percent of the immigrants from what later became Yugoslavia were Croats. Croats first settled in Louisiana and California, and many became seafaring workers. By 1910, however, they began to become more established in the iron and steel industry of Pennsylvania. Pennsylvania had more people of Croatian ancestry than any other state, as of the 1980 Census. The steelmaking cities of Ohio also had large numbers of Croats, as did Kansas City, Kansas, where Croatians made up almost 90 percent of the workers in the slaughterhouses.[3]

HOLIDAYS AND CUSTOMS

Croatian Day—May 30—This holiday is vibrantly celebrated in Western Pennsylvania with parades and festivals.

St. Nicholas Day—December 6—This is celebrated with gift-giving in a Christmas tradition.

Easter—spring—This is the Croats' biggest day of celebration in anticipation of spring's advent as well as the celebration of Jesus Christ's resurrection (among Croats who are Catholic).

St. George's Day—April 15—This patron saint of the Croats is honored with church services and parades in Croatian-populated areas of the U.S.

Croatians also celebrate traditional **Christian** holidays.

Traditional Croatian dress is worn on holidays and special occasions by Croatians in the United States. Women wear fine embroidery, white linen dresses covered by a colored apron and a shawl over their shoulders. Men wear dark linen pants with high leather boots or knee socks.

It is difficult sometimes to separate customs of the Croatian and Serbian communities throughout the United States. For example, *Tamburitza* music, which is mandolinlike and often accompanies poetry readings, is not just a performing tradition but a profound symbol of ethnic identity. The music, the instruments, the dances and the songs have played a central role in the traditional cultural life of the Croatian and Serbian communities in the United States. With its mines and mills, southwestern Pennsylvania was one of the earliest and strongest centers for Croatian and Serbian immigration. Ethnic churches such as Croatian Catholic and Serbian Orthodox and ethnic clubs were established, and national federations and fraternal unions of both ethnic groups are headquartered in Pittsburgh.

WEDDING CUSTOMS

One of the Croatian wedding customs in the United States is performed at the end of the wedding reception. The Croatian bride's veil is removed by her mother and replaced by a kerchief and an apron, signifying that she is no longer a maiden but a married woman.

The 1990 Census listed 120,000 people in the United States of Serb ancestry. Some Serbs arrived in the United States as early as 1880. But when those who emigrated to the United States did so after World War I, it was from what had been established as Yugoslavia. Serbs differed from Croats by their use of a different alphabet, the Cyrillic alphabet, and they were predominantly Orthodox. Like the Croats, they first settled in Louisiana and California, but by the first decade of the twentieth century, they tended to migrate toward the large industrial cities of the East, and their work was concentrated in the iron and steel industry around Pittsburgh and Steubenville, Ohio. According to the 1980 and 1990 Censuses, those two cities had the largest concentration of Serbs in the United States.

Serbs immigrated to the United States in the mid-1800s through the turn of the century. Like many European immigrants, they were peasants seeking a better life. They worked in the iron mines and steel mills in the Midwest and fought in both world wars on the American side. They erected Serbian Orthodox Christian churches; even today in those churches, the liturgy is said in Serbian.

Many of the immigrant Serbs' sons and daughters are now doctors and lawyers and engineers—or other professionals—living in well-to-do suburbs of cities such as Chicago and Pittsburgh and Cleveland. Their sons and daughters were joined after World War II by the Serb intellectuals fleeing Communist repression in Yugoslavia.

Like Cuban emigres, the Serb immigrants are staunchly anti-Communist and tend to vote Republican, according to a 1993 report by Isabel Wickerson in the *New York Times*.[4] Like the Greeks and Armenians, many of them still nurse a century-old hatred of the Ottoman Turks, who dominated all three groups.

Until the early 1990s, the Serbs were an obscure ethnic group, little-known to most Americans. In Midwestern rustbelt cities, where, according to the United States Census Bureau about 116,000 people of Serb ancestry lived as of the 1990 Census, the Serbs' ethnicity was often confused with Syrians and Siberians, according to an article in the *New York Times*.[5]

When the civil war in the former Yugoslavia raged during the early 1990s, Serbian-Americans were forced to account for atrocities an ocean away in a land many had never seen. Some Serbian-Americans became very angry at what they considered to be one-sided media coverage, which they said was biased against Serbs, of a war where no side is innocent. According to Wickerson's article, they say the Serbs have been unfairly blamed for every act of violence committed in the former Yugoslavia, known as Bosnia-Herzegovina. (Also, later in Kosovo)

Some Serbian-Americans say that whenever they hear or heard the word "Bosnia," or "Kosovo" they draw closer to the television, anxious for word on what many consider to be their homeland. For almost all Serbian-Americans, interest in the war was not merely political but personal, since many had parents, grandparents, uncles, aunts or cousins in Zagreb, Sarajevo, Belgrade or Kosovo.

A visit with a Serbian-American will invariably lead to an impassioned lecture on Serbian history going back to the fourteenth-century occupation by the Ottoman Turks that lasted until the nineteenth century. The Serbs sided with the Allied forces in World War II. The murder of tens of thousands of Serbs at the hands of Rome-Berlin Axis-allied Croats is something many Serbs describe as their own Holocaust, Wickerson wrote.[6] For many Serb-Americans, it seems as if the fifty years between World War II and the breakup of Yugoslavia never happened. Some have not forgotten the Croats allied with the Nazis.

Tradition, as the basis of the Serbian culture, created national and familial unity during centuries of adversarial rule. Today, traditions are kept by the Serbians as a statement of who they are and what they represent.

One traditional holiday unique to the Serbs is *Krsna Slava*, or **St. Slava Day** (their patron saint day). Celebrated on January 27, the Slava tradition dates from the ninth century, when the Serbians became Christians. Each Serb chose a patron saint for his family. He or she was baptized on the saint's holiday, which then became the Slava. Slava has been passed generation to generation, from father to son, for many centuries, uniting the past with the present by recognizing the family's Christian heritage. The celebration is a festive gathering of friends and relatives, but the religious aspect of this day is never forgotten. Slava is foremost a religious observance, and a ritual is performed to make the day complete. The religious elements of Slava are the icon of the patron saint of the family, a candle, wine, *zito* (wheat) and *kolach* (holiday bread), which must be cut by a priest. There is a prayer service and a blessing in the home with the entire family involved. The holiday reinforces the Christian character of the family and is celebrated with honor, dignity and benevolence.

St. Slava Day is one holiday that exemplifies the power of identity that tradition has brought to the Serbian people.

Many Serbs celebrate traditional **Orthodox** holidays.

The 1990 Census shows 125,000 people of Slovenian ancestry in the United States: 40 percent in Ohio, 12 percent in Pennsylvania, 12 percent in Illinois and 10 percent in Wisconsin. The number of Slovenian-Americans in the U.S. has probably been underestimated because many identify their ancestry as either Austrian or Yugoslavian. Slovenians came to the United States primarily before World War I. They worked mainly in manufacturing jobs in Pennsylvania, Ohio and Illinois, which still have the largest concentrations of Slovenes in the nation. Cleveland, Ohio, in particular, had the highest concentration of any metropolitan area as of 1990. Slovenes are strongly Roman Catholic in religion, yet few Slovenian parishes remained in 1995,[7] and most have blended into the Roman Catholic community.

HOLIDAYS AND CUSTOMS

Some Slovenian customs survive, such as the old **St. Nicholas Feast** on December 6, when the good saint exhorts children to be good. **St. Martin's Feast**, on November 11, celebrates the custom of the good saint changing lowly grape juice into wine. This is done with a banquet that includes wine tasting, waltzes and polkas.

The 1990 Census counted 1,110,000 people in the United States of Greek ancestry. The first group of Greeks to come to the United States arrived in Florida in 1768. Many of the immigrant Greeks arrived during the period 1880 to 1924. Like other groups of immigrants, they typically went to cities and towns where friends or relatives were living and took whatever jobs they could find. For Greeks, this usually meant becoming a peddler, bootblack, dishwasher, porter, miner, factory worker or railroad laborer. A Greek version of the *padrone* system, described in the Italian-ancestry section, operated in larger cities. After a few years working at menial jobs, some immigrants saved enough money to open small businesses such as dry cleaning establishments, lunchrooms or candy or grocery stores. Many Greeks opted to enter the restaurant business.[8] In 1950, Greeks were thirty times more likely to be cooks or restaurant managers than were other foreign-born men.

The textile and shoe manufacturing towns in Massachusetts and southern New Hampshire first attracted Greek immigrants in the 1890s. Nearly all Greeks arrived through the port of New York, the city of the largest Greek settlement throughout this century. The women who immigrated and married seldom worked outside their homes. In Greek communities the coffeehouse was a popular meeting place, and the Orthodox Church was the spiritual focus of ethnic identity.

On the Pacific Coast, the Greek arrivals were often sailors, and San Francisco attracted the largest settlement of Greeks. As of 1980, a vast majority—93 percent—of the descendants of Greek immigrants and the later arrivals were urban.

In the early 1920s, the largest and most distinctive settlement for the Greeks in the South was in Tarpon Springs, Florida. In that town, originally a winter retreat for the wealthy, local people were employed to harvest sea sponges using long poles to hook them. Greek immigrants soon changed the method of harvesting by becoming divers, which changed the town's economy, according to an article in the *Tampa Bay Tribune*.

The religion of most Greek-Americans is Orthodox, but some members of the population are Byzantine Catholics, sometimes referred to as Eastern Rite Catholics or Greek Catholics.

HOLIDAYS AND CUSTOMS

Greek Independence Day—March 25—Commemorated with parades in areas such as Queens, New York, and with big dinners.

Much of Greek culture in the United States has been kept alive in their religion, the center of Greek community life. Other Greek holidays are included in the **Orthodox** part of the religion section of this book.

January 6—**Epiphany**—Epiphany is a Greek word meaning a showing forth or manifestation. It is also known as the Blessing of the Waters. The events that occur on this day are intended to commemorate the baptism of Jesus Christ in the River Jordan, when many Christians believe it was revealed that he was the son of God.

A special ritual that occurs in many Greek communities, especially in coastal towns, on this day throughout the United States is "the tossing of the cross." This ritual dates back 1,600 years and is a central part of the celebration of the baptism of Christ. Some historians say the rite stems from the day that Christ's baptism took place. Others say it has to do with the miracle of changing water into wine.

An example of this ritual is the one that takes place in Tarpon Springs. It has taken place each year since the turn of the century and begins with the blessing of the waters of the spring bayou by the local archbishop. During the blessing the teenage boys of the community await the moment when the archbishop tosses a golden cross into the water. The boys then traditionally dive into the water to retrieve it. The boy who finds it is thought to be spiritually blessed for the rest of his life, and so whoever gets the cross is very proud.[9]

Greek Christmases emphasize the spiritual. The holiday is second in importance only to Easter. On **Christmas Eve**, groups of children aged 5 to 15 go singing through the streets. In the Greek language they sing the same time-honored songs Americans sing. Sometimes they are rewarded with nuts, money or dried fruit. At about 7 a.m. on **Christmas** morning, church bells sound, calling the parishioners to the Greek Orthodox equivalent of the Catholic Mass. According to some legends, the early ceremony is supposed to correspond to the hour of Christ's birth. A meal follows the services: roast pig, grilled whole lamb (if pig isn't available), spinach pies, sweet bread called *Christpsomo*, and honey-sweetened cakes. No one eats alone. Those who are poor are invited into other people's homes.

WEDDING CUSTOMS

The Greek Orthodox religion is unique in its marriage ceremony. During the service the priest leads the newlyweds three times in a circle representing eternity, by which they make an oath to preserve their marriage bond forever. Greek couples wear crowns of flowers and pearls tied together by a white satin ribbon. Prior to this the couple has made no vows, and after the last circling of the table, the couple shares some wine from a silver cup and perhaps a plate of sugar-coated almonds that represent fertility. At a Greek reception, the bride and groom share bites of the same piece of cake, signifying their union.

The 1990 Census reported 14,665,000 people of Italian ancestry in the United States. In the years before 1880 the Italian immigrants to the United States were usually from northern Italy and were well-educated professionals and skilled craftspersons, such as stone cutters and masons.

In nearly all U.S. cities, however, the character of those early settlements and American impressions of Italians were changed by the arrival after 1880 of large numbers of illiterate and extremely poor peasants of southern Italy and Sicily.

Ties between Italian immigrant enclaves in the U.S. and their native regions were strong. People from rural villages in the "old" country lived together or near one another once they arrived in the U.S. Many felt safer and more comfortable by virtue of their proximity to other Italians. In fact, they sometimes even brought their own priests.

An estimated 97 percent of Italian arrivals after 1880 landed in New York City. If no job opportunities awaited these immigrants elsewhere, they could easily sign up for non-skilled construction jobs through a labor agency. Many stayed in New York City, and it became the largest center of Italian immigrants in the country. By 1920, New York City had five times more people of Italian stock than any other American city.[10]

The Italian immigrants used a labor contracting system called the "*Padrone* System," which involved a "boss" or "*padrone*" who acted as the intermediary or contractor between the laborers and the company or government agency that needed construction or other work done.

Immigrants often sought out a "Little Italy" as a result of the hostility they encountered in the broader American society, and, like other immigrant groups, they often suffered from discrimination in housing and employment.

Jobs for men in the garment industry were filled by more Italians and Jews than by other immigrants partly because many men of other ethnicities considered needlecraft to be women's work. Therefore, garment manufacturing cities such as New York, Philadelphia and Chicago attracted Italians. Travel between New York and Philadelphia was easy, and Philadelphia had many Italian immigrants who arrived before 1880. Some became merchants, skilled workmen and musicians. Pennsylvania also attracted immigrants because of the availability of railroad work. By 1920, 95 percent of San Francisco's Italians had migrated directly from Italy. Italian immigrants to New Orleans and San Francisco became successful in business well before many migrated to eastern cities. However, in the early twentieth century, newcomers from southern Italy came in such large numbers and with so little money or skills that they often could only get menial jobs. Few Italian immigrants planned to farm when they came to the United States, but some ended up having to in order to support their families.

By 1980 Americans of Italian ancestry typically resided in the larger metropolitan areas, both in suburban communities and in older, more established working-class neighborhoods. The stability of the Italian community and its dominance in some businesses and political life has opened key avenues for occupational advancement. By 1980 the greater New York area still had five times as many people of Italian ancestry as any other metropolitan area.

Unfortunately, like other ethnic groups, Italian-Americans continue to suffer from stereotypes. With Italians, the stereotype (as with any stereotype, especially among uneducated Americans) is of being involved with organized crime and the Mafia. Yet research has shown time and time again that the rate of Italian-Americans' association with organized crime is no higher than in other segments of American society. Nevertheless, into the 1980s and 1990s, television and Hollywood have perpetuated this stereotype.

Despite the hurdles Italians have had to jump, their rich culture along with its many contributions to Western civilization encompass all aspects of human endeavor. Innovative genius and handiwork have always been the Italian and Italian-American trademark.

Italian-Americans have tried to keep Italian traditions alive in the United States, but with the desire to become assimilated into the mainstream culture and with intermarriage, it has not been easy. Younger Italian-Americans often neglect customs and traditions. However, results of studies by the National Italian American Foundation and by Professor Phillip J. DiNovo[11] of Fairleigh Dickinson University show that later in life they come to value traditions and culture, and the ancient customs have been passed along.

In recent years, many of the tightly knit Italian-American communities of the early twentieth century and into the 1940s and 1950s have become watered down, more generically Italian-American. The immigrants have either passed on or have aged, and legal immigration has slowed to a trickle. Like the elders of other immigrant ethnic groups, many officials of the old Italian fraternal societies fear that, unless more people come from Italy, the traditions and culture that many grew up with will fade.

Second- and third-generation Italian-Americans are not as dependent on their countrymen as they once were upon arriving in the United States. Today, with much success having been achieved in many parts of American life, economically, politically and socially, Italian immigrants now join broad ethnic groups like the National Italian American Foundation, where the emphasis is on Italy as a country rather than on one little town.

HOLIDAYS AND CUSTOMS

As in Italy, many Italian-American traditions revolve around family, religion and food. In many of the older Italian neighborhoods of the United States, the Italian religious procession continues to take place. Traditionally during this procession, homage is paid to the Blessed Virgin Mary, St. Joseph and the local church's patron saint. Prior to the procession, a Mass is celebrated, and following the service men of the parish hoist up statues of the Blessed Virgin and other saints and carry them through the streets around the parish. Several stops are made along the procession route so people can pay homage to the statues. The Catholic Rosary is recited in unison and monetary offerings are made to the church.

Italian holiday customs celebrate saints and take on a festive, almost carnival atmosphere, with feasts, bagpipes (yes, they are a Neapolitan tradition) and games. But the biggest celebration is the commemoration of the birth of Jesus. At **Christmastime** a manger scene is always set up, usually separate from the Christmas tree, and on Christmas Day a baby Jesus doll is placed in the creche. The Christmas season, which is called *Natale*, traditionally begins eight days before Christmas. Either in front of or inside their homes people display their manger scenes, which are the primary Italian Christmas decoration. December 24, **Christmas Eve**, is usually the biggest night of the year. Family members, including aunts, uncles and cousins, gather to eat supper and talk and play games, and they usually go to midnight Mass. Supper traditionally consists of several fish dishes, because prior to Vatican II, Christmas Eve was a day of abstinence, meaning that eating meat wasn't allowed.

The evening has an air of solemn festivity. The Italian-American Christmas menu varies depending on what region the family's ancestors came from. At an Italian-American dinner table, the tradition is *A tavola non si invecchia*—in other words, at the dinner table you never get old.

As for Italian-American weddings, a Neapolitan Dance called the Tarantella is sometimes danced as a celebration of ancestral customs.

Columbus Day—October 12—This is a holiday that has become the quintessential Italian-American national holiday, though it originated in the U.S. in the nineteenth century not just as a celebration for Italians but for the whole nation. There are elaborate dinners and banquets among Italian-Americans in most major American cities. Cities also hold large festivals in honor of patron saints of the villages that immigrants came from.

Italian-Americans, in addition to having strong familial bonds, are exceptionally proud of Italian and Italian-American contributions to the United States. It is perhaps best described in the essay "I Am an Italian-American," by Angelo R. Bianchi.

"I am an Italian-American. My roots are deep in an ancient soil, drenched by the Mediterranean sun, and watered by pure streams from snow-capped mountains.

I am enriched by thousands of years of culture.

My hands are those of the mason, the artist, the man of the soil.

My thoughts have been recorded in the annals of Rome, the poetry of Virgil, the creations of Dante, and the philosophy of Bennedetto Croce. I am Italian-American, and from my ancient world,

I first spanned the seas to the New World.

I am Christofor Colombo.

I am Giovanni Caboto, known in American history as John Cabot, discoverer of the mainland of North America.

I am Amerigo Vespucci, who gave my name to the New World America.

First to sail on the Great Lakes in 1679, founder of the territory that became the State of Illinois, colonizer of Louisiana and Arkansas, I am Enrico Tonti.

I am Filippo Mazzei, friend of Thomas Jefferson, and my thesis on the equality of man was written into the Bill of Rights.

I am William Paca, signer of the Declaration of Independence.

I am an Italian-American. I financed the Northwest Expedition of George Rogers Clark and accompanied him through the lands that would become Ohio, Indiana, Illinois, Wisconsin and Michigan. I am Colonel Francesco Vigo

I mapped the Pacific from Mexico to Alaska and to the Philippines. I am Alessandro Malaspina.

I am Giocomo Beltrami, discoverer of the source of the Mississippi River in 1823.

I created the Dome of the United States Capitol. They called me the Michelangelo of America. I am Constantino Brumidi.

In 1904, I founded in San Francisco the Bank of Italy, now known as the Bank of America, the largest financial institution in the world. I am A.P. Giannini.

I am Enrico Fermi, father of nuclear science in America.

First enlisted man to win the Medal of Honor in World War II, I am John Basilone of New Jersey.

I am an Italian-American. I am the million-strong who served in America's armies and the tens of thousands whose names are enshrined in military cemeteries from Guadalcanal to the Rhine.

I am the steel maker in Pittsburgh, the grower in the Imperial Valley of California, the textile designer in Manhattan, the movie maker in Hollywood, the homemaker and the breadwinner in 10,000 communities.

I am an American without stint or reservation, loving this land as only one who understands history, its agonies and its triumphs can love it and serve it.

I will not be told that my contribution is any less nor my role not as worthy as that of any other American.

I will stand in support of this nation's freedom and promise against all foes.

My heritage has dedicated me to this nation.

I am proud of my full heritage, and I shall remain worthy of it.

I am an Italian-American."

The 1990 Census showed 1,153,000 people in the United States of Portuguese ancestry. This population includes those from the European continent and islands belonging to Portugal in the Atlantic Ocean, but immigrants from the mainland of Portugal have generally gone to Brazil. About 70 percent of the Portuguese immigrants to the United States were originally from the Azores, approximately 900 miles west of the Portugal mainland. Another source of Portuguese immigrants has been the Madeira Islands, about 400 miles west of Morocco.

The Portuguese initially began to arrive in the U.S. in the late 1800s. And thanks to those who came to the United States early on, the Portuguese started coming in greater numbers after a change in the Immigration Law of 1965 gave preference to relatives of immigrants already in the United States. Then, the largest flow of Portuguese immigrants arrived after the 1974 military coup in Portugal, which sparked a new migration of urban professionals, tradespeople and entrepreneurs.

During the late nineteenth century New Bedford, Massachusetts, was the largest whaling port in the eastern United States and soon became the major settlement of Portuguese immigrants. Some continental Portuguese began working in the steel mills of Pennsylvania. In contrast to most immigrants, this group had motivations that were not primarily economic. In the 1840s, Madeirans who had recently converted to Protestantism found a refuge from their homeland's religious persecution in the United States, often in Illinois. Interestingly, Portuguese from the Azores began migrations to Hawaii in the early whaling days (around 1878). Later, many more came to the islands to work on the sugar plantations. By 1980, they made up 5 percent of the Hawaiian population. At that time, the descendants of early immigrants to California were still strongly represented in the San Diego fishing operations. Twenty-nine percent of the Portuguese-ancestry population lives in California, whereas 30 percent settled in New York and New Jersey, according to the 1990 Census. The remaining and largest percentage settled in Massachusetts and Rhode Island.

In Newark, New Jersey, many Portuguese illegal immigrants started settling in what was a gritty neighborhood of factories and small shops called "Ironbound." Many of these illegal immigrants were subjected to raids by the prowling "Immigration van," especially as the 1960s wore on. Many of those who scattered down the street to hide are now legal residents and own many of the stores and bakeries in the area. In the space of thirty years, the "Ironbound," a name drawn from the two railroad lines that made its boundaries, has been transformed from a dingy industrial haven to a thriving enclave of Portuguese life. The transformation comes in large part from the entrepreneurship of thousands of Portuguese immigrants.

Since 1986, the economy has improved in Portugal, and there are fewer and fewer immigrants coming from there to the United States. During the 1980s and 1990s, many Portuguese began returning to their native land, according to the *New York Times*.[12]

A variety of Portuguese folk beliefs and celebrations have been revived by Americans of Portuguese ancestry. The three main revivals have been:

The Festival of the Blessed Sacrament—This is a four-day festival celebrated in New Bedford, Massachusetts, on the first weekend of August. It is the largest Portuguese-American celebration in the United States and annually attracts 150,000 people. The festival, patterned after the custom of the island of Madeira, includes a special mass, music and costumes.

The Festival of the Holy Ghost—This is modeled after an Azorean festival and is celebrated on a weekend sometime between Easter and the end of July. For seven weeks prior to the final day, a symbolic royal crown is placed with a family, as determined by a drawing. On the final day, the crown is brought to the mass and is included in the religious procession. During the procession an Azorean folk dance called the *Chamarrita* is performed. The festival of the Holy Ghost in Fall River, MA is considered the largest gathering of Azoreans in the world. Events include a beginning procession of dancers and singers winding through the streets of the city on their way to a park, where volunteers pass out sweetbread and milk in a tradition that dates back over 600 years, to the time of Queen Elizabeth of Portugal.

In her observance of the Catholic holy day of Pentecost, Queen Elizabeth (1271–1336) would invite the poor into the castle to eat bread and drink milk. It was a symbol of the Catholic Church and of generosity of spirit.

The ***Festa de Senhor da Pedra***—This is celebrated the last Sunday of August and is also based on an Azorean celebration. It emphasizes the religious aspect of Portuguese-Americans' lives. The sculpture of various saints is carried through the streets of New Bedford (including the image of Senhor da Pedra, also known as Saint Peter). It is a religious procession with music. Some neighborhoods decorate the streets with sand paintings and flower petals over which the procession will pass.

Other holiday festivals include one on May 12 called **San Cristo** in Fall River, Massachusetts. Also, many communities celebrate the festival of **Our Lady of Fatima** in May or October. It commemorates the reported appearance of the Virgin to two children in Fatima, Portugal, in 1917 with religious services and the recitation of the Rosary.

A Portuguese **New Year's Eve** custom is to have family or friends eating in groups of twelve at midnight. This assures twelve months of happiness in the new year.

Almost all Americans of Portuguese ancestry are Roman Catholic and also celebrate the traditional Christian holidays.

The large Portuguese-language newspaper *Luso-Americano* has reported that the Portuguese National Day Parade on June 10 has drawn larger crowds in New Bedford, Massachusetts, and Newark, New Jersey, than in Lisbon, Portugal.

St. John's Eve—June 23—This celebrates St. John the Baptist and the Portuguese tradition associated with water. Basically, it blesses those making a living through the sea: sailors, fishermen and navigators, for example.

The first Spanish immigrants to the United States settled in Florida, followed by settlements in New Mexico, California, Arizona, Texas and Louisiana. The descendants of the first 1,000 Spaniards who by 1598 had settled north of Mexico now number 900,000. Since the founding of the United States approximately 250,000 more immigrants have come from Spain.

The Spanish presence (meaning specifically people in the United States with ancestry from Spain) has steadily declined in the United States. Many of the immigrants have either moved back to Spain or to another Hispanic country. In the 1990s, the areas that have the most Spanish-Americans include New York, Florida, California, the mountain west and parts of the Midwest. Many of the rural Basques went to California, and some raise sheep in Nevada.

The Spanish-Americans in the United States are the European segment of the American Hispanic population. In the 1960s, 1970s and 1980s, the decline of immigration from Spain, combined with the ability and willingness of the people of this ethnic group to become part of the Hispanic population and the society at large, has obscured any specifically Spanish presence in the United States.

HOLIDAYS AND CUSTOMS

Most are shared with the **Christian** (predominantly Catholic) Church.

January 6—***Dia de los Reyes Magos***—This is the day of the Three Wise Men (known as Epiphany in Greek). Gifts are given to children on this day as well as Christmas.

Flamenco, the Spanish dance, is seen in Spanish festivals, such as the Adams Morgan Festival in Washington D.C. and others, to celebrate their heritage.

Also, Spanish customs are on display during the annual Gasperilla Festival in Tampa, Florida, in February.

Many Spanish-Americans have kept their native language alive by speaking it at home.

[1] *We the People*

[2] *We the People, Gale's Encyclopedia of Multicultural America, Harvard Encyclopedia of American Ethnic Groups*

[3] *We the People*

[4] May 5, 1993

[5] Isabel Wickerson, May 5, 1993

[6] the Serbian Literary Association of New York

[7] *Gale's Encyclopedia*

[8] *We the People*

[9] Karen Long, *Tampa Tribune*, January 6, 1990

[10] *We the People*

[11] as reported in the *Italian Tribune Newspaper* of Newark, New Jersey

[12] Ashley Dunn, January 17, 1995

CHAPTER V:

FROM EASTERN EUROPE CAME AMERICANS OF BYELORUSSIAN, ESTONIAN, GYPSY, JEWISH, LATVIAN, LITHUANIAN, POLISH, RUSSIAN AND UKRAINIAN ANCESTRY

Belarusans first came to the United States from Byelorussia, which on August 21, 1991, became the Republic of Belarus, one of the independent states of the former Soviet Union.

More than 1,000,000 immigrants from Byelorussia came to the United States, but, according to a study done by the Belarusan Institute of Arts and Sciences, only 650,000 permanently settled in the U.S. The discrepancies between these numbers arise because upon their arrival Byelorussians were routinely registered as Russian if they were Orthodox and as Polish if they were Roman Catholic (Belarus shares a border with Poland). Many of the immigrants who were recorded in the Census as Russians were primarily of Belarusan background. Those who arrived from Byelorussia after World War I came to the U.S. for political rather than religious or economic reasons. The 1990 Census contained no category for Byelorussians; they most likely were contained in the Russian count of 2,952,000. About 80 percent of Belarusan-Americans follow the Eastern Orthodox faith; the remaining 20 percent are either Roman Catholic or Eastern Rite Catholic.

HOLIDAYS AND CUSTOMS

The Eastern Orthodox Church celebrates the **Easter** season with a priest blessing colored eggs, sausages and breads at church services.

Christmas for Belarusans includes special customs, including the Christmas Eve dinner, which is a blessed and large occasion.

St. Euphasuynia of Polacak—May 23—Celebrated in honor of the patron saint of Belarus with religious ceremonies.

St. Cyril of Turdu—April 28—Marked by religious ceremonies.

Mother God of Zyrovicy—May 20—She is the patroness of Belarusan churches.

All the Saints of Belarus—May 20—The third Sunday after Pentecost, this day is commemorated with religious ceremonies.

Our Lady of Vostraja—November 16—Celebrated by Roman Catholics with religious observances.

In the United States Estonian-Americans have been closely associated with other Baltic groups, such as Lithuanians and Latvians. The 1990 Census listed 27,000 people of Estonian ancestry in the United States. Little has been written about their immigration to the United States.

Estonians in the U.S. and abroad have remained closely knit through Estonian festivals held throughout the world. Estonian-American groups participate in these gatherings to hold on to their culture through music and religion. In the United States and Canada, national song festivals have been organized and held periodically to honor Estonia.

There are over 1 million Latvians, Lithuanians and Estonians in the U.S., all from the Baltic states at the eastern end of the Baltic Sea. They number more than 250,000 just in Chicago.

Many have assimilated into American society; some have specialized in technical areas.

HOLIDAYS AND CUSTOMS

Most Estonian-Americans celebrate traditional **Christian** holidays. In addition, many celebrate:

Victory Day—June 24—Commemorates the defeat of the Soviet armies in 1918-1920.

Midsummer or St. John's Eve—June 21 and June 22—This is celebrated with bonfires and parades to mark the beginning of summer. (It is sometimes combined with Victory Day.)

Estonian Independence Day—February 24—Marks the day in 1918 when Estonians declared their independence from the Russian empire.

Scholars disagree widely on the number of Gypsies there are in the world and in the United States, but authorities[1] say there are probably between 6 and 7 million worldwide and at least 250,000 in the United States.[2] Some estimate that in the U.S. there are as many as 1 million Gypsies, who call themselves "*Rom*" and their culture "*Romani*." One of the reasons for uncertainty about how many Gypsies there are is that many entered the United States illegally. Many Gypsies also avoid the Census out of fear: during World War II it provided Nazis data that helped identify them.

The Gypsies' ancestors were nomads who are believed to have left Northern India around the year 1000, and their dialects are still rich with Sanskrit words. The name "Gypsy," a corruption of Egyptian, was given to them by outsiders confused about their origin. Despite the similar names, the Romany language is unintelligible to most Romanians, whose language and culture derive from the Roman Empire.

Gypsies have resisted assimilation and education in the United States.[3] Prejudice against Gypsies has strengthened their resistance to conforming to American norms. But with time their traditional skills as blacksmiths, weavers and horsetraders became increasingly outdated. Many Gypsy-Americans have remained mobile, often because of harassment and prejudice that they encounter.

Stereotypes of Gypsy-Americans as fortune-tellers have endured. Much of the mysticism surrounding them is represented in fortune-teller costumes and props such as crystal balls and tarot cards and has had some influence on American culture.

More important, though, is the impact the rest of the world has had on Gypsy culture. Ian Hancock, a Gypsy historian, says in his book *The Pariah Syndrome* that there is no doubt that Gypsies have been oppressed throughout Europe. The Gypsies were enslaved in Romania for more than 500 years, despised as nomads and thieves. Gypsies have been widely persecuted throughout the world over many centuries. They were incarcerated, enslaved and killed in virtually all of the Nazi death camps, and some were subjected to medical experiments at Auschwitz.

Gypsies were forbidden to settle or ply regular trades throughout Europe, and even in the United States they were required until at least the late 1980s to be licensed in many states simply because of their ethnicity.

Political activists representing the United States' Gypsies have worked to bring attention to their people's tragedy. Gypsies tried very hard to gain representation on the U.S. Holocaust Memorial Council to bring attention to the half-million Gypsy lives lost during the Second World War. Many feel their story remains untold.

HOLIDAYS AND CUSTOMS

Many Gypsies are Christian, others are Zoroastrians; thus some of them celebrate religious holidays. At funerals, Gypsies encourage large community gatherings because they usually live in groups. Many Gypsy weddings follow introductions that are arranged by parents. Once married, the bride subjects herself to the groom's family until she gets pregnant; when the child arrives she is considered to have entered womanhood.

It is important to note that although Jews constitute a significant ethnic group in the United States (approximately 6 million), Census data on them have not been collected because questions about religion are prohibited from any Census. Therefore, in order to distinguish this ethnic group from those of the predominantly Christian population of various European countries, the data that are available have been collected though various Jewish organizations. In a 1991 study conducted by the Council of Jewish Federations, 60 percent of those polled identified their Jewishness as an ethnic group, 75 percent as a cultural group, and slightly less than 50 percent as a religious group

The four major branches of Judaism are Conservative, Orthodox, Reconstructionist and Reform. When American Jews were asked as part of a 1991 study by the Council of Jewish Federations what branch of Judaism they followed, 41.4 percent said the liberal "Reform" branch, 40.4 percent said the moderate "Conservative" wing and 6.8 percent said the religiously strict "Orthodox" group. The "Reconstructionist" branch is the smallest and is sometimes included with Reform and Conservative data as Progressive Judaism. Conservative Judaism is the middle ground between the Reform and Orthodox branches. The Reform movement freely adapts Jewish practices to changing times; Orthodox Jews see ritual as commanded by God and thus unchangeable. The reconstructionists emphasize democratic culture and humanistic values. They value Jewish traditions not merely from the religious view but because they reflect Jewish culture.

The first Jews to migrate to the United States were Sephardic Jews, a term that refers to their Spanish and Portuguese heritage. They came in the mid-1600s after their expulsion from the Iberian peninsula in the 1500s. These early arrivals were successful cosmopolitan merchants who adjusted easily to the United States and to its commercial opportunities.

Ashkenazic Jews, from the Hebrew word *AshKendz,* whose origins were in Germany and Poland, also came to the United States in the seventeenth century. By the 1770s they made up the majority of Jews in the United States.[4] Through the years, because of much intermarriage between these groups, a distinctive Sephardic Jewish population ceased to exist for a period. In the early twentieth century, however, some new Sephardic Jews started to immigrate, and most settled in New York City. Some spoke Spanish or Arabic. A Syrian Jewish group settled in Brooklyn, New York; many became importers or retailers, and some ran camera and electronics stores to cater to tourists in New York City. By the 1970s there were about 100,000 Sephardic Jews in the United States.

Two major groups among the Ashkenazic Jews immigrated to the United States: German Jews who dominated immigration until the 1880s and Eastern European Jews (from other Eastern European countries) who came in large numbers in the decades before World War I. (According to J. Higman, author of *Send These to Me: Immigrants in Urban America*, until the late nineteenth century, Americans thought of German Jews as essentially Germans of a particular religion. Their Jewish identity, Higman wrote, became emphasized as many acquired wealth, prompting a surge in anti-Semitism.) When Russian Jews began to arrive in American cities, German Jews behaved just as descendants of other Western European groups toward the new arrivals because they upset the favorable social position German Jews established. This rift dissolved in recent decades.[5] German Jews became small business owners, often starting as peddlers. By 1860 large Jewish communities developed from St. Louis to Boston, and by 1890 Jewish communities spread and appeared in most American cities.

Beginning in the 1880s hundreds of thousands of Eastern European Jews began to arrive in New York City. Until 1914 more than 75 percent of Jewish immigrants were from the Russian Empire. In contrast to the Russian Christians, who in Russia were often farm workers, Russian Jews lived in towns or cities. When they arrived in the U.S., many Russian Jews settled in New York's Lower East Side. They brought with them more skills than many other immigrants. Many were watchmakers, hatmakers, furriers, tailors, bookbinders, tinsmiths, glaziers, bakers and carpenters. They had skills that promised employment in cities. The United States garment industry, which became the most important occupation for many immigrant Jews, expanded rapidly. It paid well compared to other industries and required only a small capital investment (sewing and pressing machines plus the need for many hand-sewing workers constituted less investment than large and expensive manufacturing equipment required in heavier industries). Space and building requirements were flexible and operations could be transferred easily from one building to another. Seizing the opportunity, some went so far as to borrow pushcarts to go into business.

With crowded conditions in New York City at the turn of the century and between 1907 and 1922, especially in the Lower East Side, many Jews moved to Boston and Philadelphia. By 1915 almost 28 percent of New York City's population was Jewish. Some who left their original New York homes simply moved to Brooklyn. Since 1971, more than 40 percent of Russian Jewish immigrants from the Soviet Union settled in New York City.[6] Years later, many Jewish-Americans are reaping the fruits of their labor: as an example, though Jews represent only approximately 2.7 percent of the United States' population, they constitute 60 percent of the workers in the entertainment industry.[7]

The Los Angeles area is the second-largest Jewish-American center. The third-largest concentration of Jewish-Americans is in Florida, between Miami and West Palm Beach. Most came from the New York City area, and a high percentage of Florida's Jewish population is elderly.

In general, Jews have lived in large metropolitan areas that offer the best business and educational opportunities. Jews, like other ethnic groups, experienced some discrimination when they moved into the suburbs from the city.

A major change in recent decades is the geographic distribution of American Jews. In 1966 Judaism was centered almost exclusively in the Northeast, which was home to 84 percent of American Jewry. This figure dropped to 65 percent in the late 1970s, to 56 percent in the late 1980s, and then to 41 percent in 1991, according to a study by the Council of Jewish Federations.

Jews are one of the most upscale American groups in terms of education and income.[8] Approximately 70 percent have attended some college or technical school, compared with less than 45 percent of the general population. In a 1991[9] study by the Council of Jewish Federations, 50 percent of American Jewish men, compared with 24 percent of the general population, had graduated from college. Family incomes were also considerably higher among American Jews than in the general population, according to the council's study.

The study also reported that 140 scholarly studies of public attitudes toward Jews have been conducted since 1948. Though some negative attitudes about Jews persist, anti-Semitism, according to the study, continues to decline in the United States. A broad range of measures indicates that anti-Semitism is steadily declining, according to a study by Tom Smith at the University of Chicago Opinion Research Center.[10] Negative stereotypes about Jews have diminished, social interaction between Jews and Gentiles, including intermarriage, has become more commonplace and acceptable; organization and institutional discrimination has abated; and anti-Semitic political movements have been restricted to small but dangerous extremist groups, Smith concluded.

Jewish-Americans follow a lunar-solar calendar. All holidays and the Sabbath begin at sundown prior to the date of the holiday.

Rosh Hashanah—The New Year on the Jewish calendar, Rosh Hashanah, marks the beginning of the High Holy Days. It is the most significant holiday in the Hebrew calendar. The holiday begins at sundown. Reformed or Liberal congregations celebrate the holidays only for one day, but Conservative, Orthodox, Reconstructionist and Hasidic congregations celebrate the holiday for two days.

Rosh Hashanah is not as solemn a holiday as **Yom Kippur**, which follows ten days later. Rosh Hashanah is celebrated by festive meals, while Yom Kippur ("a time to remember") is marked by fasting. One of the traditional foods for Rosh Hashanah is pieces of apple dipped in honey, to symbolize a sweet new year. The synagogue also reflects the grand and solemn worship, and special prayers and melodies are offered.

During Yom Kippur, Jewish-Americans fast completely, eating and drinking nothing, not even water, for nearly twenty-five hours. Yom Kippur is part of the period of the High Holy Days when Jews believe their actions will be judged by God. It is a time when Jews look to the upcoming year and strive to improve their lives.

For Jews around the world Yom Kippur is a day that calls people back to their roots. This holiday also attracts Jews who are alienated from Judaism and who do not practice much throughout the year. Although most employers, including the federal government, do not recognize Yom Kippur as an official holiday, most Jews take the day off from work.

For many Jews, Yom Kippur is a time of family and introspection, a day for fasting, prayer and community with others of their faith. The day is often followed by the break-the-fast gatherings of friends and relatives of every generation that help ease the way from the solemnity of the holy day back to everyday life.

Hanukkah is a Jewish observance of religious freedom. It has no Christian counterpart. This eight-day celebration marks the first battle in history for religious freedom, fought more than 2,150 years ago. Hanukkah begins every year on the twenty-fifth day of the Hebrew month of *Kislev*. That puts the festival anywhere from late November through early January on the Gregorian calendar.

The holiday dates from 164 B.C., when Judah Maccabee and a small band of devoted followers fought to free their temple in Jerusalem from Greek domination and restore their right to practice Judaism. With victory over Greek domination, Maccabee removed the image of Zeus and constructed a new altar. The Greek word *Hanukkah*, which means "dedication of the altar," was adopted to commemorate this historical event and the eight-day celebration that followed.

Legend has it that a one-day supply of sacred oil used in the temple miraculously burned for eight days, until additional supplies arrived. Now, legend has interwoven with history, and this "miracle" (as it is referred to by many Jews) has become the most widely known reason to celebrate Hanukkah.

Like other Jewish scholars might, Washington D.C.'s Rabbi Jeffrey Wohlberg told the *Washington Post* in 1986 that "we are not a religion that celebrates miracles or military victories." The purpose of Hanukkah, he explained, is to "rededicate ourselves to the principles the Maccabees fought for—religious freedom, Jewish independence and worship of God."

Since the first Hanukkah, Jews annually celebrate Hanukkah by lighting a Menorah, a candelabra with eight branches, one for each night of the festival. Each Menorah has an extra branch known as a *shamas*, which is used to light the other candles. In addition to kindling the Menorah, Jewish children play with spinning tops known as *dreidels* (in Yiddish) or *sivivons* (in Hebrew). A *dreidel* is a top inscribed with four Hebrew letters that stand for "great miracle happened there."

In the United States, after lighting the candles each night, some people may exchange gifts, but this is a departure from the traditional celebration of Hanukkah. Hanukkah is not a major religious holiday, but rather a minor celebration. Some people have been tempted to transform it into a major holiday because it comes so close to Christmas. Many American Jews exchange cards and gifts and many give children gifts each night of the festival. Also, many decorate their homes with brightly colored symbols.

Sukkoth is an eight-day holiday when Jewish families construct a temporary hut or booth and decorate it with fruits, flowers and tree branches to celebrate the world of nature and harvest (*Sukkoth* coincides with harvest time). The structure is called a *Sukkah*. The holiday comes only five days after Yom Kippur. Religious laws require that a *Sukkah* be a temporary structure to reflect one of the themes of the holiday—the impermanence and fragility of man. According to an article in the *New York Times* by Terry Trucco in September 1990, this holiday is a feast of thanksgiving. Those observing *Sukkoth* celebrate the Jewish people's travels in the desert after their escape from slavery in Egypt and eat all their meals in *Sukkah*. The *Sukkah* (sometimes spelled *succah*) symbolizes the huts the Jewish people built in the desert as described in Leviticus in the Old Testament.

Shemini Atzeret—Falls on the eighth day of *Sukkoth* and is a day of contemplation.

Simhat Torah—Concludes the *Sukkoth* festival and celebrates the end of the public reading of the Pentateuch and a new beginning, thus affirming that the study of God's word is an unending process. It symbolizes, too, the respect for God's law.

Purim—This is a one-day holiday that begins at sundown and celebrates the foiling of a plot to destroy the Jews in ancient Persia. It is celebrated on the fourteenth day of *Adar*, the sixth month of the lunar Jewish calendar, which falls around February or March on the Gregorian calendar. A food traditionally eaten at the Purim festival is called "*hamantaschen*," a three-cornered pastry. Purim is a light-hearted celebration that commemorates the saving of the Jews of ancient Persia by Queen Esther and the defeat of the wicked Haman, who sought to kill the Jews. Purim is a favorite of children, who are encouraged to reenact the story and cheer or make noise at the names of the villain and heroine as the story is read from the *Megillah*, the special scroll containing the book of Esther.

Kosher—Also called the laws of Kashrut, "kosher" describes the Jewish dietary laws originally stated in Leviticus, the third book of the Bible that treats the offices, ministries, rites and ceremonies of the priests and Levites. The Hebrews call it *Vaicra*, from the word with which it begins. The two best-known customs are proscriptions against eating pork and shellfish, and against eating milk and meat at the same meal. For food manufacturers, that means that they must not use both dairy foods and meat products in the same item. The laws carefully spell out the proper manner of breeding and slaughtering animals: they must be killed and cleaned by hand and must be certified as completely disease-free.

The **Sabbath**—This is the seventh day of the week and is observed as a day of rest. It comes from the Hebrew word *Sabbat*, meaning devoting a day each week to rest. It is celebrated by Jews from sundown on Friday until the stars come out on Saturday, though it has declined over the years because of assimilation.

Passover—When Jews around the world usher in Passover, they repeat a story told for thousands of years. That story is far more than just a story about freedom, of the Jews' exodus from slavery in Egypt. It is a journey that Jews are directed to take as they follow the words of the Haggadah. They are instructed not only to say its prayers and carry out its rituals but to feel as if they were slaves in Egypt, so they can taste anew the joy of being free.

Passover is primarily a home celebration. There are special religious services, but the major service, the ***seder***, takes place at home.

Amid song and ceremony, the seder, the Passover feast, is recreated each year. Seders have been conducted in Jewish homes since the first century. The story has never changed. During the evening the seder participants are asked to understand the symbolism of such foods as bitter herbs (for the bitterness of bondage), *haroseth* (a pastelike combination of apples, walnuts and wine that represents the mortar that the Jewish slaves in Egypt had to use in construction) and matzo, the bread that was baked in haste and without leavening by the Jews before they fled. Lamb is usually also served.

The ritual recounting of the history of the Jews begins with the youngest child at the table asking four questions about why the night is different from all other nights. The family's oldest members answer the questions. A cup of wine is set out in hopes that the prophet Elijah might appear. A piece of matzo, the *Afikomen*, is hidden so children can hunt for it at the end of the meal.

Passover, which accounts for as much as one-third of Kosher food sales, has an additional set of requirements. During the holiday, leavened bread is forbidden, as are corn, peanuts, peas and other legumes, as well as food containing products derived from them. Additionally, any food item that comes in contact with these products is no longer considered Kosher for Passover.

Yom Ha'atzmaut—Israel Independence Day—[11] Commemorating the establishment of the state of Israel, an event of deep significance to the world's Jewry.

Yom Hashoah—A day set aside annually to memorialize the 6 million Jews who died in the Holocaust. It emphasizes respect for human dignity; the observance is not limited, however, to Jewish people. The day is sometimes called Holocaust Remembrance Day.[12]

Holocaust Days of Remembrance—April 23 - April 30—The last full week in April commemorates the victims of the Holocaust.

Sitting Shiva—This is what Jewish-Americans call the seven-day mourning period following a death in the family. Families open their homes to visitors who come to offer sympathy.

The Torah—The Torah is the compilation of the five books of Moses, which captures the essence of Jewish law and life. All 304,805 words of the Torah scroll are copied by a process dictated by millennia of tradition. Copying a Torah scroll is a special skill relatively few people have, according to an article by Peter Steinfels in the *New York Times* in 1994. Scripture from a scroll that is handwritten on parchment by a religious scribe has greater meaning for Jews than text read from the Bible. A Torah can cost tens of thousands of dollars. The scripture is read from the scroll on the Sabbath and at other religious services..

Talmud—From the Hebrew, Talmud means teaching, study, learning. The Talmud is a collection of Hebrew and Aramaic interpretations of stories, rabbinical traditions, legal teachings and exposition of scripture. It is from oral law.

Jewish law as codified in the Talmud, written between the first and fifth century, teaches that in every generation there lives a person possessed with superior moral leadership who has the potential to become the Messiah if the world is spiritually perfected for his arrival. While most Jews interpret this symbolically, the Lubavitches, an ultra-Orthodox sect, take it literally. Jewish law says the Messiah must come by the year 6000. In 1999 the year was 5760 in the Jewish calendar, according to an article by Laurie Goldstein in the *Washington Post*.[13]

Hasidic Jews—These people comprise an ultra-Orthodox sect rooted in Eastern Europe who live by a strict interpretation of the 2,000-year-old Talmud. The men wear long black coats, wide-brimmed hats and their hair has long side curls. They are sometimes referred to as "the Hasidim."

Tisha B'av—Commemorates the destruction of the first temple in 580 B.C. and the second temple in 70 A.D. and other calamities in Jewish history, including the expulsion of the Jews from Spain in 1492 and the Nazi Holocaust in World War II.

The term "Diaspora" refers to the areas of the world other than Israel to which Jews have dispersed (this is also a generic term for the forced dispersion of an ethnic group).

The **Lubavitche**—The 250-year-old Lubavitchen movement is distinguished from other ultra-Orthodox Jewish sects by its energetic proselytizing, and it claims some 300,000 followers, 1,800 schools and institutions in thirty-eight countries and $100 million in annual contributions. Many members believe that the late "Rebbie," Grand Rabbi Menachem Mendal Schneerson, was the long-awaited "Messiah" who would lead them to redemption.

At age 13, Jewish boys demonstrate that they have reached the age of religious maturity by reading from the Torah in Synagogue. This is called the *bar mitzvah*, and it is usually followed by a large party. There was no comparable ceremony for Jewish girls until American Jews developed the *bat mitzvah*, which became popular starting in the 1950s (it was created by an American rabbi, Mordecai Kaplan, sometime in the 1920s).

In a Jewish wedding the *"Chuppah,"* or marriage canopy, offers shelter to the wedding party (and symbolically establishes a new home). The bride and groom share wine as part of the ceremony.

Before the marriage ceremony many Jewish brides and grooms sign the *"Ketubbah,"* the marriage contract. Today, rather than just being a legal document, this is increasingly valued as a piece of art, commissioned from an artisan who produces a unique artistic expression of the couple's visions and beliefs.

Hasidic Jews who are determined to preserve their culture continue the practice of arranged marriages, as arranged by a matchmaker. For a match to be made, a couple need only like each other enough to be willing to live together. Marriage, the Hasidim believe, is an expression of religious observance for the purpose of increasing the size of the community through procreation.

Lubavitche and Hasidic weddings have much joyous music, and the guests play an important role in performing a good deed to both the bride and groom. The men and women are separated by a *Mechitzah* (a sort of room divider), and the bride and groom are carried into the reception on chairs in the men's and women's sections. They both are eventually raised while music plays and guests dance atop tables, and they both are pelted with napkins as they look at each other over the divider.

The 1990 Census reported about 100,000 people of Latvian ancestry in the United States. The first immigrants in the United States who came from Latvia were sailors, artisans and peasants. Another group, which came after a revolution in Latvia in 1905, was much more educated. The largest group of Latvians to arrive in the United States came after World War II, when the Soviet Union incorporated Latvia. The early groups of Latvians entered the U.S. through Boston and eventually settled in Massachusetts and Connecticut. The later groups often settled in Milwaukee, Wisconsin, and Cleveland, Ohio.

Latvians belong to the Baltic group of people of Indo-European stock. Since prehistoric times (about 6,000 B.C.) Latvians lived on the eastern shores of the Baltic Sea in northeast Europe, where present day Latvia stands. Of the original Baltic group, only Latvians and Lithuanians, who inhabit the territory south of Latvia, have been able to maintain their ethnic and cultural identity.

There are over 1 million Latvians, Lithuanians and Estonians in the U.S., all from the Baltic states at the eastern end of the Baltic Sea. They number more than 250,000 just in Chicago.

Americans from the Baltic republics, including Latvians, waited fifty years for recognition of their homelands' independence from the Soviet Union, which allowed for free elections. And, when Latvia got its independence in 1991, its residents finally uncorked the champagne, sang national anthems and unfurled the flags they saved just for that day.

For decades, the Latvians, Lithuanians and Estonians in the United States worked on the same team in the fight for their homelands' independence in marches and rallies and in letter-writing campaigns. When it happened, they went their separate ways to celebrate and are likely, some note, to find their homelands rivals for scarce development resources now that freedom has come.

HOLIDAYS AND CUSTOMS

Beginning in 1953 in Chicago, song festivals in Latvian communities were organized to celebrate their culture. Especially valuable in Latvian culture are the "*Dainas*," the Latvian folk poetry and songs that depict every aspect of ancient Latvian life. *Dainas* are regarded as the expression of Latvian religious beliefs and rituals. Over 900,000 such tales have been transcribed. Most Latvians are Protestant, Lutheran or Baptist, and small groups are Catholic.

Many Latvian traditions are based on agricultural life because most of their ancestors came from a rural society.

The holidays are of **Christian** origin, and **Easter** (as with other East European countries) has always had special significance. They color eggs using onion skins rather than paint, and they play games to determine the strongest egg. At Christmas, Latvians open gifts as somebody recites a line of poetry or of a song.

Many Latvians also celebrate:

Midsummer or St. John's Eve—June 21 and June 22—This holiday celebrates nature's fertility with bonfires and songs.

New Year's Day—Latvians have a custom called "Pouring One's Fortune." They pour molten lead into a bucket of cold water. When it hardens, it's examined to determine one's future in the New Year.

Traditionally, Latvian weddings take place in the fall, as a throwback to times when there was more time for celebration (post-harvest, plus food and barley for brewing beer were plentiful to help the festivities).

The 1990 Census reported 811,000 people in the United States of Lithuanian ancestry. The five counties with the largest Lithuanian populations were: Cook County, Illinois; New York City, New York; Los Angeles, California; Worcester, Massachusetts; and Luzerne County (Wilkes-Barre) Pennsylvania.

Lithuanians represent an ancient nation of Europe. Their language has ancient forms and several universities in the United States have courses in Lithuanian for linguistic purposes. Like Greek and Latin, the Lithuanian language has many old forms. It is one of the ancient Indo-European languages. Some maintain that it has similarities to Sanskrit.

There are over 1 million Latvians, Lithuanians and Estonians in the U.S., all from the Baltic states at the eastern end of the Baltic Sea. They number more than 250,000 just in Chicago.

Lithuanians began to arrive in the United States in the late 1860s. The period between 1880 and 1914 saw the greatest number of Lithuanian arrivals in the U.S. About 500,000 emigrated during this time, but the exact figures are unknown because incoming Lithuanians were listed as either Poles or Russians. They did not get their own immigration category until 1931.

The majority of immigrants from Lithuania were farmers or farm workers and had few skills but found jobs in coal mining and manufacturing. The earliest settlement of immigrant Lithuanians was in northeastern Pennsylvania's anthracite coal region during the 1870s. In fact, the last coal mine that operated in Scranton, Pennsylvania, listed an emergency exit sign and accident information in Lithuanian.

The Lithuanians first came to the coal regions to displace the earlier English-speaking miners. Most of them settled in the southern anthracite regions of Pennsylvania, whereas other immigrants settled mostly in the northern regions, around Scranton. In Shenandoah and Mahanoy City in Schuylkill County, Pennsylvania, Lithuanians made up a quarter of the population in 1980.

Other Lithuanian communities are found in Massachusetts and Connecticut, where they became workers in textile and shoe factories.

Chicago became the largest Lithuanian center in the United States. By 1901 Lithuanians were second to Poles in the numbers of new immigrants in Chicago. By 1980 Cook County, Illinois, still had three times the Lithuanian ancestry population of the next largest center, which was New York City. Chicago, the cultural center of national Lithuanian life, is home to the U.S.'s two largest Lithuanian-language newspapers.

Lithuanians tended to settle in areas first established by Poles due to the connections between the two groups in the "old" country. Also, Lithuanians were predominantly Roman Catholic in religion, which aided their closeness to the Poles.

After World War II a group of markedly different Lithuanians arrived in the United States. These 35,000 immigrants arrived after spending years in German refugee camps. They came from Lithuanian proper after escaping the terror of Nazi and Soviet occupation. Some came from Poland, but the majority emigrated to the United States through Germany, South America and even Australia. These Lithuanians, among them intellectuals, were more literate than their predecessors to the U.S. and began to provide leadership in Lithuanian-American ethnic life. Some of the earlier Lithuanian immigrants resented them because of their link to Europe and their professional success.[14]

HOLIDAYS AND CUSTOMS

As Roman Catholics, most Lithuanians follow and celebrate the traditional **Christian** holidays, as well as cultural holidays including:

February 16—**Lithuanian Independence Day**—Lithuanians celebrate their independence, gained from Russia in 1918, with dinners and parades.

March 4—**St. Casmir Day**—Lithuanians honor their patron saint with church festivities and religious observations.

WEDDING CUSTOMS

One of the traditions from Eastern Europe kept in Lithuanian-American weddings is that newlyweds traditionally receive bread and salt, wine and sometimes honey from their parents when they return home after the ceremony.

The symbolic meal of wine represents joy, salt represents tears and bread represents work and is served to Lithuanian couples.

Brides wear crowns or wreaths of myrtle rue or flowers during the wedding ceremony as symbols of maidenhood.

Lithuanian newlyweds enter the reception under a badge of sashes held by their attendants.

According to the 1990 Census, there were almost 10,000,000 people in the United States of Polish ancestry. Polish immigrants began to arrive in the United States in large numbers after 1850, and they came from what were originally German-controlled areas in Europe. Most early immigrants embarked from German ports and upon arriving in the United States were guided by German acquaintances who had immigrated earlier to such cities as Milwaukee, Cleveland, Chicago and Buffalo, where there were large German populations. Very few Polish immigrants settled in the South—there was nobody familiar there to greet them. By 1890 the new arrivals came from the Austrian- and Russian-dominated parts of Poland. Upon arrival in New York City, many of them were recruited to work in the coal fields of Pennsylvania. Many of their children remained in northeastern Pennsylvania in what are now Luzerne and Lackawanna counties. An unusually large population of Polish-Americans remain in that area.

Polish-Americans are predominantly Roman Catholic. In the conflicts of the 1970s and 1980s in Poland they supported the church over Soviet control. Polish-Americans were loyal to the home country of their ancestors and supplied much-needed economic and political support. Polish-Americans created many large fraternal and religious organizations, such as the Polish Union, the Polish National Alliance and the Polish-American Congress. Polish-Americans have also played a vital role in the United States labor movement.[15]

The story of the Polish National Catholic Church of America, which today has about 250,000 members (compared to the near 10,000,000 who are Roman Catholic), is that of twentieth-century reformation on American shores. By 1900 there were nearly 200 Polish Roman Catholic parishes scattered throughout the United States. Nearly 1 million Poles streamed into the United States in the decade preceding World War I. The demand for new parishes outstripped the Roman Catholic Church's ability to create new ones. Many of these Polish immigrants knew that there were no Polish bishops in the U.S. and felt that the Irish-German hierarchy had little concern for their welfare. They could not establish a church of their own without securing the bishop's approval; they had to accept the pastor he appointed. They particularly resented orders to give up teaching the Polish language and culture in their parish schools; consequently, discontent blazed into open revolt and upheaval in Polish communities.

In response, the Polish National Catholic Church was founded in the United States. Missionaries from the U.S. returned to Poland to establish branches of this independent "national" church. Almost 200 churches have been organized in the United States, and by 1951, when communism cut off the diocese in Poland, it had 122 parishes in that country.

When the bishop denied a parish delegation of Polish anthracite miners' and factory workers' in Scranton, Pennsylvania, request for lay representation in parish affairs, they blocked their appointed priest from the church entrance. The police came and a riot ensued. Within weeks, the alienated groups organized a new parish. They invited a young, Polish-born priest, Father Frances Hodur, to accept leadership of their flock. On March 14, 1897, he came to Scranton and took charge of St. Stanislaus, the mother church of the new movement. In the next few years, Hodur struggled for Rome's recognition of Polish-American problems. The differences between the church and Rome were not about doctrine; they were questions of jurisdiction and pride. When Hodur was unsuccessful on a trip to see church leaders in Italy, he returned and distanced his parish from Rome. He began making church activities and administration more suited to his Polish parishioners. Other parishes followed suit, and in 1904 Hodur was chosen Bishop-Elect for the New Polish National Catholic Church.

Pulaski Day—October 11—More than 100,000 people parade through New York City and other cities. Many of them wear traditional dress commemorating Casimir Pulaski, a Polish patriot who served in the American Revolution.

Candelmas Day—February 2—Candles blessed in church are taken home to protect family members from sickness and bad fortune.

Paczki Day—Day before Ash Wednesday—The word *Paczki* refers to a fruit-filled type of doughnut. On this day families bake these in order to use up the sugar and fat in the house before the long fast of Lent.

Easter—Easter is especially important as a holiday to Polish-Americans because they were originally an agrarian people; Easter marks the beginning of the farmer's year. It is celebrated with meat, traditional cakes and colored eggs.

Christmas Eve—December 24—Dinner on this evening is called *Wigilia* and begins when the first star of the evening appears.

WEDDING CUSTOMS

Some Polish people continue to celebrate weddings with much partying, including drinking and dancing polkas. Some involve parts of the seven steps of marriage: inquiry and proposal, betrothal, maiden evening and the symbolic unbraiding of the virgin's hair, baking the wedding cake, the marriage ceremony, putting to bed and removal to the groom's house.

The 1990 Census shows a total of 365,000 people of Romanian ancestry in the United States. Romanians (also spelled Rumanians) did not begin to arrive in the United States in any large numbers until about 1895. A few, mostly Romanian Jews, arrived prior to that date. They came with few personal contacts, and most worked as laborers. They settled primarily in the Midwest in Detroit, Cleveland and Chicago.

A large Romanian Jewish population remains in New York City and its suburban counties. The religion of Romanians was primarily Romanian Orthodox, but some were Greek Catholic and Protestant.

HOLIDAYS AND CUSTOMS

Romanian Christians celebrate the traditional **Christian** holidays, focusing on **Christmas**, **New Year's** and **Easter** because of its significance in the **Orthodox** religion. Other holidays celebrated include:

Reunification Day—December 1—This day when Transylvania united with Romania is commemorated with dinners by members of the Romanian-American community.

Romanian National Day—January 24—For special occasions the Romanian National Dance, called the "*Hora*," is observed. In this dance, men and women hold hands in a circle. The tradition spread from Eastern Europe across the Atlantic—many Jewish-Americans, too, do this ceremonial dance.

The United States and Russia have never been at war, which is one of the paradoxes of the Cold War. Yet the two nations have never developed the rapport that historically has existed between the U.S. and so many other nations. Russians, distinguished from other ethnic groups from the former Soviet Union, never contributed a numerous contingent to the American melting pot. However, there was some influx from the upper and professional classes after the revolution in 1917 and a trickle of dissidents after Stalin's death. The state of Alaska was a Russian territory first visited and settled by Orthodox missionaries in the early 1800s. It was a very small settlement, and few settlers remained when the U.S. acquired Alaska in 1867.

A group of Russian immigrants known as the "Old Believers" started arriving in the United States in about 1885. They came, as many others before and after them, seeking religious freedom and economic opportunity. They were among the earliest immigrants from Russia, and most settled in New Jersey, Pennsylvania and Michigan. Others came in waves in the 1960s and settled in Oregon. In later years, many of the communities that were made up of the "Old Believers" established closer ties with the main Russian Orthodox Church of the United States. However, many of the groups have maintained their traditional language, lifestyle, clothing and dietary habits. Singing continues to play a central role in the rituals of the "Old Believers."

A second group of Russians unique to the United States arrived in California in the first decade of the twentieth century. They were known as the Russian "*Molokans.*" They found work in San Francisco in the aftermath of the great earthquake of 1906. Many of them still reside in the Potreno Hill district of San Francisco. There are three main branches of *Molokans* in the United States. They are "Steadfast," who claimed to have preserved the original doctrine, the "Jumpers," who recognize the Holy Spirit in prophecy and physical manifestation, and the "Maximists," a group that respected the teachings of Maxim Rudometrina. A fourth group of *Molokans*, in Oregon (Reformist), has adopted English as its liturgical language and has introduced new approaches to the church.

HOLIDAYS AND CUSTOMS

Most Russians celebrate **Orthodox** religious holidays. **Easter** is celebrated more than other holidays: there are midnight services at church, candlelight processions and the early morning blessing of Easter baskets filled with foods and eggs.

The 1990 Census showed 741,000 people of Ukrainian ancestry in the United States. From 1880 to 1914 the Ukrainian settlement pattern was established in the United States. Before World War I hardly any of the immigrants thought of themselves as Ukrainian but rather as Russian or Ruthenian (refer also to the section on Byzantine Catholics in the chapter on Religions and Ethnicity). After that period, an evolution of identity labels resulted in more of them calling themselves Ukrainian. In the 1920s separate Ukrainian organizations in the United States were created for both the Byzantine Catholics and the Orthodox believers (the dominant religions of Ukrainians). Ukrainian Catholics were chiefly from the western Ukraine, specifically from a region called Galicia, which during history had changed hands between Russia and Poland. Poland claimed most of Galicia after World War II; and Poland's communist government suppressed the church.

Ukrainians settled in the anthracite counties of Pennsylvania, where they were recruited as coal miners. In the early years, mining was the most common job for them.[16] Today, New York City has more people of Ukrainian ancestry than anywhere else in the United States.

Joseph Stalin, the communist leader in the former Soviet Union, disbanded the Ukrainian Catholic Church in 1946, accusing it of collaborating with Nazi occupiers in the war, and handed its churches and property to the Orthodox Church, whose leaders stood by him in World War II.

Millions of Catholics were forced underground, but in 1990 the new political climate under former Russian leader Mikhail Gorbachev allowed them control of their churches.

Ukrainian Catholics consider St. George's Cathedral in Moscow the seat of their church, and the dispute over ownership came to symbolize their battle with the Russian Orthodox authorities over the return of hundreds of churches, monasteries and other buildings used by Catholics before 1946.

HOLIDAYS AND CUSTOMS

One of the oldest Ukrainian customs is observed on **Christmas Eve**, when the family, led by the father, rushes outside as darkness falls, in order to catch a glimpse of the first star. When the stars arrive the father gathers the family and passes out morsels of bread dipped in honey and says, "*Khrystos Razdayetsia*"—Christ is born.

When guests are present, the host at a dinner will introduce *Sviata Vechera*, the Holy Supper, and the guests are served the honey-dipped bread. Usually carols are played as the Christmas Eve dinner begins. A loaf of bread with a cross swathed across its midsection sits in the center of the table. The bread, called *Kolach*, is not eaten until later during the meal, but remains as a centerpiece symbolizing Jesus as the light of the world and the living bread who nourishes the soul. The bread, bordered by two candles, rests upon a bed of hay that commemorates the manger scene. By night's end, those gathered for the dinner will eat twelve courses that stand for Jesus's twelve disciples. The foods include borscht, three types of fish and pierogies (which are pasta dumplings stuffed with vegetables, potatoes, rice or meat).

Still a folk art in Eastern Europe, decorating **Easter** eggs today is closely identified with Ukraine, where it is a complicated ritual and where folklore is full of stories linking the egg with biblical figures.

96

There are two legends surrounding the origin of the custom of decorating eggs at Easter. The first concerns Simon of Cyrene. According to the ancient tale, Simon was obliged to put down a basket of eggs he was carrying so that he could help carry the cross of Jesus. When Simon returned to his basket, he found the eggs decorated with colors and patterns.

The other legend concerns the Blessed Virgin Mary. It is said Our Lady went to Pontius Pilate to offer a basket of eggs as a ransom for her son. When Pilate refused to see her, Mary wept over the basket and her tears fell on the eggs, forming colors and patterns.

Ukrainians continue the tradition of richly decorating their Easter eggs. Patterns vary from country to country and region to region; however, there has been a multi-step process in trimming the eggs and it has basically remained the same.

Dyeing the elaborate Ukrainian **Pysanky**, or egg, is done in secret, so no two will be alike. It begins with a prayer. The egg is then presented at church for the priest's blessing before it is given to a friend or loved one.

For Ukrainian-Americans, *Pysanky* is a ritual experience that integrates religion, ethnicity and artistic expression. It is a craft that contributes to the community solidarity, which helps maintain their identity as Ukrainian, among themselves and to outsiders.

Like many such customs, *Pysanky* was a pre-Christian practice into which Christian symbolism was introduced. Decorated eggs were given as gifts and sometimes placed at key points near the house, barn and fields to bring prosperity for the coming year and to ward off evil.

Ukrainian *Pysanky* designs are still mostly pagan and geometric, but they also incorporate Christian symbols such as the fish and the cross. Stripes represent eternity, the sun represents renewal, a comb or rake represents harvest, pine needles represent eternal youth, and a hen or rooster represents fertility. Colors are applied by waxing on a design, similar to the method of dyeing batiks. A special tool, the *kistska*, is used to apply the wax.

Ukrainian-Americans celebrate Orthodox religious holidays following the Julian calendar. They also commemorate the anniversary of Ukraine's independence on January 22, 1917.

WEDDING CUSTOMS

A traditional ritual called *Umykannia* at Ukrainian weddings involves a mock abduction of the bride and a skirmish between the families of the bride and groom. The groomsmen kidnap the bride during a Ukrainian wedding reception and return her for ransom. A bread called *Rorovai* is served and is decorated with symbolic motifs representing eternity and the union of the two families.

Ukrainian couples also receive religious icons from their parents before the ceremony.

[1] The U.S. Romani Holocaust Council

[2] The U.S. Romani Holocaust Council

[3] according to Ian Hancock, a professor at the University of Texas and an authority on Gypsies in the U.S.

[4] *We the People*

[5] *We the People*

[6] *We the People*, U.S. Census, *Harvard Encyclopedia of American Ethnic Groups*

[7] *The World of Jewish Humor* by Leo Rosten

[8] according to a survey done and reported by George Gallup Jr. and Jim Castrelli

[9] according to a survey by the Council of Jewish Federations

[10] as reported by Richard Morris in the *Washington Post*

[11] The date varies according to the Jewish calendar.

[12] The date varies according to the Jewish calendar.

[13] June 19, 1994

[14] *We the People*

[15] *The Harvard Encyclopedia of American Ethnic Groups*

[16] *We the People*

CHAPTER VI:

FROM THE FAR EAST CAME AMERICANS OF AMERICAN PACIFIC ISLANDER, BANGLADESHI, CAMBODIAN, CHINESE, FILIPINO, HMONG, JAPANESE, KOREAN, LAOTIAN, PAKISTANI, SIKH, SUBCONTINENT INDIAN, THAI, TIBETAN, VIETNAMESE AND AUSTRALIAN AND NEW ZEALANDER ANCESTRY

Asian-Americans, though sometimes dealt with as if they are monolithic, are a diverse group. About 70 percent of the Asian population in the U.S. arrived after 1970, according to 1990 Census reports. But that doesn't mean their influx has ended. Many more are expected as Hong Kong reverted to Chinese rule in 1997. In fact, their numbers are expected to exceed 10 million by the year 2000.

In terms of past immigration into the U.S., one of the largest streams of refugees from Southeast Asia began in 1975, after the fall of Saigon at the end of the Vietnam War. The influx was originally seen as temporary, but the flow continued into the 1990s as new political upheavals and natural disasters drew more refugees to the United States. Through the early '80s, the Vietnamese were followed by a more diverse group of Cambodians, ethnic Chinese from Vietnam and Laotians.

Many of the later refugees who came from rural areas of Asia came with few skills to survive in the U.S. and had to acquire them after their arrival. In general, before arriving in the United States they spent longer periods detained in refugee camps in Thailand. Since they were coming out of Vietnam and Cambodia, people were reluctant to take them, which further prolonged their adjustment to American society, according to a 1990 U.S. Census report. Their transition also has been hampered by the trauma of their war experiences. A study based on information from the Census Bureau, the Immigration and Naturalization Service and state governments[1] showed that Asian-Americans are the fastest-growing segment of the U.S. population. Their presence in the U.S. rose from 1.4 million in 1960 to more than 7 million in 1990; they represent 3 percent of the nation's total population. Regardless of obstacles they faced upon immigrating to the U.S., the study pointed out that Asian-Americans have the lowest divorce rate of any racial group (3 percent), the lowest rate of teenage pregnancy (6 percent) and the lowest rate of unemployment (3.5 percent).

Asian-Americans have significant representation in professional fields, such as medicine and engineering.[2] Among Asian Indians, for example, 47 percent hold professional or managerial jobs, compared to 22 percent of Korean-Americans. (This compares with 24 percent for whites.) Japanese and Chinese also rank very high.

Though many are successful, some immigrants from Asia still languish in poverty. Nearly twenty years after the end of the war in Southeast Asia that brought thousands of Cambodian, Laotian and Vietnamese refugees to the United States, many still haven't found economic success in their new homeland. In fact, as of 1994 Southeast Asians had the highest rate of welfare dependency of any racial or ethnic group in the U.S. By 1994, more than 30 percent of all Southeast Asian households in the U.S. depended on welfare for survival, according to one study on the economic diversity of Asian-Americans. Among some groups, such as Cambodians and Laotians in California, the percentage of those on welfare reached as high as 77 percent. Nationwide, only 8 percent of all households received public assistance in 1991.

The makeup of Asian-American families on welfare differs from some other ethnic groups. Nearly 90 percent of Southeast Asian families on welfare have both parents present, making them ineligible for some U.S. programs that are designed to help the more common welfare population of single-parent families and families headed by teenagers.

According to a *New York Times* report,[3] marketers said in 1994 that more than 68 percent of Asians speak their native tongue. This is in contrast to the 20 million people in the United States who identify themselves as being of Hispanic descent, who mostly speak Spanish or English or both: basically, two-thirds of Hispanic Americans speak English while one-third of Asian-Americans do. By contrast, the nation has one-third as many Asians, and they speak a variety of languages. In 1995 there was no national television for Asians and only a few local stations, whereas there were two national television networks with Spanish-language programming.

As a result of the ethnic conflict in some Asian countries, the fastest-growing subgroups among Asian-American immigrants are Vietnamese (134.8 percent growth between 1980 and 1990), Asian Indians (125.6 percent) and Koreans (125.3 percent). Professor Lawrence Fuchs, who teaches American civilization at Brandeis University, points to the enormous diversity among Asian immigrants: "You have variety within variety—more variety of class, more variety of skill, more variety in origins."

According to Fuchs, more than 60 percent of the 1.6 million Chinese-Americans in 1994 were born overseas, and the figure climbs in some areas to more than 80 percent, as in New York City's Chinatown. Nearly 23 percent of Asian-Americans are of Chinese heritage, and about 19 percent, or 1.4 million people, trace their roots to the Philippines. Japanese-Americans, who thirty years ago represented 52 percent of the Asian-American population, now represent 11.7 percent, just ahead of East Indians at 11.2 percent and Koreans at 10.9 percent.[4]

Asian-Americans' growing presence has intimidated some Americans, who in turn have sometimes responded with prejudice. A group called Chinese for Affirmative Action (CAA) in San Francisco reports that Asian-Americans are facing what Jewish people once faced in the United States: the resentment reserved for outsiders pressing for a fair share of the status conferred by elite institutions. Like American Jews before them, Asian-Americans have an intense desire to achieve social mobility by means of education, respect for which is inculcated by cohesive families.

The CAA points out that race-conscious policies in place in certain American institutions may place ceilings through which some Asian-Americans are not allowed to rise.

Asian-Americans, many of whom speak English as a second language, are viewed by some universities as academic "overachievers." In 1994 about 9 percent of California's high-school graduates were Asian-Americans, yet nearly 25 percent of the undergraduates at the University of California at Berkeley were Asian-American.

While Asian-Americans make up just 2.8 percent of the American population (as of 1994), at Harvard, for example, they represent about 12 percent of students; at Stanford they represent about 20 percent; and at the University of California at Berkeley about 30 percent. Asian-American students, far more than members of other minority groups, see earning advanced degrees as the only surefire way to overcome discrimination.

Entrepreneurship by ethnic groups in the Asian-American community has grown enormously, according to the Census Bureau. For example, among other Asian-Americans, Koreans and Indians each more than doubled their business ownership from 1980 to 1990.

Here's what the Census Bureau said about entrepreneurship by Asian ethnic groups in 1987: Chinese-Americans owned 87,717 firms, up 84 percent from 1982; Japanese-Americans owned 53,372 firms, up 23 percent; Filipino-Americans owned 40,412 firms, up 73 percent; Hawaiians owned 4,279 firms, up 46 percent; and other Asians and Pacific Islanders owned 20,310 firms, up 117 percent.

Asian-Americans have increasingly come to be viewed as a "model minority." If Asian-Americans can make it, many politicians ask, why can't others? The "model minority" image homogenizes Asian-Americans and hides their differences. But Asian-Americans are not all the same, and, as with every other group in the U.S., there are myths unduly associated with them. For example, figures on the high earnings of Asian-American relative to whites is misleading because many Asian-Americans (about 40 percent) live in high-income states such as California, Hawaii and New York.

Relatively few Asian-Americans have risen to national or even local prominence in politics, a fact sometimes attributed to the combination of their scattered constituencies, the lack of union among Asian nationalities and a cultural reluctance to push themselves into the limelight. Asians make up about 1 percent of registered voters in the U.S., one-third their portion of the total population. Only a handful, including five members of Congress, hold elective office. To reiterate the point of their lack of political participation, consider that the first Korean-American didn't get elected to Congress until 1992.

Michael Woo, who ran for mayor of Los Angeles in 1992, points out that you can't assume unity consensus among Asian-Americans themselves due to the long history of warfare, invasions and cultural competition, which separates the countries of the Pacific Rim. Also, the Korean-American representative said that you have to be pushy to raise the kind of money you need to run countywide or statewide office, and "It's not in the nature of Asians to do that," which is a statement that to some extent homogenizes Asians.

Daniel Goldman wrote in the *New York Times*[5] about academic success among Asian-Americans. He stated: "As researchers seek to explain dazzling academic performances by Asian-American students, they are uncovering diverse forces at work: a drive to escape discrimination, a cultural belief in the unique value of education as a path to upward mobility, family pressures to succeed and just plain hard work."

According to Goldman, nationally, Asian-Americans in 1990 had a high-school grade point average of 3.25 on a scale of 1 to 4, compared to an average 3.08 for all other students.

There is also a hidden advantage for some Asian-American students who have performed their best: in many cases their immigrant parents were professionals in their native countries and instill in their children motivation to strive for the status they lost upon leaving their homeland.[6]

Dr. Stanley Sue of the University of California at Los Angeles told Goldman that the impressive academic success of Asian-Americans is largely a result of their strong belief in education as an escape route from the social and economic limits imposed by prejudice—a belief they hold more strongly than do other minorities, according to a study of 10,000 Asian-American students conducted by Sanford Dornbusch of Stanford University.

The more Americanized Asian-Americans have become, Dr. Sue told Goldman, the less they worry about being denied access to good jobs because of their ethnicity.

Leonard Gordon, a sociologist at Arizona State University, points out that, while black and Hispanic students had the same life goals as did Asian-Americans, there was a great different in their expectations. "They didn't have the same hope of success as did Asian-American students. Their history leads them to be pessimistic about reaching their goals," Gordon said.

That attitude marks one of the strongest differences in outlooks between Asian-American students, African-Americans and American Indians.

Most Asian-Americans are voluntary immigrants, drawn to the U.S. in part by the dream of success. Such immigrants see cultural differences as something to overcome, while involuntary groups tend to cherish differences, said John Ogbu, an anthropologist at the University of California at Berkeley.

Steven A. Holmes, writing in the *New York Times*,[7] discussed in some detail how Asian-Americans felt about immigration as an issue in American politics. Asians view immigration and some of the proposals to scale it back in the early and mid-1990s with some anxieties. Asians made up 36.6 percent of the immigrants in 1994, though they represent just 3 percent of the total U.S. population.

Asian-Americans sound just like many other ethnic groups when congressional bills are introduced concerning immigration. They want relatives to be able to join them from overseas. They want their culture replenished with new arrivals. Asian-Americans also have special memories and fears: Asians are the only ethnic (racial) group in this century to have been specifically barred by law from entry or naturalization. Immigration laws in the early 1920s either limited or barred immigrants from Asia from entering the U.S. They remember the simple issue of their race being thought not good enough even to be allowed into the United States, much less to equal other people.

In the early 1990s, Asian-American advocates had a grass-roots political awakening concerning governmental matters that affected them. This is unusual for people who have roots in societies with little tradition of political participation and could be in part because they tended to have higher levels of skills and education than some other immigrant groups.[8] According to the Census Bureau, nearly 46 percent of immigrants from the Philippines had college degrees, as did 42 percent of immigrants from China and 36.1 percent from Korea. (By contrast, only 14.7 percent of native-born Americans had college degrees at that time.)

Advocates for the immigrant Asian community, such as the National Asian Pacific Legal Consortium, say the educational and professional credentials of the 1990s Asian immigrants gave them the skills and financial resources to organize themselves politically and the temperament to stand up for themselves in the political world. The leaders of the consortium point out, "Thirty years before this period the Asian community was so small and segregated that it had to force itself on making money just to support their families. For the Chinese it was just restaurants or small businesses. So they didn't have much time to think about the whole society or the whole picture."

By 1995, Asian immigrants arrived with more education and money and found themselves more adaptable to U.S. society, according to Qingsong Zhang, executive director of the Asian-American Association in Los Angeles.

According to an article in the *New York Times*,[9] a study by the Los Angeles-based nonprofit group Leadership Education for Asian-Pacifics showed that Asian Pacifics are the fastest-growing immigrant group in the U.S. The study, "Asian-Pacific Americans," said the number of people whose origins are in Asia or the Pacific increased 385 percent from 1971 to 1990 and is expected to reach 11 million by the year 2000.

The number of businesses owned by Asian-Americans grew by 90 percent between 1989 and 1996, the report said. In fact, in 1996, of the estimated 2,000 high-tech companies in California's Silicon

Valley, nearly 500 were run by Asian-Americans. The report also pointed out that fifteen of the United States' most successful high-tech companies were founded by immigrants of Asian ancestry.

The report also found that, among Americans 25 to 38 years old in 1990, Asian-Pacific Americans were twice as likely as non-Hispanic whites to have received a post-undergraduate degree. The number of second-generation Asian-Americans receiving welfare is much lower than other groups' averages. Asian-Pacific families are also more likely to have both parents present and have higher average incomes than any other ethnic group or race.

In a study of 7,836 high-school students in the San Francisco area, Asian-Americans spent over 40 percent more time doing homework than did other students—about seven hours a week versus five hours among other groups. Also, they did almost 50 percent more homework than their peers, from grammar school on. "That is the first and most important reason for the differences," said Dr. Sanford Dornbusch of Stanford University. "Asian-Americans work harder." Behind the harder work lies another basic difference between Asian-Americans and other students. "They are oriented toward their families, not just their friends," Dornbusch added.

"Those Asian-Americans who seem to be super whiz kids are mostly from professional families," said Dr. Ronald Takaki, professor of ethnic studies at Berkeley. "Over 50 percent of African-American kids are from impoverished single-parent families. They don't have an intact family with highly educated parents, like many Asian-American students."

American Pacific Islanders are a small but distinct component of the Asian and Pacific Island population. The 1990 Census counted 365,024 Pacific Islanders in the U.S., a 41 percent increase since the 1980 Census. Pacific Islanders include diverse populations who differ in language and culture. They are of Polynesian, Micronesian and Melanesian backgrounds. The Polynesian group is the largest of the three and includes Hawaiians, Samoans, Tongans and Tahitians. The Micronesian group, the second-largest, is primarily Guamanian (or Chamorros), but also includes other Mariana Islanders, Marshall Islanders, Palaians and several other groups. The Fijian population is the largest Melanesian group.

Hawaiians are, of course, native to the United States. People born in American Samoa are U.S. nationals with the right to free entry in to the U.S., and, since 1950, natives of Guam are U.S. citizens. Although some groups are small in number, all Pacific Islander groups make continuing contributions to the diversity of the United States.

Approximately 75 percent of Pacific Islanders live in just two states—California and Hawaii. Only 13 percent of Pacific Islanders were foreign-born, much lower than the 63 percent for the total Asian and Pacific Islander population. The average Pacific Islander family in the U.S. had 4.1 people in 1990, larger than the 3.2-person average American family. Of Pacific Islanders who are 25 or older, 76 percent were at least high-school graduates.

The ethnic population statistics for American Pacific Islanders as of the 1990 Census were as follows:

Hawaiians: 57.8 percent, or 140,885

Samoans: 17.2 percent, or 35,336

Tongan: 4.8 percent, or 9,666

Guamanian: 13.5 percent, or 49,345

Melanesian: 1.9 percent, or 7,195

Other Pacific Islanders: 3.8 percent, or 14,000

The first Hawaiians immigrated to the United States from Polynesia. A monarchy ruled until Queen Liliuokalani was overthrown in 1893.

In multiracial Hawaii, much public debate has centered around what constitutes a "Native Hawaiian." There are about 50,000 Native Hawaiians, compared to about 200,000 Hawaiians—those with less than 50 percent native blood.

Hawaii has a complicated land grant program for those with at least 50 percent Hawaiian blood. But some want to expand participation to include anyone who had ancestors in the islands when British explorer Captain James Cook arrived in 1778, which would allow for more recipients of funding from staff agencies.

In racial and ethnic relations, Hawaii is normally a gentle place, a mosaic of Hawaiian, Japanese, Chinese, Filipino, Caucasian and other Americans living in amity. The Hawaiian way, the state's residents say, is to be gentle, patient and circumspect. Hawaiian residents give several reasons for the relative racial harmony. The most important, they agree, is that everyone there is a minority. In addition, the good feeling conveyed by "*aloha*," a word that is hard to translate—it means hello and goodbye at the same time and alludes to human warmth that is still alive.

In a population of just over 1 million, Hawaii's population is 24 percent white European ancestry, 23 percent Japanese-American and 20 percent ethnic Hawaiian and part-ethnic Hawaiian. Filipinos, at 11 percent, are the fastest-growing group in Hawaii, and other ethnic groups round out the population.

Despite the seemingly harmonious society, under the surface exist undeniable tensions rooted largely in economics. White and Asian-Americans are the most prosperous of Hawaiian residents, while ethnic Hawaiians and Filipinos are the least prosperous.[10]

Native Hawaiians are statistically at the bottom rung on Hawaii's socioeconomic ladder. In the early 1990s, they had the largest families, the lowest incomes and the highest mortality rate and were disproportionately represented in state prisons, according to the state office of Hawaiian affairs.

The Hawaiian word "*haole*" originally meant foreigner but is now widely used to mean a white person. According to Professor Haunani-Kay Trask, director of the University of Hawaii Center for Hawaiian Studies, only new arrivals resent the term, because many of them have not experienced being part of a minority.

HOLIDAYS AND CUSTOMS

In the days before World War II, Hawaiians in various ethnic groups worked together but lived largely in separate neighborhoods and did not socialize much outside their group. People in Hawaii say that everyone gets along because they celebrate each other's holidays. **Christmas** by non-Christians, **Chinese New Year**, Japanese holidays and Hawaiian holidays like **Kuhio Day** and **Kam Day**.

The main holidays include:

Kamehameha Day—June 11—Honors the memory of King Kamehameha III and his chiefs, who created the first state constitution and a legislature that set up a public school system. Each year the holiday is celebrated with parades and people from all five Hawaiian islands coming to Oahu, the main island, for celebration.

Kuhio Day—March 26—This is a state holiday in Hawaii and celebrates the birthday of Prince Jonah Kuhio Kalanianole, who left Hawaii when its monarchy was overthrown in 1893. He returned after Hawaii became part of the United States and was the state's first territorial representative to Congress. He did everything he could to protect the rights and traditional ways of the Hawaiian people, and they now honor him with the Prince Kuhio parade and festival, which includes outrigger canoe races and traditional hula dances.

Lei Day—May 1—Celebrates the spirit of *aloha*. Everyone wears a flower lei; men wear *aloha* shirts with characteristic bright floral patterns and women wear Hawaiian dress to work and social activities.

Newly arrived Bangladeshi immigrants who know no one in the United States search out any Bangladeshi they can find to ask for help, which is often given in the tradition of their country, according to a *New York Times* article.[11] There are approximately 50,000 Bangladeshis in the United States according to the Census, and most live in New York City.

Many of the new immigrants came to New York after winning visas in a lottery that the U.S. State Department began in the late '80s. The lottery was an effort to increase the ethnic diversity of immigrants. Most Bangladeshis have settled in Jackson Heights, Astoria and Corona in Queens, New York, and many work in restaurants or delicatessens, and as taxicab drivers.

There are three Bengali-language newspapers in the city. The community has eight mosques.

One of the problems experienced by Bangladeshi immigrants, like other ethnic groups, is that their dreams of economic prosperity sometimes quickly dissolve into a nightmare of economic, social and cultural deprivation. After leaving a land cursed by recurrent and massive natural disasters such as earthquakes and floods and beset by extreme poverty and unemployment, they find themselves in a community without many job skills, access to job training, or second-language programs and plagued by a high unemployment rate.[12]

HOLIDAYS AND CUSTOMS

The Bangladeshi are **Muslim** and the holidays they celebrate in the United States are those of Islam, which are explained in the section on Religion and Ethnicity.

There are approximately 150,000 people (147,411 in the 1990 Census) of Cambodian ancestry in the United States. Almost all were refugees fleeing the slaughter of the late '70s and early '80s in their native country. Over 80 percent of them arrived between 1980 and 1990. The Cambodians make up approximately 2.1 percent of all Americans of Asian ancestry. Over half of the Cambodians have settled in Southern California. The median age of this group is 19.4 years, and 95 percent of them speak the Cambodian language, which is Khmer.

Many Cambodian women came to the United States not only as refugees but also as widows because their husbands and most of the males in their families were massacred or starved to death by the Khmer Rouge government, which caused the deaths of a million people in the 1970s. Yet many of these women, some who have married American men, find solace in preserving Cambodian culture. Hanging on to their culture has been a help in relieving stress. The local Buddhist temple serves as a refuge. Cultural preservation, like with other groups, provides a sense of identity for the Cambodians. After surviving hell on earth, they have come to the United States with a fierce commitment to make life whole again.

The conflicts of biculturalism have deeply affected families and communities. Many parents need help to understand their children, whose American ways are often difficult to cope with. The parents want the children to know who they are and where they came from.

One of the areas in which this is evident is in the language spoken by the Khmer people. Although many adults speak Khmer to their children, the children do not necessarily respond in kind.

The United States Office of Refugee Resettlement has provided funds to the Cambodian Network Council to undertake domestic programs that have helped Khmer refugees and their Khmer-American community leaders to become more self-reliant. Family respect is a proud etiquette in the Khmer culture, and when this is lost among the children, it brings great shame and disgust. Because the Khmer community has dispersed in the U.S., it is difficult for many of them to carry on much of their social and traditional events. The Cambodian Network Council is trying to correct this by trying to put Cambodian families together.

While Cambodians are happy to be part of the American melting pot, they are determined to maintain some of their rich traditions. They are grateful for business opportunities, prospects for home ownership and access to education.

The Cambodian refugees, with little recognition, have virtually taken over a certain business in California and have made it their primary route into the local economy. That business is the making of doughnuts, according to an article in the *New York Times*. Like Koreans, Sikhs and Asian-Indians in other business segments of the regional economies of parts of the United States, they did this by a cooperative effort within their own community by extending credit to one another, and by inspirational leadership. The Cambodians have opened up one small shop after another, cutting deeply into the profits of large doughnut chains. By 1995, Cambodian refugees owned about 80 percent of the doughnut shops in California. While these refugees, survivors of the Khmer regime, brought with them memories of one of the twentieth-century's great horrors, they were able to start a doughnut boom in the 1980s. They used their family as a working unit (like many other ethnic groups before them) to work and manage the business, pulling themselves up from the poverty that affected many of the refugees.

The word "transition" is not new to Cambodian-Americans. For decades, Cambodians have been in transition. In 1975 Cambodia became victim to the Communist regime of Pol Pot and the "Year Zero" marked the beginning of the traumatic transition. Cambodians became migrants in their own country, forced through evacuation to do hard labor. Families were broken up, murdered and separated from each other through forced labor camps.

In 1978, when Vietnam invaded Cambodia, her people were once more uprooted and in limbo. Cambodians became displaced people, seeking refuge along the Thai-Cambodian border, fearful of persecution to their already lost souls. Cambodians lived in these refugee camps for years, despaired and hopeless, awaiting a destination to the first world—United States, Canada, France, Australia, and other developed nations.

During the 70s to the late 80s, once Cambodians got across the vast sea to one of these countries they were called refugees. For many Cambodians, being refugees was the best thing that happened to them. They felt fortunate to be alive, and to be given a second chance to rebuild their lives.

Cambodians accepted the identity of a refugee and for awhile they felt blessed and comfortable, because for the time being they were able to live their lives in stability. Once the 90s approached it was felt that due to necessity, Cambodian-Americans must reconstruct their identity as Asian-Americans and as part of the various immigrant communities.

The Cambodian people are one of the world's most traumatized ethnic groups ever to come to the United States. This follows decades of civil war, genocide, loss of home and family in their homeland. Since their resettlement in the United States during the 70s and 80s, the Cambodian-American community has grown by 1997 to approximately 300,000 nationwide. To deal with this growth there are over 200 Cambodian community based organizations formed to help members achieve economic sufficiency and well-being, and to better integrate into the American mainstream. The Cambodian Network Council (CNC) has been established as a national umbrella organization to advocate for the interest of all Cambodians as well as to coordinate and facilitate their resettlement in what they see as a land of opportunities.

As they approached the millennium the results of the endeavors of this group has been generally very positive. There are many successful Cambodian professionals in all fields and many flourishing Cambodian businesses catering to both the Cambodian-American community and others outside the community. There are Cambodian-Americans studying and graduating from top American universities such as Harvard, Yale, Stanford and MIT, just to name a few. Consequently, there are more Cambodians than ever with college educations competing fiercely in America's highly skilled market. With the support from their parents, most of the high school graduates choose higher education as the ticket to future success and fame. From 1977 to the approaching of the millennium Cambodian-Americans have achieved a level of economic sufficiency that is commendable by any American standards.

Some of the customs carried on by Cambodians in the U.S. include:

The most important holiday is **New Year's**. It is celebrated on April 13 and lasts for three days. One of the traditions is the playing of the game *bosenhoung*. This involves a young man and women. A scarf is thrown around the woman the man is interested in. During New Year's ceremonies, young people dance traditional Khmer dances and offerings are made to ancestors. Visits to the temple are made to pray for the New Year's blessings. The ceremony of praying for the deceased is called *Pehum Ben*.

The religion of the Cambodians is **Buddhist**, and they follow the Buddhist religious holidays and customs of the Theravada Sect.

Once Cambodian-Americans felt more settled in the United States they started to take part and produce replicas of festivals that use to take place in Cambodia. Once such festival is the "Water Festival" that takes place in Southeast Asia and in Cambodia. It celebrated the beginning of the harvest season. The festival takes place on a river and its banks. Boat races are held and men and women wear colorful costumes. Food stalls line the river bank and live music is performed. One of the first to stage such a festival was by the Cambodian and Lao-American community in Lowell, Massachusetts along the Merrimack River.

May 18th Cambodian-Americans celebrate the Cambodian National Day.

In Cambodian marriage ceremony receptions, guests tie holy strings to the hands of the bride and groom, symbolizing a long and happy marriage. Previously, the strings had been blessed and immersed in holy water.

Chinese-Americans are part of a larger worldwide phenomenon of "overseas Chinese" who are spread from Southeast Asia to the Caribbean and South America. Chinese-Americans have always been a tiny part of that worldwide phenomenon.

The major period of Chinese immigration into the United States began in 1850, and by 1851 there were 25,000 Chinese in California. By 1870 the Chinese-American population grew to 63,000 in the U.S., most of whom were on the West Coast. They mostly came from the Pear Delta area of the Kwangtung Province, on the southeast coast of China. The Chinese who spoke Cantonese came along with them. Many first worked in the gold industry in the Sierra Nevada foothills. When the Chinese first came to the West, they were seen as badly needed labor, but within a short period of time they were seen as threats to the wages of white Americans.

After working in the gold mines the Chinese became construction workers, railroad workers and workers in small shoe, garment and cigar factories. Some ran hand laundries, others fished (shrimp, abalone, ocean fish) and others worked in the sweat shops of the garment industry. Some of the sweat shop work, in fact, has continued for Chinese immigrants in the 1990s.

It should be noted that some Chinese businessmen came to Hawaii early in the nineteenth century, and sugar in Hawaii was first produced by those Chinese investors. When native Hawaiians refused to harvest the cane or work in the fields, they imported Chinese workers.

During the 1960s immigration increased from both Taiwan and Hong Kong, although many immigrants who came from Hong Kong were thought to be refugees from mainland China, which was communist. The Chinese population in the United States in 1980 was almost ten times its size of 1920. Sixty-three percent of the Chinese in the United States in 1980 had been born abroad. Also in 1980, the distribution of Chinese-Americans was 97 percent urban—extremely high compared to other ethnic groups. Three large metropolitan areas were home in 1980 to most of those of Chinese ancestry in the U.S.: the San Francisco Bay area, with the most; the New York City area, including Nassau and Suffolk Counties; and, third, the Los Angeles and Orange County areas in Southern California. According to the 1990 Census, there were 1,505,245 people of Chinese ancestry in the United States, and 42.6 percent lived in California.

One of the aspects of Chinese culture brought to the United States was the secret societies or "*Tongs*." The secret societies became powerful economic and social forces in American Chinatowns in cities such as San Francisco, Seattle, New York and Los Angeles. Chinatowns developed their own community organizations and leaders to conduct their affairs and until the late 1980s, these leaders deliberately kept out of the courts and out of mainstream politics.

Much of the initial economic rise of Chinese-Americans was not in professions but in businesses that had their roots in Chinatowns.

As part of these ethnic organizations, when Chinese-Americans were denied access to capital contained in a bank or in another financial institution, they formed a credit association known as a *Hui*, which was an old institution among Chinese who came from Southern China. This device was quite simple—each member in his turn had access to the pooled resources of all—but what made it successful was that default on repayment was extremely rare.

One characteristic of the Chinese culture maintained in the United States was respect for learning. In the 1990s children and young adults of Chinese ancestry did extremely well in American schools, colleges and universities and in California became the largest ethnic group in that state's university system.

HOLIDAYS AND CUSTOMS

There are vast differences among Chinese people who hail from the mainland, Taiwan and Hong Kong versus those who come from a number of other Asian areas. There are differences in ethnic origin, in dialect, in political affiliations and among generations. Most holidays follow a lunar calendar, and consequently the dates change from year to year.

The Chinese lunar calendar is made up of twelve-year cycles, with each linked to an animal. Every animal has its own elaborate lore, with the horse, for example, signifying energy and vitality.

Chinese New Year, the date of which varies from year to year but is around January or February, is a time for family gatherings and gift-giving and, like New Year's celebrations in other cultures, a time for merriment, reflection and resolution. More specifically and most visibly, it is a time when fire crackers explode relentlessly and lion and dragon dancers happily parade through the streets of Chinatown areas of most major American cities.

Food is an important symbolic part of any Chinese New Year celebration, with particular foods chosen because their names sound like words or expressions heralding good fortune.

Chinese New Year is the most important festival of the Chinese calendar. While it is a family festival, it is also a time for clearing debts and buying new clothes. Some businesses close for two or three days to enjoy the festivals.

The Lantern Festival—This festival officially marks the end of the Chinese New Year celebrations. Lanterns in various traditional designs appear on market stalls and are brought to decorate homes, restaurants and temples.

Ching Ming Festival—This annual festival marks when families visit the graves of ancestors to perform traditional rites including placing flowers on graves, if possible, and praying.

Birthday of Lord Buddha—Buddhist temples hold religious observances and bathe statues of Buddha for Buddhists and many others.

Maidens' Festival—This celebration, also known as the Seven Sisters' Festival, is held on the seventh day of the seventh moon. It is essentially a celebration for unmarried young girls and young lovers and has its origins in Chinese folklore dating back more than 1,500 years.

Mid-Autumn Festival—This is one of the major festivals of the Chinese calendar, similar to the Western harvest festival and lasting for a day or two. It is also known as the Moon Cake Festival for special cakes eaten around this time.

Confucius's Birthday—Celebrated in temples and schools—referred to by some as Teacher's Day—citing and honoring the great wisdom of the Chinese philosopher Confucius.

113

With regards to religion, most Chinese are **Buddhists** and are of the Mahayana sect. Thus, they celebrate the religious holidays associated with Buddhism as described in the section about that religion.

Dr. Sun-Yat-Sen Day—October 10—Celebrated primarily by those Chinese with Taiwanese affiliation. He united the country through nationalism.

WEDDING CUSTOMS

The importance of family is still evident in Chinese-American weddings in the ceremony of obligation. First bowing to heaven and earth and to their ancestors, the bride and groom then bow to their grandparents and parents, serving each a cup of tea and receiving in return gifts of jewelry and lucky money.[13]

A Chinese custom requires an elaborate tea service after the ceremony, just for the couple, hosted by the groom's parents. Seaweed soup, snow peas and noodles are traditional fare.

The total number of Filipino-Americans in the U.S. at the time of the 1990 Census was 1,406,770. The average size of the Filipino family in the United States, 4.2 people, was above the median for all U.S. families. Filipinos make up 20.4 percent of the Asian-American population, with heavy concentrations in California and Hawaii. Approximately 21.7 percent arrived before 1975, and the Filipino population that is 25 and older has attained a higher degree of education than many other Asian groups. More than 89 percent of Filipino males and 85.6 percent of Filipino females 25 and over graduated high school, and more than 41 percent of females and 36 percent of males have a bachelor's degree or higher.

Ethnically and culturally, Filipinos are different from other Asian groups. Yet government agencies have sometimes lumped them together. In the early 1990s in California, Filipinos demanded that they be separated from the category of Asian-Americans as an ethnic group.

The vast majority of Filipino-Americans, about 95 percent, are Roman Catholic, and most of the remainder are Islamic.

The great influx of Filipino farm workers occurred in the 1920s, after anti-Asian immigration laws barred the importation of Japanese laborers then working the California fields. In need of workers, growers sent recruiters to the Philippines, which as an American territory was exempted from the law.

Approximately 100,000 Filipino men flocked to the United States in the years before the Depression, seeking education and wealth, but they instead found impoverished lives of stoop labor and racial codes that forbade them to own land or to marry. They were called *manongs*.

Though the Filipino experience is part of the larger story of American farm workers, it comes with its own especially lonely twist. Forbidden by state anti-miscegenation laws to marry whites, and separated by an ocean from Filipino women, most Filipinos, when compared to their Mexican counterparts, did not form families. The Filipinos found such discrimination especially painful because they saw themselves as Americans.

The Depression shattered most Filipino hopes for fortune; with farmers no longer needing the labor, the government even offered to pay the workers' way home.

One characteristic of the decade was the labor radicalism in which many of the young Filipino workers played prominent roles. Growers grew adept at breaking Filipino strikes with Mexican workers, and vice versa, a pattern that persisted into the 1960s. It was Filipinos, for example, who called the historic 1965 grape strike in California that prompted the famous labor leader Cesar Chavez and his union of predominantly Hispanic workers to follow.

Filipinos, while no longer one of the most rapidly growing Asian minority groups, still increased their numbers by 81.6 percent in the 1980s. Filipinos tend to have less difficulty adapting to a new culture than other immigrants from Asia, in part because most arrive able to speak English.

Filipinos in the U.S. are less likely to congregate in easily identifiable ethnic enclaves than some other ethnic groups. You don't find the establishment of "Manilatowns." They tend to be much more assimilated into the mainstream economy than other immigrants from Asia.

Most holidays that Filipino-Americans celebrate are the **Christian** ones. There are many cultural and social organizations which have evolved from a common region of origin, school, church or neighborhood in the Philippines. Therefore, many festivals are affiliated with such organizations.

Filipino-Americans participate in the Adams Morgan festival in Washington, D.C. and the Nations Festival in St. Petersburg, Florida.

Rizol Day—December 30—Honors the Philippine national hero and commemorates his execution. He was an exiled leader and writer.

PHILIPPINE FESTIVALS

Carabao Festival. Filipino farmers honoring their patron saint San Isidro de Labrador, dress up and adorn their carabaos, which is the farmer's best friend in plowing the ricefields.

Turumba Festival. A movable holiday either in March or April due to the calendar days of the Holy Week; the Turumba festival is a seven-day feast of Our Lady of Sorrows.

T' boli Tribal Festival. Usually celebrated during the third week of September. The celebration is an expression of hope to recapture the past and serves to inspire the people to work for this coveted state of life.

Black Nazarene Festival. Celebrated in the ninth day of January. The holiday honors the patron saint of Manila.

Pahiyas Festival. Another fiesta in honor of San Isidro de Labrador and is the most colorful of all Philippine festivals.

St. John the Baptist Feast Day. Cavite City's Water festival or St. John the Baptist feast day is celebrated every 24th day of June.

Since the United States began accepting Hmong (pronounced "mung") as refugees in 1980, more than 100,000 have come to the United States, clustering in such places as Montana, Wisconsin, Virginia and central California. Some settled at the invitation of church or community groups, while some looked for small farm plots.

The ancient traditions of Southeast Asia and the laws of the twentieth-century United States have increasingly caused conflicts in the lives of the Hmong and Mein tribespeople who settled in the United States after fleeing Laos, Thailand and Vietnam. In the first years after their arrival, they ran into conflicts with American law because some engaged in the medicinal use of opium, the kidnapping of brides or the ritual slaughter of animals. A few have leaped the cultural divide, but most remain poor. Many Hmong, because of their nomadic origin, are not sure how old they are.

The Hmong are a clan-based people whose culture had no written language until recent times. However, theirs is an oral tradition that goes back thousands of years and has enabled the Hmong to maintain ethnic integrity while moving and living among people like the Chinese and Vietnamese.

The Hmong were the battlefield allies of the United States in the secret Laos campaigns of the Vietnam War. They helped rescue many American pilots shot down over Laos. Also, they helped to block the supply trail from North to South Vietnam. The Hmong suffered greatly as a direct result of their alliance with the United States. Although they lived in the remote, mountainous northern regions of Laos, the Hmong are not ethnically Laotian and had virtually no participation in the governance of Laos, according to Jean Hamilton Merritt, a journalist who covered the war for the *Washington Post*.

"There was no group that did more for the United States war effort or paid a higher price and that put more of its faith in the premise that the United States was going to stand by them as a people" said Lionel Rosenblatt, president of Refugees International, an independent advocacy group based in Washington.

The Hmong have been some of the least adapted immigrants America has known, because they were former slash-and-burn farmers, almost none of whom could read or write and few of whom were familiar with electricity, indoor plumbing or telephones.

The Hmong did not come to the U.S. as economic refugees but almost as if they were prisoners of war who fled to Thailand after the U.S. exited and were later permitted to enter the United States as political refugees.

The Hmong have had inevitable problems adapting to a foreign culture. Confronted with a new language, new occupations and new educational systems, household management and transportation, the Hmong turned to their own community support networks based on systems of reciprocity and family relationships. An extensive system of family groupings called clans, whose lineages trace back as far as six generations, established structural relationships with attendant obligations.

Hmong religion recognizes the existence of a spirit world that interacts directly with humans. The spirits of one's ancestors retain a particular importance; each man must shoulder the responsibility of caring for his family's spirit in death as well as in life.

According to federal estimates (in 1988), 63 percent of the approximately 100,000 Hmong immigrants were dependent on welfare. Few adults, according to Ruth Hammond, a Minneapolis-based journalist covering the Hmong since 1984, have assimilated fully into mainstream American culture. Most retain a strong sense of clan identity and are struggling to preserve the traditions of their mountainous homeland. Most live clustered in poor inner-city neighborhoods with large families they find difficult to support without government help. Yet, many Hmong believe in a radiant future, expecting to return to a liberated Laos. Some believe they will be granted government posts in a new government. Some of them look forward to returning to Laos to regain what they lost for supporting U.S. involvement in Southeast Asia. And thousands of the Hmong are committed to productive lives as U.S. citizens. For many Hmong, the generation gap is one of the most disturbing signs of their alienation from their adopted country. The very concept of teenage years, as Americans know it, is alien to the Hmong, who traditionally began working as farmers, or as soldiers during the war, when they were 13 or 14 years old.

"The Hmong go from childhood to adulthood. Here, you have teenagers and adolescents," Nu Ying, a Hmong leader in the U.S., told the *New York Times*.[14] "We never had to raise our own children in that way, so it's very hard for people to grow up there."

Hmong practices conflict with American policies forbidding polygamy, common law marriages in which the bride is a minor, fishing , hunting and driving without a license.

Other conflicting practices include building charcoal fires indoors and slaughtering animals. More serious, legally, are charges of opium possession in which conviction can mean jail followed, under federal law, by mandatory deportation.

Job opportunities are few for first-generation Hmong immigrants because of high rates of illiteracy. They were guerrilla fighters coming from the most remote villages anywhere in Asia.

Among the Hmong, a high fertility rate, reportedly 9.5 children per woman, is attributed partly to the traditional culture, which prizes large families and favors sons, to very early marriages and to a lack of knowledge about contraception. People believe the bigger your family, the better and luckier. The Hmong would have to be counted as one of the more prolific groups in the world.

HOLIDAYS AND CUSTOMS

The Hmong New Year, which varies according to the lunar date, is a spring tradition in which Hmong gather from all over the country to strengthen friendships and reaffirm their cultural identity. Documenting traditions that now live mostly in memory is an important task.

The Hmong practice of marriage by capture has led to charges of kidnapping and rape in the U.S. Most cases have been resolved in juvenile courts.

Couples meet and carry on a courtship that often begins with the celebration of the New Year and a ball-tossing game for eligible young people. Eventually the young man "captures" the young woman in the presence of an older relative while the young woman ritually protests that she does not want to go with him. He takes her to his family home where she is met by relatives for a brief ceremony at the door, and remains for three days in which the marriage is consummated, and his relatives visit her family to pay a "bride price" for her.

Elaborate negotiations about bride price, a ritual practice with many rules, is the most essential ingredient of a Hmong wedding. After the ceremony, representatives of the bride give an accounting to the groom's negotiators of gifts bestowed on her by her own family, the only belongings she will take to her new home.

The Jains make up a separate Asian-Indian Hindu sect, most resembling Buddhists, that is devoted to non-violence. Jains, concerned about harming any creature, sometimes wear surgical masks so they will not breathe in and thus kill insects or bacteria.

An Indian religion that originated in the sixth century B.C.E. about the same time as Buddhism, its founder is usually given as Mahavir, the 24th and last chain of great teachers called *Tirhankaras*, which means "pathfinder" or "makers of the river crossing." Jainism shares many of the same gods as Hinduism, but teaches that the Tirhankaras, who lived over a period of 9 million years, have superiority over those gods. Jains are best known for their belief that harm to any living creation, even a tiny insect, can negatively affect one's karma in the cycle of birth and rebirth, or reincarnation.

The holiest shrine of the Jains is the statue of Bhagwan-Bahubali, which is one of the tallest and most striking monoliths in the world. The statue of Ghagwan Bahubali, considered by art historians to be one of India's greatest treasures, was built when the Jains were at the height of their power in southern India. But the attraction of the faith has declined steadily, and today there are about 5 million Jains worldwide, mostly in India. The statue—with shoulders twenty-six feet across, a nine-foot wide face and thirty-foot-long arms—is about twelve feet shorter than the great Sphinx of Egypt. It was chiseled from a solid piece of granite at the pinnacle of a 450-foot-high hillock. Its colossal size befits the exploits of Jainism's greatest saint. According to Jain theologians, Bahubali and his brother fought a tremendous battle thousands of years ago over the inheritance of their father's kingdom. At the moment of his victory, however, Bahubali realized that greed and pride had debased him, and he renounced his kingdom and other worldly things. The statue depicts him after the battle, when he meditated for so long that ant hills piled up around his feet and vines grew up his legs and arms. Perfectly naked, with a serene and benevolent smile etched on his face, he is the picture of self-control, detachment and spiritual enlightenment.

The statue, wearing only an aura of spiritual bliss, is meant to symbolize that renunciation of worldly goods and base desires is the only means to salvation. Every twelve years a purification ritual is performed at the site of the statue. It commemorates the first sacred bathing of the statue after it was carved in the year 981. In the ceremony the gathered crowd rollicks in emotional and spiritual euphoria as hundreds of gallons of water, milk and mixtures of sandalwood paste, tumeric and other sacred fluids are poured over the 1,000-plus-year-old colossus—transforming it from white to yellow to bright red.

There are about 50,000 Jains and fifty Jain temples in the United States, and just as many people in the United States wonder if the sect's spirit has been lost in commercialism. Jains in the United States question whether commercial considerations are eclipsing the true meaning of the bathing ceremony and the concept of renunciation.

The holidays observed by the Jains in the United States include:

Mahavir Jayanti—The birthday of the last Tirhanakar (*Mahavir*) or great teacher of the Jains. After his scriptures are read, a happy feast follows. This is a lunar holiday.

Paryushana Parva—Mendicant teachers give sermons about Mahavir. Celebrated during an eight- or ten-day period. On the last day confession of all sins is made and forgiveness of friends and relatives is sought—may be celebrated twice a year. This is a lunar holiday.

Rakhi—A celebration of love and friendship. Women tie a "*Rakhi*" to sisters, brothers, and/or friends to ward off evil.

Jains also celebrate certain **Hindu** holidays, such as **Diwali** and **Dusserah**, which are described in the section on Asian Indians.

By any measure, Japanese-Americans have enriched the U.S. Their household incomes and educational levels surpass the national average. They excel as professionals, managers, musicians and artists. These achievements largely stem from their devotion to virtues often prized by Americans—hard work, patience, discipline and, above all, close family ties.

From their earliest arrival, almost 150 years ago, Japanese immigrants were deprived, through a series of laws, of the most elementary civil rights: citizenship, owning or leasing land and interracial marriages, for example. In 1924, Congress halted all further Japanese immigration.

Japanese-Americans, like other Asian-Americans, have had to hurdle formidable obstacles in their struggle to gain acceptance. As recently as 1952, federal law denied Japanese immigrants the right to naturalization, which in turn barred them from owning property under discriminatory legislation enacted in California and other Western states. But, despite these early obstacles, there were many positive aspects of the Japanese-American experience. The true picture is one of enormous progress, much of it propelled by successful legal challenges to prohibitions and restrictions they faced.

One of the Japanese-Americans' worst ordeals followed Pearl Harbor, when 120,000 Japanese-Americans—two-thirds of them U.S. citizens by birth—were interned in camps on suspicion of disloyalty. In February 1942, President Franklin D. Roosevelt signed Executive Order 9066, which authorized the internment of Americans of Japanese ancestry. The policy was blatantly racist, as evidenced by the fact that Americans of German and Italian backgrounds were spared similar mistreatment. Not until the late 1970s did President Gerald Ford officially apologize for the order for internment, prompting Congress to embark on the tortuous road to indemnify the victims.

The first generation of Japanese immigrants were called "Issei"; the second generation were American-born "Nisei." After the Pearl Harbor attack the "Nisei" as well as their parents were treated as aliens (they spent two years or more in wartime internment camps) and were denied constitutional protection and due process. Their property was confiscated, and men were compelled to carry cards with a 4-C designation, the same as enemy aliens.

In 1992, which marked the fortieth anniversary of the Japanese internment, survivors of the camps retold their stories. They told of being taken from their homes as their Caucasian neighbors waited to loot them, of scraping manure from the horse stalls where they were housed until the camps were built, of being called traitors even as they sent their sons off to fight and die with the U.S. Army in Europe.[15]

Executive Order 9066 set in motion the mass removal of people of Japanese ancestry to internment camps where everyone ate in the same mess halls, lived in the same rude rectangles, slept on mattresses they had stuffed with straw, shared toilets with hundreds of others, and covered knot holes in the flimsy wooden barracks walls with tin cans to keep out the dust, as they lived under watch towers and search lights. During the internment many Japanese-Americans lost their homes, their property, as well as their dignity.

During the fiftieth anniversary year, stories were told about the 422nd Regimental Combat Team made up of second-generation Japanese-Americans. The World War II unit was recruited in part from the camps and became one of the most decorated in American history. The members of the 422nd also participated in the liberation of the Nazi concentration camp at Dachau.[16]

During World War II more than 33,000 Japanese-Americans joined the U.S. Army. Nearly 10,000 fought in North Africa, Italy and France with the 442nd team and 100th Infantry Battalion, all-Japanese units that earned more than 18,000 individual citations in battles such as Anzio, Salerno, Cassino and Vosges Mountains.

What these veterans accomplished after the war was just as profound. With new determination and far less tolerance for ignorance, discrimination and bigotry, many went to school on the G.I. Bill and forged successful careers in fields largely previously off-limits to Japanese-Americans—law, politics, engineering, education. For many of them, World War II was not just a fight for a new order overseas, but for freedom at home in the United States.

California, Oregon, Washington and Hawaii are home to more than three-fourths of the nearly 1 million-strong Japanese-American population, and it is in those states that the lives and experiences of the Nisei form a significant part of the cultural and social mosaic. It was these Nisei who fueled the drive to attain a formal apology from the U.S. government and $1.5 billion in reparations from the U.S. government for their detention and loss of property during the war, legislation that finally passed in 1988.

In 1994, the final one-third of the 60,000 surviving Japanese-American internees received their $20,000 checks from the federal government along with apologies. The payments and letters were approved under the Civil Liberties Act of 1988 to redress what the Federal Commission on Wartime Relocation and Internment of Civilians concluded was the "grave injustice" motivated by "racial prejudice and war hysteria." It is important to point out that no Japanese-American was convicted of espionage.

Glen Kitayama, curator of collections, Japanese-American National Museum in Los Angeles responding to an article in the *Washington Times* on May 13, 1997, pointed out that in the view of most scholars, the "wartime hysteria" argument implies that government officials acted in a rash manner, thus leading them to make a "mistake" by incarcerating Japanese-Americans. Both Peter Irons *(Justice of War)* and Micki Weglyn *(Years of Infamy)* dispute this casual interpretation. Both argue that government officials knew that Japanese-Americans were loyal but made a conscious and level-headed decision to intern them anyway.

Micki Weglyn produced evidence of a government report prepared by Special Investigator Curtis Munson that cleared Japanese-Americans of any fifth-column activity—evidence that was read by top government officials, ignored and then kept from the public. Professor Irons demonstrated in his book how the government knowingly suppressed evidence from the Supreme Court to support its case that the internment of Japanese-Americans was required by "military necessity."

Many Japanese-American scholars have referred to internment camps as "concentration camps" because they were surrounded by barbed wire and were guarded by armed sentries. They contend the camps were not "relocation centers," "temporary havens" or "wayside stations" created for the benefit of Japanese-Americans, as the War Relocation Authority wanted people to believe.

In September 1998, the federal government announced it was closing its books on the $1.6 billion reparations program for Japanese-Americans who were forced into internment camps in World War II.

A 10-year effort by the Justice Department to find and compensate internees ended in August 1998.

More than 81,000 Americans of Japanese ancestry received payments, an estimated 98 percent of those eligible under the Civil Liberties Act of 1988, which set up the reparations program. Individual payments of $20,000 were available to internees and others who were relocated or whose property was seized by the government.

By 1994 the Japanese, lumped under the broad label Asian-Americans, were part of the largest group at the University of California at Berkeley and the University of California at Los Angeles. This success has engendered some resentment because many Americans still based their image on stereotypes from World War II. Even Nisei, second-generation Japanese-Americans, and Sansei, third-generation Japanese-Americans, are still asked: "Are you Japanese or American?" David Mura, a Sansei, points out in his book *Turning Japanese—Memoirs of a Sansei.*

In the 1980s, there was a sharp rise in anti-Asian prejudice (namely anti-Japanese sentiments) in parts of California, where nearly 40 percent of the approximately 850,000 Americans of Japanese ancestry live today. Because 75 percent live on the West Coast, anti-Asian and anti-Japanese sentiment has always been felt more intensely there than in other parts of the U.S.

There are many explanations for such bigotry. Japan's economic successes have engendered resentments that peaked when, for example, Japanese interests bought movie companies or part of Rockefeller Center. Also, Asians are the fastest-growing minority group in the U.S., and many people do not distinguish between Asians and Asian-Americans.

In *Strangers from a Different Shore, A History of Asian-Americans*, Ronald Takaki examines the composite Asian-American experience in its 150-year entirety. For the general reader, it is a helpful volume. Takaki argues that every Asian immigrant group has been forced in varying degrees to struggle against the idea of the U.S. as a fundamentally white society, a concept initiated by the Founding Fathers and subsequently codified by discriminatory laws on citizenship, marriage, property ownership and the definition of "Caucasian." Many Nisei stated, "we are getting an inkling of what our parents went through because of being confused with criticism of a country we've never even been to."

Some Japanese-Americans have noted the ambiguous relationship that the U.S. has had historically with Asian-Americans. Takaki quotes Dale Minammi, a lawyer who worked to overturn the Supreme Court decision that upheld internment: "The United States has always had difficulty considering Asian-Americans as true citizens and confusing political allegiance with racial ancestry."

A Japanese-American National Museum opened in 1995 in Los Angeles that includes much archival film and items depicting the Japanese-American experience.

Holidays celebrated by Japanese-Americans (in addition to the **Mahayana Buddhist** religious holidays found in the religion section) are as follows:

Mochitsuki Day celebrated on January 1

Adults' Day celebrated on January 15

Vernal Equinox Day celebrated on March 21

Children's Day celebrated on May 5

Respect For The Aged Day celebrated on September 15

Emperor's Birthday celebrated December 24

WEDDING CUSTOMS

Drinking *sake,* a rice wine, is a tradition for Japanese couples. Executed in its most serious form, this custom requires each to take three sips from three different, graduated cups. The entire process is repeated at the reception by family members, connoting that the families are now bound.

If Koreans seem to have burst suddenly onto the American scene, it's because they have. In 1960, before national immigration quotas were lifted, there were 10,000 Koreans in the United States. By the 1990 Census there were 800,000, one-third of them in California. Many came with what Harvard University Korea expert Carter Eckert has called "an understandable post-colonial mentality: a view of themselves as an embattled people who won't be pushed around." Many also brought attitudes common to homogeneous East Asian societies—a wariness of other peoples and a fear of blacks.

Like Jewish and Italian immigrants before them, Koreans have gravitated to retailing in urban areas, where their willingness to work long hours and use low-paid family labor compensates for their limited English and capital, according to *U.S. News and World Report*.[17] But Koreans are different from their predecessors and from many other recent immigrants in that they are mostly well-educated and relatively well-off. Some 75 percent of Korean entrepreneurs have college degrees; many of them sold their homes in Korea to invest in their American ventures. For them, running a store is both a first step on the American ladder and, often, a downward step from higher-status professional jobs back home.

Despite their considerable progress, the Korean economic experience in the United States is not all good news. They have a higher rate of entrepreneurship than any other Americans—nearly 40 percent of Korean families own a business. But the average income for Korean-Americans is still lower than those of white and some other Asian-Americans. Koreans also earn less than other people with equivalent education, which is why many are so determined to protect their hard-won gains and to ensure that their children do still better. Koreans, like other Asians, resent the term "model minority." They would rather be called old-fashioned seekers of an old-fashioned dream, according to the *U.S. News* article.

The contrast between Koreans and their Asian neighbors is striking. Having suffered invasions and a long period of colonization by Japan in the twentieth century, Koreans have had to fight for their lives to retain their language and culture—in that way, Koreans are feisty. They certainly don't fit the subservient or docile Asian stereotype.[18]

Koreans live by what they call "*cheong*." "*Cheong*" is love, respect, affinity and loyalty rolled into one. It comes only with time.

Culturally and socially, and especially because of the language barrier, some Korean newcomers are ill-equipped to run businesses in America's inner cites. But because they, like other immigrants, are sometimes denied mainstream jobs, they pool their resources and start mom-and-pop stores. Like all immigrants, they go through an "American passage" that requires cultural insight on both sides.

Koreans, like other Asian-Americans, learn from Confucius' teachings how to be good parents, sons and daughters, and how to behave with other people. But Confucius' teachings have not necessarily prepared them for living in a democracy. The Confucian ethos lacks the social conscience that makes democracy work. As one Korean grocer in San Francisco noted, "Koreans must learn to participate in this society."[19]

For work, some Koreans have started as sidewalk vendors. Many then have graduated to corner groceries, then to larger stores in better areas. For capital, they often draw on the proceeds of hundreds of monthly "money clubs." In such a club, about twenty people, for example, contribute a given amount to a common pool. Each month a different person takes all the money in the pool. The month-to-month order is determined by lot, and the money must be repaid into the pool. This informal banking system is called "*Kye*" which is used instead of banks by a majority of Korean immigrants. For labor, at least in the early stages of a business, many Koreans rely on family and friends.

Korean merchants have become a visible lightning rod for the discontent of the African-American community. For example, in Los Angeles, African-Americans have remained poor as, one after another, immigrant groups have arrived and climbed past them to prosperity. "It's illogical, but it's convenient to target the Koreans," said Lawrence Aubrey of the Los Angeles County Human Relations Commission. It is estimated that in 1992 there were about 6,000 Korean retail outlets in Los Angeles County, a main source of livelihood for the 300,000 to 400,000 Korean-Americans who live there.

When Jewish shop owners left the South-Central area after the Watts riot of 1965, Asian businesses began to move in, and, during the '80s, Koreans became overwhelmingly dominant among business owners there, while also developing an area called Koreatown in Watts.

Across much of the poorest parts of the city, the only shops in which to buy groceries or liquor or gasoline, or to have clothes cleaned or a car repaired, are owned by Korean immigrants. Koreans have a quasi-monopoly on running and owning gas stations in Los Angeles.[20]

In major cities such as New York, Philadelphia, Los Angeles and Washington, D.C., Korean immigrants' presence has made a big impression. In the '80s, Koreans opened stores of every kind in virtually every New York City neighborhood, including some forsaken by other merchants, becoming emblems of the new immigrant entrepreneurs.

In response to social problems in New York, Koreans started moving into the suburbs as their businesses grew and evolved. In New York City, as they branched out from fruit and vegetable stands to fish stores, dry cleaners, liquor stores, nail salons and a dozen other businesses, the number of Korean-owned stores is reported to have reached a peak of about 10,000 in 1990, according to the *New York Times*.[21] An estimated 100,000 Koreans have come to the New York City metropolitan area since the 1970s, and 40 percent of Korean families own at least one business. No other ethnic group is as highly self-employed, according to *U.S. News and World Report*.

Few Korean greengrocers owned such stores in their homeland. By 1993 in New York City more than 85 percent of the 1,600 greengrocer stores were owned by Koreans. The grocery stores were attractive because, although they required long, hard hours, they could be run with only basic knowledge of English. The snowballing success of Korean grocers in New York City, Philadelphia and Washington, D.C. is due in part to an extensive and well-organized support system. For example, in some areas new arrivals can rely on Korean business directories that are hundreds of pages long. By the early 1990s, as a visible testimony to the phenomenon of ethnic success, Koreans had begun hiring Central Americans and Mexicans to perform the menial tasks in their stores, and many first-generation Koreans who have succeeded in their businesses will not allow their children to work in the stores. They want them to become managers or lawyers. Employing Central Americans, for example, is cheaper than hiring Korean laborers.[22]

In Philadelphia, thousands of Korean immigrants have moved beyond the greengrocer trade for which their countrymen are noted in New York City. They operate grocery stores, dry-cleaning shops, discount stores, seafood stands and small clothing factories, for example.

As of the mid-1990s, they have formed some seventy churches, have made their own internal lending arrangements, and have established closely knit community organizations. They publish at least two newspapers, and they have set up a radio network, the Korean-American Broadcasting Company, which began broadcasting to Koreans across the country in the 1990s.

Philadelphia's 40,000 Koreans have become widely recognized not only as the fastest developing minority in town, but also as one of the most energetic and successful groups in a city whose ethnic makeup has become much more diverse in recent years. They have built this reputation in a mere decade, and the speed of their success has both startled and impressed many Philadelphians.

For a long time, Koreans here moved, talked and worked in their own circles, kept there largely by language and custom. This isolation, which some Philadelphians saw as aloofness, as was noted in Los Angeles, was said to have contributed to nasty conflicts between Koreans and African-Americans in the largely black neighborhoods where Koreans opened many grocery stores.

In Washington, D.C., the majority of lottery agents are of Korean ancestry.[23] In 1992, of the over 275 liquor stores in the District of Columbia, 127 were owned by Koreans or Korean-Americans. More than 700 dry-cleaning establishments in the D.C. area were Korean-operated. Koreans also held nearly one-third Washington's 3,000 street vendor jobs and licenses and, through their two dozen wholesalers, control much of the tourist merchandise sold on the street. In the poorer sections of Washington, Korean immigrants dominate the world of mom-and-pop stores, deli-style takeouts and no-name fast-food eateries. Wherever in D.C. there are everyday human needs, Koreans have become ubiquitous.

"They and other Asians are changing the social landscape of industrialized society," said Hyung Chan Kim, author of *The Korean Diaspora* and professor at Western Washington University.

Brad Edmondson, editor in chief of *American Demographics* magazine, said of Koreans, "They own more businesses per household than any other ethnic group, including non-Hispanic whites. That's really incredible."

"They have taken advantage of a situation where they have progressed economically off of the backs of the African community," said Reverend Willie F. Wilson, the influential pastor of Union Temple Baptist Church in Anacostia, part of the District of Columbia.

According to the *Washington Post*,[24] Korean-Americans have long been viewed by African-Americans with a mixture of admiration, envy and resentment in poorer neighborhoods where they dominate the marketplace.

The story of how Koreans came to transform the face of many United States cities, however, starts with a people as severely oppressed as any civilization in history. As recently as 1942, Korea was colonized and occupied by its Japanese neighbors.

Perhaps no one is as surprised as the Koreans themselves by their transformation into America's entrepreneurs. First, they have very little history of being scattered about the globe, ethnologists say.

Not only is South Korea smaller than Virginia, but Koreans readily describe themselves as provincial. The United States is one of the first countries to which any Korean migrated voluntarily.

Koreans did not have generations of ancestors with worldly experience to advise them on what they would be facing upon settling in the U.S. They are making up their responses to the United States as they go along. Many of those responses surprise even them.

Many knew nothing of business before arriving in the United States. However, many were educated people—choir directors, nurses, doctors of philosophy. Their work ethic is so keen that some of them refer to Japanese as "the lazy Asians."

In the same year that Congress passed the Voting Rights Act of 1965, the United States immigration law was overhauled to reflect a new order and admit more people of color. The spirit of the time is clear in the congressional testimony concerning new immigration policy—an attempt was made to create a new United States without regard to race, color, creed or national origin.

Soon after the immigration law changed, Koreans discovered the United States. At that time the Korean wage levels were 15 percent of that in the United States. If you as an American were earning $15,000 per year and you thought you could earn $100,000 per year for the same work you were doing in Korea, what would you do? That was the calculation they made.

United States immigration policy put a premium on Koreans who had significant skills and advanced degrees, and they flocked to fill skilled jobs. But they ran into an enormous problem: the Korean language is one of the most difficult in the world. Koreans have a terrible time with language in the United States, even more so than the Chinese and Vietnamese. Even the most educated and sophisticated struggle learning English because of the vast differences between the two languages.

Thus, in the early '70s, Koreans found that once they got here, they were stunned by how thoroughly language, among other things, blocked their professional careers. They did find, however, that not much money was required to be a store owner. "Probably one or two months for the security deposit. That's how we all started," said one successful Korean wholesaler.

Desperation was important in motivating some Koreans to work. They didn't have a choice. They had families to support. And, besides, they had already changed their lives so radically by coming to the United States that the shock of the new occupation was mild by comparison. Stubborn pride had something to do with it, too.

"These were people who'd gotten Ph.D.s and just couldn't get a job. They felt incredibly unfairly treated. So rather than undergo the humiliation of doing something that normally a Ph.D. wouldn't do, they decided to be their own bosses," said Young-Key Kim Renaud of the Korean Studies Department at George Washington University.

It didn't take long for these educated Koreans, many of whom started working in the United States as convenience store clerks, to quickly learn the ropes of basic retailing.

Then came the key observation: if they could buy a small store cheap and keep it open eighteen hours a day, seven days a week, with little or no hired help, just by putting in vastly more hours of family labor than the typical American was willing to contribute, they would have significant advantage over, say, that same typical American who refused to live such a life.

They learned to shun competition with the large U.S. retail juggernauts. No way could their simple grocery go head-to-head with giant supermarkets. Nor could their takeout take on McDonald's. Instead, they sought out niches that were too small for these leviathans. That is how Koreans came to see opportunity precisely in those markets that chains did not consider worth servicing, many of which were poor and black.

One successful Korean-American businessman put it this way: "I knew the United States to be not a land of paradise, and that there are certain conflicts among the races. But most importantly I was convinced that I should be able to provide my kids with opportunities that weren't available in Korea such as education, and getting ahead in their lives."

The crisis of December 1997 in Korea sparked many Korean Americans to send money back to Korea to their families rather than gifts during the Christmas season of that year. There are many Koreans Americans in the United States who are referred to as the 1.5 generation. That is, they are people who were born in Korea but grew up mostly in the Los Angeles area and other US cities. So consequently, they do not know much about Korea but they do remember the fact that they were born there. By 1989 Korean-American banks appeared in the United States, that is, they were started by a few hundred immigrants pooling their money. In the Los Angeles area known as Koreatown, many Korean Americans have rehabilitated many old housing areas and there are many boutiques, trendy, bohemian cafes, billiard halls, discos, and music studios, and even Korean karaoke bars. Many of the members of the 1.5 generation speak Korean and English—one foot in each country. Its members are far different from the 1.0 generation which is the familiar Korean grocer with very broken English and the 2.0 generation of Korean Americans who were born here to Korean parents but highly Americanized in fashion, education and outlook. In 1970 for example, there were only 10,000 Koreans living in Southern California. By 1997 it was one of the largest populations of Koreans outside of Korea. The Korean American chamber of commerce estimated that in Los Angeles county alone, there were probably 25,000 businesses owned by Korean Americans. They have transferred the neighborhood now known as Koreatown displacing African Americans and for blocks the visitor is greeted by signs in boxy Korean script for restaurants, banks, trading companies, beauty parlors and so forth. The Korean-American community has now graduated and become more sophisticated and Americanized. In the early years, many Koreans could not get traditional loans so they participated in the system known as "kye," which was a form of lending clubs. Today, there are banks that will be only too happy to loan money to the children of the 1.0 generation who have less allegiance to the mother country and more to the United States of which they are citizens. In the 1970s and 80s, the Koreans who came to America were seen as the cream of the crop, the elites, and people back in Korea were somewhat jealous of them, said Edward Chang, a professor of ethnic studies at the University of California, Riverside, and a Korean American who studies that community. But beginning in the 1990s the Korean economy rose so sharply and the value of the dollar fell, that many Korean Americans felt that Koreans were celebrating too much and too early when referring back to the people in Korea.

By January of 1998, many Korean Americans who were interviewed believed the home country would in time weather its economic storms but change is coming to Koreatown. Close ties with family and finance are changing. The signs advertising services to immigrants and Korean tourists, once all in Korean, are beginning to include English in the hopes of luring new, non-Korean customers.

One of the biggest problems facing the Koreans as store owners in poor African-American neighborhoods was the perception by African-Americans that Koreans comprise a rude population. Many African-Americans read Koreans' cultural signals or fractured English as rudeness. The Koreans didn't understand that they had to smile. Koreans equate being solicitous as being insincere. The Korean demeanor is the absence of a demeanor. Koreans have a name for it: "*mu-pyoqung*." It means "lack of expression."

Even in South Korea officials have urged citizens to greet visitors with a friendly smile. At the Seoul Olympics in 1988, according to a *San Francisco Examiner* article,[25] some tried but found it difficult.

African-Americans also complain that Koreans take money out of the community and hire few non-Koreans. This perception seemed to be true in the early 1990s. Koreans move to be near good schools, just like other middle-class Americans.

Southern California has at least 500 Korean churches to serve the 75 percent of local Koreans who are Christian.

By necessity, Korean immigrants have come to "understand the role of politics in our society." Many Korean businessmen now contribute generously to the political campaigns of office holders in both parties, though they typically lean to the right. In the meantime, the Koreans continue to prosper and to expand their community.

HOLIDAYS AND CUSTOMS

"*Chusok*," or "Autumn Night," is one of the major holidays for Koreans and for Korean-Americans. In Korea it is called *Hangawi-Nai* (Big Day). In the United States people call it "Thanksgiving." Its date follows the lunar calendar and changes each year. Just like Thanksgiving, special dinners are also a part of *Chusok* festivities. Koreans prepare and offer the best fruits or grains of the harvest to their family shrines, and eat their symbols of the harvest: rice, *Song-pyon* (rice cakes) and fresh fruit, and they drink wine (*Maggoli*) made from the new grains.

Religion is a big part of this celebration. It is a time that promotes the spirit of common heritage. *Chusok* offers some important concepts that are truly beautiful. *Chusok* is an ancient ritual, beginning more than 4,000 years ago, and originally called "*Han-ka-wee*" or "Full Moon in Autumn." The full moon symbolized plenty and a promising crop. It was time to thank god that bestowed grains on the human race.

In 1932, the purpose of *Chusok* changed. King Taecho designated the day as a time to worship one's ancestors, according to the doctrine of Confucianism. It became, most importantly, a time for worshipping ancestors. Koreans dress in their best clothes and visit family and family burial sites if possible. The oldest male representative of the family hosts the ancestral worship after burning incense and placing food on a stone table in front of the tomb. Koreans believed that the burial site visits renew their bonds with the past.

Two other important holidays for Koreans that are celebrated in the United States are **New Year's** (Lunar) and "**Tano Day**" or "Swing Day."

Like other new groups in the U.S., Koreans have had their share of difficulties, among them learning a new culture, speaking a new language and getting along with new neighbors. However, they have kept some of their wedding customs, one of which is the "*p'yebaek*" ritual. As part of the "*p'yebaek*" ceremony, the Korean bride's mother-in-law gives her "*jujubes*," or red dates, to eat, symbolic of the grandsons who will hopefully be born. It is sometimes performed at the end of the wedding banquet on "*Tatami*" mats spread before a screen.

The English language is only one of the myriad problems of adjustment that Lao refugees have encountered since their migration into the United States since 1975. According to the 1990 Census the Laotian population in the United States numbered 150,000.

Lao children entering the United States public school system have found adapting especially difficult. Lao culture taught children to place teachers in a different light than American students. For example, teachers are placed on a pedestal, and questioning a teacher's credibility would be unacceptable. Also, Lao culture would never embarrass, contradict, offend or confront one's superior, thereby causing the recipient to lose face, especially in the presence of others.

Social mixing of the sexes is uncommon to Lao culture, and dating as in the American custom is rare. Parents are very careful concerning unchaperoned activities. Also, Laotians have had difficulty adjusting to American food primarily because of their unfamiliarity with dairy products (as they are not readily available in Laos).

As children have become more Americanized they have caused Lao parents to be taken aback as they see their children forsake many of the traditional Lao values in the home. One of the most common causes of this shock or disappointment is disrespect shown toward parents and elders, and a greater sense of independence. However, the bigger area of change that is evident is in the matter of language. As the children have become more fluent in English, the image of the parents as the ultimate authority in the family has become tarnished. Lao parents want to try to maintain their culture but at the same time must face the fact that their children must be enrolled in programs that will allow them to become proficient in English so they can keep the pace with American students. The children, on the other hand, once they are exposed to American culture, complain that their parents are too conservative.

HOLIDAYS AND CUSTOMS

There is a diversity among the Lao people who came to the United States. This is demonstrated between those who came from rural area versus those who came from urban areas, between male and female, the poor and the wealthy. The religion of the Lao is **Buddhist**, and they are of the Theravada sect and observe the holidays noted for this group in the section of this book on religions. Many Lao also have French rather than English as a second language.

WEDDING CUSTOMS

A Laotian wedding custom is for the couple getting married to have their wrists tied with *Siquan* (spiritual string) which has been blessed by a Buddhist priest, and their free hands are raised in a gesture of respect for the words being spoken.

Very little has been written about this ethnic group. They have usually been lumped together with the Asian-Indian community. Yet Pakistanis are a distinct ethnic group. This lumping together might also be because they are Muslims and thus they have been mistaken for Asian Indian Americans.

There are, according to the 1990 Census, approximately 100,000 Pakistanis in the United States. As a community, they are large enough to stage an annual Pakistan Day Festival and Parade each March 23 in Brooklyn, New York, where about 40,000 Pakistanis live. As one of their community leaders stated, "Most came in the early 1970s. We are a big enough community now, and most of the people have no intention to go back to Pakistan. We have to participate in the political life. So we decided to establish his day, which celebrates Pakistan's independence over forty years ago, and as a day to establish our independence politically as a community."

The top occupations for Pakistani immigrants listed in the 1990 census were taxi driver, truck driver and construction worker. While there appeared to be anecdotal evidence that an increasing number of Pakistani immigrants are moving into retailing, the trend is too recent to show in official statistics.

Pakistanis themselves by 1997 say they have observed that many of their fellow immigrants, who have now worked long enough to amass some capital, are leaving cab driving and construction for other pursuits, which describes a path typical of many immigrant entrepreneurs.

One of the areas has been in small retailing and in the New York City area where a large number of Pakistanis have settled they have become evident by their ownership of the "99¢" stores. While in 1997 it was too early to conclude that the Pakistani proprietors have cornered the market on 99¢ stores, they did control what appears to be the city's only multistore network of 99¢ discounters, which sell everything from air fresheners to Zwiebacks.

A vast majority of Pakistanis are Sunni Muslims and celebrate the holidays of Islam, which are found in the section on Religion and Ethnicity. They worship in mosques along with other Muslims.

The Pakistanis have many things to offer their communities. They know their rights and their duty as Americans. Many feel, like other Muslims in the U.S., that there should be more culturally sensitive schooling for Muslim children.

HOLIDAYS AND CUSTOMS

Pakistani Hindus celebrate **Diwali** and **Holi**.

August 14—**Independence Day** is celebrated. The day the country of Pakistan was created.

December 25—Celebrates the birthday of **Jinnah**, the founder of the Pakistani nation.

Ethnic dress is common during Pakistani parades and festivals. Men wear shirts and pants-like *hagwars*, and women dress in brightly colored *dubattas* (scarves) and *kameezes* (blouses). Cricket remains a highly popular sport for Pakistani-Americans.

Sikhism began in India in the fifteenth century with Nanak, a Hindu and first Sikh guru. He studied under Muslims and Hindus, and he felt followers were dissenting from both faiths. The nine gurus who succeeded him shaped Nanak's teaching into a separate group of believers with their own monotheistic religion, language, literature and traditions. Sikhism borrowed from the subcontinent's two major religions, Hinduism and Islam. It has a humanistic tone, largely free of ritual and opposed to the Hindu caste system. There are more than 20 million followers worldwide of the religion, and there is no place holier or more sacred than the Darbar Sahib, a complex in India. The Sikhs are a warrior clan that lived and died by the sword, and they have seen their holy precinct overrun more than once by marauding armies, beginning with the Moguls. Today there are 16 million Sikhs in the Punjab of India.[26]

The Sikhs form a religious community that traces its origins to the first of its ten gurus, Nanak, born in 1469, whose words are preserved in the principal Sikh scripture, the Adi Granth or Granth Sahib. To become a "*Sant*" (one who knows the truth), it was necessary to practice a regular discipline of inward meditation directed to the timeless being (*Akalpurakh*), the creator and sustainer of the universe. True religion was interior.

Guru Gobind Singh founded the military order of the *Khalsa*, whose male members are baptized early on by water stirred with a two-edged sword, and thereafter they never shave their beard or touch tobacco and always carry arms.

The departure of the British and the partition of the Indian subcontinent into Pakistan and India in 1947 produced a seismic crisis among the Sikhs, for the border between the two countries divided the Punjab, leaving many Sikhs in hostile Pakistan. The Sikhs have retained many of the features of Hinduism, including the caste system, though it differs from that of the Hindus. Jat Sikhs are the largest caste.

Sikhism emphasizes a personal relationship to God and an obligation of believers to work for social justice. Observant male Sikhs never shave as a sign of respect for the natural order of God. The Sikh worship centers are called *gurdwaras*.

A Sikh temple on Gudwara is where Sikhs who are isolated by geography, language and religion practice their faith, share a meal or exchange information and news of their native India. Sikhs in the U.S. are something of a bachelor society. Many came to the United States without their families, hoping to make enough money to bring their wives and children, siblings and parents from India. Many came to the U.S. to escape the strife in their native Punjab, where, they say, they were persecuted by the Hindu majority. Many who came to the New York City metro area found jobs at gas stations and garages owned by more established Sikhs.

In the summer of 1994, the estimated 150,000 Sikhs in the U.S. held camps in Pennsylvania, New York, New Jersey, Michigan and California to discuss their situation in the United States.

Sikhism is a monotheistic religion, blending elements of Islam and Hinduism, whose stronghold is Punjab, in Northern India. Its adherents, most of whom have the word *Singh*, or Lion, in their names have beliefs that are familiar to most Westerners. One is "Life is continuous"—it came from God and it will go back to God. The real person is in the soul, which does not die.[27]

One thing that worries some Sikhs in the United States, such as Harmohindar Singh of North Carolina, more than the situation in India is the fear that either Christianity or secularism will lure their youth to forsaking their religious traditions. For example, a male Sikh is supposed to wear a turban without cutting his hair. Due to peer pressure, many Sikhs in the U.S. don't keep with that custom.

Among Sikhs, unshorn hair neatly kept in a turban and a full beard are signs of respect for "the natural order of God." The practice is one of several external Sikh symbols. Sikhs also wear iron or steel bracelets to bind them to God and remind them of their duty. Every male Sikh takes the name Singh, every female the name of Kaur. In the United States, many use them as their last names. Sikh women wear a "*Kada*," a steel bangle which is a religious symbol. Many Sikh women say it is against their religious tenets not to wear the *Kada*.

Historically, Sikhs in India have been known as good farmers, committed soldiers and religious worshipers who practiced equality in a society where the caste system prevented rich and poor from eating and socializing with each other.

Sikhs in India are also known as transporters and mechanics. The largest fleet of trucks in India is owned by Sikhs, who control more than 80 percent of the bus service throughout the country, stated W.H. McLeod in his book *The Sikhs*. "Sikhs are very enterprising, and they don't mind going into areas where no one else will work," wrote McLeod.

While many Sikh immigrants are blending into the American mainstream, many still hold on to their native culture. Many wear a long beard and turban, symbols of the Sikh religions, and teach their children to speak Punjabi at home. Some are active supporters of a Sikh separatist movement that the Indian government has tried to suppress.

HOLIDAYS AND CUSTOMS

Sikh holidays must be adjusted each year because many of them are lunar. The principal holidays are:

GURU NANAK'S BIRTHDAY—Guru Nanak was the founder of Sikh religion. His birthday is celebrated generally in November, but the date (A.D.) varies from year to year on account of following the traditional dates of the Indian Calendar. The birthday celebrations usually last for three days.

GURU GOBIND SINGH'S BIRTHDAY—His birthday generally falls in December or January because it is calculated according to the Indian Calendar. The celebrations are similar to the three-day schedule of the celebrations of Guru Nanak's birthday.

INSTALLATION OF SRI GURU GRANTH SAHIB (SIKH SCRIPTURE) AS PERMA-NENT GURU—The word "Guru" literally means one who gives light or guidance. This day generally falls in October, but the date varies as per calculation according to the Indian Calendar. On this day, a special one day celebration is held. Sikhs rededicate themselves to follow the teachings of the Gurus contained in the Scripture.

BAISAKHI (VAISAKHI)—*Baisakhi* called *Vaisakhi* is the birthday of the *Khalsa* (The Pure Ones). Guru Gobind gave a call for the devoted Sikhs who would be prepared to die for the faith. Five Sikhs answered his call and they were baptized by him with *Amrit* (water of immortality). They were ordered to keep the five symbols—unshorn hair, drawers, comb, steel wrist band and *Kirpan* (sword). *Baisakhi* is generally celebrated on 13th April every year.

DIWALI—The Sikhs celebrate *Diwali*—generally regarded as a Hindu festival—because Guru Hargobind came back to Amritsar on this day in 1620, after his release from Gwalior jail. The Sikhs on this day, which generally falls in November, hold a one-day celebration.

GURU ARJAN'S MARTYRDOM ANNIVERSARY—Guru Arjan, the fifth Guru of the Sikhs compiled Sikh Scripture called Adi Granth in 1604 and also built the Golden Temple at Amritsar. This anniversary generally falls in summer (May-June).

GURU TEGH BAHADUR'S MARTYRDOM ANNIVERSARY—His martyrdom anniversary generally falls in Winter (November-December). Usual one day celebrations.

Sikhs in the United States also commemorate what they refer to as the "Golden Temple Massacre" which occurred on June 4, 1984 when Indian troops attacked the Golden Temple at Amritsar, the center and seat of the Sikh religion.

Many devout Sikhs wear a small brass and steel dagger called a "Kirpan" as a symbol of readiness to defend the faith.

Because of the Sikh tradition of not shaving, they have at times been discriminated in applying for jobs where an employer requires its employees to be clean shaven.

WEDDING CUSTOMS

A Sikh wedding ceremony is when the bride's "*Palu*" (a type of scarf) is pulled well forward to shadow her face before the actual ceremony takes place.

According to the 1990 Census, the population of Americans of Asian Indian-American ancestry totaled 815,000, of whom more than half have migrated to the United States since 1970.

Asian Indian immigrants make up 11.8 percent of the Asian population in the United States. Of this number 75.4 percent are foreign-born, of which 43.9 percent came to the United States between 1980 and 1990. According to the 1990 Census, Asian Indians were making progress on the economic ladder, having achieved a median household income of $44,696, the highest of any major immigrant group and well above the overall median household income of $30,176. They're educated, they have good jobs, and they're working hard, according to an article in *USA TODAY*.[28]

Indian immigrants often credit their success to strong family and religious values. Other factors:

- Many Indian immigrants can speak or read English before they arrive in the U.S. English is India's second official language.

- Many already have college degrees and professional training when they arrive.

- Most Indians aren't refugees; they come by choice. The well-off are more able to afford the costly journey.

Indian immigrants often settle in suburban communities and rarely form ethnic enclaves. That's partly because they don't share a single culture. India is home to dozens of ethnic and religious groups.

The experience of Indian immigrants offers a stark contrast to other Asians. Although most Indians who came to the United States in the 1960s and 1970s were professionals who spoke English, the arrivals since then are not as well-educated. They come from the small towns and the countryside, many for economic reasons. As their families have reunited in the United States, many have recreated the extensive social and familial networks they had in India.

Various communities in India are devoted to certain occupations. One example is the Indians working in the Diamond District in New York City, many of whom are Guierati Jains, renowned as traders and merchants throughout India. Their growing presence in the jewelry trade has made them the second-largest ethnic group—other than Hasidic Jews— in the Diamond District.

In a *New York Times* article on March 21, 1996, Edwin McDowell wrote about Indian-Americans, saying that, from 1971 to 1996, people of Asian-Indian ancestry have been emigrating to the United States in sizable numbers.

One of the businesses in which they have emerged as having a large presence is the hotel industry. They have carved out a steadily bigger ownership share of the nation's hotel industry for themselves. Starting with ownership of no-name motels, they soon graduated to Days Inn, Econo Lodge, Rodeway and other economy franchises.

By the spring of 1996 Indian-Americans owned more than 12,000 properties, or 46 percent of American's economy hotels and 26 percent of the nation's total 45,000 lodgings. They are also moving up. A new generation is buying properties (in 1996) like Sheratons, Radissons and Hiltons, adding an upscale chapter to an immigrant success story.

The first wave of motel ownership was propelled by the Asian Indian-Americans' strong family ties, close-knit communities and a willingness to invest years of sweat. The latest wave represents a break with tradition and a willingness to tackle bigger, more complex challenges. But the original community still provides the backing, as entrepreneurs pool the resources of extended families and borrow from fellow Asian Indian-Americans, for whom a handshake is often sufficient collateral.

"These Indians are modern Horatio Algers," says Joel Kotkin, a senior fellow at Pepperdine University's Institute for Public Policy in Malibu, California. "They're willing to start in marginal and sometimes risky areas that native-born Americans are not interested in going into, and working incredibly long hours."

Many Asian Indian-American hotel keepers came to the United States by way of Africa, where, in some cases, their families had lived for many generations. In the early years, some Asian Indian-Americans had problems typical of many newcomers in trying to get financing and insurance, McDowell wrote. By some immigrants' account, insurers in the early 1980s suddenly canceled property insurance to all Indian hotel owners, believing them to be part of an Indian conspiracy to buy properties and burn them down to collect insurance money. "They were turned down by about 200 insurance companies, until we convinced underwriters that these immigrants were outstanding risks," says Ron Thomas, a vice president of United Insurance Agencies, in Muncie, Indiana.

Asian Indian franchises have been the engine of growth for the entire economy hotel sector. They have generally stayed away from luxury hotels and five star resorts, and often from full-service hotels, mainly because of their cost but also for cultural and religious reasons. (Most are Hindus from the Gujarat state in India and as part of their religion are vegetarians and don't consume alcohol.)

In the United States, many Asian Indian immigrants turned to lodging as a business because they could buy cheap motels, they could live rent free, and the family could work the front desk, clean rooms, do laundry and make repairs. However, parents instilled in their children the need for education and trust between families and among their own ethnic group.

"We work together as a team," said Arvind Patel, a native of Tanzania. "A lot of families give you $10,000, even $30,000, without charging you interest and without any collateral. They figure one day, you may help them."

When Asian Indian-American children graduate from America's universities and colleges, many have chosen to become doctors, engineers, lawyers and accountants. But in most families at least one son or daughter will become a hotelier, because he or she realizes it will not be the hard work it was for his or her parents, said J.K. Patel, a former Barclays banker. "The difference is, we used to man the desk ourselves. The new generation likes sitting in the office and delegating the work."

Also in New York City, for example, ownership of gas stations reflects the enormous ethnic transformation of the city during the 1980s. With 1 million newcomers, the latest wave of immigration is the second-largest in New York City history. Just a decade earlier, gas station ownership usually mirrored the ethnic makeup of the surrounding neighborhood. But by 1994, about 40 percent of New York City's stations were run or owned by South Asians. And their entrepreneurship isn't limited to gas stations. Indians and Pakistanis - close to 95,000 of whom reside in New York City - have a virtual monopoly on newsstands.

The religions of Asian Indian-Americans follows closely those of their home country. The percentages of religious beliefs and followings in India are as follows:

Hindu - 83.5 percent

Muslim - 11.0 percent

Christian - 3.5 percent

Sikh - 1.9 percent

Buddhist - 0.7 percent

Other - including Jains 0.3 percent

HOLIDAYS AND CUSTOMS

One of the Asian Indian-American holidays that is widely celebrated among the Asian Indian community in the United States is the **Festival of Lights** (sometimes referred to as Dassara and sometimes as Diwali). It marks the culmination of Ashwin, which lasts ten days in October or November. There is a time-honored belief that if any new venture or important undertaking is started on this day it is bound to succeed. So any undertaking, be it laying the foundation of a new building, opening a new shop or factory or even sending a child to school, is likely to start on these days.

Each year, Asian Indians in the United States celebrate their independence from Great Britain. Elaborate arrangements are made by several organizations to celebrate the anniversary of Indian **Independence Day** on August 15. In some states it is called **India Day** and celebrated often on the weekends. Religious and commercial groups join in the celebration, creating colorful parade floats. Food stalls are set up either along the parade route or at a gathering place for the celebration. Cultural programs that include music and dances are also held as part of the celebrations.

Another festival, sometimes celebrated in its mild form, is *Holi*, an annual rite of spring in India, symbolic of fertility and decoration and steeped in Hindu mythology. In its most innocent form, *Holi* (pronounced holy) is an occasion when families, friends and neighbors smear brightly colored liquid dye on each other, gaily sing and dance and celebrate the onset of summer and the harvest season. The origins of *Holi* have been obscured by time, but the festival has been associated with several gods of Hindu mythology, including Kama, the God of Pleasure.

There are many "deities" in Hinduism; three of them are Sanaswali, Lakshmi and Parvoli, or Dunga, who are believed to confer knowledge, prosperity and valor, respectively. There is also the God Rama, the hero of the epic Ramayana (the triumph of good over evil).

The Hindu temple in Lanham, Maryland, "The Sri Siva Vishnu Temple," a structure of over 12,000 square feet, is the largest of its type in North America. It is an example of the effort by Hindus to recreate the culture of their Indian homeland, some 10,000 miles away, for themselves and their children.

The temple experience is taken much more seriously in the United States than in other parts of the world because the temples are built the way they are in India. In England, for example, there are a lot of temples, and they're mostly in other buildings or converted churches. Although young Hindus in the United States don't spend much time in places of worship, temples remain a focus for Hindu communities in most U.S. cities.

As with other ethnic groups, Hindus are concerned about young people forgetting their culture and religion as their people assimilate into American culture. The temple at Lanham is one of such high profile that people think of it even when they're not looking to, a reminder of their heritage. Unlike churches or synagogues, Hindu temples have no fixed membership, and anyone, Hindu or not, is welcome to come in and pray at any time.

What follows is a brief description of the many other Hindu holidays and festivals that are celebrated by Asian Indians and by some other Southeast Asian immigrants from Sri Lanka and elsewhere. There are no fixed dates for these holidays and most are lunar holidays. Calculations are based on a formula dealing with the bright and waxing side of the moon.

Mahavir Jayanti—This festival is dedicated to Mahavira, the twenty-fourth Tirthankara (reincarnation) of the Jains who have a large following in Gujarat.

Buddha Purnima—This full moon day is celebrated as the day of birth, enlightenment and Mahaparinirvana, or salvation, of the Buddha.

Ratha Yatra—One of the greatest temple festivals of India, in Washington, D.C., profusely decorated chariot cars resembling a temple structure are drawn by thousands of pilgrims. Similar celebrations on a much smaller scale in other cities.

Teej—Teej is an important festival in Rajasthan and welcomes the monsoons. It is essentially a women's festival. The presiding deity is Goddess Parvati, who, in the form of a bride, leaves her parents' home for that of her husband. A procession of the goddess is taken out with a retinue of elephants, camels and dancers.

Naag Panchami—Celebrated to revere the Cobra (*Naag*) all over India, this day is dedicated to the thousand-headed mythical serpent called Sesha or *Anant*, which means infinite. Vishnu, the Hindu God of preservation, reclined on him in contemplation during the interval between dissolution of one aeon and the creation of another. For people from Rajasthan huge cloth effigies of the mythical serpent are displayed at colorful fairs.

Ganesh Chaturthi—Ganesh, the deity with an elephant head (son of Lord Shiva), is the god of good omen and is worshipped by most Hindus. The festival of Ganesh is celebrated with enthusiasm. Clay models of the deity, sometimes as tall as eight meters, are worshipped and taken out in a procession to the accompaniment of cymbals and drums and finally immersed in the sea.

Durga Puja—Durga Puja is mainly celebrated by those who came from Calcutta and the region of Bengal. The devotees don new clothes and entertain with music, dance and drama. On the last day, images of the warrior goddess are taken out in procession and immersed in the river or sea.

Dussehra/Ramlila—This is a joyous Indian festival that celebrates the victory of truth over evil.

Diwali/Laxmi Puja—The Festival of Lights—The gayest of all Indian festivals, Diwali marks the start of the Hindu New Year. Every city, town and village is turned into a fairyland with thousands of flickering oil lamps and electric lights or candles illuminating homes and public buildings.

Basanta Panchami—This festival is celebrated in honor of Goddess Saraswati, the goddess of knowledge.

Shivaratri—Celebrated by Hindus all over, Shivaratri is a solemn occasion devoted to the worship of the most powerful deity of the Hindu Pantheon—Shiva. It is purely a religious festival at which devotees spend the whole night singing his praises. Special celebrations are held at important Shiva temples.

Gangaur—This festival is held two weeks after Holi in honor of Parvati, the consort of Lord Shiva. In their invocation to Gauri, they ask for husbands like the one she has been blessed with. The festival, during which gaily attired young girls proceed to the temples, culminates in rejoicing with the arrival of Shiva to escort his bride Gauri (PaNati) home, sometimes accompanied by horses and elephants.

Vaisakhi—This is the Hindu Solar New Year's day observed virtually all over Northern India and Tamil Nadu. It is a religious festival when people bathe in rivers and go to temples to worship. The river Ganga is believed to have descended to the earth this day. For the Sikh community Vaisakhi is of special significance, as on this day in 1689 Guru Gobind Singh organized the Sikhs into the "*Khalsa*," a military order who never shave their beards or touch tobacco and always carry weapons. In the Punjab, farmers start harvesting with great jubilation.

Ramanavami—Birthday of Lord Rama, the ninth reincarnation of the Lord Vishnu. This festival is celebrated all over India. The epic Ramayana is recited for days in the temples and homes of the devotees.

WEDDING CUSTOMS

Hindu weddings are usually arranged by parents or relatives. Advertisements or announcements of availability, and a dowry perhaps, are placed in various Asian Indian-American publications. There also is an increasing awareness of "Love Marriages," which are not arranged by parents. In the Hindu marriage ceremonies the newlyweds are required to share a plate of food.

Thais, who came to the United States from Thailand, make up only 1.3 percent of the recent Asian immigrants who have come to the U.S. The 1990 Census showed a Thai population in the U.S. of 112,000 people. They had a median age of 31.8 years, and 75.5 percent were foreign-born. About 27 percent entered the U.S. before 1975, 16.2 percent entered between 1975 and 1979. The largest number entered between 1980 and 1990, when 32.2 percent entered the United States. The average Thai family in the U.S. is 3.5 people, which is larger than the national average for U.S. families but among the smallest of families of Asian ancestry.

The educational achievement of Thais, like other Asian groups, is above the U.S. average (88.6 percent of males graduated from high school, 66.2 percent of females). A large part of the Thai population in the U.S., 79.1 percent, speaks a foreign language at home, and more than 70 percent of the population 16 or older work in the labor force. Like other Asian immigrant families, many Thais have families (21.3 percent) in which three or more members are in the work force.

HOLIDAYS AND CUSTOMS

Thais' predominant religion is **Buddhist** (mostly of the Theravada sect, see section on Buddhism), and it deeply affects their lives. Traditionally, all young men are expected to become Buddhist monks for at least three months of their lives.

Families are close-knit, and grandparents live with the family if at all possible.

The Thais celebrate their **New Year**, as well as many other groups in the United States from Southeast Asia, according to the Solar New Year known as **Songkran**, celebrated in mid-April. The day is traditionally given over to meditation and reflection on the moral teachings and examples set by Gautama Siddhartha, who became the first Buddha. Thais traditionally wash statues of the Buddha. They also throw water on each other, as it is considered a blessing to be soaked because the water washes away all the evils of the old year. Also, to give animals new life as well, people sometimes release birds from their cages and pour fish from their bowls into rivers.

Another day that is marked reverently by Thai Buddhists each year is called Kaopansa. It is a day on which Thais pledge themselves to renew spiritual vigor, in the ancient Buddhist tradition. Thais also realize that in the Buddhist religion there is no dogma, no single entity, and that Buddha was an enlightened teacher, not a god. To Thais this means there is no clearly defined right or wrong—whatever works is okay. As a result, nothing is urgent. Consequently, most Thais are essentially pragmatic and open to new experiences.

Queen's Birthday—August 12 and **King's Birthday**—December 5—Commemorative days.

Chulalongkorn Day—October 24—Celebrates a former monarch beloved for having abolished slavery and reformed Thai laws and customs.

WEDDING CUSTOMS

One Buddhist Thai wedding tradition is to pour holy water blessed by a Buddhist monk over the hands of the newlyweds, who wear linked wreaths (*mongkhon faet*) of unspun threads, in a ceremony of congratulation after the wedding.

Tibet, a country of 6 million on the northeast border of India, was annexed by China in 1951 but had considerable autonomy until a Communist crackdown in 1959.

During the Cultural Revolution in China, Tibet remained virtually sealed off from the rest of the world.

The Tibetans are one of the smallest ethnic groups in the United States—there are less than 10,000 of them. But they remain tightly knit and culturally and politically active. Most live in the New York-New Jersey area, according to the 1990 Census.

Some of the Tibetan Americans went to Maine as lumberjacks in the late 1960s, but now they mostly work in different professions: as plumbers, teachers, translators, exporters or importers, for example.

Despite their small numbers, the Tibetans are well-organized and increasingly vocal. There are at least a score of Tibetan cultural and social organizations in the U.S. and Canada, some thirty Tibetan Buddhist centers, and a number of Mongolian temples where Tenzin, Gyatso and the fourteenth Dalai Lama are also worshipped.

The Tibetans are scattered but manage to get together for important occasions: the American and Tibetan New Year (the date of which varies), National Day on March 10, and Dalai Lama's birthday on July 6. They also organize lectures, art exhibits, Tibetan-language courses and bazaars, with the proceeds going to Tibetan refugees who live mainly in agricultural settlements in India.

"Most Tibetans in exile would return if His Holiness the Dalai Lama went back, and Tibetans were given their rights and freedom," Tenzin Tethong, a representative of the Dalai Lama in the Office of Tibet in New York City, told the *New York Times* in 1985.

A fundamental tenet of Buddhism is that the path to salvation runs between the extremes of self-denial and self-indulgence. Therein lies a hint of the path by which the Dalai Lama, spiritual and temporal leader of Tibetan Buddhists, eventually hopes to return from exile.

On the day the thirteenth Dalai Lama died, June 6, 1935, a son was born to peasant parents from the Kokonor region of northeastern Tibet. By Mayahana Buddhist tradition, the Dalai Lama's death inspires a wide-ranging search by most venerated monks for the next god-king.

And so, two years later, when an array of objects was placed before the child and he immediately grabbed one that belonged to the thirteenth Dalai Lama, it was the awaited sign that the Dalai Lama had been reincarnated. On February 22, 1940, in the holy city of Lhasa, he was enthroned and immediately moved into the Potala, a 1,000-room palace overlooking the city.

But there was a prophecy at the time that the fourteenth Dalai Lama would one day leave Tibet, to return later. In 1950, the twelfth year of his reign, China invaded and grabbed power from the Dalai Lama. Then, after the Chinese crushed an uprising in 1959, he trekked across the border into India and was soon followed by 100,000 other refugees. Since then, he has headed a government in exile based in the Himalayan town of Dharmsala.

As of the 1990 Census, there were approximately 950,000 Vietnamese-Americans living in the United States. Most of them came to the U.S. as political refugees from their native land's communist regime. They include highly educated professionals and elite members of the former U.S.-backed South Vietnam government who fled after the capital city, Saigon, fell in 1975. They include boat people who were of more modest backgrounds, who numbered in the tens of thousands and who escaped between the late 1970s and the early 1980s. This group also included Amerasian children of U.S. servicemen and Vietnamese women, and some political prisoners who in the late '80s and early '90s were jailed by the communists because they held military or government positions in the former South Vietnamese government. This is different from the majority of immigrants in U.S. history, who were drawn to the U.S. more by economic rather than political forces. Consequently, political exiles, especially the Vietnamese, found it difficult to accept the United States' August 1995 reestablishment of diplomatic relations with Vietnam's government, according to the *New York Times*. After all, Vietnamese-Americans were part of the largest refugee resettlement program in U.S. history. They were resettled in all fifty states, partly to avoid a concentration in one city, as happened with Cubans in Miami. Over the years, however, many have settled in California, Texas and Washington, D.C. Like other immigrant groups, many Vietnamese prefer to live close to relatives as a means of raising their comfort level.

On April 29, 1975, the fall of Saigon sparked the largest refugee wave to the U.S. since World War II—an exodus that is an enduring legacy of the United States' long involvement in Vietnam. And from 1975 to 1992, more than 824,000 Vietnamese made their way to the States, according to the Census Bureau. The tide of Vietnamese immigrants that began with the military collapse of South Vietnam included many who lost their property to the new government and were charged huge fees to leave the country. Many of the people leaving were those who had a capitalistic stake in Vietnam, and when they came to the U.S., they came with an inclination to start businesses of their own.

Forty percent of the Vietnamese immigrants in the U.S. obtained their business capital from savings. They worked for others, saved money and used it to open their own businesses. About a quarter of them, according to the Vietnamese Chamber of Commerce, got their money from family, either as loans or gifts. Vietnamese-Americans often go into business to stay close to their families and to provide jobs for members of the family who can't find work elsewhere. A typical Vietnamese business hires a member of the family—a brother, sister or parent.

Two-thirds of the Vietnamese-American firms nationwide are either in retailing or services, according to Census data.

According to Census Bureau reports, half of all Vietnamese households in 1994 earned more than $38,205—$3,000 more than the median for the population as a whole in the U.S. But Vietnamese-Americans are almost twice as likely as other Asian immigrants to live in poverty—23.7 percent compared with 13.2 percent of all Asian-Americans. Their families are more than four times as likely to receive welfare, 24.5 percent, compared to 5.6 percent of other Asian-Americans.

Even as recently as 1995 in the Vietnamese refugee communities throughout the country, usually referred to as "Little Saigons," people still struggled to come to terms with history. Many have adapted only halfway to their new country, taking on the ways and pace of American life but with their hearts still in Vietnam.

Those who have come to the United States have inspired others. New arrivals sent for family members, who either made a dangerous escape from Vietnam by boat or joined the long list of people petitioning the State Department to come to the United States.

Many immigrant Vietnamese in the U.S. describe the Little Saigons as cauldrons of political intrigue, much like the Saigon of the past, with plenty of daily and weekly newspapers and an array of political tensions that sometimes flare into violence. The major issue among Vietnamese in the U.S. before 1995 was whether Washington should open diplomatic relations with Hanoi (in the hope that the Communist government there would become more liberal) or continue to work for the Vietnamese government's collapse.

With time's passage, generational divisions changed the character of Little Saigons, and they have become the scene of culture clashes that are purely Vietnamese. One leading Vietnamese businessman in Orange County, California, told the *New York Times*, "When people come here to find Vietnam like Saigon before 1975, they are making a mistake, because we are not the same. We are Vietnamese, but we are not Vietnamese."

"Living in a new country, we change and we don't even know it," he added. "Sometimes they try to deny that we are Americanized, but we have changed. How we have changed I don't even know. But at some time we changed."

The Vietnamese feel a strong urge to cluster. Unlike immigrants who uprooted themselves, many of the Vietnamese are refugees from war, devastation and political repression, and some continue to be traumatized by their perilous escapes. Some are tormented by an almost obsessive nostalgia for a native land that many fear they will never see again. Though most have shown extraordinary resilience, others have failed to adjust fully to the United States, and their problems have strained their mental stability as well as their family ties. As one Vietnamese social worker explained, "We are survivors, grasping each other for support. A place like Little Saigon provides that support."

As noted, the U.S. government, striving to avoid a repeat of the massive Cuban refugee crisis in Miami, originally attempted to disperse the first Vietnamese arrivals in 1975 around the U.S. The policy failed. Seeking to be closer to their relatives and friends, and lured by a warm climate reminiscent of home, more than a quarter of the nearly 1 million Vietnamese refugees who poured into the United States after 1975 migrated to California. At least 70,000 settled in Orange County, giving it the largest concentration of Vietnamese people outside Vietnam.

The 1,500 or so businesses in Orange County's Little Saigon are typical of Vietnamese-American enterprises. They're small, family affairs serving the Vietnamese-speaking community.

"The 1975 refugees—the first wave—have done well because they have some education," said Nhu-Hao Duong, Orange County's refugee coordinator. "The recent refugees—the second wave—come with less education, very limited exposure to Western culture, and the majority come from a rural background."

The second wave came between 1978 and 1993. Among the latter group are the Amerasians, 80 percent of whom are illiterate, Duong said.

In 1987, according to an analysis of U.S. Economic Census figures, William O'Hare of the University of Louisville found there were forty-nine Vietnamese-owned businesses for every 1,000 Vietnamese-Americans.

Probably the most celebrated holiday for Vietnamese-Americans is "Tet," the start of the **Vietnamese New Year**, which is on the same date as the Chinese New Year. A traditional Vietnamese New Year invocation is performed at the Tet celebration, in which tea and incense are offered for those who died during the previous year. The colorful Lion Dance is the climax of the ceremony marking the start of the new year.

The religious holidays are **Buddhist** (Mahayana Sect) and Christian. See more details in the religious section.

Two Trung Sisters Day—Sometimes referred to as Trung Nguyen, which is celebrated in the middle of the seventh lunar month.

Trungthu—the mid-Autumn festival on the fifteenth day of the eighth lunar month.

A SPECIAL COMMENT ABOUT ASIAN-AMERICAN BURIAL CUSTOMS

To Asians the idea of a flat grave, which is a Western custom, is repulsive. Older Asians can't imagine being buried in underground tombs where people can step all over remains. They consider it very disrespectful. Asians prefer a raised tomb on graves. In many Asian countries, the dead are buried under a large mound, often on a hill, so that revered ancestors can watch over their descendants and bring them good luck. Customs differ by Asian ancestral groups, and privacy is appreciated. For example, Koreans hold annual memorials in the front of the tombs during which family members pay tribute to ancestors by drinking and eating. A recent development in the U.S. is to have either Asian cemeteries or sections of community cemeteries set aside for different Asian groups.

To mirror immigration and other statistics, these two groups will be considered together.

U.S. immigration from both Australia and New Zealand followed the ethnic population statistics of both countries. The people who have come to the United States have been predominantly English, Irish and Scottish in ancestry. Although people of Australian and New Zealand backgrounds have been in the United States for almost 200 years, their numbers have been relatively small. Many originally came to the United States because of the gold strike in California around 1850, and others who were on their way to England decided to stay. The 1970 Census counted 82,000 people of Australian and New Zealand backgrounds in the United States. Later statistics indicate that from 1971 to 1990 immigrants from both countries to U.S. shores totaled more than 86,000. However, data from the 1990 Census indicated only a little more than 52,000 Americans reported having Australian or new Zealander ancestry. It is not clear what happened to the other 30,000-plus people. There are some theories or thoughts concerning this. One is that many were not Australian to begin with and consequently thought of themselves as something else, such as Scots, Irish, etc., and others feel many may not have intended to stay or only were visiting, then didn't like it and moved on to England or somewhere else, often Canada.[29]

According to Laurie Pane of the Los Angeles-based Australian-American Chamber of Commerce (of which there were twenty-two chapters in the U.S. in 1995) there are over 15,000 people of Australian ancestry living in Los Angeles area. She feels there is no constant pattern of settlement and they are well-scattered across the United States and that there may be many more than shown in the Census. She continues by saying, "Australians are not the sort of people to register and stay put. Australians aren't real joiners, and that can be a problem for an organization like the ACC. But they're convivial. You throw a party, and Australians will be there."

Dr. Henry Albinski, director of the Australian-New Zealand Studies Center at Pennsylvania State University, theorizes that because their numbers are few and scattered, and because they are neither rich nor poor, nor have they had to struggle, they simply do not stand out. "There aren't stereotypes at either end of the spectrum."

According to Harvard professor Ross Teirell, Australians and New Zealanders have a great deal in common with Americans when it comes to outlook and temperament, and are easy-going and casual in their relationship with others.

HOLIDAYS AND CUSTOMS

The holidays celebrated are predominantly those of the Christian tradition.

January 26—**Australia Day**—commemorates the 1788 arrival of the first convict settlers in Australia.

April 25—**Anzac Day**—honors the memory of the soldiers who died in World War I at the battle of Gallipoli.

[1] prepared by the Asian Pacific and American Public Policy Institute, based in Los Angeles and the Asian American Studies Center at the University of California, Los Angeles 1990

[2] by the Asian Pacific and American Public Policy Institute, based in Los Angeles and the Asian American Studies Center at the University of California, Los Angeles 1990

[3] Paul Sladers International Corp., a New York City advertising agency that specialized in ethnic marketing, November 11, 1990

[4] Felicity Barringer, the *New York Times,* 1991, as well as Census data

[5] September 11, 1990

[6] Ronald Takaki, a professor of ethnic studies at Berkeley, speaking to Goldman of the *Times*

[7] December, 1995

[8] reported in a study by National Asian Pacific American Legal Consortium

[9] March 31, 1996

[10] Richard Hallaran, the *New York Times,* December 26, 1990

[11] Donatella Lorch

[12] Donatella Lorch

[13] *Ethnic America* by Thomas Sowell, *We the People*

[14] Seth Mydans

[15] David Margolick, the *New York Times*, May 18, 1994

[16] Neil Henry, the *Washington Post,* May 28, 1995

[17] Emily MacFarquhar, May, 1992

[18] K. Connie Kang, *San Francisco Examiner*

[19] K. Connie Kang, *San Francisco Examiner*

[20] Donatella Lorch, in the *New York Times,* talking about the Korean American Grocers Association

[21] December 27, 1990

[22] The *Washington Post*, July 5, 1992

[23] The *Washington Post*, July 5, 1992

[24] July 5, 1992

[25] K. Connie Kang

[26] *The Sikhs, History, Religion and Society*, by W.H. McLeod

[27] Richard Perez-Peda, the *New York Times*, November 28, 1994

[28] November 5, 1993

[29] *Gale's Encyclopedia*

CHAPTER VII:

FROM THE CARIBBEAN AND CENTRAL AND LATIN AMERICA CAME AMERICANS OF CUBAN, DOMINICAN, GUATEMALAN, HAITIAN, JAMAICAN, MEXICAN, NICARAGUAN, PANAMANIAN, PUERTO RICAN, SALVADORAN AND WEST INDIAN ANCESTRY

The ancestors of American Hispanics were among the early explorers and settlers of the New World. In 1609—eleven years before the pilgrims landed at Plymouth Rock—the Mestizo (Indian and Spanish) ancestors settled in what is now Santa Fe, New Mexico.

Over the years, several historical events increased the presence of Spanish-speaking people in the United States: the Louisiana Purchase; the admission of Florida and Texas into the Union; the Treaty of Guadalupe Hidalgo, which ended the Mexican-American War; the Spanish-American War; the Mexican Revolution; labor shortages during World War I and World War II; the Cuban Revolution; and the political instability in Central and South America during the late twentieth century.

In 1990, there were 22.4 million Hispanics in the United States, almost 9 percent of the total U.S. population. This population grew by 53 percent between 1980 and 1990, according to Census data. The Cuban and Puerto Rican populations grew at a rate at least four times as fast as the rest of the nation. By 1999 the Hispanic population in the U.S. grew 35% since 1990 and numbered 30.3 million. This accounted for 11% of the U.S. population and it is projected to grow to 14% by the year 2010.

In 1990, nearly nine of every ten Hispanics lived in just ten states.[1] The four states with the largest populations of Hispanics were California, Texas, New York and Florida. The Hispanic population grew by 45 percent in Texas, for example, from 1980 to 1990. Reasons prompting the growth included immigration and family size. Hispanics are more likely to have large families than non-Hispanics, which helped boost the Hispanic population by 7.7 million in the 1980s. The average Hispanic family size is made up of 4.1 people, compared to 3.1 people in the overall national average-sized family. In fact, Census projections say the Hispanic population could surpass the black population in the United States by 2014.

In 1990, Spanish was spoken by about one-half of all non-English speakers in the United States. The median age of Hispanics is 7.5 years younger than other American groups, an interesting fact, considering its impact on elections, education and the make-up of the work force.

Economically, the Hispanic community is not homogeneous: Cubans have the highest income levels; Puerto Ricans and Mexicans have the highest poverty rates. As Rafael Valdivieso, director of the United States Hispanic Policy Development Project, pointed out, "It's not a monolithic group, and you won't be able to pigeonhole Hispanics politically or economically."

The Latino National Political Survey, conducted in the early 1990s, was the most extensive effort to measure Hispanic attitudes to date. It showed that on immigration issues, as well as on other social and political questions, economic self-interest and a driving commitment to be part of American society— more than a sense of ethnic identity—shape attitudes among Hispanic groups.

According to the Latino National Political Survey, a majority of the Hispanic population in the United States say there is too much immigration, and a large proportion of Hispanic citizens and residents—more than 50 percent—say people who live in the United States should learn to speak English. In fact, the survey found that a majority of Hispanic people born in the United States speak English better than Spanish.

Ethnic population statistics of "Hispanics":

(1990 Census data)

Mexican:	61.2 percent	13,647,600
Puerto Rican:	12.1 percent	2,700,000
Cuban:	4.8 percent	1,070,000
Dominican:	2.4 percent	535,200
Other Hispanics:	3.9 percent	869,700 (Includes those who reported Spanish)
Spaniard:	4.4 percent	981,200
Central American:	6.0 percent	1,338,000
Salvadoran:		571,326
Guatemalan:		271,614
Nicaraguan:		204,714
Honduran:		132,462
Panamanian:		93,660
Costa Rican:		57,534
Other Central American:		28,098
South American:	4.7 percent	1,048,100
Colombian:		380,460
Ecuadorian:		193,898
Peruvian:		177,128
Argentinean:		101,665
Chilean:		69,175
Other South American:		122,627

Clearly rejecting labels like "Hispanic" or "Latino" that lump together groups from different nations, a large number in each group said they believed they had little in common with the others. In addition, the survey found some deep social bonds within each national group but a surprising lack of interest among respondents for most Hispanic groups, leaders or causes. "The implication is that there is a growing gulf between the Latino leadership and the community," the report stated. In the survey, Hispanic citizens readily identified themselves by their nation of origin and said they were most likely to socialize with other people from that area.

A number of contrasting attitudes and values among the various Hispanic groups emerged in the findings. The most notable thing about Hispanics, though, is that they are a diverse group in thinking and in behavior.

With regards to religion, Catholicism is dominant for Hispanic-Americans. However, the Catholic Church is losing members to evangelical Protestant denominations. While 90 percent of Hispanic-Americans were Catholic twenty-five years ago, in 1994 only 70 percent were, according to the *Yearbook of United States and Canadian Churches*. [2]

David Gonzalez, writing in the *New York Times* on November 15, 1992, pointed out that each year when Americans celebrate Hispanic Heritage Month, from mid-September to mid-October, differences in how this diverse group wants to be identified are confirmed. "The term Hispanic can be misleading, giving a picture of a behemoth with a single mind," Gonzalez said. "In reality, the term encompasses Mexican-Americans in the Southwest, conservative Cuban exiles in the Southeast, liberal Puerto Ricans in the Northeast, and increasing numbers of Dominicans and newer arrivals from Central America."

Many people of Spanish-speaking ancestry would have preferred "Latino," and feel that the Census Bureau imposed the label "Hispanic" upon them. Young people in some cities, especially, find Hispanic archaic, if not downright offensive. They say it recalls the colonization by Spain and Portugal and ignores the Indian and African roots of many of the people it was used to describe. By comparison, the word closest to Hispanic that exists in the Spanish language is "*hispano,*" or Spanish-speaker. "To say 'Latino' is to say you come to my culture in a manner of respect," says Sandra Cisneros, an author. "To say 'Hispanic' means you're so colonized you don't even know for yourself, or someone who named you never bothered to ask what you call yourself. It's a repulsive slave name."

According to Jorge del Pinal, chief of ethnic and Hispanic statistics at the Census Bureau, his agency began grappling during the 1970s with how best to describe the diverse groups that had been called "Spanish-speaking" or "Spanish-surnamed." As a result, he said, the final category came to be designated "Spanish/Hispanic Origin," preferably used in tandem. Most Hispanics/Latinos prefer to identify themselves according to their country of origin—as, for example, Puerto Rican, Colombian, Dominican or just plain American.

The larger question suggested by the study[3] was whether a label for the larger group is useful at all in characterizing a population that is not monolithic. Indeed, in Miami, there are bumper stickers that proclaim, "*No soy hispano, soy Cubano*" ("I am not Hispanic, I am Cuban"), a sentiment echoed among other groups who do not want to see their achievements and struggles vanish in the swirl of the American melting pot. Lisandro Perez, director of the Cuban Research Center at Florida International University, said,[4] "They [Cubans] find out they're Hispanic when they get here. The mega label is widely used in the United States, but people have an identity of where they migrate from."

Earl Shorris, author of *Latinos: A Biography of People*, has written: "The use of a single word to name a group including people as disparate as Mexicans and Cubans conflates the cultures and raises a serious issue. And whatever conflates cultures destroys them. Nevertheless, there will have to be a name, for political power in a democratic society requires numbers, and only by agglomerating does the group become large enough to have an important voice in national politics."

He added, "The group cannot be defined racially, because it includes people whose ancestors came from Asia to settle in the Western Hemisphere thousands of years ago, as well as people from Europe, the Iberian Peninsula and Africa. Religion won't do, either. The group comprises Roman Catholics, many Protestant denominations, Jews and people who still have deep connections to Mixtec, Nahua and other native American religious rites and beliefs."

As evidenced by the continuing controversy just outlined, the terms Hispanic and Latino have taken on political, social and even geographic meaning. Latino is used in California. Hispanic is used more often than Latino in Texas, but neither word is used much: Mexican and Mexican-American and Chicano dominate there. In Chicago, which has a mixture of people from the Caribbean, Mexico and the U.S., Latino has been adopted. According to Shorris, Hispanic belongs to those in power; it is the choice of establishments, exiles, social climbers and kings. Latino is used by almost everyone else. A demonstration of how the terms and cultures can be misunderstood was when a reporter in the *Washington Post* on May 6, 1996, wrote a story about a civil disturbance that took place in a distinctive neighborhood populated by Spanish-speaking peoples. The newspaper story referred to the "Cinco de Mayo" holiday as the starting date for the disturbances in the section of the city known as Mount Pleasant. A person with even peripheral knowledge of the Spanish-speaking people who live in Washington would know that most of the Spanish-speaking community in the city is made up of Columbian, Ecuadorian and Salvadorian peoples who do not recognize, much less celebrate, Cinco de Mayo. By referencing the Mexican holiday, the story diminished the real frustrations and problems borne by that particular community. Mexican Americans were disturbed by this passing of misinformed references.

A 1992 survey called "Latino Voices: Mexican, Puerto Rican and Cuban Perspectives on American Politics"[5] offers valuable insight into the position of various Hispanic groups.

People often lumped together as "Hispanics," the survey found, don't consider themselves Hispanics but rather Cubans or Mexican-Americans or Puerto Ricans, showing a tie to their native country, but also to the United States: "A majority in all three groups is more concerned with U.S. politics than with the politics of their country of origin," the study showed. "And big majorities say they feel 'very strong' love for the U.S. and that they are 'very proud' of this country."

Nevertheless, friction among different Hispanic ethnic groups often flares. For example, Dominicans in New York in the early 1990s complained that Puerto Ricans were unfairly dominating city government jobs. On a broader scale, some Puerto Ricans gripe that Mexican-American organizations have the franchise on the term "Hispanic" and have used it to attract the lion's share of federal funding. In the 1980s, Cuban-Americans backed United States policy in Central America, often at odds with traditionally liberal Hispanic groups.

In many American cities with large Hispanic populations it is quite common to have "Latino or Hispanic festivals." These so-called festivals point out that the Hispanic community is united only by language but divided by national origin, income levels and legal status. Also, at these festivals it is interesting to see the differences in food. You will find Mexicans filling tacos next to Guatemalans preparing tamales, Chileans making fried cheese empanadas, elbow to elbow with Peruvians dishing out seco de rez, and Puerto Ricans serving arroz con ganules across from Salvadorians peddling pupusas. You will also hear the music of the pipestrains of the Ecuadorian Andes mingled with the syncopated rhythms of Central American cumbia, Bolivian ballads and Puerto Rican salsa. The festivals always serve as a vehicle for political as well as cultural expression.

During every major immigration—from Ireland or Italy or the ghettos of Eastern Europe—you heard the same thing about the immigrants: "They will keep to themselves and never become real Americans." But all of these groups have become part of the majority—the majority of minorities—and have made their contribution to American society. As with other immigrants whose main language was other than English there comes a time when variations of language start to appear.

A new hybrid lingo of the Spanish language being used by those other than first generation Hispanics is starting to appear in conversations across the United States. It is known as *Spanglish*—the language of choice for a growing number of Hispanic-Americans who view the hyphen in their heritage as a metaphor for two coexisting worlds.

Ms. Nely Galan, the young president of Galan Entertainment, a Los Angeles television and film production company that focuses on the Latino market, says, "It's a phenomenon of being from two cultures, for those who speak English perfectly and Spanish perfectly. They choose to speak both simultaneously."

Spanglish has few rules and many variations, but at its most vivid and exuberant, it is an effortless dance between English and Spanish, with the two languages clutched so closely together that at times they actually converge. Phrases and sentences veer back and forth almost unconsciously, as the speaker's intuition grabs the best expressions from either language to sum up a thought. Sometimes entirely new words are coined.

Many Spanish-language purists denounce Spanglish as a debasement of their native tongue.

Lizette Alvarez, reporting in the *New York Times,* wrote: "There are two basic approaches to Spanglish, with countless variations: switching and borrowing. Borrowing words from English and Spanishizing them has typically been the creation of immigrants, who contort English words for everyday survival. But it is also true that as Spanish gets fuzzier to American-born Hispanics, they come to rely on English words to fill the gap."

Ana Celia Zentella, a linguist at Hunter College in New York, says that Spanglish is a sign of "linguistic dexterity." Some who speak English mostly and often switch into Spanish when they want to convey anger, joy, love or embarrassment, because Spanish is a more descriptive language than English—not because they don't know the word.

A SURVEY IN HISPANIC BUSINESSES

A 1994 study in one New York county (Westchester, just outside of New York City) showed a dramatic increase in "Hispanic"-owned business. Cuban, Peruvian and Mexican restaurants abound as well as grocery stores that sell chili peppers, green tomatoes and tender cactuses. There were also travel agencies, social clubs and *bodegas* that cater to Spanish speakers that were owned by Hispanic-Americans.

Hispanic residents are filling the economic niche of mom-and-pop operations and other small proprietorships in the way that Italians, Jews and other ethnic groups did more often in previous generations.

Hispanic immigrants are following the same path as other ethnic groups. However, larger business ventures among Hispanic-Americans are still in the minority. The businesses tend to be small, and they are often started by people who have used their savings to go into business.

Many Hispanic merchants (like different ethnic groups before them) have relied on relatives to get their fledgling enterprises off the ground. Mirroring the ways of preceding immigrant merchants, such as the Korean grocers of New York City, they depend on financial support and even free labor from their spouses, children, siblings, parents and other relatives. The whole family helps out; sometimes they get paid, sometimes they don't. The important thing is that the business does well, because then the whole family does well.[6]

In July 1997, Lou Cannon, a well-known California writer/author/reporter, penned a story he had researched concerning the emerging Latino middle class in Southern California. The Latino middle class was leading the economic and real estate boom, and in the process was transforming the culture of that region.

By 1997 Latinos were buying more than half the homes in Los Angeles County and owned more than a quarter of all businesses in the Los Angeles-Long Beach metropolitan area. An academic study, meanwhile documented that 50 percent of U.S. born Latinos in the five county Los Angeles region had household incomes above the national average. Also, by this time Latinos, native born and immigrants, made up 42 percent of the 10 million population of Los Angeles County.

Gregory Rodriguez, a Latino scholar, stated, "We are redefining what it means to be an American in Southern California, the center of the cultural matrix that was traditionally Anglo-American is shifting to Latino-American."

An example of this is the town of Huntington Park, a thriving community that a generation prior to 1997 was 80 percent Anglo and is now 80 percent Latino and had more signs in Spanish than English. Rodriguez states further, "A poor Latino who once modeled himself after middle class whites as he moved up the economic ladder now has plenty of Latino models."

The Cuban ethnic population in the United States was small before 1959. Some were political exiles and others were cigar workers in factories that had moved to Florida from Havana after the 1959 overthrow of the right-wing Cuban government. Members of the old Cuban elite fled to the United States, mostly to Miami (Dade County), Florida. Later, when the communist policies and practices were instituted by Fidel Castro, hundreds of thousands moved to the United States, again mostly to Florida. Many were from middle-class business families who were not sympathetic to Castro's cause. Although a quarter of Cuba's population is black, about 95 percent of those who have come to the United States have been white, a factor that has eased the adjustment for many, according to *We the People*. Most black Cubans have settled in New York City and New Jersey, partly because the Cubans and other whites in the Miami area have been less accepting.[7]

A section of Miami called "Little Havana" has become a thriving center of Cuban cultural and business life that has served the large Cuban population. By 1980, Cubans made up 42 percent of Miami's population; Hialeah, the second-largest city in Dade County, was 60 percent Cuban. The total Cuban population in the U.S. in 1990 was 1,070,000.

The Cuban revolution spurred the first large-scale Latin migration to Miami, and waves of immigrants transformed the city from a sleepy, seasonal tourist town to a city often called the crossroads of the Americas. Many of the early immigrants had been traders and entrepreneurs in Cuba, and they urged old clients in Latin America to do business with them rather than shipping to New Orleans or New York. That shift accelerated Miami's development of commercial links with Latin America and the Caribbean.

Among the first businesses established were those catering to Latin tastes: the *panaderias* (bakeries) with guava pastries; the stands serving potent Cuban coffee; and the restaurants. Then the Cubans branched out into auto repair shops, gas stations, dry cleaners, boutiques and many other small businesses. Eventually they opened law offices, medical and dental practices, public relations firms and banks.

A copyrighted story in *USA Today* written by Del Jones on January 18, 1999, reported how Cuban-Americans have thrived in the United States and how successful many of them have become in business. Cuban-American executives say they are driven by a consuming work ethic, but admit that is common to immigrant groups. What's unique is that their parents were already successful in Cuba. They arrived here broke but brought education and know-how that could not be confiscated.

Many Cuban-American business owners say that seeing their millionaire parents lose everything has made them more entrepreneurial. They have less fear of risk, and many have traded comfortable careers to start ventures in untested waters.

Their background also tends to make them more politically conservative than most other Hispanics. "Anything that goes in the direction of socialism is distasteful," says Emilio Alvarez-Recio, vice-president of global advertising for Colgate-Palmolive.

According to *Hispanic Business Magazine,* by the end of 1998, 27 percent of the 500 largest Hispanic-owned businesses were owned by Cuban-Americans who make up only 4.8 percent of the 13.7 million Hispanics age 15 and older in the United States. They are more educated and more than twice as likely as other Hispanics to be earning $50,000 a year. Of the 50 largest Hispanic businesses, Cuban-Americans owned 38 percent. They owned 40 percent of the top 25.

Most Cuban-American executives were children or young adults in 1959, but some say their drive to achieve has an element of revenge. They're forever trying to prove capitalism superior to communism.

By 1999 the *New York Times* reported Cuban-Americans and the latest Cuban immigrants were the single largest Latin American group in southern Florida, making up about 60 percent of the total Hispanic population, which accounted for more than half of Florida's Miami-Dade County's population.

The people from an earlier Cuba, and their children, have grown into a Miami's who's who. By 1999 the mayors of the city and county of Miami, the county police chief and the county state attorney were all Cuban-born or of Cuban descent. So was the president of the largest bank, the owner of the largest real estate developer, the managing partner of the largest law firm, nearly half of the county's 27-member delegation in the legislature and two of its six members of Congress.*

In the mid-1990s, Cuban exiles continued to arrive in south Florida at the fastest pace in a decade, revising some hopes that Fidel Castro might soon be forced out of power. Cuban-Americans in 1994 said they believed Castro's government might soon fall, according to a survey conducted in the Dade County area. However, in late 1999 Castro was still in full power.

Many of the new exiles tell tales of hardship about economic and political pressures that led to their perilous trip over ninety miles of sea. Many came in homemade vessels—some made of light wood strips tied over inner tubes. In 1980 the rafters, called *balseros*, washed up onto U.S. shores at the highest rate since 125,000 left the port of Miriel.

More Cubans live in south Florida than anywhere else in the United States. By 1994 about 49 percent of Dade County's population was Hispanic, and most of them were Cuban. Although many arrived empty-handed, Cuban exiles have steadily increased their economic and political clout.

Cubans, who, according to the Latino National Political Survey of 1990, have fared better economically in the United States than any other Hispanic group, are more than twice as likely as Mexicans or Puerto Ricans to believe that job placement and college admissions should be based strictly on merit rather than quotas.

Although a great deal of political activity in Cuban communities has long focused on the prospects of overthrowing Fidel Castro and returning to the island, only 5.6 percent of the foreign-born Cubans in a 1994 survey said they intended to return to Cuba.

Cuban-American political leaders, in contrast to Mexican-Americans and Puerto Ricans, describe themselves as ideologically conservative rather than liberal.

HOLIDAYS AND CUSTOMS

Jose Marti Day—January 28—This day honors Jose Marti, a Cuban revolutionary leader and poet who was killed while fighting for Cuban independence from Spain. Cuban-Americans celebrate with dinners and banquets.

Cuban-Americans also celebrate other **Christian** (mostly Roman Catholic) holidays; most of them are either Roman Catholic or non-religious.

* *NY Times*-Mineya Navarro 2-11-99

The Dominican Republic is a Caribbean country that shares an island with Haiti and traces its much interrupted independence to 1844. The residents of this small nation have been exploited for centuries by outsiders and sometimes by their own people such as the brutal dictator Rafael Trujillo, who ruled with an iron hand for three decades. The United States has had an ambiguous and complex relationship with the Dominican Republic, intervening with troops twice in the twentieth century—ostensibly to preserve civil order and keep the Dominicans from suffering an even worse fate than Yankee occupation.

It is thus no surprise that many Dominicans have had to deal not only with rural poverty but also with the absence of a political culture that could provide them with hope for a better future in their country of birth. After decades of coups, assassinations and political corruption, cynicism is rampant. One result is that despite the ambivalence of many Dominicans about the United States, immigration to the shores of this country has boomed: Only 90,000 Dominicans came here in the 1960s, and 140,000 came in the 1970s, but in the 1980s so many came that some estimates say there are now one million Dominicans in this country. (This from a nation with a little less than eight million people.)

However, according to the 1990 census there are approximately 500,000 Dominicans in the United States of which 400,000 live in New York City.

As for legal immigration to New York City, the Dominican Republic has become the largest source, with an annual flow that has risen 50 percent over the last decade as reported by a *New York Times* article in February 1997. The article by Larry Rother further pointed out that from 1990 to 1994 the Dominican Republic accounted for one of every five new immigrants to New York City, or more than 110,000 people in that short period of time.

As a result, the ties between the United States and the Dominican Republic are ever more binding and complex. It is said in that country that by 1999 half of all Dominicans have relatives in the United States and more than two-thirds would move to the United States if they could.

In the book entitled *Muddy Cup,* written by Barbara Fischer (Scribner) in 1997 she asks the question: What makes these families leave behind the roosters, the dirt roads, the sheep, the churches, and the faith healers of their homeland and brave the streets and sidewalks of New York. In a word, the answer is jobs. Typically, one family member hears that by driving a taxi or working on a construction site or cleaning houses, a Dominican can make enough money in New York to send most of it back home and eventually to bring the rest of the family over as well. Although families may have to be separated for years, the expectation that they will someday be reunited is enough to keep them going. Meanwhile, those who are in the United States become more and more American every day.

Because New York remains a city in which ethnic neighborhoods are often matched by ethnic industries, where Greeks own many of the diners, many diamond merchants are Jewish, and greengrocers are often Korean, one of the business areas that Dominicans staked out for themselves was that of grocery stores different from Korean fruit and vegetable markets. By 1994 the Dominicans formed grocery store chains, which were called "voluntary associations." Ask the Dominican store owners what brought them together, and they sketch a story of traditional immigrant virtues and of fourteen-hour workdays in poor neighborhoods. They came to New York to get rich, and some have succeeded. Often, they plant their stores in tough neighborhoods where major chains have pulled out or seldom ventured.

Like other ethnic groups, Dominicans began with small stores serving their own communities, then they branched out. They put their relatives on the job, recruited other Dominicans at near-minimum wages and worked countless hours themselves. One-third of the Dominican business owners started their careers as employees in other businesses owned by Dominicans. They learned the ropes, got the skills and moved up.

HOLIDAYS AND CUSTOMS

In addition to the usual **Christian** holidays, Dominicans in the United States celebrate **Altagracia Day**, January 21, which is St. Agnes Day, the patron saint of girls. Also, they celebrate **Duarte Day** on January 26, **Independence Day** on February 27, and **Dominican Restoration Day** on August 16.

Because as of 1995 Dominican-Americans were one of the newer groups coming into the United States and because they are still in the process of creating a unique place for themselves, their relationships to the United States and its culture and to the Dominican Republic are still evolving.

Baseball is an active sport among Dominican-Americans, as it was in their homeland. Many Major League Baseball players are Dominicans.

Guatemalans didn't start arriving in the United States until the late 1970s and 1980s. They came because of political unrest, high inflation in Guatemala and for economic reasons. Also, a population explosion in Guatemala created lifestyle problems.[8]

In 1980 the Census reported only 62,000 of Guatemalan ancestry in the U.S., but most arrived later, and the Census in 1990 reported 268,000 people (of which 225,000 are foreign-born) of Guatemalan ancestry. Also, it is estimated that an additional 300,000 have entered the United States illegally.

The United States has not recognized Guatemalans as political refugees, and recent immigrants are considered economic immigrants. Guatemalan-Americans are a culturally diverse group, coming from twenty-three different ethnic groups with different languages and customs. The majority are Mayans and Latinos or Hispanic Guatemalans and constitute a separate population both in Spanish language and customs. Because of this diversity, it is not easy to generalize about this ethnic group as a whole. Its largest populations are in California, Houston, Chicago, Washington, D.C. and Florida.

HOLIDAYS AND CUSTOMS

Among the most unusual cultural celebrations immigrant Guatemalans have brought to their new home are the events of **All Saints' Day** and **All Souls' Day** that had been conducted in many small towns and villages of their native Guatemala. Guatemalan-Americans are Christian and celebrate the American and Christian holidays.

According to an article in the *Washington Post*[9], on the first day of November, All Saints' Day, people gather at cemeteries with armloads of flowers and baskets of the favorite foods of buried family members. Children and adults alike launch hundreds of colorful kites intended to ward off evil spirits while the souls of the dead make their annual twenty-four-hour escape from the bodies buried in the graves. They believe that the souls return to their original homes for a visit during the night, so they set up altars with candles, flowers, a statue of the Virgin Mary and glass a of fresh water for the thirsty soul.

The next day, All Souls' Day, the families return to the cemeteries, where they beat cans and drums and shout to help the souls find their way back to the graveyard.

Guatemalan-Americans celebrate the **Quinceanera** (see section about Mexican-Americans).

Semana Santa—A Catholic tradition on the week before Christmas, participants cover the streets with *Alfombias*, which are carpets made of sawdust and arranged in intricate patterns. The parish priest leads a procession at the end of the week across the *Alfombias* to prepare for the birth of Jesus.

San Miguel Acatan—Celebrated September 29 by Guatemalan *Kanjohals* in Los Angeles and Florida. A ritual called the Deer Dance is performed by people dressed as animals.

Haitians first settled in the United States after the late eighteenth-century revolution, when white sugar planters, free blacks and slaves came. A small number of Haitians came to the U.S. after 1915, and in the 1960s and 1970s many professionals, students and politicians came because of opposition to the Haitian government. By 1980 close to 90,000 people of Haitian ancestry were in the United States, and more than 50 percent lived in New York City. The largest settlement is in Brooklyn. Many have worked as taxi drivers,[10] and some have started the same businesses they were in on the island, serving a Haitian clientele. Since the 1980s and another revolution in Haiti, thousands have ventured on hazardous voyages in small ships to try to land in Florida. There, many requested political asylum and were refused. In the late 1980s many boats carrying Haitian refugees were turned back. However, some have entered the United States illegally, which has caused some resentment, particularly in South Florida, toward Haitians.

By 1995 New York's Haitian Diaspora was at a delicate point of transition. Most fled the bloody oppression of the Duvalier regime, then, brick by brick, built a new life in the U.S. They got a foothold but, like many immigrants, live on the precarious margin where danger is greatest. And they face prejudice from both whites and native blacks. Many say they feel they have never really belonged.

When the U.S. government banned Haitian blood donors in the late 1980s, fearing many were at risk as HIV-virus carriers, tens of thousands of Haitians protested, suggesting to a people who had long felt powerless that they could exercise influence through their protest against discrimination.

Haitians, mostly Catholic, proudly mention that Pierre Toussaint, a Haitian-American buried in the United States, is moving steadily toward becoming the first black American saint.

HOLIDAYS AND CUSTOMS

Haitians celebrate **Carnival** (two days before Ash Wednesday), the **Christian** Catholic Holidays and **Discovery Day**, which is December 5. They also celebrate **Flag and University Day** on May 18 and **Independence Day** on January 2.

Haitian Voodoo—Among Haitians, Voodoo is a prominent aspect of religion, a means of influencing the culture, according to Donald J. Consentino, who was the co-curator of a traveling exhibition in 1996 of Haitian Sacred Arts. It was a religion that was transported by enslaved Africans who adapted their beliefs and rituals to a new world. Another specialist in Haitian art, Nicole Smith, who owns an art gallery in Chicago, says the word "Voodoo" often is misunderstood. " 'Voodoo' means spirit," she says, and has nothing to do with black magic or devil worship.

Some of the art of Haitian Voodoo is expressed by audio or visual effect, temples, altars, sculptures, sequined flags, sacred bottles, painted calabashes, medicine packets, dolls and paintings.

The 1990 Census showed a Jamaican population in the United States of 435,000. The population of Jamaica represents the descendants of slaves brought centuries earlier from Africa as laborers. Most who came to the United States were blacks from Jamaican heritage who spoke English (British) or Creole with an English-language foundation. Many were Episcopalians. During World War II many Jamaicans came to the United States under contract to pick fruit and vegetables in various Eastern and Midwestern states. Between 1967 and 1979 legal immigration increased substantially.

Jamaicans, like other blacks from the West Indies, have mostly settled in parts of larger black sections of American cities, particularly in New York City, western Virginia and in and around Hartford, Connecticut.

HOLIDAYS AND CUSTOMS

West Indian/American Day—Carnival and parade are celebrated in late summer in New York City. See also section on West Indian ancestry.

WEDDING CUSTOMS

For Jamaicans, slices of dark Caribbean-style wedding cake are soaked in rum and mailed to friends who were unable to attend the marriage ceremony.

The 1990 Census showed 11,586,983 people of Mexican ancestry in the United States. After 1970, people of Mexican origin represent by far the largest group of settlers among all ethnic groups immigrating into the United States. Because of the early Mexican ethnic settlements in the United States, 74 percent of the Mexican-origin population counted in the 1980 Census were born in the United States.

The U.S. population of Mexican ancestry is heavily concentrated in the Southwestern United States, some parts of which had originally been part of Northern Mexico. The Mexican-American population is particularly large in Texas, and then north to Colorado and west into California. In fact, the largest single barrio by far in 1980 was in East Los Angeles, which had a population that was 90 percent Mexican-American. Earlier in the twentieth century, Texas was the major center of Mexican settlement. Its Mexican-American population comprised most of the unskilled labor force in the Southwestern United States, according to U.S. Census reports. By the 1920s, immigration laws and restrictions in California and the cutoff of Asian immigrant labor meant that Mexicans replaced Asian farm workers. After the Depression and the great growth of California, people of Mexican origin found work in manufacturing and in other areas. By 1980, more than half, 52 percent, of the country's population of Mexican-origin was living in California and only 21 percent were residing in Texas. While this indicates a large migration from Texas to California, the immigration directly from Mexico to California in recent decades has been much greater, and in 1980 there were six times more Mexican-born people in California than in Texas. However, in the 1990s Mexican workers started traveling to new areas other than the Southwestern United States and California. They were crisscrossing the United States in ways that break dramatically with traditional patterns according to Jorge Durand, a University of Guadalajara demographer who has studied migration since 1980.

The dispersion of Mexicans into virtually all 50 states has increased since 1986, when passage of the Immigration Reform and Control Act legalized the status of more than two million Mexicans who had been working in the United States without documents. This enabled them to migrate to remote regions without risking arrest.

Mexicans were in the last years of the twentieth century America's largest immigrant group, constituting 28 percent of the foreign born population up from 7 percent in 1970. There is an identifiable presence of Mexicans in states where there's never been any before. Prior to this California had been their main destination.

The high mobility of Mexican workers across the U.S. during the early decades of the twentieth century was similar to that of many Eastern European immigrants. People of Mexican ancestry have worked in the Southwestern mining settlements in Arizona and New Mexico and have been cowboys and sheepherders and agricultural workers in Texas and California.

As with other Hispanic groups, Mexican-American families are usually larger than those of other ethnic groups. The father is leader of the family, but the mother is in charge of the household. Family unity and family responsibilities are paramount in Mexican-American families.

One of the biggest holidays celebrated by Mexican-Americans is **Cinco de Mayo**. Cinco de Mayo, or Fifth of May, can best be compared to the Fourth of July celebration in the United States. A celebration of tradition. A celebration of community. At the Cinco de Mayo festival Mexicans celebrate with bands, dancers—and lots of tacos, tamales, fajitas and margaritas. The holiday commemorates May 5, 1862, when a band of Mexicans led by farmer-turned-general Ignacio Zaragosa defeated Napoleon III's French Army at Puebla. Even though two years later the French installed Maximilian as Mexican emperor, the day is still a celebration of Mexican independence and courage.

One Mexican-American tradition that is well practiced by Americans at **Christmas** is the inviting glow of *luminaria*—stumpy candles in sand-filled paper sacks lining curbs, sidewalks and walkways like rows of landing lights for Santa Claus. The tradition is anything but local or new. It dates at least to early seventeenth-century Spain. In one version of the legend, people burned cedar boughs along town paths, symbolically lighting the way to Bethlehem for Mary and Joseph. A slightly different version suggests that *luminaria* were intended to brighten the way for the Magi (the Three Wisemen). The tradition is a feature of Christmas festivals in the American Southwest. All day on Christmas Eve, neighbors meet neighbors as they emerge from their homes to place the sacks at two- or three-foot intervals along sidewalks and curbs.

Also at Christmastime, Mexican-Americans enjoy "*Las Posadas*," the reenactment of the holy family's search for an inn. The solemn tradition starts December 16 and continues for eight days, through Christmas Eve.

Feliz Navidad—Spanish for Merry Christmas—is a greeting heard from Thanksgiving weekend until early January. For many among the Mexican-American population, it is celebrated with the arrival of Pancho Claus, Santa's black-bearded cousin from the South Pole. Many families also gather for piñata parties and the Blessing of the Animals (both stuffed and live) by Pancho Claus.

In addition to these, another cultural holiday that is important to Mexican-Americans, celebrated annually, is **St. Anthony's Day**—January 17. St. Anthony is the patron saint of animals, and it is a day when children take their pets to receive the blessing imparted by St. Anthony.

Considering that 90 percent of Mexican-Americans are Catholic, note that religious holidays of significance include: **Candlemas Day**, on February 2, which is the Blessing of the Candles; Corpus Christi, celebrated eight weeks after Easter (in May or June); **All Saints' Day** on November 1 and **All Souls' Day** on November 2. Mexican-Americans celebrate "***El dia de Los Muertos***" or "Day of the Dead," on November 2. In the Roman Catholic tradition it is known as "All Souls' Day." Mexican-Americans celebrate the lives of their loved ones who have died by visiting cemeteries where they are buried. They remember the person by remembering the departed's life.

Prior to the late 1980s these family reunions, traditions and gatherings at the cemeteries were kept alive by the Mexican elderly, mostly women. The traditions have been revised, and today in cities like San Antonio, where the fast-growing Hispanic population constitutes a majority, rituals on November 2 that schools once shunned are now embraced. Some teachers build small classroom altars—ethnic, not religious—and bring in "*pan de muertas*," or cookies shaped like corpses with folded arms and raisin eyes.

Mexican Independence Day—September 16—Parades, festivals, dinners.

Revolution Day—November 20—Parades, festivals, dinners.

The day of the Virgin of Guadalupe—December 12—This day honors the Catholic patron saint of Mexico.

Day of the Holy Cross—May 3—Many Mexicans celebrate this day by raising a cross decorated with flowers.

The Ritual of **Quinceanera**—The *quinceanera* is a cultural ritual that makes a 15-year-old girl of Hispanic ancestry feel like a "queen for a day." It is a centuries-old Latin American tradition that both marks a young girl's passage into womanhood and celebrates her innocence. It also highlights the powerful role that age-old rituals play in modern American society. The *quinceanera*, celebrated from Mexico to Argentina, is as much a family statement as a reaffirmation of cultural identity in a new world.

The tradition comes when a young girl of Hispanic ancestry in her teenage years faces contradictions in her life, when other types of parties may seem more attractive than dancing something like a waltz with her father, a *quinceanera* tradition. The tradition also includes a reaffirmation of the young girl's baptismal vows and commitment to chastity. In the United States it's called the quince, and the tradition endures. In 1996 Roman Catholic priests in and around the Houston, Texas, area, where the population is about 30 percent Hispanic, said there are more *quinceanera* blessings than weddings.[11]

Going along with the religious flavor of the tradition, a Roman Catholic Mass starts off the day's celebration. In many areas of the United States that have a high concentration of Latin Americans, the Church has promulgated guidelines through its dioceses but lets each parish adapt the guidelines to tradition. For example, in Texas, some parishes perform *quinceanera* blessings by the dozens with no requirements, while others require lengthy religious preparations. Still other parishes refuse to have *quinceaneras* altogether because of the sectarian feel to the ceremony—priests want the religiosity of the event to endure.

Though some families cannot afford to uphold the tradition because of its costs, many others who believe strongly in it spend a large sum of money by day's end. It is reported extravagant *quinceanera* parties can cost as much as $50,000; some families even go into debt for a quince. Quinceaneras are particularly popular among first- and second-generation Hispanic immigrants. The tradition tends to dissipate by the third generation.[12]

Mariachi music—The tradition of Mariachi music was brought to the United States by Mexican immigrants and continues to flourish today in regions populated by Mexican-Americans. The music originated in West Central Mexico in the 1850s. It is an intimate part of Mexican family life. (The word "mariachi," whose origins are in dispute, is a nineteenth-century term referring to a party.) While most other Latin countries have adopted some version of the tune of the American "Happy Birthday," Mexican-Americans sing a Mariachi song.

A tradition Mexican-American men take from their ancestors is to bring a Mariachi band when making a marriage proposal. Baptisms, weddings and the rites of passage are accompanied by Mariachi brass and the thump of the big acoustic bass guitar.

The uniforms of the Mariachi players is a symbol of stubbornly independent machismo and at the same time of a sentimental Mexican identity. The suits, inspired by rural rodeos, are made up of bolero jackets, silk bow ties, tight pants with silver buttons down the sides, sometimes accompanied by a flashy pistol. For fancy occasions, the players don huge velvet-lined sombreros. Sometimes the music is plaintive, and sometimes it includes hymns bemoaning romantic conquests and humiliations of everyday life. Mexican-Americans, like their ancestors, have a deep need for music to be present in their emotional moments, either to show great joy or to vent great sorrow, Jesus Jauregui, who has written a book about Mariachis, told Juls Preston of the *New York Times*. [13]

More than 100,000 Nicaraguans came to the United States, and specifically to the Miami area, fleeing war, economic hardship and a leftist government in the 1970s and 1980s.[14]

According to Mireya Navarro of the *New York Times,* "Like Cuban exiles before them, the Nicaraguans have spent their years in exile in Miami building new lives, setting up businesses and settling into neighborhoods with streets and schools named after Ruben Dario, their most famous poet." Navarro went on to write, "In fact, each year members of former Nicaraguan President Anastasio Somoza Debayle's National Guard don their uniforms for a parade along Ruben Dario Avenue. In 1995 many Nicaraguans found themselves in a legal limbo, immigrants caught between a recovering country that said it could not yet absorb them and an adopted one that had never given them a blanket welcome. What still eludes many of these Nicaraguans is a certainty about where their futures lie. Some feel as if they have one foot in the U.S. and the other in Nicaragua."

The Nicaraguans were almost invisible before the 1980s. Yet they are believed to be the second-largest Hispanic group in the Miami area, after Cubans. Although the 1990 Census counted fewer than 75,000 in Dade County, Florida, estimates that include both legal and illegal Nicaraguans run closer to 150,000 (which would make Dade's concentration of Nicaraguans the highest in the U.S.).

Nicaraguans, much like Cubans, moved into Miami in waves. The Cubans regarded them as fellow refugees from communism and welcomed them with open arms after the Sandinista revolutionary victory over Somoza, a military dictator, in 1979. The bulk of them, and the poorest, came in the years of U.S.-financed armed resistance to the Sandinista government.

Many in the Nicaraguan community do not want to go back because, they say, their country's democracy is too young and the economic and political problems are too big. Some say they fear political reprisal. Others await the settlement of property claims. And still others say they do not want to return because they no longer believe they belong there. A spokesman for the Committee of Poor Nicaraguans in Exile also states, "Now the situation is different because the children who are protesting are Americans."

The Nicaraguan exodus strained education and health services around Miami, but a multitude of small businesses, newspapers and professional organizations, and other areas of the country with a distinct Nicaraguan imprint, attest to the success of a large part of the exile community.

HOLIDAYS AND CUSTOMS

La Purisima—From the end of November until the night of December 7—December 7 is called the "Night of the Shouting." The centerpiece of the holiday is a small statue of the Virgin Mary covered with decorations of flowers, fruits, lights and candles. Each night the family prays together in front of the statue. It is a celebration of Mary's conception.

Semana Santa—Holy Week—This major summer holiday celebrated by some Nicaraguan-Americans includes a parade sometimes led by symbolic characters of Hebrew elders and Apostles.

Velorios—This is the funeral party families hold after a person's death.

In 1990 there were approximately 93,000 Americans of Panamanian ancestry in the United States. This constituted one of the largest immigrant groups from Central America. Most live in New England, on the Gulf Coast and in the New York metro area, where the largest Panamanian population exists. Most are Roman Catholic in religion, and the majority are non-white.

HOLIDAYS AND CUSTOMS

Most Panamanians celebrate the traditional **Christian** holidays. They also participate in the **Caribbean Day Festivals** and **Hispanic Day** in New York and Washington, D.C. For these celebrations they wear distinctive and formal Panamanian dress and traditional costumes.

November 3—Many Panamanian immigrants celebrate **Panamanian Independence Day**, commemorating their independence from Spain.

The island of Puerto Rico was taken over by the United States when it assisted the islanders in their fight for independence from Spain in 1898. Today, the island is a self-governing commonwealth of the United States, with its people having U.S. citizenship.

A large influx of Puerto Ricans, starting in the 1920s, settled in the East Harlem section of Manhattan in New York City. Very few came during the 1930s, but when direct air service started around 1945 between New York and Puerto Rico, a highly mobile population circulated back and forth between New York City and the home island.

The work of the Puerto Ricans usually has been in low-wage occupations, according to *We the People*. The men have worked in economically marginal factories, as waiters, porters, dishwashers, attendants in hotels, in restaurants and in hospitals. Many of the women born in Puerto Rico have worked in the garment industry, while those born in the United States have done clerical or sales work. As a result of several factors, Puerto Ricans have been the poorest of New York City's ethnic groups.[15]

Puerto Rican communities in the Western states date from 1900, when Puerto Ricans were recruited to work in the sugarcane fields of Hawaii.[16] There have been some Puerto Rican settlements in the Chicago area, but most concentrations are in the New York City, northern New Jersey and Philadelphia areas.

In 1990 there were 2,700,000 people of Puerto Rican origin in the continental United States. Many Puerto Ricans, who are United States citizens by birth, nonetheless express greater concern with events in their ethnic homeland than on the mainland of the United States. According to the Latino National Political Survey in the early 1990s, proportionally more Puerto Ricans who were born on the island express an intention to return there, and Puerto Ricans were the only group in the 1980 Census in which a clear majority said the history of their ethnic homeland should be taught in schools along with American history.

Since 1970 Puerto Ricans have been pouring out of the New York area faster than they have been pouring in. Between 1985 and 1990 New York experienced a net out-migration of 87,000 Puerto Ricans, according to the 1990 Census.

Kenneth T. Jackson, a professor of history at Columbia University and author of *Crabgrass Frontier*, points out, "Virtually every ethnic group that has come into New York has in some measure left it, and Puerto Ricans are now the old immigrant group."

The places that Puerto Ricans have fled to include little cities like Lancaster, Pennsylvania, the epicenter of Amish tourism, and Reading, Pennsylvania, the real-life basis for the middle-American city in John Updike's "Rabbit" books. These two cities are among the most Latin in the Northeastern U.S. In Reading, Latinos make up 40 percent of the public school student body and 30 percent of the overall population; in Allentown, Pennsylvania, they make up about one-fifth of the population.

There has always been a streak of urban discontent in the Puerto Rican migrant experience—a bitterness given voice by the "Nuyorican Poets" of the 1960s and 1970s. Miguel Algarin, a poet, phrased it well by telling the *New York Times*, "It's a Caribbean impulse, an island impulse, and the Puerto Rican discomfort with the urban landscape has finally found its way out."[17]

Puerto Ricans, who mostly live in large urban areas, have created tiny tropical worlds out of many vacant urban lots in cities such as New York and Philadelphia. They are called "*Las Casitas.*" They see their gardens and *casitas*, Spanish for "little houses," as both a link to simpler times and an oasis from the encroaching blight. The houses may look like Caribbean Hoovervilles, but they reflect long-standing features of Puerto Rican peasant architecture. The wooden porches with railing supported by crossbeams, the shutters made from wood panels and the open space in front of the houses can be traced to the shanties that once dotted Puerto Rico's mountains and seaside. "These are cultural safe houses," wrote David Gonzalez in the *New York Times.*[18]

More than a sentimental backdrop for the garden, the *casita* is a workshop where craftsmen carve drums and speckled carnival masks and where local children learn dance steps to rhythms that first came to this hemisphere aboard slave ships. On religious feast days and at spontaneous parties, drummers gather in a circle outside the house and pound out a rhythm while dancers gyrate in a swirl of billowing white skirts and fiery red sashes. Often, pigs are roasted crispy brown on a makeshift spit, and the bounty of the garden is shared with friends and strangers.

Puerto Ricans, like many of their fellow Caribbeans, are very fond of devotional art known as *Santos*. These are carved and wooden holy images from the Caribbean.

The Santos are modeled on sculptures of saints and angels brought by Roman Catholic colonists from Spain in the sixteenth and seventeenth centuries. These religious sculptures are sometimes grandly scaled for display in churches. Many though, are only inches high and were made for worship in village homes.

Holland Cotter reported in an article in January 1997 that the Santos were sometimes set up on altars in kitchens and bedrooms and asked to intercede in heaven at times of birth, death or marriage. But they were also treated familiarly as family members, alternately coddled and scolded as seasons and fortunes changed.

At **Christmas**, Puerto Ricans, like many other Roman Catholics, attend a solemn, music-filled midnight Mass, the "*Marisa Del Gatt.*" At 2 a.m., after the Mass, a door-to-door celebration, called the "*parranda*" in Spanish, begins. The celebrants shout "*abre me la puerta*" ("open the door") and wait for their potential hosts to allow the festivities to begin. They sing Christmas carols (called "*aguinaldos*"), eat, drink and share stories of Christmases past. One of the foods that is traditionally served is *pasteles*, which are green banana tree leaves, boiled, seasoned and mixed with meat, potatoes or other vegetables.

That most cherished of American Christmas traditions—opening presents on Christmas morning—for Puerto Rican families is sometimes delayed until **Three Kings Day** on January 6, which is called the "*Dia de los tres Reyes Magos.*" The origin of this tradition dates back to the Old Testament's tale of the Three Wisemen bringing gifts to the baby Jesus. Yet another round of Christmas celebrations for Puerto Ricans is called "*las Octivitas*," the eight days after Three Kings Day.

Other holidays of importance to the Puerto Rican community in the United States include:

de Hostas' Birthday on January 11 (honoring the discoverer of Puerto Rico).

Constitution Day—July 25—Commemorated with a parade.

Puerto Rico Day (Discovery Day)—November 19—Also commemorated with parades.

All Souls' Day—November 2—Marked with attendance at Mass and visits to graves.

One million Salvadorans, equal to one-fifth of the current population of El Salvador, live in the United States, though, like with other ethnic groups, not all of them are legal immigrants. Three-fourths of the Salvadoran immigrants arrived in the United States after 1979, when the civil war in El Salvador intensified. Almost half, or 48.8 percent, arrived after January 1, 1982, the cutoff for an amnesty program that was part of new U.S. immigration laws.

According to the *Washington Post,*[19] the Washington, D.C., area is believed to have 80,000 to 150,000 Salvadorans, the second-largest concentration in the country after Los Angeles. In 1994, United States Salvadorans sent an average of $113 a month to relatives back home, for a total of $1.3 billion a year. The family remittances are one of the three largest sources of foreign exchange for wartorn El Salvador. Most of the money is channeled through unofficial transfer houses.

According to surveys by the Salvadoran ambassador and by Professor Segundo Montes of Georgetown University, 36 percent of the Salvadorans who arrived in the U.S. after 1980 said they had emigrated for economic reasons, 28.5 percent for political reasons and 20 percent for both political and economic reasons. The surveys also found that among the Salvadorans in the United States, 46 percent said they would like to return to El Salvador, and 57 percent said they intended to become legal residents.

Among immigrant groups in a 1991 Census Bureau survey, those from El Salvador have the hardest time with English. Almost three-quarters of Salvadorans say they don't speak English well. Much of the difficulty stems from the fact that most Salvadorans are recent immigrants, and growing numbers had little formal education in their native Spanish. Almost one-third of Salvadoran adults who arrived between 1987 and 1990 have less than a fifth-grade education.

During the week of May 17th 1999 the Clinton Administration issued new regulations that make it much easier for thousands of Salvadorans to become permanent, legal residents. These new regulations would mean a chance to return to El Salvador and visit relatives many have not seen in years. It could mean better jobs and higher wages, access to federal loans for college, finally putting down permanent roots, or even starting a business.

Most of all, it could mean peace of mind for people who have been living with uncertainty for years.

The regulations allow these Salvadoran immigrants, to avoid deportation without having to prove they would suffer extreme hardship if they were sent back. Instead, the government will presume they would suffer such hardship, a key step to being allowed to stay as legal immigrants.

The immigrants from El Salvador have settled primarily in the Los Angeles area (the largest) and the Washington D.C. area. Many are permanent residents or U.S. citizens, including almost all of those who arrived before 1982 and were given amnesty under the 1996 Immigration Reform and Control Act. Others, many of whom arrived after 1991, are here illegally.

But between 1982 and 1991, with the war still raging in El Salvador, an entire generation of Salvadorans converged on the cities of Los Angeles and Washington D.C. and ended up in legal limbo, permitted to work here but not to stay permanently.

The new regulations marked the end of a long journey of these Salvadorans, who during the 1980s made their way across Mexico and then the U.S. border. Many applied for political asylum, but most were rejected by an administration that backed the government in El Salvador. The Salvadorans sued, winning the temporary residence they held for nearly a decade.

The new rules don't provide amnesty to all Central Americans, but only make it easier for certain Salvadorans and Guatemalans who arrived before October 1990 and their families to obtain residency. More recent arrivals, and those from other nations, are not included.

One way some El Salvadoran families manage to afford a home is by sharing costs and space with relatives. While this practice may alarm their more established neighbors,[20] the new homeowners say it is perfectly natural in their culture, and even expected, to rent a basement to a cousin or cosign a mortgage with a brother or other relative.

HOLIDAYS AND CUSTOMS

Salvadoran-Americans celebrate the traditional **Catholic** holidays.

During the last twenty-five years, hundreds of thousands of immigrants from Haiti, Jamaica, Trinidad, Guyana and other islands and nations of the Caribbean basin have settled in the Crown Heights section of Brooklyn, New York, and in the adjacent communities of East Flatbush and Flatbush. They usually experience wrenching changes in the course of their migration. Many, for example, leave a small, airy house beneath nutmeg trees for a cramped apartment in a crime-plagued building in our major cities, according to an article in the *New York Times*. [21]

Many immigrants from the West Indies are in the country illegally, and most who are legal are either not yet citizens or are not registered to vote, the *Times* article went on to say. Caribbean community leaders assert that there is harmony among the immigrants, yet they acknowledge wide cultural differences separating Creole-speaking Catholic Haitians, English-speaking Protestant Jamaicans and Trinidadians, and Spanish-speaking Dominicans and Panamanians.

"To the white and Hasidic communities, black is black," states the Reverend John Bolduc, a Catholic priest who serves the West Indian community. But the African-American and Caribbean-American communities are so diverse, it's inaccurate to say or even imply that they speak with one voice. He continues, "It would be advantageous for them to unite on common issues like housing, education and racism, but the only thing that holds them together is the color of their skin."

The West Indian-American Day Parade, the largest annual street celebration in New York City, is an explosion of colorful costumes, a haze of spiced food and a thunder of steel band music. It represents one of the city's already large and burgeoning immigrant groups. In the early 1980s this was just a large but local ethnic festival. There's a growing recognition that the West Indian community has become one of New York City's most important political forces. For New York's Caribbean immigrants, the parade of calypso and reggae bands, floats and costumed marchers as well as those in Rastafarian dreadlocks is the most visible sign of their community's tremendous growth in the last generation; in recent years it has drawn more than a million spectators and participants annually.

Dr. Lameul Stanislaus, a former ambassador from Grenada who lives in Crown Heights, told Andrew Yarrow of the *New York Times*: "There may be three-quarters of a million Caribbeans in Brooklyn, but many are undocumented, and they remain unorganized." He added, "If Caribbean political power were integrated with African-American power, it would be even a greater force."

Caribbean immigrants call the parade a mass, which some say is a corruption of the word "masquerade," indicating the costumes. Others say it derives from an African word for a festival of celebration. Much of the carnival, they say, originated in the Yoruba culture of West Africa and that which evolved in the islands.

During the parade, usually held the first week in September, the pungent smell of barbecue hangs over the carnival, and a soft thin pita-like pastry called roti filled with goat, chicken and other meat and vegetables is served.

The parade casts into sharp relief the Caribbean immigrants' complicated relationships with both American-born blacks and Hasidic Jews in Brooklyn.

The often-cited axiom that Brooklyn, New York, has become the largest Caribbean island outside the Caribbean masks the considerable differences evident within the borough's Caribbean population. While Haitians and Jamaicans represent the largest segments of Brooklyn's Caribbean population, immigrants from Trinidad and Tobago have always been heavily involved in running ethnic activities, partly because the carnival traditions are older in Trinidad, dating back several hundred years.

"Few people in the English-speaking Caribbean—the term itself is an inexactitude—really speak standard English at home. Most think they do, and therein lies a problem," states Lawrence Carrington, a linguist at the University of the West Indies in Trinidad. Caribbean linguists say most people communicate in a variant of English-lexicon Creole, even though some consider it either a dialect of "bad" or "broken" English.

Creole languages were cooked up as linguistic stews when European colonizers brought African slaves to the Caribbean islands. Mixing syntax, grammar and vocabulary from West African languages with English, French, Spanish and Dutch, they became, by a second generation, languages in their own right, linguists say.

In New York City and on Long Island, the problems of some Caribbean immigrants have become clearer in recent years as their numbers increased. For example, in the school systems, there are children from nineteen Caribbean countries where English is the official language. Many of the children speak a language halfway between Creole and standard English. "It's been a very, very long struggle to get people to understand this as a problem," said Joyce Coppin, the superintendent of Brooklyn's high schools, in 1992. And educators are deliberating whether Jamaican, Guyanese and other Caribbean students should be entitled to schooling in English as a second language or English as a second dialect.

The music of most Caribbean-Americans is Calypso, a buoyant rhythmic music that traces its roots to Africa and began as a mode of communication for slaves. It was used to make fun of the masters, to relieve oppression and to bring the news of the day. "It finally emerged as the mouthpiece for the underprivileged," said Slinger Francisco, better known as the Mighty Sparrow, the leading Calypso performer in the United States.[22] "The music is mostly unwritten; the arranging is done in the head, and you play by memory." The Calypso drummers, mostly men who learned from an older generation in their native Trinidad, practice throughout the year in backyards or basements and perform at parties, nightclubs and festivals. From an outcast art form in 1940s Trinidad to a herald of ebullient celebration on the late-summer streets of Brooklyn, steel-band music has come a long way.

The Caribbean parades are the year's festive high point for many United States residents from Trinidad, Haiti, Jamaica, Grenada, Barbados and other West Indian countries. The music is an infectious concoction of dueling rhythms, social commentary and an unrelenting call to dance.[23]

Music has been an essential part of those traditions from the earliest West Indian carnivals, when slaves and poor people performed with makeshift costumes and improvised instruments. Steel-drum music spread rapidly throughout the Caribbean, making its way to the United States in the 1950s. It became more common in the 1970s after hundreds of thousands of West Indians emigrated to the United States. The carnivals were shifted from late winter to late summer and have evolved into a more secular celebration. The immigrants from "the islands" including Haiti, the Dominican Republic, Jamaica, Barbados, Guyana, Trinidad and Tobago—who speak deeply accented English—often wear colorful head wraps and threefold skirts and prefer the rhythms of reggae and calypso, or salsa and merengue, to American rock.

Trinidad and Tobago (Caribbean) West Indian carnival-style celebrations, which achieved their highest expression in the twin-island nation of Trinidad and Tobago, are related to the celebration of Mardi Gras in New Orleans and elsewhere, but they also have roots in African village festivals and in spontaneous celebrations of liberation from slavery in the islands during the 1800s.

One of the Caribbean musical instruments familiar to many Americans is the steel pan, which is used in Caribbean steel bands. It is said that steel bands evolved from bamboo bands that utilized various sized struck bamboo lengths and were formed in the late nineteenth century as a reaction to a ban on African drumming. Steel bands are used in community dances, weddings and large carnival celebrations.

In addition to roti, other foods of the Caribbean include beef patties, rice and beans, kallaloo and crab or fish cakes, Trinidadian coconut bread, Jamaican jerk pork and chicken, and drinks such as ginger beer and sassafras-like mauby.

Estimates of the Caribbean population in the Eastern United States run as high as 500,000 to 1,000,000, and it is reported that from 1982 to 1989 about 153,000 people from twenty-three Caribbean countries moved to New York City alone. In the 1980s, more immigrants came to New York from Jamaica than from any other country except the Dominican Republic.

The West Indians who came to the United States by choice came to make money. Many hailed from urban rather than rural backgrounds, which gave them greater familiarity with commerce. Economist Thomas Sowell points out that, while the American slave remained completely under the control of his white master, West Indian slaves were allowed to tend their own small private plots and sell their surplus in the marketplace.

By 1901, West Indians owned 20 percent of Manhattan's black enterprises. As with many Asian and Hispanic immigrants today, entire families pitched in to run these proudly ethnic businesses, keeping labor costs low and ensuring that the instinct of enterprise would be passed on to the next generation. Virtues like thrift and hard work were part of this West Indian ethos.

Census data from 1980 show Jamaicans enjoying rates of self-employment nearly 60 percent higher than blacks of other ethnicities. And by 1990, the median income of all West Indian black families exceeded that of American white families, according to the 1990 Census.

HOLIDAYS AND CUSTOMS

The West Indian-Americans celebrate holidays in addition to the traditional **Christian** holidays that include **Emancipation Day** on August 1 and **Independence Day** on August 31, as well as **West Indian/American Day**, all of which are celebrated with parades and festivals.

[1] U.S. Census report, 1990

[2] Abington Press

[3] Latino National Political Survey

[4] in Miami in 1992

[5] Rodolfo de la Garza

[6] the *New York Times,* July 15, 1994

[7] Perez study, 1980

[8] *Gale's Encyclopedia*

[9] October 8, 1995

[10] *We the People*

[11] Donatella Lorch, the *New York Times*, February 1, 1996

[12] Donatella Lorch, the *New York Times*, February 1, 1996

[13] January 22, 1996

[14] Mireya Navarro, the *New York Times*, March 28, 1995

[15] *We the People*, which quoted Fitzpatrick, 1971

[16] *We the People*

[17] the *New York Times*, May 16, 1994

[18] the *New York Times*, September 9, 1990

[19] September 23, 1988, report of study of Georgetown University Hemispheric Migration Project

[20] the *Washington Post*

[21] Andrew Yarrow, August 30, 1991

[22] September 6, 1992

[23] the *New York Times*, September 3, 1990

awaiian-American cutting pineapple — Honolulu, HI

Making danish "aebleskiver" pancakes — Solvang, CA

Swedish-American children celebrate St. Lucia Day — Portland, OR

Appalacian women at festival — Western Maryland

The "story teller" American Indian - Papago Reservation, Arizona — BNA Photo

Eskimo American doll exhibit — Festival of Nations, St. Paul, MN

Vietnamese-Americans demonstrate embroidery —
Festival of Nations — St. Paul, MN

Colombian-American dancer — Washington DC parade

Trinadian-Americans in costume — Arlington, VA

Swiss-American alpine horn blowers from Wisconsin

Polish-American dancers — New York City, NY

Haitian-American dancers — Brooklyn, NY

German-American children at "kids korner" — Festival of Nations, St. Paul, MN

Cuban-American children at festival — Ybor City, Florida

Dancing the Irish Jig — Irish-Americans at Norfolk, VA festival

English-Americans doing an English country dance — Glen Echo, MD

Jewish-American child making a Jewish star — Potomac, MD

Racing the Saints - Italian-American religious procession — Jessup, PA

El Salvadoran-American demonstrating corn grinding — Washington, DC

Croatian-Americans celebrating St. Georges Day, Pittsburgh, PA

Saudi-Arabian American children — Maryland

Scottish Americans tossing the caber highland games — Alexandria, VA

Young Welsh-Americans at Gymanfa Gamu — Pottstown, PA

Armenian American showing dolls and lace "project save" — Watertown, MA

Pennsylvania Dutch boy eating funnel cakes — Kutztown, PA

Japanese-American Cherry Blossom Lantern Lighting — Washington, DC

Lithuanian-American playing the "kankles" — Chicago, IL

Chinese-Americans doing the dragon dance — San Francisco, CA

Spanish-American musicians at festival — Washington, DC

*Making the pateno toy papier mâché - Mexican American —
San Antonio, TX*

Asian-Indian (Hare Krishna) celebrate Rath Yatra — West Virginia

An Amish Wedding — Paradise, PA

African-American gospel singers — Washington, DC

CHAPTER VIII:

NATIVE TO NORTH AMERICA ARE AMERICAN INDIANS. EVOLVED AS ETHNIC GROUPS WITHIN NORTH AMERICA ARE AMISH, APPALACHIANS, CAJUNS, CREOLES, MENNONITES, MORMONS AND PENNSYLVANIA DUTCH AMERICANS

For a full and accurate description of American Indians and their culture, one must first have an understanding of the term "American Indian" and the reasons for its usage as an alternative to "Native American." The question of "Native American" versus "American Indian" has been addressed by several different sources. For example, in his column "On Language," William Safire of the *New York Times* wrote the following:

"Native American, adopted by many American Indians, causes semantic difficulty because all citizens born here are native Americans, as against naturalized Americans; indeed, nativism means 'immigrant-baiting.' You can't call an American Indian an Indian-American, (as other hyphenated ethnic groups) because that refers to an immigrant from India. Therefore many institutions have come to use the term "American Indian."

American Indian remains a proud and dignified term as does black American, but both may be relegated to second-reference status in the coming years or perhaps not, since in the lexicon of self-identification, usage calls the shots."

For the purposes of this book, the term American Indian will be used. With that in mind, let's get to the crux of this chapter—the description of American Indian history and traditions.

American Indians and Alaska natives are the original inhabitants of the United States. Joy Hakim, a former teacher and journalist, has written a ten-volume history of the United States called *The History of Us for Children Ages 8 to 13*. Her first volume, *The First Americans*, begins with the appearance of the first settlers—the ones who crossed the Bering Strait while woolly mammoths still roamed what would become the United States. (We were all, Hakim remarks, once immigrants.) No one is quite sure exactly when the first journey occurred; some archaeologists say at least thousands of years ago. Joanne Takebayashi of FYI—County of Los Angeles Library, reported in an article in *Modern Maturity* magazine in July 1992 that, according to her research, the ancestors of today's American Indians migrated from Asia at least 20,000 to 40,000 years ago. In many American Indian and Alaska native lands across the country, they still hunt, fish and gather from the land, river and sea, much as they have for thousands of years. Before 1492 and every year since, they have burned sage and sweetgrass and sung songs, whether people have heard their voices or not. The long and proud American Indian heritage is manifest in the usage of many of their traditional foods, medicines and names by all Americans. But their legacies haven't meant that American Indians and Alaska natives haven't had troubles: they have survived numerous disruptions of their lives and dislocations from their native habitats. In general today, in addition to maintaining their tribal traditions and languages, they strive to accept new technologies that address their needs.

The 1,959,000 American Indians, Eskimos and Aleuts living in the United States in 1990 represented an increase of 38 percent over the 1980 total. As of the 1990 Census there were 437,500 American Indians, 182 Eskimos and 97 Aleuts living on 314 reservations and trust lands. In 1990, nearly one-half of the American Indian population lived in the West, 29 percent in the South, 17 percent in the Midwest and 6 percent in the Northeast. The more than 500 American Indian tribes vary greatly in size, with only the Cherokee (308,000), Navajo (219,000), Chippewa (104,000) and Sioux (103,000) having populations of more than 100,000. The four states with the largest populations of American Indians are: Oklahoma (252,000), California (242,000), Arizona (204,000) and New Mexico (134,000).

By many measures, American Indians are the poorest ethnic group in the country. On some reservations, unemployment exceeds 70 percent, while it averaged 4.2 percent for the whole U.S. population in 1999. Of the ten poorest U.S. counties in the 1990 Census, four were Indian lands in South Dakota. On the Navajo lands, unemployment ranges from 30 percent to 40 percent, and shacks are more common than houses. Income among Indians did not grow between 1980 and 1990, according to Census data.

Also, the proportion of American Indians (including Eskimo and Aleut individuals and families) living below the official government poverty level in 1989 was considerably higher than that of the total population (31 percent versus 13 percent). Senator Ben Nighthorse Campbell, the only American Indian serving in the U.S. Senate in 1995, wrote an op-ed piece in the *New York Times* on March 30, 1995, pointing out that in the 1980s the American Indian average household income fell by 5 percent, while that of all three major racial and ethnic groups rose. In 1994 the average income of American Indians living on reservations was less than $5,000.

Besides low incomes, some Indians face problems with infrastructure in their communities. After years of neglect, some reservations lack running water, sewers and trash removal. More specifically, in Alaska, 80 percent of the Indian villages cannot be reached by roads. And the problem extends to the lower forty-eight states: for example, Navajos in Chinle, Arizona, must drive seventy miles to reach a bank.

A NOTE ABOUT ALASKA NATIVES

The Alaska native population in 1990 numbered approximately 86,000. More than half, 51.8 percent (44,548), were Eskimos, about 36 percent (31,390) were American Indians and about 12 percent (10,320) were Aleuts. The two main Eskimo groups, Inupiat and Yupik, are distinguished by their language and geography. The former live in the north and northwest parts of Alaska and speak Inupiaq, while the latter live in the south and southwest and speak Yupik. The American Indian tribes in Alaska include the Athabaskan in the central part of the state and the Tlingit, Tsimshian and Haida in the southeast. The Aleuts live mainly in the Aleutian Islands.

WHAT IS AN INDIAN TRIBE?

Each Indian group is unique. But different Indian tribes share common bonds, including personal characteristics such as a spiritual attachment to the land; sharing with others; a lack of materialism; a belief that a supernatural power exists in all objects, animate and inanimate; and a desire to remain Indian and to retain culture and language.

Before anything else, an Indian tribe is a cultural entity. Formed by a common history that often stretches back too far to measure, it is a group that shares the same race, religion, language, traditions and values. Of these facets, values are probably the most important common element.

What culture really means is that, as a result of sharing ways of life and experiences, the members of the group have common values. They look at the world in the same way and regard the same things as important. They make similar judgments and have a common definition of right and wrong.

The term "cultural entity" is a bit vague and is difficult to define. We might say, for example, that a single Hopi Indian village in Arizona is a "culture," different from other Hopi villages. Or we might say that all the Hopi people are a "culture," different from non-Indians. Since there are many ways to define a culture, it's important to note what boundaries and characteristics you're using when talking about a group as a cultural entity.

But Indian tribes are something more than cultural entities. They also are political entities, and this makes them special. A political entity is a group of people living within a certain territory under a government that has some sovereignty. Federally recognized Indian tribes fall within this definition. Congress, which may terminate tribes from federal recognition, may likewise restore tribes to the rolls and does so on occasion.

In 1990, there were 542 federally recognized tribes in the U.S. In addition, 197 Alaskan-village communities boasted the same designation. Leaders of most tribes are called "chairmen." Some are called "president." Most tribal governing bodies are called "councils," but there is varying terminology and some are called "business committee," or "general council" or "executive committee." As far as internal matters are concerned, tribes are self-governing. The Navajo tribe has the country's largest governing body.

An "Indian reservation" is a specific area of land that has been reserved, set aside or acquired for occupancy and use by an Indian tribe. The earliest reservations were created by treaties. Later, many were set up by an executive order issued by the president. A large number have been designated by acts of Congress. Some reservations were created by a combination of these methods.

Throughout American history, Indian reservations have been created for several purposes. Initially, they were created to reduce the area of land used by Indians. Later, many reservations were set up as sites for the relocation of Indian tribes being moved westward to make room for white settlers.

Indian reservations are affected by many of the same factors that affect the economies of other areas. Natural resources—timber, water, oil and gas, rich agricultural soil—can play a critical role in economic development.

But there are other factors unique to Indian reservations. The trust status of the land, the sovereignty of the tribe, the tribal government and the way it operates, jurisdictional questions—all these can have an effect on the success or failure of a tribal economy. Court rulings have made it clear that tribes on reservations are not subject to state civil and regulatory laws. In the late 1980s and early 1990s some tribes used their sovereignty to their economic advantage by opening and operating legal gambling operations. But for some of the tribes of the High Plains, life has not proved to be much more promising for them than it was for their ancestors a century ago, when official policy held native tribes on vast and vacant reservations.

Long after blacks, Jews, Roman Catholics and other ethnic and religious groups had established colleges to serve their special needs, American Indians founded their own. The first tribal college, the Navajo Community College, was founded in 1968 on the Navajo reservation in Tsaile, Arizona. Fifteen are fully accredited. All but three (which are four-year institutions) are two-year community colleges. The *Washington Post* reported in July 1997 that the number of tribal colleges increased to 30, and most are in remote rustic outposts. The same article, written by Rene Sanchez, spoke of the fact that the severe lack of education has long been a root cause of the economic crisis afflicting tribes. For many Indians, completing high school is still a feat. The powerful links between education and opportunity are hard for many families to grasp. However, in the decade of the 1990s enrollment in the tribal colleges doubled to 25,000. Many of the colleges battled great odds to succeed. Budgets are tight and teachers are difficult to retain and many of the students have other serious worries beside classes. Two others are operated by the U.S. Bureau of Indian Affairs. The American Indian Higher Education Committee is a group that represents tribal colleges.

Historically, formal education had been imposed on tribes by outsiders, often with disastrous effects, tribal leaders and educators say. So creating their own system of higher education facilities made sense. "They provide an institution that is sensitive to their culture and focuses on the needs of the communities that they represent," wrote Michael Marriott in an article in the *New York Times*. [1] That sensitivity was the original motivation for tribal colleges, which were created because Indians living on reservations had few opportunities to obtain a post-secondary education near where they lived. An article in the *New York Times* on July 3, 1994, noted that Indians view school as "a new transformation." In the past, some Indians' views of education were not so positive: "For generations, Indians have been suspicious of formal education, a legacy that dates to the government boarding schools, where native languages were forbidden, and teachers denigrated tribal culture," the *Times* article said.

While precise numbers are sketchy, about 13,000 full- and part-time students attended the thirty tribal colleges in 1997. The average tribal college student is 30 years old, female and has children. Of the thirty American Indian colleges, twenty-four are on or near reservations. Indian tradition dictates that women teach women and men teach men, according to one Navajo tribal college official. Tuition is generally low, considering that many students come from areas steeped in multigenerational poverty, alcoholism and unemployment rates as high as 80 percent, according to the report by Michael Marriott in the *New York Times*.

Laurie Oueuette, writing in the *Utne Reader* in 1992, emphasized that, since the sixteenth century, Indian people have been surrounded by a paternalistic mythology, getting lost in someone else's political agenda, and that American Indian people are forever being "discovered" and rediscovered, "being surrounded by thicker and thicker layers of mythology, so that every generation predicts the inevitable and tragic disappearance of the American Indian." However, after five centuries, Indian people are still here, resisting and surviving in whatever ways they can.

Some important data obtained from the 1990 and later (1997) U.S. Census provide the most thorough count and demographics yet on American Indian tribal populations:

- American Indians (in what is now the U.S.) when Europeans first landed (estimate): 9.8 million; current population: 2.4 million in 1999.

- American Indians who live on reservations: 22.3 percent; in poverty: 31 percent.

- Indian tribes in the U.S.: 557; largest: Cherokee, 308,132; smallest: Siuslaw, 44.

- Indian chiefs who are female: 5 percent.

- Amount of land (in what became the U.S.) that was populated by Indians in 1492: 1.9 billion acres; today: 46 million acres.

- Year the U.S. government first sent Indians to reservations: 1830; year it recognized tribal autonomy: 1974.

- Year Congress granted citizenship to all American Indians born in the U.S.: 1924.

- As of 1990, nearly 20 percent of Indians were younger than 10, twice the national rate, which showed that their population is growing.

- Welfare payments account for a great share of the money on some reservations, according to the U.S. Census Bureau.

Rates of American Indian suicide and alcoholism far exceed the national average. And, yet, many Indian people, while poor, are hardly broken. Indian officials state, "It is important not to impose the non-Indian values of poverty on Indians." Many of them value traditional ways more than modern contrivances, and no federal or state program could persuade them to follow a new way, even if it seems easier to those who are not Indians. Many still barter goods and services for items such as car needs or repair work.[2]

An article on April 9, 1998 *New York Times* James Brooke reported an Indian language story. Despite five centuries of population decline, assimilation and linguistic oppression, most of the North America's Indian languages have survived to the end of the twentieth century. Of the approximately 300 Indian languages that existed when Europeans first arrived in what is now the United States and Canada, 211 were still spoken in 1998.

Of the 175 Indian languages still spoken in the United States in 1998, only 20 continued to be spoken by mothers to babies, said Michael Krauss, a linguist at the University of Alaska who surveys native languages. In contrast, 70 languages are spoken only by grandparents, and 55 more are spoken by 10 tribal members or fewer.

Belonging to 62 language families, American Indian languages are as dramatically different as German, Chinese and Turkish. However, among American Indians many of the languages are in the process of disappearing. This is true among both large and small tribes.

In Arizona among the Navajo, the most populous tribe in the United States, the portion of native speakers among first graders has dropped to 30 percent by 1998 from 90 percent in 1968.

By spring of 1998 there appeared to be a belated movement among American Indians to rescue their languages from extinction.

The language revival effort has taken many forms. In 1997 the Crow Tribal Council adopted a resolution declaring Crow the official language of the reservation, honoring fluent speakers as "tribal treasures."

In Montana, the Northern Cheyenne started offering tribal children a summer language camp. In Missouri, summer language classes are offered in Blackfeet.

Idaho State University offers Shoshone for foreign language credit. Many of the tribal colleges now require language study. The Mohegan and Pequot of Connecticut are studying written records in their languages in an effort to revive languages that have not been spoken since the early 1900s.

Some tribes started in the 1990s to put electronic communications to work. The Hopi of Arizona expanded Hopi language radio broadcasting, the Choctaw of Oklahoma have produced native language video dramas, the Sioux of South Dakota maintain a Lakota language Internet chat room, and the Skomish of Washington have produced a Twana language CD-rom.

WHO'S A REAL INDIAN? DEFINITION SPURS CONFLICTS

David Foster, in an Associated Press researched article for publication in 1997 reported that one of the most divisive issues facing American Indians was deciding who is a "real" Indian. One of the reasons raising this issue is the "gambling profits" that Indian tribes are enjoying from the operation of gambling casinos that has proliferated on Indian reservations during the decade of the 1990s. Consequently, the stakes of tribal membership have risen.

The issue that has become quite nettlesome for the nations over 550 tribes is not what to do with their own sons and daughters, because most often, their Indian ancestry is unquestioned, but generations of intermarriage have crowded their family trees with non-Indians as well.

Many tribes in the later years of the twentieth century were easing membership requirements just to survive, prompting worries that tribal traditions will fade along with blood levels.

One federal study estimated that the percentage of Indians who are full-blooded—60 percent in 1980-will fall to 34 percent by the year 2000 and to 0.3 percent in 2080.

But even as bloodlines thin, being Indian has never been so popular as it was in 1999. The number of people identifying themselves as American Indian has tripled since 1970 to 1998, rising from 827,000 to more than 2.4 million, census figures show.

A renaissance of Indian pride is partly responsible. Some examples concerning tribal membership are:

• In Connecticut, the 383 members of the Mashantucket Pequot tribe share profits from a casino that clears more than 1 million dollars a day from slot machines alone. The tribe has received as much as 50 calls a day from people who figure they must have some Pequot blood. While it was easy to brush off such wannabes, it did cause the Pequot to look at their own families and they realized that many of their children and grandchildren wouldn't qualify for membership.

Consequently, in November 1998, the tribe dropped its eligibility requirement of one-sixteenth Pequot blood. Applicants now must prove only that they are descended from someone listed on the tribal census rolls of 1900 or 1910.

Even without big money complicating things, a decision to relax membership requirements can prompt soul-searching. Oklahoma's Fort Sill Apache, a tribe of 379 members descended from Geronimo's band, looked into the future and saw its own demise.

"Everybody was saying that before long, we're just not going to have people left," tribal chairwoman Ruex Darrow said. Consequently, in November 1997 the tribe voted to reduce the level of Fort Sill Apache blood needed for tribal membership from one-eighth (1/8) to one-sixteenth (1/16).

Some tribes, however, still tow a hard line on membership. The Miccosukees of Florida, for example, require one-half Indian blood. But more seem to be heading the way of the Cherokee Nation, which has no blood requirements and which from 1987 to 1997, has more than doubled its membership to 182,000.

Of course, legal membership doesn't guarantee social acceptance. In some tribes, light-skinned members aren't invited to sacred ceremonies, says Jerry Bread, a professor of Native American studies at the University of Oklahoma. Some parents tell their children they'll drown them if they marry outside the tribe, even to other Indians.

However, such purists seem to be bucking the trend. With half of all Indians living off the reservations, continued intermarriage is likely.

Another example worth mentioning is the Kaw Nation because the tribe stopped looking at blood levels years ago, now requiring only proof of descent from a 1902 tribal roll. Among the 2,186 members in 1997, the only full-blooded Kaws left are two old men.

However, as a 22-year-old member of the Oklahoma's Kaw Nation who has only one sixty-fourth Kaw blood has said, "There's more to being an Indian than a pedigree. What you feel inside of you is what's important."

NATIVE RELIGIONS AND TRADITIONS

American Indians still perform native religious ceremonies as a tribute to their way of life and the strength of their beliefs. Tom Bahti, in his book *Southwestern Indian Ceremonies*,[3] pointed out that no Indian group presumed its religion to be superior to another, and no tribe ever conducted warfare against another for the purpose of forcing its religious beliefs upon them. Sometimes, one tribe borrowed traditions from another, and if one group performed a particularly effective ceremony, it could be copied and performed. Dances, songs and rituals are freely shared among tribes. "It was not uncommon for even traditional enemies to borrow each others' ceremonials," Bahti wrote. Much of the Navajos' mythology and their use of sand painting, for example, was adapted from Pueblo tribes, and the Hopi possess a number of *Kachinas* (doll-like figures that are not gods but the symbolic representation, in human-like form, of the spirits of plants, animals, birds, places or ancestors) they recognize as being of Navajo origin. The similarities in the emergence of myths of many Southwestern tribes also indicate a sharing of legend.

The European invaders of the Southwest made a special effort to stamp out native beliefs in order to impose their own religious doctrines upon the tribes. Civil and church authorities regarded the native people as "barbarians," completely devoid of civilization, government and religion. They saw native ceremonies not as expressions of religious faith but as mere "idolatries." They felt a duty to teach the "savages" civilization and Christianity. It was not a matter of replacing one culture with another—they didn't believe the Indians had a culture to begin with. The invaders destroyed *Kachina* masks and religious paraphernalia whenever possible. But, instead of stamping out native rituals, they merely drove them underground.

In the 1870s and '80s, the U.S. government turned over the task of educating and "civilizing" Indians to the churches, and assigned various Christian denominations to specific reservations. The practice was discontinued in the 1890s. About this same time, the Bureau of Indian Affairs made a number of attempts to suppress native religion with a series of departmental regulations. It is ironic that the very people who took pride in the fact that their immigrant ancestors came to this country to escape religious persecution participated in or even tolerated such activities. This anti-Indian movement culminated in 1889 with a set of regulations known as the Code of Religious Offenses. It was used as late as the 1920s in an attempt to crush Pueblo religion, restricting the times of the year and days of the week that could be used for religious observances. It even restricted the number of participants and set age limits—all in an attempt to deny younger Indians the opportunity to participate and learn. It was not until 1934 that this policy was reversed, when the Bureau of Indian Affairs issued the following directive: "No interference with Indian religious life or ceremonial expression will hereafter be tolerated. The cultural liberty of Indians is in all respects to be considered equal to that of any non-Indian group." Freedom of religion, the goal of so many white immigrants, was finally extended to the United States' original inhabitants.

Christianity, however, did have an effect upon Southwestern Indian religions, which can only be broadly summarized. A minority accepted Christianity, which for some was the new religion, to the complete abandonment of native practices. Meanwhile, a majority merely accommodated the Christian doctrines by modifying them to fit with native beliefs—this way they lost nothing of the old but gained the new. This was the case, for example, with the Rio Grande Pueblos. The Yaquis, who lived in Southwestern states such as Texas, Arizona and New Mexico, modified Catholicism into a form that suited their own needs, but they were not recognized by the Roman Catholic Church because their modifications were deemed too extreme. According to Bahti's book, others, such as the followers of the Native American Church (the Peyote Cult), combined native and Christian beliefs to form an entirely new religious movement. Many of the Hopi and Zuni practice their native religion to the total exclusion of Christian beliefs.

Going into detail about all of the religious practices and traditions of different tribes of American Indians would yield enough information to fill a whole book, so rather than such a detailed account of the varied tribes' practices, a set of examples follows, as presented in *Southwestern Indian Ceremonies*:

APACHE

In 1996 the most important and elaborate ceremony given by the Apaches is the girls' puberty rite, their coming out party. Four days and nights of rituals are observed. There are dancers accompanied by a drummer, along with musicians and a chorus that accompanies a medicine man.

HOPI PUEBLOS

The Emergence Myth—Each Hopi village has its own particular version of the Emergence Myth, but in general it alludes to social disorder caused by evil people. Life began in four underworlds, some depict life as good, others as dark and overcrowded.

197

The Snake Dance—The most widely known of all Hopi ceremonies is this dance, which is one of the most ancient of all Pueblo rituals. It is a 16-day ceremony that is of lesser importance to the Hopi but the one that draws the largest tourist crowds.

NAVAJO

Afterworld—The Anglo concept of an Indians' "happy hunting ground" does not apply to the Navajo (nor to many other Indian tribes, for that matter). The life currently being lived is the one that is important.

Curing ceremonies—The Navajo have more than fifty chants or ways of curing that deal with specific illnesses.

The Emergence Myth—In the beginning there was First Man, a deity transformed from an ear of corn. It was he who created the Universe. There is no supreme being, according to Navajo religion.

NAVAJO PEYOTISM

Ever since white Americans first recognized the use of the peyote plant on Indian reservations in the 1880s, government officials, medical researchers and missionaries have tried to stamp it out as a dangerous hallucinogen. Nevertheless, it has become the cornerstone of an Indian religion that has spread from western Oklahoma to the Western states. The Navajos use it for many purposes, the Indians say, as it prompts visions. It is also used during elaborate rainmaking ceremonies.

Somewhat analogous to communion wine in Christian tradition, peyote is called "the sacrament" by Native American churchgoers. Drawing on pan-Indian traditions of the Plains, the ceremonies take place in teepees, where a fire is kept burning and drumming and chanting last through the night. As the Road Man, or leader, takes followers down the Peyote Road, the cactus buttons of peyote plant are sliced into pieces and eaten, or ingested as a tea. Though large amounts can induce visions or hallucinations, participants say the amounts taken are so small that the peyote only brings on a spiritual, introspective mood that puts them closer to God.

Such rituals go back 10,000 years, but American law has taken time to recognize their validity. After decades of being caught between laws protecting freedom of religion and those prosecuting illegal drugs, Indians who use peyote in religious ceremonies were given full protection by Congress in 1994, through amendments to the American Indian Religious Freedom Act of 1978.

RIO GRANDE PUEBLOS

Corn Dance—Corn has always been the basis of Pueblo life. The maintenance of the precarious balance of an agricultural economy in this arid land requires the cooperation of all forces, natural and supernatural. Therefore, all religious ceremonies (except for curing rites) revolve around the cultivation and propagation of corn.

Creation and Cosmos—These Indians thought woman, the deity who created all things by thinking them into existence, is responsible for the world as it appears.

Hoop Dance—This tradition may have originally been a symbolic reenactment of man's emergence from the Underworld. Its origins are unknown.

ZUNI

The Zuni, a tribe in New Mexico, have probably the most complex of all native religions. Every aspect of Zuni life is completely integrated with their religion. Among Indian tribes, the Zunis retain more of their original culture than most, according to an article in the *New York Times* in January 1995. Some of the tribe's religious ceremonies, such as the winter *Shalako* Dance, which features towering costumed figures, have long been popular among tourists—so popular, in fact, that in recent years the tribe has taken measures to dissuade outsiders from attending them. The *Shalako* is usually referred to as a house-blessing ceremony, as well as a prayer for rain, for the health and well being of the people, and for the propagation of plants and animals.

The Zuni tribe provides a good example of the resolution of conflicts that arise when American Indian traditions clash with modern U.S. culture. In August 1990, Robert Suro, writing in the *New York Times*, reported that the Zuni were quietly trying to regain religious idols, which could alter views of Indian art.

"There is a secret shrine on a sage-covered hill in the heart of the Zuni reservation where Indians exercise a radically new concept of their property rights every time it rains or snows, every time the sun bears down with the heat of the day," Suro wrote. "There is a small building, and inside of it sit thirty-eight rare wooden statues of Zuni war gods, two to three feet high, austere and cylindrical, with rounded heads and stark, sharp faces. All belonged to museums and private collections. The war gods, once dutifully protected by curators, have been deliberately exposed to the weather by Zuni priests so they will decay into dust."

This is a rare story of American Indians getting back what was taken from them, and it may presage broad changes in the ways that Indian artifacts are bought and sold, in how they are studied and exhibited. By force of persuasion, the Zunis have won the right to have their war gods treated according to the tenets of their religion rather than the norms of Western culture. Edmund J. Ladd, curator of Ethnology at the Museum of New Mexico, states, "This makes sense if you consider them religious objects...rather than cultural artifacts or works of art."

The Zunis are trying to regain every war god known to be in the hands of an American museum or collector—more than fifty statues in all, in twenty-one museums and five private collections. Scholars and policymakers regard this push to regain an entire category of objects as a turning point in a process that is rapidly redefining the concept of ownership of objects sacred to Indians. No longer a matter simply for museum trustees to decide, the question of who owns human remains and sacred objects went before Congress. In 1990, Congress passed the Native American Graves and Repatriation Act and in 1992 passed further legislation that required the Museum of American Indians to notify the tribes of their holdings and the holdings' availability to them.

It has been about 1,000 years since the Zunis first inhabited their homeland of sandstone mesas and thick forests of runty pinyon and tall ponderosa pines, about 140 miles southwest of Albuquerque, New Mexico.

Like many other Indian tribes in recent years, the 7,000 Zunis, on their 40,000-acre reservation, have suffered from underemployment and the abuse of alcohol and drugs. Farmers by tradition, most of the Zunis must now live off government assistance, sometimes subsidized by jewelry-making.

In just a few decades the Zunis have lost some religious practices, such as sword swallowing and nose piercing, that had been passed from generation to generation by word of mouth. More threatening to the tribe is the fact that there are now only three members of the Bow Priesthood, while not long ago there were as many as forty. The priests are an important repository of esoteric Zuni traditions, which are passed only by word of mouth. Incidentally, the priests are the only ones allowed to touch the idols.

One tradition that has persisted is devotion to the war gods, known in the Zuni language as *Ahayuda*. Two war god idols, representing twin brothers who are the guides and guardians of the tribe, are carved every year in an all-night ceremony on the winter solstice; others are made on special rare occasions. They are then taken to caves and other age-old hiding places in the mesas surrounding the Zuni pueblo, the tribe's primary residence.

"Each *Ahayuda* serves as guardian for the tribe until he is relieved by a new one, and then the old ones must remain there, contributing their strength until they go back to the earth," says Desanclio Lasiloo, the tribe's lieutenant governor.

The statues have faces that are suggested only by the hollow of the eyes, the jutting nose and the cut of a jaw. They are distinctly phallic in appearance, for the war gods bear the attributes of young men: strength, aggression and an Olympian sense of mischief.

When the first white scholars and museum collectors started visiting the Zunis in the late nineteenth century, they found a dozen or more war gods lined up in each of numerous shrines. According to the practices of the time, they took specimens home. But the Zunis started trying to retrieve their statues in 1978 after they stumbled across documentary evidence showing how a nineteenth-century surveyor had taken a statue that ended up in the Denver Art Museum.

Other groups, such as the Pawnee tribe and some Hawaiian islanders, have won back human remains and persuaded the Smithsonian to sign a formal agreement on the subject in 1989. "We explained that the war gods were created in a communal process for the use of the entire tribe and that the entire tribe owns them," says Barton Martza, head councilman of the Zunis, "so no individual Zuni has ever had the right to give them away or sell them, and no outsider has been given permission by the tribe to take them away."

Although there is wide acceptance of the idea that sacred artifacts obtained illicitly from the Indians should be returned to them, debate persists over how permanent institutions such as museums can cooperate with ever-changing tribes to ensure the preservation of the nation's cultural heritage.

Historically, the Amish stemmed from the Anabaptist movement. Anabaptists, or "rebaptizers," trace their roots back to the Swiss Brethren. Around the year 1525, they formed their own sect on the premise that other reformers had not accepted all the doctrines taught in the Bible. The Anabaptists rejected infant baptism and insisted that the church should be a voluntary brotherhood of adult believers. They also taught separation of church and state, a concept unheard of in those days. The Anabaptists were later called Mennonites after Menno Simons, an influential leader and writer who unified the movement.

In the late 1600s, Swiss Mennonite Jacob Ammann felt his church did not administer strictly enough a shunning (or excommunication) of disobedient or negligent members. Over this and other issues, Ammann broke from the Swiss Mennonites, and he and his followers became known as Amish.

As radicals, Mennonites and Amish suffered persecution by Protestant and Catholic officials. Both plain groups therefore welcomed William Penn's offer to settle in Pennsylvania and participate in his "Holy Experiment" of religious tolerance. The first sizable group of Amish arrived in Lancaster County, Pennsylvania, as early as the 1720s or 1730s.

Since both groups share common historical origins, many Amish consider themselves conservative cousins of the Mennonites. Differences among the various Amish and Mennonite groups through the years have almost always been ones of practice rather than basic Christian doctrine. While Amish restrict technology and limit education to grade eight, most Mennonites regard education and technology as positive opportunities and encourage growth of the fellowship through worldwide missionary activities.

The Amish are a private people. They believe God has called them to a life of faith, dedication and humility. It is the belief of God's personal interest in their lives which holds them together, in spite of many forces in a modern world which could pull them apart.

A strong and deep-set religious faith shapes their world, which excludes electricity, television and automobiles. The Amish express their religious values through the use of the horse and buggy for transportation, their style of dress and their strong sense of community and family. But their simple lifestyle is not totally distanced from society as a whole. Due to constant pressures from the "outside world," the Amish may make certain concessions to their traditional values but still restrict themselves to comply with their faith. Therefore the culture and tradition described in this section may change and should not be interpreted literally.

There are three families of Anabaptist related churches: the Amish, the Mennonites and the Brethren. Anabaptists believe in making a conscious choice to accept God and therefore only baptize adults. There are eight Amish, twenty-one Mennonite and nine Brethren groups. All of these groups share the same beliefs concerning baptism, nonresistance and basic biblical doctrines, but differ in matters of dress, technology, language, form of worship and interpretation of the Bible.

A majority of Brethren and over half the Mennonites dress much like the broader society. Smaller groups of Mennonites and Brethren wear distinctive clothing but partake of other "worldly" conveniences like cars, electricity and telephones. This is also true of the Amish Mennonites or Beachy

Amish. Old Order Mennonite groups are considerably more restrictive concerning various areas of technology like their Old Order Amish counterparts. The Old Order Amish are the most conservative and best known of the "plain" groups. For purposes of simplicity, the information in this section will refer to the Old Order Amish.

On the surface, the lifestyle of the Amish appears to be staid. However, it is primarily based on a literal interpretation of the Bible and a set of unwritten rules called the Amish *Ordnung*, which prescribes behavior, appearance and other aspects of the Amish culture.

The Amish style of dress is symbolic of their faith. Amish men wear dark-colored suits, straight-cut coats with no lapels, broadfall trousers, suspenders, solid-colored shirts, black socks and shoes, and black or straw broad-rimmed hats. While men's shirts fasten with conventional buttons, suit coats and vests fasten with hooks and eyes.

Amish women wear modest dresses made from solid-colored fabric. The dresses are usually made with long sleeves and a full skirt (not shorter than halfway between their knees and the floor) and covered with a cape and apron. Women's clothes are fastened with straight pins or snaps. Their hair is never cut. It is worn in a bun on the back of their head and concealed by a white prayer covering. Amish women are not permitted to wear jewelry or printed fabric. Children's clothes are smaller versions of adult clothing. Only slight differences exist depending on age and marital status.

Farming was originally not a tenet of Anabaptism, but agriculture became important when persecution drove the Amish to the remote regions of Europe. The Amish believe that practical knowledge, hard work and long hours create a good living from the soil. They practice a life of hard work, thrift and self-sufficiency, which they believe is substantiated by the Bible. Their closeness to the land comes from generations of experience. The Amish attribute their success in farming to divine blessing. In recent years, as land has become scarce and high-priced, many Amish have had to turn to non-farming occupations such as construction, woodworking and craft making.

The Amish are reluctant to accept any technology that weakens the family structure. Progress is not assumed to be better in the Amish community. Nonconformity to American culture is a fundamental Amish belief. The conveniences that the non-Amish take for granted such as electricity, television, telephones and tractors are considered to be a tempting force that could lead away from their close-knit community.

The Amish believe that photographs in which they can be recognized violate the biblical commandment "Thou shalt not make to thyself a graven image, nor the likeness of anything that is in heaven or in the earth beneath." They also believe that agreeing to pose for photographs is an act of pride. Visitors to Amish areas are asked to respect these values and to refrain from taking photos or video images of the Amish.

Sometimes their traditions have made things difficult for the Amish. For instance, the horse-drawn buggies seen daily in Amish farming communities have caused problems for the group. About 1,000 primarily Old Order Amish who migrated to Minnesota, according to an Associated Press report in 1988,[5] won a significant victory in the Minnesota Supreme Court in 1989 about the buggies. The Court ruled unanimously that the Amish had a constitutional right to refuse to affix safety emblems to their horse-drawn buggies. The state had required orange-red slow moving vehicle signs or an alternate black triangular emblem on their black buggies. The Amish were unwilling to compromise their belief that the "loud" colors and the "worldly symbols" (the triangular shape) represented a conflict or conflicts with admonitions found in the Apostle Paul's Epistles. To them, to recognize such emblems would be putting their faith in "worldly symbols" rather than in God. Instead, the Amish said they understood the matter of road safety and agreed to outline boxes on their buggies at night with silver reflective tape or to display red, lighted lanterns to supplement the tape.

Amish children attend school until the eighth grade. In 1972, the U.S. Supreme Court exempted them from state compulsory attendance beyond the eighth grade based on religious precepts. The Amish build and maintain their own church-funded one-room schoolhouses. The children study reading, writing, English, mathematics, geography, history, German, music, art and the Bible. Surprising to most people, an Amish teenager and his average American counterpart probably know about the same number of facts. While the Amish child knows less about science, technology and the arts, he knows more about soil, animal and plant care, carpentry, masonry, clothing and food preparation.

The Amish believe classroom learning is only half of the preparation needed to make a living as an adult. Therefore, farming and homemaking skills are extremely important to an Amish child's upbringing. Old Order children are usually taught by a young unmarried Christian woman.

The Amish are principally trilingual. At home and among their community, the Amish speak a dialect of German called Pennsylvania Dutch, from the word *"Deutsch,"* meaning German. Amish children learn to speak English at school and High German at worship services.

The Amish are Christians. They do not worship in churches as is customary in other faiths, but take turns holding services in each other's homes. The Amish community is divided into church districts of 150 to 200 people. Each district gathers at a different member's home every other Sunday for a three-hour religious service. Worship is solemn; hymns are sung slowly in German without musical accompaniment or harmony. Scripture reading and sermons in High German follow.

The five tenets of faith that separate the Amish from mainline Protestantism are:

• Believer's Baptism—The members believe the church should be a group of individuals who voluntarily repent and request baptism for the remissions of sins. Baptism occurs by choice usually around age 18. Although a few people outside the Amish community have joined the church, the Amish make no effort to evangelize or proselytize.

• Brotherhood—The Amish believe in a close community. When the need arises, the Amish voluntarily help each other as well as their non-Amish neighbors. The elderly are not sent to nursing homes, but are cared for at home. And the Amish look out for neighbors outside the family, as well. For example, when a member experiences a disastrous barn fire, his neighbors and relatives hold a barn-raising to rebuild it. After the fire, a date is set to erect a new structure on the site. On the day of the raising, hundreds of men gather to supply the labor to build a new barn while women bring food and prepare meals. In a matter of only one or two days, the job is complete. In addition, a social gathering has taken place and everyone has enjoyed each other's company while achieving a mutual goal. No man is ever paid for his work, but each knows he can count on the same help under similar circumstances.

• Non-resistance—The Amish do not take part in violent actions, whether in self-defense or during times of war. This stance represents much more than a policy of biblical non-resistance. Although some Amish vote, any type of political involvement or use of the court system is extremely rare. Two notable exceptions involved the Supreme Court provision allowing the Amish their own parochial school system and exemption from making Social Security payments if they are self-employed. Many Amish vote and are especially conscious of local school, land zoning and health concerns. Also, the Amish pay taxes, but generally do not accept welfare. The Amish faith provides not only religion but a way of life that stresses separation from the world, caring for others of faith and self-sufficiency. As a result, besides not accepting Social Security payments or welfare, the Amish will not purchase life insurance.

• Non-conformity—The Amish have been able to preserve their distinctive subculture by practicing the traditions of their ancestors. The Amish encourage members to remain distant from people who do not hold similar convictions in order to preserve the church's beliefs and values. However, the Amish bend in some instances to meet the demands of the ever-changing world around them.

• Authority of the Bible—"Religion is diffuse and all-pervasive"[6] among the Amish. Bible teachings are accepted by simple faith. Their interpretation of the Bible influences every aspect of their lives and faith.

While the Amish shun "worldliness," they are not ignorant of world events. Many subscribe to local daily newspapers, farm magazines and *Die Botschaft*, or *The Budget*, a weekly newspaper published to serve as a communications network for the Amish in thirty states.

In recent years, the Amish have had increased contact with outsiders, or "English," as the Amish term them. The Amish often encounter visitors in towns and villages that dot the Pennsylvania Dutch countryside. A greeting by a stranger will probably be answered by a friendly smile and a wave of the hand, attesting to the hospitable nature of the driver of an Amish buggy.

Despite the progress surrounding them, the Amish continue to thrive and membership in the church had an annual growth rate of about 2.5 percent. Although change is inevitable, strong, ancient religious tradition, limited acceptance of progress and emphasis on practical arts taught in parochial schools and in the home primarily account for Amish continuity.

The family is the most important social unit among the Amish. In Amish families, a large number of children are considered desirable. Large families with seven to ten children are common. This is reflected in the Amish population, which has doubled in recent decades. Children not only provide necessary farm labor but also old age care for their parents and insurance that the farm can be passed on to still another generation.

Family values are important in the Amish home. Often the children will spend their playtime mimicking their parents' tasks. Thriftiness and the church's cautions against indulgences have led the Amish to look within the family circle for toys for their children. You will not find the youngsters lounging in front of televisions because in Amish homes there are no televisions. There are also no radios, nor any video games; in fact, sometimes there's no electricity. Instead, the children use creativity during playtime. A simple broom becomes a horse. Empty store boxes and cans become the perfect props for playing house, peddler or storekeeper.

Mothers or older sisters bring fabric scraps to life as stuffed dolls or animals. Animals are created from gourds and corn cobs. Fathers and brothers craft doll beds and furniture from spare wood found in the barn. The dolls sometimes lack faces and cascading blond hair, but they are not loved any less by the children.

The faceless dolls can be attributed to the same Bible passage that prohibits the Amish from having their pictures taken. There is no written rule to enforce the anti-graven image principle in the Amish community, but it is still widely respected, especially among the more conservative Amish. Today, however, it is not unusual to find store-bought dolls in Amish homes, but they will be dressed anew in traditional Amish clothing.

Stilts are a common toy among the Amish. They can be conveniently and economically made from scrap wood. Scooters, wagons and kiddie cars are also widely popular. Bicycles, however, are generally disapproved of because they provide easy access into town and away from home.

Toys are looked upon as valuable learning tools. Playing with dolls, for instance, can teach a young girl what is expected of her as an adult. Making clothes for her doll is the first step in learning how to make her own clothes. But often Amish children play without toys. Ice skating, swimming and water play are highly rated playtime activities. Since Amish families are rather large, loneliness among children is uncommon.

HOLIDAYS AND CUSTOMS

Christmas for Amish children is a time of simple pleasures and family unity. There are no bright lights, Santa Claus or piles of expensive new toys. Instead, the children look forward to a huge home-cooked meal, reading the Christmas story from the Bible and playing outdoors with cousins and siblings. The parents give them just a few useful items, such as clothing or dishes, and perhaps one home-made toy.

The children partake in the gift exchange by making presents for their parents. They may use scraps of materials from home to make things like quilt patches, doormats or needlepoint. Youngsters also construct family records. One of the few decorations permitted in the Old Order Amish home is a beautiful needlepoint or handwritten wall hanging that traces the family roots. Children often make a record of the immediate family by pasting alphabet noodles on a piece of cloth or board. Another gift the children make is cloth flowers. They shape flower petals from craft thread. They paste cloth on top of the thread and cut the flower pattern out of cloth.

The Amish exchange their gifts without ceremony on Christmas morning. The rest of the day is spent quietly at home, walking in the woods, sledding and reading from the Bible.

December 26, celebrated as **the second day of Christmas**, is a day to visit and feast with extended family members. Since many Amish families consist of nearly a dozen children, there is quite a crowd.

More than anything else, Amish children are taught the spirit of thankfulness. "We try to keep our old faith," said one Amish father. "We want them [the children] to believe the Lord gave the gifts to us to give to them."

The Amish celebrate **Reformation Day** on the last day and Sunday in October. The day commemorates the sixteenth-century movement in Western Europe that aimed at reforming some doctrines and practices of the Roman Catholic Church and resulted in the establishment of the Protestant Christian Churches.

One of the Amish's better-publicized traditions, shunning, is used as a way to discipline transgressors. Shunned persons cannot eat with members, sleep with their member spouse, give favors to or conduct business with members. Some examples of transgressions include using a tractor in a field, posing for a TV camera, flying on a commercial airliner, filing a lawsuit, joining a political organization and spurning the advice of elders. Conversation and other contact between shunned and other members is kept at an absolute minimum. Shunning lasts until the person repents, which in some cases means all of a person's adult life. It serves as a powerful deterrent to disobedience in a community so thoroughly linked by family ties.

The most important social events for the Amish are weddings, which traditionally take place on Tuesdays and Thursdays in November, most often at the home of the bride. Wedding ceremonies, like regular worship services, or "meetings," are held in homes, as the Old Order Amish do not build churches. Depending on the size of the district, more than a hundred members may journey to the Sunday meetings held every other week, while wedding guests frequently number 200 to 400.

Nine out of ten adult Amish people get married, usually between the ages of 22 and 25. Divorce and birth control are taboo; the average Amish family has 8.6 members. Although there is adolescent rebellion among the Amish, four out of five Amish children will remain in the church.

The Amish reject the use of special wedding clothing (which most other ethnic groups wear). Maintaining their belief in simplicity, the Amish still marry in new but ordinary Sunday clothing. The Amish are the only ethnic group that continues to celebrate weddings exclusively after the harvest and marry mid-week as their tradition dictates.

After the wedding ceremony, an elaborate dinner is served to everyone and usually includes roast duck and chicken, dressing, mashed potatoes, gravy, cooked vegetables, cold ham, sweet and sour relishes, homemade bread, jam, fruit pies and several kinds of cake.

While a period of visiting friends and relatives will follow the festivities, the new couple takes their place in the Amish community without a typical honeymoon. In the Amish faith, a marriage is an important affair, for it means a new home, another place to hold preaching service and a new family committed to rearing children in the Amish way of life.

Single women in their teens and twenties wear black prayer coverings for church services. A white covering is worn after they marry. Men do not grow mustaches and wait to grow beards until after they wed. In parts of the United States outside Pennsylvania, men are permitted to grow beards after baptism.

According to the Balch Institute, many Amish brides are given bridal showers by their friends. The purpose of this party is to let friends "shower" the bride with useful items for her new household, such as tablecloths or dishes.

The Amish community has another way of helping young people set up their own homes. Their custom, maintained even in the 1990s, is to present the bride and groom with a dowry, which means "gifts from home." To the Amish, a dowry is a collection of objects needed to furnish a household and to continue the family business. The dowry includes many things the young couple will need: from cows to beds, dried beef to hats. Some Amish families have been known to keep dowry lists in an account book, recording each item, its value and which child would receive it upon his or her marriage.

Appalachian Americans speak different regional dialects and accents that enrich American English. These varieties of the language result from distinct patterns of migration and settlement, isolation and interaction. The speech of residents of the Southern Appalachians is perhaps the most familiar of these marked regional dialects. Our familiarity, though, is often based more on stereotypes created by popular media than on the real speaking styles of Appalachian residents.

Some parts of northwestern North Carolina are typical of contemporary Appalachia, so let's consider these parts and their people as an example of this group of Americans. Settled primarily by people of English, Scotch-Irish, German and African origin, the region, like much of Appalachia, which stretches 1,600 miles from southern Quebec to northern Alabama, is dotted with mountain settlements, small communities and a few larger urban centers. Many residents are self-employed farmers or work in local public-sector jobs in schools, building roads or in public works, for example, or in private-sector jobs in construction, retail and other trades. Other residents commute to factory jobs in the textile and furniture industries. Most families also have some members who left Appalachia to work in the industrial cities of the East and Midwest but who return for family occasions and sometimes in retirement.

Appalachian speech is subject to numerous contradictory stereotypes, most of which have little factual basis. Like any speech style, dialect or language, it follows certain discernible rules, and the forms that strike a casual listener as curious or unusual are in fact orderly and consistent. In popular media, these "curiosities" are exaggerated, misused, overused or invented, conveying the patently false impression that Appalachian speakers are ignorant and their speech improper. An equally pernicious— and equally untrue—stereotype presents Appalachian English as some miraculous relic of Elizabethan English that has survived intact in the wooded isolation of the Southern highlands.

Many Scotch-Irish descendants are reflected in the Appalachian image. One of the many "hillbilly" legends portrays the Appalachian residents as ill-clad, barefoot bumpkins who are, with Daisy Mae and her family, fond of moonshine whiskey. Much of this image spread with the Lil' Abner comic strip, which began in 1932 and was followed by a television series starting in the 1950s. The Great Depression of the early 1930s and its hard times brought many of the Appalachian people to the cities and created "hillbilly ghettoes." However, a more accurate image has emerged, one with more respect for rural life and rural people by the establishment of arts and education centers. One such center is in Whitenburg, Kentucky, which exemplifies the effort to preserve the Scotch-Irish heritage of Appalachia.

The quilting bee, a tradition of Appalachian women, allowed them to enjoy each others' company. Today quilting is both a hobby and a folk art. In many areas Appalachians such as newlyweds, or members of the community who are rebuilding after a fire, get together and hold a barn raising, followed by a dance, which is a tribute to the tradition of the early pioneer spirit.

In an essay in 1971,[7] Raymond W. Mackm, an educator and historian, wrote that an Appalachian characteristic that distinguished them from other minority groups was that they were English-speaking as well as being native-born. Furthermore, they were white. Mack pointed out that nonetheless they were an ethnic minority, unprepared by their upbringing and by their mores for life beyond Appalachia. But they have learned to assimilate into urban life. They are Southern whites who came from an area where the culture is different, where different behaviors are sometimes rewarded but then punished when they move to the city. Both their speech and behavior make them visible, and many people in the dominant population consider them to be inferior and undesirable, a similar reaction the dominant population has had to other ethnic minorities in U.S. history.

Hillbilly. Ridge runner. Hick. Those were just some of the names people were called after they and their family moved to urban areas from the hills of Appalachia. Many say it's more than names. They say people from Appalachia are discriminated against in hiring and housing because of the stereotypes associated with poverty in Appalachia.[8] For that reason, the city of Cincinnati decided to include Appalachians as a protected class in the city's human rights ordinance. In fact, Appalachians were the only group singled out for protection against discrimination in that ordinance.

Mountain people, as they are called, number about 250,000 in the Cincinnati area and fit the description of a minority. According to the Cincinnati government, they thus deserve special protection.

Gary Foster, a sociologist in Eastern Illinois University, who has studied the persistence of hillbilly stereotypes in the media and popular culture, has found that these caricatures endure well into the 1990s "despite the national sensibility toward tolerance and diversity" that repudiates racial and ethnic stereotyping but still overlooks class-based slurs.

Foster and fellow sociologists writing in an article for the *Sociological Spectrum* pointed out that in caricatures, hillbilly men are lanky and unkempt, have a taste for moonshine and an aversion for honest work; modern versions often update these classic characteristics to produce the hillbilly's kissin' cousin, the southern redneck.

They also point out that hillbilly women come in two divergent types: "Granny...a gaunt woman with straight, unkempt hair... wearing a tattered and patched dress and high-topped work boots or no shoes at all." Then there's the oversexed and under-dressed hillbilly babe, complete with "curvaceous hips and an exaggerated bosom. Her legs are long, her lips are full and she is barefoot, the inspiration for many of the women on the long running television show, *Hee Haw.*"

Professor Foster rightfully asked the question: Why do we tolerate hillbilly caricatures while condemning nearly every other racial or ethnic stereotype? One reason is that those who are most offended by the stereotype—poor Appalachian-dwelling whites-lack "political or economic power, or a national constituency." to effectively protest.

Another reason, he suspects, is that hillbillies are white, "so it's much easier to offer or accept these slurs without the kind of reflection that is given to characterizations of racial and ethnic minorities."

Studies by the Urban Appalachian Council have found the school dropout rate in heavily Appalachian neighborhoods in some areas of Kentucky, West Virginia and North Carolina to be as high as 80 percent. People feel some of those results stem from teachers' low expectations about Appalachian students, according to an Urban Appalachian Council study conducted in the 1980s.

HOLIDAYS AND CUSTOMS

Other than the traditional **Christian** holidays, Appalachians celebrate **Sadie Hawkin's Day**, which is the first Saturday in November. It is observed with festivals in some parts of Appalachia.

WEDDING CUSTOMS

Customs and traditions that many people associate with those from Appalachia include a courting ritual in which the bride is serenaded outside her window, the square dancing ritual and the holding of square dances, most often to the music of the Scotch-Irish instrument, the fiddle.

Cajuns are the French-speaking people of southern Louisiana. Their basic stock is descended from Nova Scotia exiles who found their way south in the eighteenth century. Today there are also black Cajuns, Irish Cajuns, German and Filipino Cajuns and others. Immigrants in southern Louisiana assimilated into the existing culture the way the Anglo-American melting pot absorbed them elsewhere.

The heart of Cajun country is the "French Triangle," an area stretching westward from the mouth of the Mississippi to the Texas border. The majority of Cajuns live outside the centers of population, but there has long been an urban elite in such centers as Lake Charles and Lafayette, Louisiana.

What makes a Cajun? Ask a Cajun and he might tell you it's "*joie de vivre*." That means "Joy of Life." Everywhere in Cajun country you hear people say "*Laissez les bon temps rouler*"—let the good times roll. In general, Cajuns love music and food, and they love sharing with others. Crawfish from the bayou is a staple, and dishes like gumbo and jambalaya are meant to serve large families and lots of guests.

There's more to Cajuns than just good food and good times. You hear it in their slow, traditional waltzes. The Cajuns' history is every bit as poignant as their music. The tragedy that brought them to Louisiana was very nearly genocidal.

French fishermen and merchants began colonizing Nova Scotia in the 1500s. The peninsula was called Acadia, a misspelling of Arcadia, Virgil's name for paradise on earth. That ended in 1710, when England took control of the region. For the next forty years, English governors tried vainly to force loyalty oaths from the Acadians. Governor Charles Lawrence began what the English call the Expulsion of 1755, according to an essay by Thomas Brown in *Continental* magazine.[9] They separated the men from their families, then shipped the women and children to different destinations far from each other. The exiles were transported slaveship-style; hundreds died of exposure, starvation and smallpox. They were scattered, mostly in the American colonies and the West Indies, but some were taken as far away as the Falkland Islands. Many became indentured workers; others were sold outright into slavery.

As Acadians escaped or earned their freedom, many made their way to Louisiana, which, although ceded to Spain in 1762, was still very French. They settled along the Mississippi River between Baton Rouge and New Orleans until the United States finalized the Louisiana Purchase in 1803. Then Anglo-American landowners, eager to extend their sugarcane plantations, forced the Acadians into a second exile in the bayous farther south. It was the American frontier drawl that changed "Acadian" to "Cadian" to "Cajun," much the same way "Indian" devolved verbally into "Injun."

These days Cajun country is a place of nonstop festivals. There are cultural festivals and oyster festivals, rice festivals and catfish festivals. And there is Mardi Gras, as Cajun as it is Creole. Cajun musicians, the most visible representatives of French Louisiana's culture, no longer have to sell their souls for a record deal. In the 1990 Census, 668,000 people said they are of Acadian/Cajun ancestry, and Lafayette, a city of about 100,000, is considered the unofficial capital of Acadiana. Cajuns are largely Catholic.

According to Bryan Miller, a food and feature writer for the *New York Times*, the Cajuns "brought with them a style of classic French cooking based on a long-cooked roux that became the culinary mortar of such dishes as seafood jumbo, chicken fricassee and Cajun crab stew. The Cajuns also brought the buoyant folk music that celebrates their way of life, their legends and their land. The Cajun language, now an amalgam of Old French, Canadian French and Louisiana shopping mall, is widely spoken on the streets of Abbeville, New Iberia, Crowley, Broussard and the other towns that dot the largely rural south-central region of Louisiana."

Cajuns have a passion for dancing and music. Sometimes there is confusion between Cajun and Zydeco music, which have common roots but distinctly different sounds. Cajun music is lyrical, often plaintive and fiddle-driven. Zydeco is the result of bucolic French music mingling with the blues tradition of native Louisiana blacks. Both Cajun music, played with a squeeze-box accordion, triangle and guitar, and its more contemporary cousin, Zydeco, have become enormously popular in recent years. This is not sit-down music.

A Louisiana state agency, the Council for the Development of French in Louisiana, reported in 1991 that 300,000 of the state's 4 million residents say they speak French at home. Some call it a unique dialect of French. Cajun French is a language that is filled with colloquialisms and slang. About 900,000 residents of Louisiana claim full or partial French ancestry, but it is not uncommon for Cajuns to have Irish, Italian or German surnames, as they have mixed with other ethnicities as generations pass.

Many Cajuns, according to an article by Sally Johnson in the *New York Times,*[10] earn their living as ranchers or raising sheep and cattle; others grow sugarcane, rice and soybeans.

HOLIDAYS AND CUSTOMS

Cajuns enjoy socializing, and telling stories and jokes are a part of their make up. Many of them also love horses; consequently horse racing is part of their lives. Of course, food is an integral part of their lives, and crawfish and gumbo are two foods closely related to Cajun culture.

Cajun Mardi Gras—Celebrated the week before the beginning of Lent—History and a touch of romance live in the reincarnation of star-crossed lovers as the official rulers of Cajun Mardi Gras. They are Queen Evangeline and King Gabriel, sweethearts separated forever during exile from Nova Scotia, when Acadians (who came to be called Cajuns) were driven from their homes for refusing to take an oath of allegiance to the British crown and to abandon the Catholic Church. Families were torn as the exiles set sail on a long search that eventually led some 4,000 of them to settle in southern Louisiana. The sad tale of lost love was immortalized by Henry Wadsworth Longfellow in his poem "Evangeline."[11]

The Bastille Day Festival—July 14—In southern Louisiana, this celebration is a bigger party than the 4th of July. They celebrate the Bastille Day Festival in Kaplan, Louisiana, by destroying a cardboard replica of the Bastille. Sometimes the Cajun National Orchestra, based in southern Louisiana, will play.

Fat Tuesday—(Mardi Gras)—Day before Ash Wednesday - Many Cajun Catholics go from house to house with a cross. Those participants wearing masks may get a chicken during their visit from which they make a gumbo. Many communities continue this practice, including smaller communities in the bayou.

Good Friday—two days before Easter—this solemn day signals the approaching end of Lent, which is the next day at noon; some communities have a religious procession referred to as the "Way of the Cross."

Christmas Eve—often celebrated in an unusual way in communities that adjoin the levees between New Orleans and Baton Rouge, Louisiana. Families light bonfires on the levees along the Mississippi River to celebrate the birth of Jesus Christ.

Cajuns celebrate other holidays that often deal with their occupations and livelihood. Since they are predominantly Roman Catholic, a priest comes to bless the sugarcane fields at harvest, as well as the shrimp boats. Other Christian holidays are also celebrated.

"Creole" is an adjective that refers to people, to culture, to food and music, and to language. Originally from the Portuguese "*Crioule*," the word for slave brought up in the owner's household, it eventually became *Criollo* in Spanish, and *Creole* in French. By the early seventeenth century the term distinguished Europeans born in Caribbean and Indian Ocean colonies from foreign-born colonists. In the United States, the term refers to Louisianans of French or Spanish descent and in the past was used to distinguish a native-born slave from an "imported" slave.

Louisianans of French and Spanish descent began referring to themselves as Creoles following the Louisiana Purchase (1803) in order to distinguish themselves from the Anglo-Americans who started to move into Louisiana at that time.

In the United States in the twentieth century, Creole most often refers to the Louisiana Creoles of color; ranging in appearance from mulattos to northern European whites, the Creoles of color constitute a Caribbean phenomenon in the United States. The product of miscegenation in a seigniorial society, they achieved elite status in Louisiana. They also have become leaders in all aspects of Louisiana life.

Louisiana Creoles of color thus constitute a self-conscious group, who consider themselves different and separate from others in their area. They live in New Orleans and in a number of other bayou towns. Overwhelmingly Catholic, the New Orleans Creoles usually attend parochial schools. Their ethnicity is exceedingly difficult to maintain outside of the New Orleans area because of their sparse population outside the Louisiana city. Over time, a great many have passed into white groups in other parts of the country, and others have assimilated into African-American communities or groups. Creole, over time, has come to include people of African, Spanish, French and American Indian descent,[12] so it would be impossible to tell from looking at an individual in Louisiana whether he or she is Creole.

Creoles are descendants of Spanish and French settlers who lived in the city, rather than Cajuns, who lived in the Bayous. Creoles have also been described as descendants of the Louisiana area's often wealthy French and Spanish settlers and their slaves.

Creole, according to some Louisiana officials and inhabitants, is one of those terms about which people love to argue. The term is most easily translated as homegrown, or indigenous to the area. Hence, there is French Creole, Spanish Creole, etc.

For example, according to Louisianan historian Fred B. Kneffin: "Creole has loosely extended to include people of mixed blood, a dialect of French, a breed of ponies, a distinctive way of cooking, a type of house, and many other things. It is therefore no precise term and should not be defined as such."

According to Helen Bush Carter and Mary T. Williams in *Gale's Encyclopedia of Multicultural America*, unlike many other minority groups in the United States, Creoles did not migrate from a native country.

Sister Dorothea Olga McCanta, who wrote *A Translator of Our People and Our Color*, gives special attention to the term "Creole." She says that the free mixed-blood French-speaking descendants from

Haiti living in New Orleans came to use the word to describe themselves. The phrase "Creole of Color" was used by these proud part-Latin American people to set themselves apart from American blacks.

"Creole" and "Cajun" are sometimes confused. Both groups are mostly French Catholics, yet that's where their similarities end. Creole identity was manifested in New Orleans or small cities where people worked, but not in manual labor. Creoles have tended to isolate themselves, even in cities, by educating their children in private schools and keeping to themselves rather than sending their children to public schools. Catholic Creoles, too, were strict in following their religion; they lived in cities rather than in the bayous, but did not marry much outside Creole community.

HOLIDAYS AND CUSTOMS

Holidays that are celebrated are those of the Roman Catholic faith. Creoles visit the graves of ancestors on either **All Saints' Day** (November 1) or **All Souls' Day** (November 2). Both holidays are especially important to Creoles in terms of having respect for the deceased.

The first permanent Mennonite colony in the United States was established in Germantown, Pennsylvania, in 1683 by a group of Germans of Dutch ancestry. Mennonites at the close of the seventeenth century had not yet secured full religious liberty. The Mennonite movement was a part of the Anabaptism movement started in the 1500s in Zurich, Switzerland, known as the party of the common people, without a religious hierarchy of any sort, basing both their faith and practice on the example of the New Testament Church, preaching a voluntary, free, independent religious organization, entirely separate from the state.

The name "Mennonite" was taken from one of the early leaders of the Anabaptists, Menno Simons, who was very influential during a critical period of the movement. He was a former Dutch Catholic priest. Anabaptists, or rebaptizers, believed that infant baptism was invalid and rebaptized all adult believers who joined the church.

The early Germantown Mennonites, coming largely from northwestern Germany, and for the most part of Dutch stock, constituted a small but steady stream of Mennonite immigration that found its way into Pennsylvania throughout the seventeenth century. The heaviest immigration of the Mennonites was between 1717 and 1727, according to the *Harvard Encyclopedia of American Ethnic Groups*. After that period fewer came from this part of Germany. A much larger migration was that of the Swiss Germans, who came from the Palatinate, a region in southwest Germany that goes east to Bavaria. Also during this period tens of thousands of Palatines of every faith known in Germany settled in southeastern Pennsylvania: Lutherans, Reformed, Catholics, Dunkards, Schwenk Felders, Moravians and Mystics, as well as Mennonites, forming the basis of the picturesque element of Pennsylvania's population known as the Pennsylvania Dutch. The cause of this immigrant tide was mainly economic pressure.[13]

The Anabaptist movement had its beginnings in Zurich, Switzerland, in 1525 as dissenters from the Reformed movement. In Holland, Menno Simons (1496-1561) renounced Catholicism in 1536 and advocated strict adherence to the tenets of the New Testament. This movement spread through Europe, and the followers became known as Mennonites.

The Mennonites were the main evangelical branch of the Anabaptist movement. The Anabaptists opposed war, military service, participation in government and the swearing of oaths. Persecution drove many of them to the Palatinate on the Rhine River, where they were permitted to worship but not to erect meeting houses. Continued governmental restrictions encouraged their emigration to America.

Mennonites arrived in Germantown (now part of Philadelphia) in 1683 and formed the first Mennonite congregation in America. During the eighteenth century, most of the Mennonite immigrants settled in Pennsylvania; later migrations during the nineteenth century brought the Mennonites to the Midwest and Canada.

The Lord's Supper was served twice a year in nearly all Mennonite congregations and typically included footwashing as part of the ritual. Earthenware cups and pitchers were frequently used as communion vessels, although pewter cups—usually beakers or mugs—were sometimes used. Pewter vessels—(not used by Amish in communion) cups or basins—were also part of the baptism service.[14]

Communion in a broad sense included the observance of the Last Supper through a "Love Feast," a celebration that included footwashing to symbolize servanthood, a meal to symbolize brotherhood and communion—unleavened bread or wine—to symbolize salvation. The communion cups were always found in pairs, because one was used for men and one for women. Pewter spoons were often used for the meal during the Love Feast, which was an important ritual in the Moravian faith that included a simple meal and music.

MENNONITE WOMEN AND THE HEADSHIP VEIL

Mennonites believe that God has chosen to employ a visible means to keep us aware of the divinely appointed man-woman headship arrangement. The divinely supplied witness is that the woman is to have long, uncut hair. They believe that scripture states plainly that it is a shame for a woman to be shorn or shaven. Long, uncut hair is a glory to the woman. Because every Christian woman wants to be in daily communion with God, she keeps her head covered as a visible witness that she is prepared to pray at all times.

The veil is an ordinance meant to preserve a New Testament principle. This principle has already been partially stated—that women are to be subjected to men. Man is the head, having been created first in God's image and glory. Man was divinely assigned to headship in the human social unit. Woman was made for man, in man's glory, and assigned to be in subjection.

Every woman who wears the special sign-covering is giving visible evidence to society that she is subjecting herself to God's order, and that she is subject to man, her head. However, due to the inclination to become formal, many women wear the covering out of tradition rather than as a spiritual conviction of obedience to God. This will only add to the condemnation of an inconsistent life. Any refusal to wear the covering, or veiling, is a public testimony of rebellion and can only bring rejection and judgment upon the individual.*

Faithful Mennonites believe that no person can be accepted by God except through confessing his son, Jesus Christ, as master, and trusting Him as savior from sin. This continued trust in Christ brings from Him power over sin in the present, and confident hope of heaven in the future.

Faithful Mennonites believe that the only spiritually successful life, the life acceptable to God, is that lived by the power of God in obedience to the Holy Scriptures. Such a life is possible only through a continuing fellowship in Christ.

Another group with Pietist as well as Anabaptist roots was the Church of the Brethren. Like the Mennonites and the Amish, they practiced adult baptism. A Reformed pietist, Alexander Mack (1679-1735), founded the sect in 1708 in Wittgenstein, Germany. The group migrated to Pennsylvania between 1719 and 1729 and settled in Germantown, where the first American Brethren congregation was founded in 1723. From there, the Brethren spread into rural southeastern Pennsylvania.

The Brethren practiced baptism by threefold, or trine, immersion. Because of this practice, they were sometimes called Tunkers, Dunkers or Dunkards, from the German word *tunken*, which means "to dip." Baptism traditionally took place outdoors in a stream, river or lake, but most modern Brethren use baptisteries or pools.

* Source: Rod & Staff Publishers, Crocket, KY.

216

The Moravian Brethren who settled in Bethlehem, Pennsylvania, were descendants of the followers of Jan Hus, who was the initiator of the Reform movement among Czechs. During the persecution of the Protestants by the Hapsburg dynasty in the seventeenth century, the Moravians, who had converted many German Waldensians, emigrated to Saxony. In time, members of this group, the majority of whom were Germans, made their way to Pennsylvania, where they purchased a large tract of land from William Penn. They established a number of schools in keeping with the precepts of the educator Comenius, who believed in equal education for women, and they founded the first American preparatory school for girls.[15]

The Unitas Fratrum, or Moravian Church, had its beginnings in Bohemia in 1457. Persecuted followers of Jan Hus (1369-1415) found protection on the estate and castle, "Litik," of Bohemian Ding George Podiebrad. A Protestant leader, Count Nicolaus Ludwig von Zinzendorf (1700-1760), provided refuge from war and persecution on his estate in Saxony. In the United States, the first Moravian missionaries arrived in Philadelphia in 1734. A failed settlement in Savannah, Georgia, was followed by successful communities in Emmaus, Nazareth and Lititz, Pennsylvania.

Moravian settlements differed from those of many other Pennsylvania German immigrants: rather than on dispersed family farms the Moravians settled in planned towns that focused on community life and education.

On a muggy June afternoon in 1844, four Mormon men waited pensively in the upper room of a primitive Illinois jail. Suddenly gunfire erupted. Men with blackened faces stormed up the stairs, shooting through the door. In an instant, one man lay dead, another shot in the leg.

Joseph Smith, the 38-year-old founder of the Mormon Church, who organized it in 1830, raced to the window, where he was hit simultaneously by bullets from the door and the ground below. He wailed, "Oh Lord, my God," fell out the window and died.

Years earlier, in 1820, Smith was a farm boy in a region of upstate New York known as the "burned-over district" because of the waves of religious revivals sweeping through it. At 14, Smith said he saw a vision of God and Jesus Christ, who told him that all churches had lost the true Christianity. During this vision, he said, Christ told him the Protestant sects were "corrupt" and an abomination. Smith became disgusted with the Protestant Christian churches and launched what he called a "restoration" of the true Christian faith. To this day, Mormons object strongly if their church is called a "Protestant" religion. Members of the church refer to others as "Gentiles"—for Mormons this term covers all non-Mormons, including Jews.

A few years later, Smith reported that an angel named Moroni directed him to find plates of gold, on which was written the history of a Hebrew family who migrated to the Americas and whose descendants were said to have been visited by the resurrected Jesus. Smith is believed to have translated those ancient writings into the Book of Mormon. As soon as Smith began telling his story and selling the book of Mormon, opposition arose among skeptics and offended Christians.

Nevertheless, within fourteen years, Smith's following numbered in the thousands. They were chased from state to state, persecuted for their theological innovations, their political unity, their communal economics and their social arrangements, which included a return to patriarchal polygamy. At the center of it all was the charismatic Smith.

Smith and his followers had been forced to migrate first to Missouri and then to Illinois. By 1844, when Smith was killed, the Mormon movement was threatened with extinction. But Smith's martyrdom renewed Mormon resolve, purged the group of all but the most determined and propelled followers on a western exodus and expansion. Brigham Young led the church's members to establish a new community in Utah, although a minority established the Reorganized Church of Jesus Christ of Latter-day Saints, which does not share the same rituals, in Independence, Missouri.

In 1847 Brigham Young led the first group of 144 persons into the Great Salt Lake Basin along what is now called the Mormon Trail. In the next 22 years, 70,000 more church members, many of them frontier converts, followed.

"This is the right place," Young exclaimed when the Salt Lake Valley came into view on July 24. The trek from Illinois had covered approximately 1,200 miles and it firmly established the Mormons in Utah and the mountains of the southwest.

In 1995, 75 percent of Utah's residents were Mormons.[16] This percentage remained stable since the 1960s despite the fact that between the '60s and the '90s the state had an influx of many newcomers. Some 1.5 million members of the Church of Jesus Christ of Latter-day Saints resided (as of 1996) in Utah—more than any other state, and about twice as many as the runner-up, California. The influence of the Mormons spills from Utah into thirteen Western states, where some 80 percent of the nation's 4.5 million Mormons live.

With 4.5 million members in the United States, Mormons outnumber Presbyterians and Episcopalians combined. According to a demographic study by Lowell C. Bennion, a Salt Lake native and geography professor at Humboldt State University in Arcada, California, those born into the Mormon culture retain strong bonds with Utah. Also, many who have gone out and lived in California, the Pacific and Northwest, even to the Eastern United States, have returned to Utah. They have long dominated Utah politics, and their influence is felt in other Western states, Bennion says.

The Mormons have been denounced and despised since Joseph Smith first organized the sect in upstate New York. The story of the Mormons' journey from state to state in search of a home, of Smith's murder at the hands of an angry Illinois mob, and of his followers' subsequent exodus across mountain and plain to a land nobody else wanted in the barren Utah territory is the most dramatic epic of religious persecution in American history.[17]

According to its own records, the Mormon Church has become one of the world's fastest-growing religious organizations, with members in 140 countries. Since 1990, membership has grown 3.8 percent annually, and in 1997 totaled approximately 9 million people. Nearly half live outside the United States. In 1950, when there were 1 million Mormons, nearly half of them lived in Utah; today, not even one in six live in Utah. By the year 2000, at the church's present rate of growth, only a minority of Mormons will be American.

According to Gordon Hinckley, counselor to the president of the Mormons, the church in the early '90s had to build nearly a meeting house a day to keep up with membership growth, much of it overseas.

According to an article in *U.S. News and World Report*,[18] the church's annual income has been estimated at $4.7 billion—more than any Protestant denomination aside from Southern Baptists, who outnumber Mormons by nearly two to one. In Salt Lake City, the church hierarchy oversees a multibillion-dollar business empire and a global welfare program. A Phoenix newspaper reported in 1990 that the Mormon Church controls at least 100 companies or businesses, has become one of the largest private landowners (with holdings in all fifty states), and appointed spiritual leaders who could double as business leaders to oversee real estate, communications, tourism, insurance and educational operations.

Until a few decades ago the Mormon Church was a small and obscure sect, a religious oddity ensconced in the inter-mountain West and isolated from the rest of Christendom by its heterodox beliefs and a history tinged by violence, persecution and characterized by polygamy.

Rodney Stark, professor of sociology and religion at the University of Washington, states, "Mormonism stands on the threshold of becoming the first major faith to appear on Earth since the prophet Mohammed rode out of the desert."

A Mormon congregation provides a sense of community, values and stability that many crave, particularly in the big and busy cities of the Northeast. When a Mormon congregation grows too big—usually larger than 600 families—it divides and members go where church leaders tell them. The members do not have a choice as to what church they will attend. Mormon congregations are characterized by missionary zeal, adherence to church discipline and old-fashioned values, such as encouraging women to stay home with young children.

Being a clergyman is a part-time job. Women do not serve in clerical roles. The communion service of the Mormons consists of bread and water (Mormons do not drink wine), which is casually passed about the chapel on silver trays. The choir sings only one hymn, titled "Testimony," and the preaching is by a guest. After the worship service, the children go to their Sunday school groups, and the adults have their own Bible study. Forty minutes later, the adults divide again, the men in one room for their "priestly meetings" (all men over 12 are eligible to be part of the priesthood of believers) and the women in another for their Relief Society meeting. The women share tips on home-making and child-rearing, and they organize programs for the needy; the men discuss management issues of the church.

The Mormon Church, whose early leaders feared the wrath of outsiders, has lately viewed the gravest threat to tradition as coming from within: intellectuals and feminists in the temples. Growing numbers of women in the church, like those in other religions with male-only clergies, are chafing at what they regard as sex discrimination.

During the 1980s and more recently, a flurry of independent Mormon publications and groups have emerged in Salt Lake, including the Mormon Women's Forum, a feminist group that says it has about 2,000 members. While women sometimes deliver sermons and lead prayers in the Mormon Church, they are not allowed to baptize, bless or distribute the sacraments or lead congregations. According to a report about the Mormon Women's Forum in the *New York Times*,[19] it galls some Mormons that boys as young as 12 can become deacons, hold an office within the priesthood and distribute the sacraments. At 16 boys can baptize. In their early 20s, men typically become bishops (the equivalent of priests or ministers in other Christian denominations), an office that is closed to women, as are other positions of authority within the church.

A long-established doctrine of Mormonism, not widely known outside the church, gives the debate concerning the role of women a tantalizing twist: the belief in a female as well as a male deity as the spiritual parents of humankind.

In recent years, Mormon feminists have pointed to a female deity as logical grounds of opening leadership to women. Indeed, some women have begun praying to "our Mother in heaven" as well as "our Father."

Gordon Hinckley, a church leader, delivered a speech in 1991 that forbade prayer to a mother in heaven but did not challenge the concept of a female deity. Citing the Sermon on the Mount by Jesus, he said prayers should be offered to "our Father."

"Every individual in the church is free to think as he pleases," says Hinckley, "but when an individual speaks openly and actively and takes measures to enlist others in opposition to the church and its programs and doctrines, then we feel there is cause for action."

The Mormon Church has changed some of its most sacred rituals, eliminating parts of the largely secret ceremonies that have been viewed as offensive to women. It has quietly dropped from its temple rituals a vow in which women pledged obedience to their husbands, the wearing of face veils by women and a portrayal of non-Mormon clergy as hirelings of Satan.

In 1993 church officials excommunicated five people who had expressed critical academic views or feminist opinions about Mormon history and teachings. The decisions were made by local officials acting to preserve church discipline. The Mormon Church also uses a practice called "disfellowshipping," which means the loss of certain privileges like receiving necessary sacraments as punishment for openly criticizing the church.

Throughout the twentieth century, leaders of the Mormon Church have sought to move the faith toward the mainstream of Christianity and at the same time to preserve the distinctiveness of its religious culture. Mormons are expected to tithe, or donate 10 percent of their income to the church, abstain from coffee, tea, tobacco and alcohol, and adhere to conservative family values.

But the profile of church members has been changing. Statistics on family size, working women and divorce rates show that Mormons are looking more like the rest of America. Through the 1970s, the size of a typical Mormon family was about 50 percent larger than the national average, but that gap has shrunk in recent years. The typical married couple in Utah today has 2.5 children, compared with the national average of 1.9.

"Mormons respond to the same kinds of social and economic conditions that others do," Tim Heaton, a sociologist at Brigham Young University, told the *New York Times*.[20] "And the fact is, it's gotten to be very expensive to have a big family."

The Mormon Church encourages women to stay home with children rather than work. "But that is an ideal," Heaton added, "and the church understands it's just not economically possible for many families to do so."

Temples are an integral part of Mormon lives. While Mormon Sunday services are held in local meeting houses, temples are reserved for sacred ceremonies such as baptisms and the making of covenants in which followers make a pledge to live up to strict moral standards. Temples are usually open only to "worthy" members of the Mormon faith. In 1994 the church had forty-three temples around the world.

By most measures, the Latter-day Saints are thriving. Mormons on the whole are a devout, happy people; they have far lower rates of divorce, suicide, alcoholism and criminal behavior than the general population.[21] Having been founded and cultivated in the United States, the Mormons have a thoroughly American flavor to their religion.

Scholars say reasons behind the astounding growth of the Mormon Church include:

- Unique doctrines and a strong emphasis on family and wholesome living that seem to strike an increasingly resonant chord among those who are looking for moral certitude yet may be disillusioned by traditional Christianity.

- An aggressive worldwide missionary effort that enlists more than 60 percent of all young Mormons in preaching the Mormon gospel door to door. The Mormon church has emphasized missionary work since its founding. By 1998 it had a missionary force of 55,000.

  Men serve 24 months, women who are 18 percent of the church's mission force, serve 18 months. Members are encouraged to participate, but they remain in good standing if they do not. Missionaries, who always work in pairs, are not allowed to go home during their two-year assignments and can call home only twice a year. They customarily pay most of their living expenses, often helped out by their families.

- Strong support of church members in committing time and money to the work of the church. Tithing, the giving of 10 percent of one's income, is a basic tenet of Mormon belief, and a high percentage of members comply.

Among Mormon doctrines, none is more attractive to potential converts than the church's optimistic view of the afterlife. In most branches of Christianity, anyone who does not embrace the Gospel and accept Jesus as savior risks eternity in hell. But, in Mormonism, only "sons of perdition"—former believers who betray the church—are destined for eternal punishment. All others are assured at least of entry into the "telestial kingdom," a sort of lesser Paradise where one spends eternity apart from God. The most faithful enter the "celestial kingdom" and then can commune directly with God and eventually may themselves become gods and populate.[22]

The Mormon Church's emphasis on strong families goes beyond its view of the afterlife. In the here and now, families are expected to conduct once-a-week "family home evenings" during which parents and children study scripture, pray and counsel together.

As Debbi Wilgoren writes in the *Washington Post*,[23] the Mormon Church has set aside the first night of the work week as a time for families to be at home together. Mondays mean no overtime and no telephone interruptions at home, and no skipping out to attend a PTA meeting or to watch a favorite TV show. Instead, Mom, Dad and children sing, pray and play together, then study the Gospel or simply catch up on the week's events. A church-sanctioned "Family Home Evening" manual provides scores of ideas for activities, but families are welcome to improvise.

Church statistics show that nearly seven of ten Mormon families with children observe the custom, according to Wilgoren. Leaders of the church say the ritual has been a mainstay of the faith for three decades and has done much to keep Mormon families strong. The evolution of the tradition parallels changes in American society. It was first proposed in 1915, but no particular night of the week was set aside for it, and it was not widely observed. It was not until the mid-1960s, when a social revolution was changing interfamilial roles and posing new challenges, that Mormon leaders mandated that Family Home Evenings be observed each Monday. They forbade the scheduling of any church activities on that night to avoid potential conflicts and began publishing new how-to manuals, which eventually expanded to include lessons geared to single parents and those who do not have children at home. The Mormon Church teaches that marriage and family bonds are eternal.

Despite its successes, the Mormon Church faces potentially crippling obstacles from within and without. One of the most persistent is an almost unrelenting controversy over the church's nineteenth-century origins and the veracity of its founder, Joseph Smith.

From the very beginning, detractors have disputed and ridiculed Smith's claim that an angel led him at age 17 to a set of mysterious golden plates hidden in the woods near his home in Palmyra, New York. The tablets were said to contain the sacred history of an ancient Israelite civilization in North America and, once translated, formed the basis of what became known as the Book of Mormon.

The church also continues to suffer in the public eye from its historical links to polygamy, a practice abandoned by the church in 1890 but still advocated by some on the Mormons' fringes.

But the doctrines with the greatest potential for divisiveness concern blacks and women. For most of its history, the Mormon Church relegated blacks to a position of inferiority and divine disfavor. In 1978, the church dropped its long-standing policy barring blacks from the priesthood. Women remain ineligible for the priesthood and for top posts in the church hierarchy.

Other unique Mormon doctrines, though not sources of division within the church, tend to divide and isolate the Latter-day Saints from the rest of Christendom, occasionally spawning accusations that Mormons are not Christian. There remain striking differences between Mormon teachings and mainstream Christian doctrine:

- The Mormon Church teaches that the Book of Mormon and other volumes, some yet to be written, are equal to the Bible as holy scripture. "Many great and important things will yet be revealed," said Neal Maxwell, one of the "Twelve Apostles"—a body of leaders of the church who met in 1992.

- Where traditional Christianity teaches that the Holy Trinity—Father, Son and Holy Spirit—is one God, Mormons teach they are separate gods, that God the Father is a former human and has a wife who begets "spirit children," that Jesus is the literal offspring of the Father and that faithful Mormons can also advance to godhood.

Joseph Smith taught that the biblical Garden of Eden was located in what is now Jackson County, Missouri—a site that still holds divine favor in Mormon belief. After his Second Coming, the church teaches, Jesus Christ will designate Independence, Missouri, as the New Jerusalem.

According to an article on April 29, 1995, in the *New York Times* by Gustave Niebuhu, one of the practices of the Church of Jesus Christ of Latter-day Saints is the baptism as Mormons of dead people by living church members, who stand in as their proxies. Although little is known outside Mormon circles about this, "baptism for the dead," in which a church member stands in for a deceased person, is a main tenet of Mormonism. The church teaches that such ceremonies were performed in the early Christian Church and work to help extend Mormon membership not just to the living, but also to the dead, who exist in what the church calls "the spirit world."

In Mormon theology, all people living and dead possess "face agency," and they either accept or reject church membership, even if they are baptized by proxy. Ceremonies take place in the faith's forty-six temples (as of 1995, a growth of three temples over 1994). A church member is immersed in a baptismal font as names of the deceased are read.

The names of those to be baptized are taken from the church's genealogical archives, which contain approximately 60 million names. Church rules obligate members to perform genealogical research so they can baptize their ancestors, thus allowing the extended family to reunite in heaven.

Church officials point out that "we ask people to be respectful of other families" and try to get permission from non-Mormons before ceremonies are performed on behalf of their ancestors.

An important ancillary to Mormon belief is that church members are encouraged to find out as much as possible about their ancestors (many of whom originally came from Europe). In years of work, Mormon researchers have compiled a databank.

HOLIDAY AND CUSTOMS

Pioneer Day—celebrated on July 24—It is a state holiday in Utah. The day honors the time Brigham Young entered the Salt Lake Valley in 1847.

Mormons celebrate most of the traditional **Christian** holidays.

The population of the Pennsylvania Dutch as of the 1990 Census was 305,000. The Pennsylvania Germans, frequently called Pennsylvania Dutch, are the descendants of colonial immigrants from the German-speaking lands of Central Europe. The terms "Pennsylvania Dutch" and "Pennsylvania German" are Americanisms; Dutch is derived from an older English usage of *Deutsch* that referred to everyone in the area from the mouth of the Rhine to its origins in Switzerland—Pennsylvania Dutch signifies a German heritage.

The history of the Pennsylvania Germans begins with the settlement of Germantown in 1683 and continues on into other parts of Pennsylvania. Their ethnic consciousness was sharpened by the political campaigning of "Dutch" governors against English opponents in the first half of the nineteenth century. The most critical problem they faced was relating to the new wave of German immigrants. Although some nineteenth-century immigrants settled among them, intermarried with them and became "Dutch," the Pennsylvania Germans never culturally, ecclesiastically or politically merged fully with later arrivals. Eventually, the Pennsylvania Germans founded their own institutions, such as the Pennsylvania German Society.

The Pennsylvania Germans developed a distinctive culture with attributes ranging from traditional peasant to elite forms. They produced a great many folk arts, including the *Fraktur*, a style of manuscript decoration. The Pennsylvania Germans had a massive repertory of secular folk songs—some brought over with the colonial immigrants, others learned from the nineteenth-century arrivals, and still others composed in Pennsylvania.

The contributions of the Pennsylvania Germans to American culture were most widespread in folk custom and domestic economy, in agriculture and in religious patterns. Pennsylvania German foods (and names of foods) include scrapple, Lebanon bologna, *Schnitz un gnepp*, hot salads and shoofly pies.

As for religion, the majority of the Pennsylvania Dutch were members of the two main European Protestant traditions: the Lutheran and the Reformed. A minority belonged to sectarian traditions that opposed established churches, the political system and the cultural environment. A subgroup of millennialist communitarians included the Ephrata Society, the Moravian Brethren and the Harmonites.

Because the Pennsylvania Germans were often the first settlers in an area of the colony and were numerous enough to be able to preserve their linguistic preferences (High German for official use in church and school, dialect for home and community use), a distinctively Pennsylvania German linguistic world took shape early in the eighteenth century. The Pennsylvania German dialect was a hybrid based mostly on dialects from the Palatine in what is now western Germany and adjoining areas, with some Swiss mixed in. In the late nineteenth century, the German language used in rural Pennsylvania became less standard and more influenced by dialect.

In the twentieth century, Pennsylvania Germans stressed the dialect as a cultural anchor. Pennsylvania German culture is, then, essentially American. The historic Pennsylvania German culture contained obvious European elements, but these, like the dialect, were modified over time to yield a hybrid American form. Pennsylvania Germans, whether in Pennsylvania, Ohio or even in Ontario, Canada or in other places where they have branched into, may still speak the dialect or English with a Dutch accent, or they may be completely Anglicized, but they are different from other German enclaves in the United States.

The Pennsylvania barn has been associated with excellence. A drive through certain counties in rural Pennsylvania will include the sights on many barns and houses of Hex signs. The Hex signs are found on the property of the "church" groups, most notably Reformed and Lutheran. Among the "plain" groups (Amish and Mennonites do not have Hex signs on their property) Hex signs, while noted mostly for their symmetrical and geometric designs, now include nongeometric designs including birds, trees of life, shamrocks, hearts and in some cases pigs, chickens, cats and angels. The Hex sign came from within Pennsylvania German culture as part of an early Pennsylvania German revival that also included a return to their designs on gravestones. In their need to make public statements concerning their ethnicity in the face of the anti-German and antiwar sentiments around World War I and II, the churched Pennsylvania Germans chose Hex designs from their past and applied them to barns and gravestones.

The Pennsylvania Germans' *Fraktur* (birth certificates) is a tradition that has enjoyed a revival. Early Fraktur was completely hand-done and included both birth and baptismal certificates, as well as rewards for merit, etc.

The Pennsylvania Germans celebrate **Fasnacht Day**, which is Shrove Tuesday, the day before Lent begins. The word *fasnacht* means "night before the fast." Fasnachts are Pennsylvania Dutch donuts, but they do not resemble the average American donut. They are made to use up accumulated fat and sugar before the Easter season begins.

[1] February 26, 1992

[2] Given the vital importance of the American Indian story to educators and librarians, the following list of publications may be useful in pursuit of additional up-to-date information about the American Indian population:

Akwwesasne Notes ($15/yr., 6 issues, Box 196 Mohawk Nation, Rooseveltown, NY 13683-0196). Newspaper featuring Mohawk Nation news as well as national American Indian news, historical analysis and book reviews.

The Circle ($14/yr., 12 issues, 15030 E. Franklin Ave., Minneapolis, MN 55404). Newspaper featuring news and commentary from the Upper Midwest American Indian community, accompanied by national news and perspectives.

Cultural Democracy ($25/yr., 4 issues plus membership, Alliance for Cultural Democracy, Box 7591, Minneapolis, MN 55407). Activist-oriented magazine promoting cultural pluralism and equal access to cultural expression. Features American Indian arts and policies; actively involved in protesting the 1992 quincentennial celebration of Columbus' "discovery" of America.

Cultural Survival Quarterly ($25/yr., 4 issues, 53-A Church St., Cambridge, MA 02138). A magazine committed to helping indigenous peoples survive in an expanding industrial society. Addresses issues pertinent to tribal peoples and ethnic minorities across the globe, including American Indians.

Huaacn ($15/yr., 4 issues, Box 7591, Minneapolis, MN 55407). Small newspaper that was devoted to challenging the 1992 quincentenary celebrations and continues chronicling various protest activities.

Indigenous Women ($10/yr., 2 issues, Box 174, Lake Elmo, MN 55042). A magazine dedicated to the issues and concerns of American Indian women.

Native Nations ($20/yr., 12 issues, 175 5th Ave., Suite 2245, New York, NY 10010). This magazine features American Indian news, commentary, arts coverage and film and book reviews.

Northeast Indian Quarterly ($15/yr., 4 issues, American Indian Program, 300 Caldwell Hall, Cornell University, Ithaca, NY 14853). Journal devoted to both historical and contemporary American Indian culture. Features academic articles, personal essays, fiction and poetry.

Whispering Wind Magazine ($16/yr., 6 issues, 8009 Wales St., New Orleans, LA 70126). Magazine devoted to preserving American Indian customs. Includes information in how to find and make traditional dress, crafts and powwows.

[3] published in 1970 and revised in 1982

[4] Information in this section comes from the Pennsylvania Dutch Convention and Visitors Bureau in Lancaster, Pennsylvania

[5] Mary R. Sandok

[6] John Hostetler, 1963, *Amish Society*

[7] *Ethnicity in American Life*, 1971, Anti-Defamation League of B'nai B'rith.

[8] the *Washington Post*, December 10, 1993

[9] February, 1988

[10] February 27, 1991

[11] *Adventure Road* magazine, Winter, 1993

[12] Smithsonian Festival of American Folklife book, 1987

[13] *Harvard Encyclopedia of American Ethnic Groups*

[14] *The Amish in Pennsylvania History*

[15] Christine Molinari, writing in *Gale's*

[16] Peggy Fletcher Stack, writing for the Religious News Service

[17] T.R. Reid, the *Washington Post*, September 22, 1986

[18] September 22, 1992

[19] Dirk Johnson, September, 1991

[20] September, 1991

[21] T.R. Reid, the *Washington Post*, September 22, 1986

[22] *U.S. News and World Report*, September, 1992

[23] July 8, 1996

CHAPTER IX:
FROM AFRICA CAME AMERICANS OF AFRICAN ANCESTRY

The 1990 African-American population in the United States was nearly 30 million people, or about 12 percent of the total U.S. population—the same proportion as in 1900. This was a growth rate of approximately 13 percent since 1980. Most of this increase could be attributed to the population growth rate and immigration from Caribbean and African countries. Less than 1 percent of this population is 65 years old or over. African-Americans live in all fifty states; there are about 2,000 in Vermont and more than 2 million in New York. From 1990 to 1999 the African American population has grown 13% to 34.4 million.

African-Americans are mostly an urban people and live in cities and large metropolitan areas. As of the 1990 Census, nearly 84 percent of the African-American population lived in urban centers (57 percent in central cities and 27 percent in the suburbs). Over one-half of the African-American population lives in the South, while 19 percent live in each of the Midwest and Northeast. Only 9 percent live in the West, according to the Census. Forty percent of African-Americans live in the ten largest consolidated metropolitan statistical areas, of which the five largest are New York, Chicago, Los Angeles, Philadelphia and Detroit. The *New York Times* of February 15, 1998, reported in an article by Isabel Wickerson about the great migration of Blacks from the South to the North which essentially started at the turn of the century but really took off probably in 1942. Many of the Blacks of the South went to the city of Chicago. Many arrived in Chicago buzzing about the big money they would make at the steel mills and packing houses and rivet factories for the war, and everyone wanting to know if Cab Calloway would be at the Regal Theater that night.

Many of them arrived at the train station with their cardboard luggage tied with string. The migration from World War I to the 1960s redistributed 6,000,000 southern Blacks who fled to nearly every major American city in the North and West. They were fleeing the racial caste system that consigned them to the lowest rung and the racial violence that came with it. The waves of people crested at wartime when factory jobs were plentiful and paid what seemed like unbelievable money to people accustomed to picking 100 pounds of cotton for a dollar. To big manufacturers, it was cheap, hungry labor. "Chicago was built on the backs of Black migrant workers," said Harold Lukens, who was president of the Black Metropolis Convention and Tourism Council. "They worked the stockyards and factories and the steel mills. Their hard work helped the country make it to the technology age."

The first migrants settled in what would become the northern tip of their neighborhoods when they arrived in Chicago, for example. Sadly, they found the North could be as hostile as the South. Many trade unions would not accept Blacks. Most beaches were off limits. Housing laws confined them to certain neighborhoods where demand was so high that small apartments were divided into one-room units spilling over with children and newly arrived relatives. The overcrowding bred many of the ills that still plague the inner cities: gangs, drugs, crime. Because the migration unfolded with little mainstream documentation much of the ills in the daily lives was taken for granted even by many of the participants. No one has the foundation for preserving the history that was made at that time. However, research in 1998 was started on a quite orderly basis in order to document this period of time.

As of 1995, 85 percent of both the African-American population and the white population 25 years old and older had completed high school. These rates were up from 1990, when 63 percent of the African-American population 25 years of age or over had completed high school and 75 percent of the white population had (the 1990s data had increased from 57 percent in the 1980s). Also, 11 percent of African-Americans compared to 22 percent of whites had earned a bachelor's degree, according to the 1990 figures.

Twenty-six percent of all African-American families had incomes below the poverty level in 1989. By 1994 nearly one-third of all African-Americans were classified as poor, having incomes below the official poverty level ($11,281) for a family of three, according to the *New York Times*.[1] By 1990, median income among families headed by African-American married couples improved and grew to 83 percent of comparable white families. The number of households among African-Americans that are headed by a female has increased since 1900, mostly as a result of divorce and higher separation rates, according to 1990 Census data.

Gary Younge, a black Englishman and a reporter for *The Guardian* in London,[2] had a three-month reporting fellowship at the *Washington Post*. He wrote an article in October 1996 that said that meeting many Americans with names like Gugliotta, Biskupic and Shapiro was refreshing because almost everybody in the United States is originally from somewhere else. He noticed that white Americans and most everybody claimed another identity—Italian-American, Irish-American, Hungarian-American—that qualified their American identity but does not necessarily undermine it.

At the National Association for the Advancement for Colored People's annual convention in 1996 which Younge attended, he pointed out three higher authorities to which speakers called upon: God, the Constitution and the American Flag. The NAACP may represent the "old school" of African-American politics, but throughout Younge's stay in the U.S. he did not meet an African-American who did not place some faith in these common reference points. He said Britain, which in contrast doesn't have a written constitution, is far less religious, and you wouldn't get a Union Jack (the British Flag) within five miles of a political meeting full of black people, regardless of how moderate the organizations may be. Black Americans who feel aggrieved can, and often do, look to the symbolism of their national flag as a form of redress. Black Britons see their flag not as a possible solution but as part of the problem. For Americans, according to Younge, this seems to breed a kind of confidence that allows a more open discussion of race issues than in England.

Younge reported he was amazed on a day trip to Harper's Ferry, West Virginia, when he saw an all-white group of cub scouts learning all about how John Brown fought alongside black abolitionists and the legacy of Frederick Douglass. White kids learning about black history on a day out during the summer holidays—at the time, "I felt like I had died and gone to heaven," Younge said.

THE TERM "AFRICAN-AMERICAN"

What an ethnic group is known as, or calls itself, is very important for its self-image, sense of worth and emotional well-being. Take, for instance, the Inuits of Canada, or "Eskimos," as they are sometimes called in the United States. "Eskimo" is a derogatory term coined by the Inuits' American Indian (another Canadian term) neighbors. It means "carrion eaters," and the Inuits have always resented it. Therefore, in the 1970s the Canadian government, reacting to repeated pleas and complaints, very wisely decided to start using the term "Inuit" for this ethnic group. "Inuit" means "the people" and is what this group has called itself for centuries.

Similarly, African-Americans in the United States have often been called derogatory names by their neighbors. "Negro," which was used until the 1960s and was the Portuguese and Spanish equivalent for "black," had a negative connotation because it served as a reminder of African-American descendants' slave experience. Rather than focusing on a negative past, African-American leaders in the 1960s decided to start calling themselves "black" to stress that they were not foreigners and to show pride in their heritage.

But "black" refers somewhat to skin color, as well. The Reverend Jesse Jackson argues that Americans need to get away from racial categories. Anthropologists no longer classify people by the color of their skin but, rather, by their culture. Similarly, Americans no longer call American Indians "Redskins," nor do people refer to Asians as the "Yellow Peril." Most Americans are becoming more mature and sensitive to the feelings of others; and their awareness means recognizing and respecting the ethnicity of African-Americans. It is perfectly reasonable, inoffensive and objective to refer to descendants of African immigrants (whether voluntary or involuntary) as African-Americans.

Going back to the 1960s, several ethnic groups demanded to be called by new and presumably more respectful names: "Negroes" became blacks; "Indians" became Native Americans; "Mexican Americans" became Chicanos and "Latinos" became Hispanics.

The power to name is frequently also the power to define. The power to name a group can be the power to position it socially and politically.

Jesse Jackson is the person most responsible for the term "African-American," according to *The New Republic*:[3] "If this label sticks, it will be the first time in United States history that an ethnic leader has single-handedly changed the name commonly applied to his or her group."

According to Jackson, "black" is inappropriate. "Just as we were called colored, but were not that ... and then Negro, but not that ... to be called black is just as baseless." He defended the term "African-American" because it "has cultural integrity" and is linked to a specific place.

(Immediately after the Jackson pronouncement, 62 percent of the respondents to a call-in survey taken by the *Chicago Sun-Times* said they preferred "African-American" to "black.")

Using the term recommended by Jackson and a small group of other black leaders is a way of affirming a heritage that predates African-Americans' ancestors' arrival in the United States as slaves; it's a way of ameliorating our cultural identity crisis. In addition, it is more consistent with other ethnic designations, such as Irish-Americans, Italian-American or Jewish-American.

Charles Freund, in an article in the *Washington Post*,[4] points out that the relationship between power and language is a direct one; whatever the social homilies a society mouths, its language reveals the realities of its power sharing. In the case of group labels, the more power held by a specific group, the less narrow its place in the language. One example is Americans of British descent who, in a nation of white ethnic hyphenates, avoided any label at all (save that of "Americans") until their hold on establishment power began to erode after World War II. Only in the early 1960s were they tagged—by others unfriendly to them—as "WASPs" (or White Anglo-Saxon Protestant).

Prior to 1989, when "African-American" became accepted usage, the terms used for identification were "colored," "Negro" and "black."

According to Edward C. Smith of American University, the use of "colored" was a realistic recognition of the fact that although "we are not white, neither are many of us black. Indeed, Smith adds, the great majority of "black" Americans range in hue from light tan to dark brown.

The term "Negro," as previously mentioned (Spanish for "black"), became fashionable during the 1940s and 1950s. Smith adds that it was welcomed by many who stated that "our Negroid ancestry and the distinctive African physical features (which many whites found offensive) were now associated with that ancestry." "Negro" was eventually eclipsed in the mid-1960s by the term "black."

However, as "African-American" becomes more universally accepted by blacks, it still creates a problem for some. The term "African-American" is not analogous to "Italian-American" or "Mexican-American," but rather to "European-American," and there are very few whites who identify themselves as such. Those American whites who choose to maintain an intimate cultural association with ancestral homes in Europe do so through bonding themselves with a specific people, location and language. Unfortunately, ancestral people, location and language were lost to blacks when the African slave trade began.

Therefore, to identify themselves as African-Americans is to associate themselves with an entire continent, where Arabs dominate the north, whites control much of the south, and in between are a host of fragile black nations formed by once-powerful European colonizers.

RELIGION AND AFRICAN-AMERICANS

African-Americans are one of the ethnic groups in the United States most closely identified culturally with religion. It is within the four walls of churches that the African-American community congregates weekly: worship bonds the African-American community.

Within the black church, there are several different denominations, including African Methodist Episcopal (AME), Christian Methodist Episcopal (CME), Baptists and Pentecostal.

The AME Church, once referred to as the Zion Methodist Episcopal, began in the late 1700s in protest of what was considered racial discrimination. Before that, blacks and whites worshipped together. The Reverend Richard Allen, the first black bishop, was told one day that he could not pray with white members of the church. The blacks protested and formed their own denomination, the AME.

While the AME Church was formed out of anger, the CME was formed in an amicable agreement between the two races in 1870. With the approval of the Emancipation Proclamation, the black members pulled away, forming the Colored Methodist Episcopal before changing its name in the late 1950s to the Christian Methodist Episcopal.

The development of the black Baptist Church stemmed from a joint effort between a black minister and a white minister in the 1700s. The largest black membership today is among Baptist churches. It was the Baptist Church that was the force behind religion during the post-Civil War era. White slave owners in the South provided places of worship for their slaves and sometimes worshipped with them.

Then, in the late 1800s, the Pentecostal churches were organized. With some alterations, the theological standards of the Methodist Church are used in Pentecostal churches.

While many denominations exist within the black churches, there is just one goal among black preachers and their congregations: "The end of the journey is heaven; we are all just using different roads to get there," Reverend Warren Atkins told a Naples, Florida, newspaper.[5]

Black churches have grown stronger because of their unity. People often ask why African-Americans don't worship with whites more often. Many African-American ministers say it is not the mentality of white congregations that keeps the races so separate, but rather the style of worship. African-American congregations are more demonstrative and more vocal than many majority-white congregations. Even in Catholic churches where the races are more mixed, black Catholics such as those who have worshipped in Haiti, for example, have found that the Mass differs in the United States. The difference is not racial, but cultural.

Whether Baptists, Methodists, United Methodists or Pentecostal, Atkins said, "most black churches follow similar doctrinal principles as white churches—belief in the Holy Spirit, salvation and redemption through Jesus Christ and the Second Coming. They also serve the needs of their members both spiritually and socially."

"We are an organization, not an organism," Atkins added. "We cannot be torn apart to be put together. We all teach the word of God, but there is a distinct difference between the Methodist and Baptist Churches. In all Methodist churches, things are done the same way, but independent Baptist churches can deviate among themselves."

A thread uniting black congregations and distinguishing them from white congregations is the verbal feedback of members during the sermon. And the service in most black churches lacks the formality of their white counterparts. Also, the sermon does not have as many philosophical references. Black ministers often preach about society's views of blacks, about alcohol, drugs and teenage pregnancy—and about how these things can be fought for the better.

HOLIDAYS AND CUSTOMS

The **Black Family Reunion Celebration Days** are held annually in various cities around the country. The goal of the celebrations is to strengthen family ties and to project positive images of black families. They are sponsored by the National Council of Negro Women, which started the program in 1987. The idea was born with Dorothy Height's (president of the National Council of Negro Women) annoyance with a TV documentary about the black family that painted a grim picture of black family life. There is a black family reunion pledge which speaks of ancestors, love and wisdom forgotten and calls on blacks to "embrace our lowliest and insist that this is but half the picture." The reunions have helped to build a sense of obligation to each other—you can't tell the homeless from the wealthy, Height says.

The space at each reunion is divided into theme pavilions that offer information on such topics as parenting skills, prenatal care, education, study habits, family values, parent-child relations, discipline, spirituality and aging. The Fifty-Plus Pavilion focuses on the changing roles of people who are 50 and older. The Diaspora Pavilion highlights the values, history and culture shared by families in Africa, the Caribbean and the United States. There are also pavilions focusing on women's issues, on fathers and on brothers.

The National Council for Negro Women, headquartered in Washington, D.C., is a social services organization that was founded by the educator Mary McLeod Bethune in the beginning of the twentieth century.

KWANZAA

In the United States many cultures have contributed to the evolution of the December holiday season, including Kwanzaa, a colorful African-American celebration of family, community and culture.

Kwanzaa, created in 1966 by civil rights activist Maulana (Ron) Karenga, is geared specifically to embrace African heritage and human values. It is an elegantly African and an aggressively American holiday of affirmation.

The word "Kwanzaa" comes from a Swahili phrase that means "first fruits" of the harvest. The seven-day festival, which begins on December 26 and ends on New Year's Day, has been steadily growing in popularity throughout the United States.

According to Karenga,[6] Kwanzaa is now celebrated by some 15 million people in the United States, Africa, Canada, the Caribbean and parts of Europe. Although it contains many spiritual elements, it is not a religious holiday. It is a cultural holiday that is observed by people of all faiths.

"It's not a substitute for Christmas," Dereca Blackman, a young black filmmaker, told the *New York Times* in 1991. "It is not a substitute for anything. It's a movement to something."

"This is a holiday based on traditions surrounding the first fruits: It adopts practices prevalent throughout Africa," Karenga, a professor at California State University at Long Beach, told *Modern Maturity* magazine.[7] "First-fruit celebrations are a bringing together of a living human harvest, a time for renewing and strengthening the bonds between people. Kwanzaa teaches respect for the family, for the community and African traditions. Its values are one of our contributions to the best of human culture."

The heart and soul of Kwanzaa are the *Nguzo Saba* (seven principles), which are guidelines for year-round living: *Umoja* (unity), *Kujichagulia* (self-determination), *Ujima* (collective work and responsibility), *Ujamaa* (cooperative economics), *Nia* (purpose), *Kuumba* (creativity) and *Imani* (faith). Each day of the festival is dedicated to one of those principles.

There are seven symbols of Kwanzaa. They are:

Mazeo: The fruits and vegetables of the harvest that are part of the celebration table.

Mkeka: The placemat on which the fruits and vegetables are arranged.

Kinara: The seven-branched candlestick that holds the candles.

Mishumoa saba: The red, black and green candles that are lit each evening.

Vibunzi: The ear of corn that is representative of each child in the family.

Kikombe cha umoja: The communal chalice from which the ceremonial libation is poured.

Zawadi: The gifts that are given at Kwanzaa.

Every evening of Kwanzaa the family gathers to discuss the principle for the day. A candle is lit and placed in the seven-branch *kinara* (candleholder) to symbolize giving light and life to the seven principles and to the ancient African concept of raising up light to lessen both spiritual and intellectual darkness. Small gifts (preferably hand-crafted) are exchanged.

The giving of modest gifts, like ethnic toys, books by or about blacks and anything in kente cloth, is as much a part of the holiday's ritual as the feast on the eve of its final day.

"Kwanzaa's most important lessons are for children because it gets them away from the commercial aspects of the season and helps them emphasize the spiritual," said Cerise Richardson, a single parent in Long Beach, California.[8]

While most Kwanzaa activities are family affairs, on December 31 family and friends join with other members of the community for the *karamu* (feast). This final event is particularly festive. The *karamu* site is decorated in rich red, black and green, the colors that have come to symbolize Africa. Adults and children wear colorful African garments, and everyone contributes dishes to the *karamu* table.

While there is no single dish or type of food that defines the week-long African-American celebration of Kwanzaa (the way turkey symbolizes Thanksgiving, for example), most Kwanzaa feasts feature the depth and range of foods culled from worldwide black culture. The dinner can be a small family affair, but many participants prefer larger potluck get-togethers where extended family and friends gather around a large table or eat off straw placemats, or *mkekas*, on the floor.

For more than twenty-five years, blacks, cautious and few in the beginning, have been looking to Kwanzaa to help them rededicate themselves to their teachings, culture and traditions. During Kwanzaa, eggnog gives way to ginger beer; caroling finds harmony with African chants, and Christmas stockings dangle next to the royal designs of West African kente cloth.

One of the principles of Kwanzaa is to encourage what is known as *ujamaa*, or cooperative economics; in other words, blacks working together to create and maintain their own stores and shops for the good of the entire community.

"Kwanzaa is a philosophy for life," says Cedric McClester, who wrote *Kwanzaa, Everything You Always Wanted to Know, But Didn't Know Where to Ask.*[9] "It is a value system."

Juneteenth Day—The history of Juneteenth, a name derived from the slang combination of June and Nineteenth, dates to June 19, 1865, when Union General Gordon Granger landed in Galveston, Texas, and declared United States sovereignty over the state. In announcing the freedom of the state's 250,000 slaves, he read President Abraham Lincoln's Emancipation Proclamation, which had taken effect January 1, 1863. When Granger arrived in Texas, the Civil War had been over for seventy-one days, and Lincoln had been dead for sixty-five. But Texas was the last Confederate state to yield to the Union, and word of the end of slavery and of the war was slow getting there. A legend among black Texans is that the message was sent from Washington by slow-stepping mule.

But year by year from 1945 to 1975, the celebration diminished. According to David Maraniss, a *Washington Post* reporter,[10] during the civil rights era, many blacks dismissed Juneteenth, saying it was a reminder of past repression and submission.

Once predominantly the domain of older citizens—initially former slaves, then the sons and daughters of slaves—Juneteenth by the 1990s was embraced by black teenagers, many of whom cannot name any ancestral slaves but understand the modern meaning of slavery and freedom. And, since then, the day has been transformed into an anniversary of deep cultural meaning.

There are signs that African-Americans in many parts of the country are adopting Juneteenth Day as their own. Cities as diverse and distant as Milwaukee, Los Angeles and Charlotte are among those holding parades and picnics to mark what once had been an event limited largely to Texans and to some blacks in Louisiana and Mississippi.

Harlem Day—Harlem Day is the culmination of the annual Harlem Week Festivities in New York City.

"Harlem Day started in 1975 as a day to promote the positive aspects of the community and offset beliefs that Harlem isn't a vibrant community," Tony Rogers, one of the festival's founders, told the *New York Times*.[11] "Over the years, the day started to grow until it turned into a fourteen-day event."

Tens of thousands of people turn out annually on 125th and 135th Streets in Harlem (New York City) to eat, listen to music, shop and socialize. Bands and theater groups perform, antique cars are exhibited, fashion shows are held and street vendors sell art prints, T-shirts and African craftwork.

THE "BLUES"

The Mississippi delta, where African-American history is considered both a grand legacy and an incurable curse, is really the home of the music called the "Blues." It was on the region's vast cotton plantations that black sharecroppers combined African rhythms and European harmony with field chants and hollers to create the blues, which became the foundation of much of twentieth-century American popular music. Almost every important folk blues musician was nurtured in the Mississippi delta region.

Jim Crow's chokehold and the great migration North beginning in the 1940s spurred many blues men to leave the delta, usually to go to Chicago to sweat out careers performing black music for black audiences. There have been two major periods in which whites "discovered" the blues, one in the 1960s and another in the early 1990s. The backroads of rural Mississippi still have the juke joints (bars in the backwoods and rural areas of the deep South) and country stores where many a top blues performer wails on his electric guitar before raucous crowds. According to the Smithsonian's Folklife Festival literature, many blues musicians are people without fixed addresses or telephones. Many of the blues musicians are self-taught, so they don't have a traditional sense of time or meter.[12]

In a column in the May/June 1993 issue of *Living Blues* magazine, Paul Garon, a founder of the magazine, stated: "It was quite clear ... that the very specific forms of torture, beating, lynching, slavery, mistreatment and general discrimination that white Americans had visited upon black Americans had—combined with the black response to this torment—produced the BLUES. The very specific sociological, cultural, economic, psychological and political forces faced by working-class African-Americans—forces permeated with racism—produced the BLUES, nothing else. The undimmed voice of working-class blacks crying out their pain and pleasure still speaks in many voices from the ghettos of America."

Garon went on to write: "Indeed, while anyone can play the blues, it is the unique engendering nature of black culture that has always been our prime concern. Only the complex web of racist oppression suffered by blacks at the hands of whites produced the blues, regardless of the many types of suffering with which the blues deals in the manifest content of its songs. The fact that white musicians are now playing the blues ... is immaterial to a focus on black culture."

Brewer Phillips, a 70-year-old African-American guitarist, puts it another way:[13] "The Blues is part of religion for me.... For black people it's something we really don't actually play. We are born with it. If we can sing or play an instrument, it just brings out the way we feel. If you ain't black and hadn't been through these things, you can't really learn what the blues is about, 'cause YOU DON'T KNOW! But if you're black, poor, living in them huts, [it's] just something to keep the rain off you sometimes. You BORN with it."

Martin Luther King Day—This holiday is an official legal American federal holiday celebrated on the third Monday in January. Reverend Dr. Martin Luther King became the national leader of the civil rights movement in 1955 after Rosa Parks, a black woman in Montgomery, Alabama, refused to give up her seat on a bus to a white man and was arrested. This led to a bus boycott and the leadership of the Reverend Dr. King. He subsequently organized the Southern Christian Leadership Conference to promote civil rights on a national level.

Before Dr. King began heading protests it was altogether fitting in the hearts and minds of many white Americans throughout the land that blacks sit in the back of the bus. In the South there were separate water fountains for blacks and whites and separate lines in bus stations. Blacks were excluded from many public facilities—movie theaters, restaurants and public swimming pools, for example. Dr. King helped prompt new laws prohibiting segregation and did something perhaps more important: he forced Americans to look at themselves and brought about a change in both consciousness and conscience.

On August 28, 1963, King led a Washington demonstration of 200,000 people (both black and white) in support of black demands for equal rights. The highlight of the demonstration was Dr. King's "I Have A Dream" speech. His dream was that the United States would rise up and live out the true meaning of its creed: "We hold these truths to be self-evident: that all men are created equal."

Dr. King's role as a leader of the civil rights struggle and his nonviolent approach had a great impact on civil rights legislation from 1955 to 1968. For this he was awarded the Nobel Peace Prize in 1964.

Martin Luther King Jr. was born January 15, 1929, in Atlanta, Georgia, and was assassinated on April 4, 1968, at the age of 39 in Memphis, Tennessee, where he was heading a strike of sanitation workers. His assassin was James Earl Ray, an escaped convict.

President Reagan in 1983 signed into law papers making the third Monday in January a holiday for remembering King and honoring his legacy.

Dexter King, speaking for the King family, said the holiday should not be thought of as only for blacks, but as a celebration of America's diversity and pledge to equality among people.

The first official legal observance of Martin Luther King Day was on January 20, 1986. It has been made one of the U.S. official holidays by an act of Congress, and each year on that day African-Americans nationwide take pride in commemorating Dr. King and his accomplishments.

Dr. King had a dream in which people would come to be "judged by the content of their character instead of the color of their skin." In a United States that was riddled with racism he achieved some portion of that for which he fought and ultimately gave his life. To deny the accomplishment is to deny his greatness and flies in the face of ample historical evidence.

Dr. King built his movement on solid principles. The son and grandson of Baptist ministers, he was himself a minister who knew that love was stronger than hatred. He adopted the powerful tactic of nonviolent, passive resistance, and he embraced the teachings of our nation's founders, especially the ideas of freedom and of equality under the law. He was an intellectual, as was demonstrated in his statement of moral philosophy "Letter From a Birmingham Jail."

Not everything in Dr. King's dream has been realized, but we celebrate his birthday as a national holiday because he and those who stood at his side ushered America closer to justice.

THE NATION OF ISLAM

The Nation of Islam was founded in Detroit in 1930 by W.D. Fard, who claimed to be the reincarnation of Noble Drew Ali, founder of the black separatist Moorish Science Temple of America.

Like the Moorish Scientists, Fard, who took the name W. Fard Muhammad, and his successor, Elijah Muhammad, taught that a mad black scientist named Yakub created the "white beast," or Caucasians, 6,000 years ago.

The Nation of Islam believes that Allah is permitting the white man to rule for a specific period of time, scheduled to end this century, and that the black man will then resume his rightful leadership role.

There are no official membership numbers for the Nation of Islam. Scholars estimate the number at no more than 20,000, according to the *Washington Post*.[14]

Orthodox Islam does not endorse racial separatism and does not recognize the Nation of Islam as a legitimate branch of the religion. But the Nation does observe some Muslim tenets, such as abstaining from eating pork, fasting during the month of Ramadan on the Muslim calendar and using the traditional call to prayer.

The Nation also employs the *Shahada*, or creed, which holds that the only God is Allah, whose messenger was the seventh-century prophet Mohammed. But the creed is usually followed by the statement blasphemous to traditional Muslims that Allah appeared through W. Fard Muhammad and that Elijah Muhammad was his messenger.

According to an article by Debbi Wilgoren in the *Washington Post*,[15] "Arabbing" is a folk term peculiar to African-Americans in Baltimore, Maryland, for the selling of goods from horse-drawn wagons, pushcarts, trucks and corner stands by hawkers of street vendors. It derives from "Arab" or "Street Arab," colloquial words for a peddler. The Arabbers live an old-fashioned life. Even their name has an antiquated echo in an ethnically sensitive era. The term comes from a nineteenth-century description of people who made their living on the streets or who were homeless children.

Selling from horse-drawn wagons was once a major means of supplying city dwellers with fresh fruit and vegetables, fish and poultry and ice, wood and coal. Today, this type of street peddling is nearly extinct in major American urban areas—except in Baltimore, where some 100 wagons worked the streets even in the early 1990s.

Over the years Arabbers established traditional routes through Baltimore and have developed many faithful customers. An Arabber takes great pride in decorating his or her wagons.[16]

BLACK GOSPEL

Black Gospel heads the list of traditional black music, even more so than the Blues. It thrives in a variety of forms in different American cities, ranging from the harmonies of traditional quartet groups to the sounds of more contemporary soloists, ensembles and choirs. Black churches have served as a primary conduit for the transmission of black music aesthetics. Hundreds of churches support numerous choirs, smaller family groups and other ensembles and soloists who provide their memberships with gospel music. Gospel music is central to a variety of black community events.

Gospel is urban black religious music of rural origin. Its roots reach back to the plantation spiritual of more than two centuries ago. As black people migrated into northern urban communities, they brought along a love for sacred song but needed musical expression that did not bear reminders of slavery. The texts of gospel music expressed a hope for freedom.

The power of radio broadcasting cannot be underestimated in nurturing the presence and ultimate acceptance of gospel music.

In most urban communities—where one can hear blues, jazz, rock, rhythm n' blues, soul and rap—black gospel music exerts a tremendous presence and influence. One effect is its role as a medium of community spirit and cultural identity for a large part of the African-American population, and, despite changes in musical style and content, gospel continues to serve a vital function in the lives of many African-Americans on all levels—spiritually, artistically, technically and commercially.

Gospel music is rooted in spirituals, blues, sharp-note songs, ragtime and the urban church revival. It emerged in the early twentieth century as traveling performers "visited" church communities, popularizing compositions by Charles Tindley and Thomas Dorsey. Gospel compositions are formally notated, but they are transformed during performances, when participation and improvisation on the part of the audience become an important part of the offering.

In a brief article accompanying the 1996 Festival of American Folklife, Jacquelyn C. Peters wrote that song and eloquent oratory are integral to African-American religious expression; they were pervasive, spiritually sustaining elements of the U.S. civil rights movement. In emotionally tense or physically threatening situations, the standard of nonviolence and a serene attitude were maintained through song, prayer and words of encouragement. Massive church rallies, picketing and demonstrations took place, and even jail houses echoed with the sounds of resolve, declaring "Just like a tree standing by the water/we shall not be moved."

Sacred African-American music provided the basis for many freedom songs. One such spiritual, "I will be all right," has evolved to become the universal anthem of protest "We Shall Overcome."

Techniques such as call and response, "worrying the line" (using vocal embellishments) and "lining out" (the song leaders singing or reciting the next line of verse before the end of the previous one) are other characteristics of African-American song.

Grounded in the tradition of black congregational song, choral quartets and ensembles transmitted the movements' musical message to audiences from the locale of the struggle.

AFRICAN-AMERICAN QUILT MAKING

Perhaps one of the most enduring African-American artistic traditions is that of quilt making. On April 4, 1996, Patricia Leigh Brown wrote in the *New York Times* a story of how a circle of African-American quilters is widening nationally among older women, for whom quilting was a rural necessity, as well as among younger urban women weaned on store-bought blankets and central heating. Many quilting groups are active each week, and the oldest and largest is the Daughters of Dorcas & Sons, based in Washington, D.C. The group is named after Dorcas, the biblical character whom Peter is said to have raised from the dead so that she continue her good words as a seamstress on behalf of the poor.

Many of the group's quilts adorn the walls of some of the most prestigious buildings in Washington, DC, including universities, libraries, museums, and the office of the mayor.

Courtland Milloy, a *Washington Post* columnist, has pointed out that most of the quilts made by the Daughters of Dorcas are at least three layers thick. Some are so heavy with fabric that you can barely turn over once you get under one. They are colorful and cottony, and they don't just warm you up, they make you feel safe and secure, like somebody really cares about you.

In a January 1999 article appearing in *USA Today,* a story was written about historian Jacquelin Tobin, a teacher of writing and women's studies at the University of Denver. She tells of a story related by Ozella McDaniel Williams of how quilts made by slaves were encoded with secret messages and hung in plain view to be used as guides by Black underground railroad fugitives. A resulting book from such stories is entitled *Hidden in Plain View; A Secret Story of Quilts and the Underground Railway.* Williams's story refers to the cooperative system that developed among antislavery activists who helped spirit fugitive slaves northward from about 1830 to 1865.

241

Ms. Tobin also reports that very few original slave quilts exist: They were washed repeatedly in lye—heavy soap, which weakened them; the original materials were humble and did not wear well.

Colors, designs and the types of knots used were all significant, Williams states. Blue and white was a protective combination, a blessing for a long trip, for example. The spacing of knots might indicate a grid with a suggestion of distances. One such design was of a bear's paw and this exhorted escapees to follow the track a bear would take on a journey north. Another was a "monkey wrench" which meant slaves should gather their tools.

Raymond Dobard, a professor of art history at Howard University and an accomplished quilter himself, has cautioned his and Ms. Tobin's interpretation of Ms. Williams's story, buttressed by their research from Africa and the southern USA, does not result in "some type of Rand McNally map" used by fugitives. And he suspects it will be challenged by scholars who are "doubting Thomases." He is satisfied that he and Ms. Tobin have an accurate understanding of Williams's references to both the monkey wrench and bear's paw designs.

Other experts who have written forewords for Ms. Tobin's book agree there will be opposition. "The oral testimony of Ms. Williams is going to generate a great deal of controversy because it is the custom of scholars to look askance at oral traditions, at anything that can't be proved by the written word," says St. Louis quilt historian Cuesta Benberry.

Maude Wahlman, who is another expert on African-American textiles and quilts at the University of Missouri says this book is important because it illuminates "an aspect of American history that has not been documented or explained." She believes the authors' interpretation of the Williams story is correct. "They studied it thoroughly from every angle."

Dr. William Ferris, the director of The Center for the Study of Southern Culture at the University of Mississippi, has spoken of the special historical resonance that quilting has. He told Brown of the *Times*, "within the African-American community, the quilt is perhaps the single most important image families have created for several centuries and often the most lasting and permanent."

"Quilts connect to memory and constitute a bond between generations. They have roots in African culture, where quilt making and textiles are important," Ferris added. "But they are critical to African-American history because much of the history of black culture has not been written down. Oral tradition and the world of the quilt constitute the most important record we have of black families."

Quilting is by nature a communal art, noted Dr. Raymond G. Dobard, a Fine Arts professor at Howard University and a member of the Daughters of Dorcas. "It has historically provided women an opportunity to come together to work, exchange ideas and share in each others' troubles," Dobard said. He continued: "In times of social fragmentation, it offers an antidote, common ground, and in many ways quilting is a healing art."

Many older women relate their quilts to contemporary African-American issues and themes, and younger quilters are creating African-American quilts that depict political and civil rights events.

Collectively these quilters are redefining tradition. The definition of an African-American quilt has been the subject of scholarly debate in recent years. Some historians have interpreted it strictly as a

Southern rural utilitarian quilt, based strictly on things remembered. In trying to understand the meaning behind quilt making and the impact of it, historians have said that African-Americans use this art form as a means of passing on historical information. Older black women tell stories to younger black women who in turn make quilts showing the events. Cuesta Benberry, a quilter and historian in St. Louis, has a simpler definition: "An African-American quilt is one made by African-Americans."

WEDDING CUSTOMS

Those African-Americans who have returned to the traditions of African religions such as Yoruba hear the priest describe their marriage as a joining of two families rather than two individuals. Many African-Americans are reinventing traditions already lost, incorporating African tribal customs into the contemporary American marriage ceremony.

At some African-American weddings, members of each family line up on either side of the room, and then meet in the middle to embrace and move to the other side. This symbolizes the new union of the couple and their families.

Take Sierra Leone and its natives as an example of how African-American communities get involved in weddings more than with some other ethnicities. If you are from Sierra Leone or from parts of the West Coast of Africa and you hear of a wedding of a compatriot, you of course celebrate. And you know you will be welcome. A wedding is a big party, and everyone is invited. Occasionally, a bride may try to limit attendance with invitations. People from Sierra Leone have an "open-door policy." Weddings may be one of the few opportunities that people from Sierra Leone in the U.S. have to get together. For get-togethers, the community at large depends on a wedding, a baby-naming ceremony or a forty-day ceremony at which the dead are remembered.

[1] February 14, 1996, based on Coalition of Civil Rights Group study

[2] writing in the *Washington Post*, October 6, 1996

[3] January, 1989

[4] February 7, 1989

[5] *Daily News*, Naples, Florida

[6] January, 1992

[7] Ken Wibecan, January, 1992

[8] December, 1992

[9] Gumbs & Thomas, 1985

[10] June 20, 1990

[11] August 20, 1990

[12] Smithsonian Folklife Festival literature

[13] Smithsonian Folklife Festival literature

[14] Debbi Wilgoren

[15] October, 1995

[16] Smithsonian Folklife Festival literature

CHAPTER X:

FROM SOUTH AMERICA CAME AMERICANS OF ARGENTINEAN, BOLIVIAN, BRAZILIAN, CHILEAN, COLOMBIAN, ECUADORAN AND PERUVIAN ANCESTRY

The people who have migrated from Argentina to the United States are a recent group of immigrants. The 1970 Census showed only 44,803 people of Argentinean ancestry in the United States, but by the 1990 Census Argentinean newcomers had more than doubled to 101,665. This means that most immigrants came in the two decades of the 1980s and the 1990s. Those who came during this period came mostly because of political persecution during the Argentinean "dirty war." The dirty war, which lasted until 1983, was one of political persecution conducted by the military junta that ruled the country against opponents of the military. People were taken from their homes and offices and were never heard from again. Many were imprisoned and tortured.[1] The people who came prior to 1970 had a higher educational level than those in the latter period. However, even the latter group had a higher educational level than the average Argentinean, according to Julio Rodriguez, writing in *Gale's Encyclopedia*.

When trying to describe the people of Argentina and other countries in South America, it is improper to use the term "Latino" or "Hispanic"—it doesn't apply. Over one-half of the Argentinean immigrants to the United States were of Italian descent or were Italian-born, so the terms Latino and Hispanic are inaccurate: the terms exclude half the Argentinean population. Also, the term "Latino" describes people who come from Latin America, which doesn't include the people of Central and South America.

The large Italian population of New York City drew 20 percent of these immigrants. These Italian-Argentineans were attracted to New York. Los Angeles was the city that drew the second-largest number of Argentineans.[2]

HOLIDAYS AND CUSTOMS

November 10—the **Day of Tradition**—This is the most popular of the secular holidays. Celebrations could include parades, folkloric shows known as *penas* and rodeos with skilled riders called *Gauchos*.

Christmas Day is celebrated by Argentinean-Americans much like the Italian or traditional Catholic way.

Epiphany—January 6—In Argentina this day is called the **Day of the Three Wise Men**. It's a big day for children, who leave their shoes, a glass of water and games at the foot of their beds along with a letter asking for special presents.

Also, some Argentinean-Americans celebrate **Los Quince**, which is discussed in detail in the section on Mexican-Americans. It is celebrated upon young girls' fifteenth birthday.

The religion of Argentinean-Americans is primarily Christian, specifically Roman Catholic, but there are also a small number of Jewish Argentinean-Americans.

See also the section on **Christian** holidays, which many Argentinean-Americans celebrate.

There are three stages to the wedding ceremony of Argentinean-Americans: first there are the showers, depending on the families' social classes (some are together and some are separate for the bride and groom); next there is a civil ceremony, which is also very formal; and, third, there is the church wedding. Customs include changing the *Liga,* which the bride wears and which the groom takes and gives to single girls.

There are only approximately 40,000 Bolivian-Americans in the United States, according to the 1990 Census. Most are recent immigrants from the highlands of Bolivia, and most are devout Catholics who still carry a touch of highland Indian culture. According to a 1990 article in the *Washington Post*,[3] a majority of the immigrant Bolivians have settled in the Washington, D.C., area. Many came to the United States for economic reasons.

HOLIDAYS AND CUSTOMS

Bolivian-Americans in general celebrate the traditional **Christian** holidays.

In Washington, each year there is a traditional festival called the **Feast of the Virgin of Urkupina** in mid-August that coincides with similar celebrations in Bolivia. Members of the Bolivian community show their devotion to the Virgin Mary with parades, dancing, music, an open-air Mass and Communion service. Some attend the festival to make new wishes. They go clad in lavender satin and adorned with gold lace and red stones. There is a statue of the Virgin in Alexandria, Virginia, which is a reproduction of a figure in Cochabamba, Bolivia. In Bolivia, they call her "the Virgin of the rich people," believing that praying to her will bring fortune.

The custom of venerating the Virgin, celebrated by hundreds of thousands of Bolivians each August 15, has its roots in a 500-year-old legend. As the story goes, a Bolivian shepherd girl tending her flock saw a vision of the Virgin Mary and the Jesus child. She told residents of the nearby village about the miracle. Some of them caught a glimpse of the Virgin disappearing into the misty hills and decided to honor her with an annual feast.

Apart from the religious and cultural significance of the annual celebration, many Bolivians say it performs an important social function in the community by bringing them together.

Also, each year many Bolivians make an extra effort to display their highland Indian culture by dressing in native costume and participating in the Fourth of July parade in Washington, D.C.

Counting the number of people in the United States who are of Brazilian ancestry is very difficult for several reasons, but the main one is that the 1990 Census form (as with other groups with insignificant numbers of U.S. residents) did not contain a category specifically for those of Brazilian ancestry. Therefore, the only way Brazilians could be counted was if they wrote "Brazilian" in the "Other Hispanic" category. But Brazilians are not Hispanic. Therefore, the number on the U.S. Census total, which is about 65,875, is probably too low. There are settlements of people of Brazilian ancestry in New York City, Boston, Washington, D.C., Los Angeles, Miami and Phoenix.

A significant percentage of Brazilians in the United States, according to *Little Brazil* by Maxine Margolis, are illegal immigrants. This is because during the 1980s many Brazilians wanted to migrate to the United States, but the low immigration quota set by the United States for their country would not allow this. Consequently, many came, and they blended into Brazilian communities and found work at very low wages. According to Margolis, there may be as many as 350,000 people of Brazilian ancestry in the United States without proper documentation.

As with other groups of immigrants, most Brazilians tend to live where other Brazilian-Americans have settled. However, second and third generations, who have attained financial independence and who have left their close-knit Brazilian areas, tend not to preserve their native culture; it is easier to assimilate.

Portuguese is the native language of Brazilian immigrants to the United States, and 90 percent are Roman Catholic.

HOLIDAYS AND CUSTOMS

Soccer (*Futebol*) is an important part of Brazilian-American life. Most Brazilian-Americans celebrate the traditional Christian holidays. Many also celebrate:

September 7—**Brazilian Independence Day**. The largest celebration is in New York City, and it includes a huge parade and street fair on West 46th Street. This is the section of the city called "Little Brazil."

Carnavel—This celebration (in the days before Lent) is considered to be the quintessential expression of Brazilian culture with its fun-loving and carefree parades and parties. The largest Carnavel celebration is in Rio de Janeiro, but festivities involving Brazilians also take place in New York City and Miami.

The 1990 Census counted 62,000 people of Chilean ancestry in the United States. Most of this population has arrived since the 1970s. Of these 62,000 people, more than 55,000 were born in Chile. Upon arrival in the United States, most settled in and around major cities in California, Florida and New York. The largest Chilean-American enclave is in California.

Many Chilean-Americans who came to the United States did so because of political repression in Chile, and most were of middle- or upper-class origin. Many had advanced educational degrees and well-developed skills. But even more, however, comprised a second group, who came for economic opportunity. These people were less educated and had fewer skills than the political exiles.

Many of the immigrants worked in domestic jobs and as manual laborers, much like other new-comers to the United States.

Chilean-Americans share the Spanish language with other Latinos, but many feel separated from Central Americans and people in the Caribbean because of differences among their cultures. Chile is home to many diverse European groups, including Germans, Italians, Irish and Greeks who brought their customs from Europe. For example, tea is more popular in Chile than coffee, and many people serve dinner later in the evening. And, for example, it has been said that prior to coming to the United States many Chilean-Americans never tasted Mexican food. More important and more distinguishing is the fact that Chilean accents are quite different from many other Latin groups. In fact, some are more comfortable with their European tendencies than those associated with Latin groups.

Chilean-Americans are primarily Roman Catholic.

HOLIDAYS AND CUSTOMS

Chilean-Americans celebrate the traditional **Christian** holidays. (See section on Christian holidays.)

New Year's Eve is the largest celebration.

New Year's Day is for family gatherings.

September 18—Celebrates independence from Spain by having fairs with singing, music and booths for people to sell food from and in which they can exhibit their crafts. One such fair is held annually in Northern Virginia.

There were 350,000 people of Colombian ancestry counted in the 1990 Census. Approximately 86,000 resided in New York City, 56,000 in northern New Jersey and 84,000 in Dade County (Miami) Florida. The immigration of people from Colombia into the United States started in the 1960s. These were immigrants who came to the United States because of the dismal economic conditions they faced in their homeland. The first groups settled in Los Angeles, San Francisco, Houston and Washington, D.C., according to *We the People*. After the late 1970s the largest groups settled in the Miami area.

For years Colombian-Americans were little noticed in the greater American society, but, because of drug-related problems and crimes, they became a target of resentment.[4] Since the 1970s acceptance of Colombian-Americans has been impeded by the prevalence of stereotypes based on the drug trade. Their efforts to squelch stereotypes have been hindered by Hollywood's frequent portrayal of them as drug lords.

Nevertheless, many Colombian-Americans have overcome such stereotypes. They have found opportunities by working within the Spanish-speaking community through informal networks. In the Miami area, for example, they have done well in business related to trade with Latin America.

HOLIDAYS AND CUSTOMS

Colombian-Americans celebrate the traditional Christian holidays as well as sharing in other Latin American festivals and cultural parades.

Colombian Independence Day—July 20—This is celebrated with traditional foods and dancing in communities that are home to large numbers of Colombian-Americans.

Ecuadoran-Americans started to arrive in the United States in the 1960s. Prior to that time very few came. The 1990 Census counted 191,000 people of Ecuadoran descent in the U.S., but as with other South American groups it is felt, and acknowledged by the Ecuadoran consulate in New York City,[5] that many more thousands who are undocumented are in the United States. The estimated number of undocumented Ecuadorans in the U.S. runs as high as 500,000.

Most Ecuadorans came to one destination: New York City. The 1990 Census showed 60 percent of all Ecuadoran-Americans live in New York City, followed by 10 percent in the Los Angeles area. Coming from all parts of Ecuador, the immigrants usually have settled where there are other South Americans.

It has been a difficult issue for many Ecuadorans to decide whether to become American citizens. For some it seems to be a betrayal to their country of birth. In addition, some Ecuadorans have difficulty learning the English language, according to Jeremy Mumford in *Gale's Encyclopedia*, sometimes because of linguistic difficulties stemming from their familiarity with Latin languages, sometimes because of intimidation at the new language, and sometimes for still other reasons.

HOLIDAYS AND CUSTOMS

Approximately 95 percent of Ecuadoran-Americans are Roman Catholic. Therefore, they celebrate the holidays associated with **Catholicism**, as well as the various saint days and festivals associated with the various regions of Ecuador from whence they came.

St. John the Baptist Day—June 24—This religious holiday is special to Otavaleno Indians, who were enslaved by the Spanish invaders. It is celebrated with all-night dancing and music.

Feast of the Virgin of Carmen—July 16—This is celebrated by people who come from the town of Cuenca, but in the U.S. this and St. John the Baptist Day are celebrated in private, with friends and relatives.

First Cry for Independence Day—August 10—In New York City on this day the Ecuadoran Parade is held in the borough of Queens.

Ecuadoran-Americans also celebrate a form of the **Quence**, as many others from Latin and South American countries. However, Ecuadorans call it "Today I am a Senorita," marking the transition to womanhood. (See section on Mexican-Americans for more information on the Quence.)

The 1990 Census counted 162,000 persons of Peruvian ancestry in the United States, but there are estimates that run much higher. The largest numbers are in the New York City area, which has an estimated 80,000 Peruvian-Americans.

Immigrants from Peru started arriving in the United States in small numbers early in the twentieth century. However, the vast majority have come to the United States since World War II. The largest numbers came between 1975 and 1990, as word about opportunities in the U.S. filtered back to Peru.

The reasons for Peruvians' immigration into the United States included, at first, the unemployment rate in their homeland, which was very high. Then, the later groups were attracted to the United States because of the unstable political climate in Peru and also the economic stability that they expected to find in the United States.

Many Peruvians of the upper classes came to the U.S. because of political troubles in their homeland. Because of their upper-class upbringing and status, many have found it difficult to assimilate into American life. Peruvians of the upper economic strata were the first to come, and people of the middle and lower classes came later. The Catholic Church, with its many services, has been very helpful to Peruvians upon their arrival in the United States. Ninety-five percent of Peruvians both in Peru and in the United States are Roman Catholic.

Many Peruvians in the United States are restaurateurs, construction workers, secretaries, physicians and other trained professionals who have been able to scrape up the money needed for airfare to initially get to the United States. They arrive with little, but it isn't long before they are financially secure. Among the new arrivals are also better-off college-bound children of Peruvians who can afford tuition at American schools, some of them in the large metropolitan areas. Many of those graduates stay and flourish in the U.S. labor force.

HOLIDAYS AND CUSTOMS

June 29—**St. Peter and Paul Day**—A Catholic feast day honoring the Apostles Peter and Paul.

July 28 and 29—**Independence Day**—Celebrates Peru's independence from Spain in 1821.

August 30—**St. Rose of Lima Day**. She is the patron saint of Peru.

Peruvians generally also celebrate other traditional **Catholic** holidays.

According to an article in the *Washington Post*,[6] the throwaway mentality of some Americans bemuses Peruvians—perhaps more than other ethnic groups. In their poor homeland, Peruvians' first impulse is always to fix something that's broken.

Most Peruvian families in the United States are very close and often work together in businesses such as restaurants or small grocery stores. Peruvian parents take care of the children until they marry. In return, Peruvian children take complete responsibility for their elderly parents.

[1] *Gale's Encyclopedia*

[2] *Gale's Encyclopedia*

[3] August, 1990

[4] *Gale's* Pamela Sturner

[5] *Gale's*/U.S. Census bureau

[6] Pat Durkin, January 25, 1991

CHAPTER XI:

FROM THE MIDDLE EAST CAME AMERICANS OF ARMENIAN, ASSYRIAN, EGYPTIAN, IRANIAN, KURDISH, LEBANESE, PALESTINIAN, SYRIAN AND TURKISH ANCESTRY

WHAT IS AN ARAB?

Arabs are a diverse people who reside in twenty-two nations in North Africa and Southwest Asia. Formerly a reference to the largely nomadic Semitic inhabitants of the Arabian peninsula, today the word "Arab" embraces many of the multiethnic and multiracial Arabic-speaking people living in the area stretching from Morocco and Mauritania in the west, to Iraq and Kuwait in the east, to Yemen and Somalia in the south, to Syria and Lebanon in the north. In addition to language, Arabs are unified by culture and several strands of common history, particularly having been part of the Islamic Empire. In the U.S. there are about 3 million Americans of Arab heritage.

Before describing specific ethnicities, a brief history concerning Arabs may be in order. There has been a great misunderstanding of Arabs in the United States that for the most part began in the late 1970s and early 1980s. The term "Arab" carries weighty cultural imagery, but it essentially means those whose native tongue is Arabic, whether they be Muslims, Christians or even Jews.

The influx of Arabs into the United States began more than a century ago, in about 1880; they were recruited as cheap labor. Many came to the U.S. very simply seeking the gold that they believed paved the streets. But the real gold they found was opportunity.

Today Arab-Americans constitute 1 percent of the United States population, some 2.5 to 3 million people in all, according to the 1990 Census. "We have the most assimilated ethnic groups in the country," says William Baroody Jr., former chief of Ronald Reagan's White House Office of Communications. "We've always been a kind of private people."

If previous generations tended to lose their identity in the melting pot, more recent generations tend to be culturally distinct parts of the mosaic.

Many Arab immigrants were natural entrepreneurs. Many of them did what they knew best: they grew and marketed fruits and vegetables. But they were also merchants, and many began peddling notions and Bibles out of suitcases from the mountains of West Virginia to the plains of the Midwest.[1]

Many people mistakenly think the Arab and Muslim worlds are the same. But many Muslims are not Arabs, and some Arabs are not Muslims. An Arab country is one in which the native language is Arabic and in which the people adhere to the Arab culture.

Nineteen countries are regarded as Arab: Algeria, Bahrain, Egypt, Iraq, Jordan, Kuwait, Lebanon, Libya, Mauritania, Morocco, Oman, Qatar, Saudi Arabia, Sudan, Syria, Tunisia, United Arab Emirates, South Yemen and North Yemen.

Because much of the land of the Arab world is desert, one of the most common conceptions people have of life there is of desert nomads traveling from oasis to oasis on camelback. But the Arab nations today also boast modern cities, built in part by revenues from vast oil reserves.

The Arab world is predominantly Muslim, but there are several million Christian Arabs, who are divided between Eastern Rite churches (Orthodox), Latin Rite (Maronites) and Chaldeans.

There are other countries that are also predominantly Muslim, but the language is not Arabic, so those nations are not considered Arab. For example, the people of Muslim Iran speak Persian and thus are not Arabs. And in Asia such Muslim countries as Indonesia, Bangladesh and Pakistan maintain their own languages and cultures.

Historians say the original Arabs were the people of the Arabian desert. In about 570, the prophet Mohammed was born in the Saudi Arabian oasis of Mecca, now a holy site for Muslims. Mohammed founded the Muslim religion and converted the Arabs, who quickly began to build an empire.

Some Arab immigrants to the United States in the 1980s and 1990s fled their homelands for their lives. Many of those who have come to the U.S. are agrarian Muslim families from southern Lebanon, but there are also Iraqi Chaldeans and some Palestinians. Many Yemenis are fleeing poverty to seek jobs in auto plants or to work in the fields of California.

Figures from the 1990 Census show that Dearborn, Michigan, has the largest concentrated Arab community outside the Middle East. According to Ismael Ahmed, who runs Dearborn's Arab Community Center for Economic and Social Services, as of 1990, within a five-mile radius of Dearborn, there were 60,000 Arabic-speaking people; six out of ten of them had been in the United States less than five years; one out of three didn't speak English; two out of three didn't read or write English; and one out of three didn't read or write Arabic. And, Ahmed points out, there were as many as 5,000 new Middle Eastern immigrants arriving in Detroit each year, many of them seeking out family.

Today the greatest concentrations of Arab immigrants outside Detroit are in Southern California, Brooklyn, New York, the Cleveland-Toledo area, Illinois, Massachusetts and Texas.

For years Arabs were an invisible minority, cloaked in ethnic and national anonymity. According to Ahmed, Arab-Americans also have "that feeling you are worth something," he says. "Your religion, your culture is worth protecting. It's stronger now among the new immigrants. It's something we work with."

Some first-generation families will never be rich, but their aim is to establish an economic springboard for their children.

Many Arabs started out as peddlers, which fostered an entrepreneurial ethic that led many others to become storekeepers or small businessmen.

A study reported in 1986 by John Zogby, a pollster and market researcher, found that, based on 1980 Census data, Arab-Americans have higher levels of education and income than other immigrant groups and the American population as a whole. The study was based on 1980 Census data.

Of those who came to the United States from Arab countries before World War II and their descendants, 90 percent are Christian. Most came from the former Ottoman Empire, from the provinces of Syria, and considered themselves Syrian. After the independent country of Lebanon was formed in 1946 many came to consider themselves Lebanese.

The second, more conspicuous wave of Arab immigration came after World War II and continues in full force. These immigrants are about evenly divided between Christians and Muslims. They include Palestinians as well as Lebanese, Syrians, Egyptians and Yemenis.

Peter Appleborne, a *New York Times* reporter, wrote in 1991[2] that because most of the 2.5 to 3 million Arab-Americans are recent arrivals, they feel a tension between their life in the U.S. and the one they left in their homeland. "We are looking out two windows," William Ali, a General Motors worker, told Appleborne. "We love our people here, but we love our people there, too. We're existing in two worlds, but one of the things that hurts most is how little people in our world here really know about our world there."

Many Arab-Americans faced that realization in 1967, when Americans sided overwhelmingly with Israel in its war with its Arab neighbors, a war that redefined the geography of the Middle East. The resentment escalated during the Arab oil embargo of the early 1970s, when many Americans reacted angrily to the notion that their economic destiny was controlled by Arab oil sheiks.

Just as the Middle East changed with the Arab-Israeli war of 1967, so did the Arab community in the United States. Bitter feelings erupted between Lebanese and Palestinian immigrants at the height of Lebanon's civil war.

Before 1967, there was almost no sense of cultural unity among Arab-Americans. But the shock of that war, the rise of anti-Arab sentiment in the United States and the continuing flow of immigrants from the Middle East have profoundly changed Arab life in the United States.[3] Many Arab-Americans are angry at the degree to which Arabs remain fair game for negative stereotypes and caricatures, of greedy oil sheiks or of crazed Arab terrorists.[4]

One way Arabs fought the stereotypes was by forming Arab organizations. Beginning in 1967 there was a surge in the formation of such groups, the first of which was the Association of Arab-American University Graduates, which was followed by the American Arab Anti-Discrimination League, the Arab-American Institute and the National Association of Arab-Americans.

Despite the differences within the Arab-American communities, there are some common concerns. First, from the 1960s through the 1990s, there has been widespread disagreement with U.S. policy toward Israel and a sense that peace in the Middle East depends on a resolution of the problems of the Palestinians, specifically, for example, defining their homeland. Second, there is a deep feeling of frustration among many Arab-Americans that the United States' picture of the Arab world is deeply distorted and antagonistic.

Some other important facts to note about the Arab-American population: the United States' most diverse Arab population is in Illinois, according to Census data. It is not dominated by Lebanese-Americans, as some other states are. Illinois' immigrants from the Middle East have come from all over their native region. Lebanese- and Syrian-Americans dominate the Arab population in the United States.[5]

Los Angeles is rapidly becoming an Arab political and cultural center. California has the largest Arab population in the country—about 350,000, mainly in the Los Angeles and San Francisco areas. Although about half of the immigrant Arab-Americans in California have attended college, one in eight lives below the poverty level, according to Census data.

While California is the state with the largest Arab-American population, the Detroit-Dearborn area of Michigan has the country's largest Arab-American community, including 60,000 Iraqi Christians. In Dearborn, four of ten Arabs are foreign-born. Also, many Arabs, particularly college students, immigrated to Texas recently. As of the 1990 Census, Texas had the highest percentage of Arab families living below the poverty level.[6] Massachusetts is home to 150,000 Arabs, most having lived two or three generations in the United States—about 82 percent were born in the United States. New York's metropolitan areas, including Buffalo, Rochester and Syracuse, host a diverse Arab population. Large concentrations of Jordanians live in Yonkers, while many Yemeni have settled in Brooklyn. New Jersey boasts a very diverse population of Arab-Americans in which a high percentage of Lebanese are joined by Syrians, Egyptians and others. Pennsylvania's Arab-American population is mostly made up of Lebanese and Syrians born in the United States. Virginia's largely foreign-born population of Arab-Americans is located in the District of Columbia suburbs, with a large Palestinian community. Family incomes are among the highest in the country.

American Muslims, and Arab-Americans in particular, are struggling to deal with a combination of new visibility and old stereotypes, the latter renewed by the Gulf War of 1991 and freshened every time a terrorist act hits the news.

Some Arab-American leaders blame Hollywood for a long tradition of stereotyping Arabs. Essam Abdullah, a Jordanian immigrant from Hickory Hill, Illinois, told the *Washington Post*, "For 70 years, Hollywood has portrayed the Arab as ... a bomber, belly dancer or billionaire." Many Arabs and Muslims feel the movie and television industries portray them as crazy, all-purpose anti-American, terrorist bad guys.[7]

According to survey results reported in *USA Today* in February 1991, Arab-Americans were virtually unanimous about one thing: Non-Arab-Americans don't understand the Arab people and their ways, and most non-Arabs don't understand the Arab world.

Osama Siblami, editor of *The Arab-American News* in Detroit, says Arab-Americans live in the United States for the same reasons others do: freedom and democracy.

Hopefully all Americans will become aware that there are Arabs in their midst who are just as American as they are: rich, bold, colorful tiles in the American mosaic.

In an article by Steven Holmes in the *New York Times* on October 30, 1996, his story revealed some changes concerning stereotyping was starting to change. Arab-Americans were not shy about using their ethnicity to persuade some political party leaders to back them for political office.

Demographic changes that began in the late 1990s forced politicians at all levels to adjust their thinking and vote calculations, and they found themselves counting emerging blocks of ethnic voters including Arab-Americans.

Gone are the days when Walter Mondale running for the presidency returned donations made by Arab-Americans to his 1984 campaign or when Michael S. Dukakis told a group of Arab-Americans in 1988 that he did not want their presidential endorsement.

"Arab-Americans are getting as much attention as any other ethnic group," said George R. Salim, a Palestinian-American lawyer in Washington, DC, who worked for the Dole campaign in 1996.

Nittad Awad, executive director of the Council on American-Islamic Relations in Washington, D.C. pointed out in a speech about stereotypes about Arabs and Muslims that careless generalizations foster racism and hate crimes of which Arab-Americans have often been the target. Those wrongheaded generalizations include:

1. Fathers forcing daughters into marriage. In reality, according to Islamic law, both parties in a marriage must approve of prospective mates.

2. Husbands abusing wives. The prophet Mohammed is an example to be emulated by all Muslims. During his married life, he never beat or abused his wives and reprimanded others when he witnessed abuse. He also performed housework and often served his guests.

3. Husbands divorcing wives quickly and easily. In Islam, divorce is the most disliked of all permitted things. Every route to reconciliation is attempted. If a temporary separation is agreed upon, mediators from both families try to help the couple get back together. If all else fails, Islamic law allows for divorce to be initiated by either the wife or the husband.

4. Muslim women being "docile." Islam encourages humility in men and women. This should not be interpreted to mean that Muslim women are "docile." Islamic history has witnessed many prominent women. The prophet Mohammed's first wife, Khadija, was a successful business-woman as well as his employer. Also, the first martyr in Islam was a woman who died under torture because she refused to recant her declaration of faith. Women took part in battles and tended to the wounded on the battlefield.

5. Dowries being paid to a bride's family. The Koran states, "Give women their marriage portions with no strings attached." In Islamic marriages, the groom must pay an agreed upon amount directly to the bride. This money or property cannot be touched at a later time by the husband or the father. It is solely for the wife's use.

6. Polygamy being unrestricted. Muslim men may marry up to four wives if they can support and treat all wives equitably—a formidable task. Although monogamy is far more common both among Muslims in general and in the U.S. Arab population, polygamy is seen as a provision that has benefits for the society at large. For example, if a war results in many widows, it is in the best interest of the community to have families provided for by capable husbands. Polygamy, according to the Koran, can never be used as an excuse for sexual promiscuity.

As with any belief system, there are individuals who follow their own desires and go against Islamic law. This is the case in some parts of the Islamic world. Unfortunately, the Western media sometimes portray social problems and cultural practices that have nothing to do with Islamic teaching as being derived from the faith itself.

Arab-Americans celebrate religious holidays: Islamic holidays for those who follow Islam and Christian holidays for Arab Christians.

Arranged marriages remain common among recent immigrants, and there is a preference for endogamy (marriage among cousins), but both customs decline among Arabs born in the United States and those who have assimilated into American culture.

Depending on her religion, an Arab woman might wear a *chador*, which is a veil that covers her hair and skin in an effort to show modesty.

The 1990 Census said that there were 308,000 people in the United States of Armenian ancestry, although Armenian organizations such as the Armenian Evangelical Social Services give estimates of between 500,000 and 800,000.

Most of the historical homeland of Armenia has been under Turkish control for several centuries, but part of it has been controlled more recently by Russia. Emigration and massacres by the Turks left only a few thousand Armenians in Turkey. Since 1920, the majority immigrated to the United States. Nearly all of the Armenian immigrants to the U.S. since the 1960s have come from predominantly Arabic countries or the Armenian republic of the former Soviet Union.

Armenian immigration to the United States has come in three waves—the first group (of about 60,000) came between 1890 and 1914, prior to World War I, as they fled Turkey. Then, from 1920 until 1924, about 30,000 survivors of the massacre came. After World War II the Turks forced about 700,000 Armenians into the Middle East. Later, in the 1980s and 1990s, about 60,000 more came to the United States, of which 75 percent settled in the Los Angeles area.[8]

Armenians were different from most Eastern Europeans but similar to Jews in that a large minority immigrated from towns and cities, rather than from rural areas, and were artisans or traders. Although most Armenian immigrants would have opened a business had they had the money and been able to speak English, they typically had to accept factory work (like other immigrants) in order to earn capital for later investment. Large concentrations of Armenians worked in the factories of New England.[9]

In all cities with Armenian settlements there were some craftsmen and entrepreneurs, particularly in Boston, New York and Philadelphia. They were especially likely to be shoe repairers, tailors, jewelers and grocers. However, their most distinctive business was that of selling oriental rugs.[10]

Migration to California was so substantial among Armenian immigrants that about 42 percent of the nation's population of Armenian ancestry in 1990 lived in that state. About 15 percent of Armenian-Americans live in Massachusetts, and 10 percent live in Michigan.

The ancient kingdom of Armenia consisted of parts of what are now Turkey, the Soviet Union and Iran. The kingdom was absorbed by the old Malmuk Empire, and for more than six centuries (except for a brief period between 1918 and 1920) the Armenians have struggled to retain their national and cultural identity without a country of their own. For more than 500 years, Armenians had no independent state.

The Armenian culture has roots in Anatolia and the Caucasus stretching back 2,500 years. The Armenians were a cosmopolitan people with strong ties to the Hellenic world, and as traders they traversed the world from Shanghai to Amsterdam to India. They were the Ottomans' architects, famous for the sensuous carvings of their churches as well as for their tiles, their rugs and their lace.

Along with Greeks and Jews, Armenians constituted a large part of the intellectual and financial infrastructure of the Ottoman Empire. They were often resented by the Turks because they were Christians, better educated, wealthier and westernized. Like Jews, Armenians were in many places forbidden to own property, so they frequently became bankers and money lenders, and like Jews they were despised. During successive waves of persecution they dispersed throughout the world, and by 1999 the Armenian diaspora extended from Australia to Jerusalem. Armenians settled on the farms and vineyards of California, and in the last quarter of the twentieth century many poorer immigrants from the former Soviet Union have settled in Los Angeles.

On April 24, 1915, several thousand Armenian artists and intellectuals in Constantinople were arrested by their Turkish overlords. The arrests marked the beginning of the series of massacres and scattering of families.

With the outbreak of World War I, the Turkish government that had replaced the old theocracy saw the Armenians as a security threat and collaborators with the Russians. As part of a systematic plan of extermination, the Armenians say, two-thirds of the Armenian people were killed, deported or sent into the desert to starve. It was estimated that 1.5 million Armenians suffered this fate.

To this day, the Turkish government disputes that genocide took place. The Turkish position has been, and continues to be, that the Armenian community was in revolt against the central Ottoman administration and siding with Russian invaders.

Armenian immigrants often kept the Turkish atrocities hidden from their children.

HOLIDAYS AND CUSTOMS

On April 24 each year, Armenian-Americans commemorate the massacres on **Martyrs' Day**. In many families, it was the practice to have photographs taken each year to send to overseas relatives. They provided a link: photographs were often a way of keeping the family together. Photos also played an important role in the so-called "picture marriages" between Armenian men fortunate enough to be in the United States during the massacres and the widows, orphans and unmarried women in the old country. Many of the women who later immigrated arrived in the U.S. with little more than a tiny picture of their husband-to-be.

In the United States a project called SAVE is an effort to alert the Armenian community to the importance of preserving memories and artifacts. For Armenians, who lost so much of their past through traumatic events in history, photography is especially important to bridge the gap created by the massacres.

Many Armenian-Americans celebrate Catholic holidays. Easter time is special because it comes close to the April 24 commemoration of the massacres. Good Friday and Easter are seen as a parallel to the genocide, to the crucifixion and to the resurrection of the Armenians themselves.

Armenian Christmas is celebrated on January 6, which dates back to the Julian Calendar. Note that even though this is celebrated on a different date than what many people are familiar with, it is still to celebrate Christ's birth.

The holiday called *Hampartzoom* refers to Christ's ascension forty days after Easter.

263

February 10—**St. Vartens Day**—Commemorates the martyr Vartan Mamigonian's battle for religious freedom with sectarian ceremonies.

May 28—**Independence Day**—Commemorates Armenia's independence from Turkey (1918-1920) with parades and speeches.

September 23—Commemorates independence from the Soviet Union in 1991.

Armenians also celebrate the various **Christian** holidays.

The 1990 Census showed 51,750 people of Assyrian ancestry in the United States. Assyrians have long been concentrated in what is now Northern Iraq and surrounding areas, where their ancient Assyrian Empire was located almost a thousand years before Christ. Assyrians have been divided by their adherence to various Christian traditions and organizations, and the differences among them have remained significant in the United States.

Most Assyrian immigrants to the U.S. have settled in the Detroit area, though percentages are tough to nail down because their population in the United States is so small. By the 1960s, more than half of the families were in the grocery business, and by the early 1980s they owned more than 400 outlets.[11]

It is estimated by Egyptian organizations that there are 150,000 Egyptian Christians in the United States, although the 1990 Census counted only approximately 78,000 of them. Professionals started emigrating to the United States in significant numbers after the 1967 Arab-Israeli war. They were drawn to the U.S. by better opportunities than in Muslim Egypt. Most, over 85 percent, were Coptics, Egypt's native Christians. The Copts are descendants of the Egyptians who remained faithful to Christianity during the almost thirteen centuries since the ascendance of Islam in Egypt. The Copts are among the oldest Christian sects in the world, yet they remain largely unknown in the West.

The great majority of Egyptian Christians belong to the Coptic Orthodox Church. So do the great majority of the 8 million Copts in Egypt, where Christianity arrived in the year 42, when the apostle Mark went to Alexandria.

The smallest group of Copts among the 150,000 in the United States are Protestants. Fed up with Byzantine taxes and interference, Coptic Christians parted company with Rome in 451 and remained separate from Rome until 1741.

Like other immigrant groups, Copts have come to the United States for opportunities not available in their homeland.

The liturgical calendar follows the three seasons of Egypt: the annual flooding of the Nile, the time of sowing and the harvest. Coptic music is the oldest church music in the world, with sounds that are similar to those that filled the temples of the pharaohs.

In the Coptic church, men sit on the left side, women on the right. The altar is screened from the congregation by an iconostasis, a wooden wall on which icons are displayed. (See section on Orthodox religion and discussion about icons.)

The liturgy includes passages in Coptic, the language spoken in Alexandria when the Egyptians played a leading role in the growth of Christianity. The Mass is chanted in either Arabic or Coptic, with some Greek responses. Once a year the Copts sing the Mass of St. Cyril, the oldest form and the most closely associated with Egypt. The burning of incense precedes Sunday Mass, which begins with the offertory. The priest wears a *tailasana*, a miter of pharaonic origin with a long veil down the back. During much of the liturgy, he holds up a small Coptic cross.

A handful of Arab horsemen invaded Egypt in 639, ending Byzantine rule and imposing their own. They introduced the Islamic religion, which was to envelop most of the Middle East. Soon, the Coptic Christians were surrounded by Muslims. To survive, the Copts clung to the cross.

The Coptic cross is made up of two bold lines of equal length that intersect at the middle at right angles. At each angle are three points, representing the Trinity of the Father, the Son and the Holy Ghost. All together, the cross has twelve points, symbolizing the Apostles, whose mission it was to spread the Gospel message throughout the world.

The Copts and the like-minded churches of Ethiopia, Syria and Armenia were declared heretical by the Western and Eastern Orthodox Churches when they rejected a reference of the Church of Rome and the Byzantine empire in 451 to Christ's having two natures: human and divine. The Orthodox churches insisted the Monophysites were denying the full humanity of Christ.

In January 1996, the Patriarch of the church announced that on December 23, 1995, a Bishop was installed for North America whose task would be to unify the Coptic community.

The 150,000-200,000 Egyptian Copts in the U.S. form about sixty congregations. The Coptic community has grown steadily since 1980, when, for example, the Los Angeles area had only three Coptic churches. By 1996 Los Angeles had thirteen Coptic churches spread across the county. There are about fourteen congregations in New York and New Jersey. This growth in the number of Coptic churches has been fueled by immigration from Egypt. While many Egyptians have said they immigrated mainly for educational and economic opportunities, others acknowledge the difficulty of living as a Christian in the predominately Muslim Egypt. Copts in Egypt have felt oppressed, as the newly appointed Bishop Serapicon pointed out in an interview with the *Los Angeles Times*.[12] He said that even a good student who was Christian would have little chance to enter a profession like teaching. In the U.S., though, that student would have an opportunity to pursue such a career.

Many Egyptian Copts living in the U.S. grew up under repressive Egyptian regimes, tended to be skeptical of the political process in the United States and were reluctant to take part. The Bishop Serapicon said he hoped to change this by encouraging voter registration and full civic participation. But, as Egyptians, the Bishop said, community leaders sometimes faced the added challenge of being stereotyped by some who believe that all Arabs are Islamic fundamentalists or terrorists. The Coptic Church in the United States is undertaking efforts to combat the stereotype.

Another pressing dilemma for Copt leaders has been to keep the Egyptian Coptic youth in the U.S. connected and interested. For children, the pressure to assimilate is great—a problem faced by many immigrant communities. One change taking place designed to help youths feel more comfortable in the church is to use English rather than Arabic and ancient Coptic at services.

HOLIDAYS AND CUSTOMS

September 11—The **Coptic New Year** is celebrated with feasts and church activities.

Christmas—Some celebrate on December 25 and others on January 7, when the Orthodox churches celebrate the Nativity.

Easter Monday (Sham Al-Nasim) is a rite of spring, and it dates back to ancient times when Egyptians ate special foods and went out to the fields and beaches. This custom is dying out in the United States because Monday is a work day (many instead celebrate it on Easter Sunday). Egyptians of all faiths get together to celebrate if possible.

Eid Al Fitr —For believers in Islam, the end of the month of Ramadan.

Eid Al Adha — The feast of the sacrifice. (For further information on these last two holidays, see description in the section on Islam.)

When it comes time to name a baby, Coptics write seven names on separate pieces of paper and place a lighted candle on top of each. The name under the candle that burns the longest is given to the baby.

The most glaring misconception concerning Iranians in the United States is that they are Arabs. They are not. They identify themselves as Persian. They are predominantly Muslim in religion, approximately 93 percent, according to *The Harvard Encyclopedia of American Ethnic Groups*. The 1990 Census showed 235,000 of Iranian ancestry. It is estimated that more than 1 million Iranians have come to the United States, the first wave between 1950 and 1972. It has been very difficult to trace a definite immigration pattern among Iranian newcomers to the U.S. Many thousands left Iran because of the 1979 revolution. Of the non-Muslim group of Iranian immigrants to the U.S., about 35,000 were Iranian Jews who settled later in Los Angeles, New York or in Europe. Those who came to the United States were the elite of Iran, and they came as political refugees. Of others who came, over 100,000 returned to Iran between 1989 and 1992. Only 240,000 Iranian-Americans were counted in the 1990 Census. But the estimate of the actual population is much higher, according to Iranian-American organizations.

The relationship of Iranians to other ethnic groups in the U.S. and to Americans in general is an unusual one. Many Iranians have felt the sting of being stereotyped as either violent Muslim fanatics or as terrorists. Consequently, many feel a deep sense of alienation from other Americans, though public relations programs are striving to stop such stereotypes.

Few Iranians immigrated until 1945, and even by 1966 they numbered only 1,000. In 1978, the peak year for Iranian visa approvals, more than 116,000 visas were issued for temporary stays to Iranian nationals. Iranians have generally lived in large metropolitan areas, especially the Washington, D.C., area and in California. In 1979 and 1980 there were more than 51,000 Iranian students in the United States, making Iran by far the largest source of foreign students studying here.

HOLIDAYS AND CUSTOMS

The language of many Iranian-Americans is Farsi (sometimes known as Persian), not Arabic. Most are Shiite Muslims. The most significant holiday is **Muharram** (the date of which varies according to the lunar calendar) and through the tenth day afterward. The holiday focuses on the seventh-century martyrdom of Husain, the grandson of the prophet Mohammed. It is a period of mourning and penitence for all Shiites. It is a period of ten days, and the first eight or nine days are the most intense. The tenth day is sometimes referred to as Muharram 10, or Ashura, and is the height of the period characterized by celebration, whereas the previous days comprise a sorrowful religious period.

Iranian immigrants in the U.S. celebrate **Islamic** holidays.

Iranian wedding customs include those followed by devout Muslims, which traditionally include having the father of the family expressing control.

The *hijab*, modest clothing for women, is a controversial aspect of Islamic culture, and public conformity varies according to the political climate that existed in Iran prior to individuals' emigration.

The immigration of Lebanese and Syrians to the U.S. first started in the 1880s and continued until the U.S. government set quotas that limited the number of incoming immigrants in the 1920s. Though Lebanese and Syrians are not monolithic, what is now Lebanon was carved out of what was in 1946 Syria, so the two groups will be considered together.

Syrian Christians were the first Arabs to immigrate into the United States.[13] Most came from a Maronite (Eastern rite) religious tradition and had been strongly influenced by the French. In the United States, the Maronites adapted readily to Roman Catholic parishes, and many became peddlers. After the independent country of Lebanon was founded in 1946, many Maronites thought of themselves as Lebanese. There were also many Orthodox Christians. Only 5.1 percent of the pre-1914 immigrants were Muslims.[14]

HOLIDAYS AND CUSTOMS

Holidays are celebrated by different sects and religions. Christians celebrate both **Christmas** and **Easter** as well as some other feasts such as St. Maron and St. Charbel (by Maronites). Orthodox celebrate **St. Nicholas Day** and **St. George Day**.

Muslims celebrate the holidays outlined in the section on **Islam**.

National Independence Day for Lebanese-Americans is November 22; **National Independence Day** for Syrian-Americans is April 17.

No one knows how many Kurds live in the United States because they have come as nationals of Iran, Iraq, Turkey, Syria and the former Soviet Union, which share the mountainous area called Kurdistan. It is estimated by the Kurdish National Congress that there are 10,000 to 12,000 Kurds in the United States, including more than 5,000 from Iraq.

Mehrdad Izady, who teaches in the Department of Near Eastern Languages at Harvard University, mentions three main waves of Kurdish immigration to the United States: after World War I with the upheavals in Turkey; in the mid-1970s after the collapse of the Kurdish revolution in Iraq; and between 1979 and 1981 in the wake of the Iranian revolution. Originally, many settled in rural areas such as North Dakota and Tennessee, but they have since tended to migrate to cities for greater opportunities.[15]

In 1991, despite a month's saturation of news coverage around the world about the suffering many Kurds endured at the hands of Iraqi dictator Saddam Hussein, the Kurds remain a people seen but not known. They have been bred to inscrutability by centuries of oppression in the five countries where most of them live but where their existence is ignored or even denied: Iraq, Turkey, Iran, Syria and the former Soviet Union.

The Kurds lost control of their homeland, Kurdistan, when it was carved up after World War I among Turkey, northeastern Iraq and northwestern Iran (formerly Persia). Forces of Iraq's Saddam Hussein crushed the Kurds' latest struggle for independence, in 1991. As an ancient Kurdish axiom goes, "The Kurds have no friends."

This much is known: The Kurds are an ancient mountain people of indeterminate number and uncertain origin whose many dialects are akin to Persian. They are mostly Sunni Muslim, with Shiite and Christian minorities. What has held them together is the oldest human tie: family.[16]

Some scholars say the Kurds are descended from the Medes, the historic foes of the Persians who lived in the same mountains. Far more elusive are the Kurds' fierce and tangled loyalties to the *agha*, or sheik; the *ashiret*, or tribe; and the *kabile*, or clan.

In 1991, when Iraq's Hussein pushed them back to the mountains and tried to starve and even annihilate them, the Kurds, whose origins reach back to biblical times, got assistance both from government and religious agencies in the United States. Yet their ordeal intensified. The United Nations estimated that up to 800,000 refugees lived along the Iraq-Turkey border.

The history of the Kurds stretches back 4,000 years in a region once known as Mesopotamia. A close-knit, fervently independent tribal people, the Kurds possibly descended from the Medes of the Old Testament, whose empire fell in 550 B.C.

Darius, Median king of Persia in the time of the prophet Daniel, may have been a Kurd. At one time, many Kurds followed a Persian form of Zoroastrianism, a little-known religion in the West that can be described as the struggle between the forces of light and darkness, with light symbolizing goodness. Most now are Sunni Muslims, converted to Islam in the seventh century.

Kurdish-Americans welcomed American and international emergency relief in 1991 for the beleaguered Kurds in Iraq, but they continue to voice anger and hurt over the refusal of the U.S. under George Bush's administration to support the 1991 rebellion, said Dr. Esfaniar Shoukry, a founder of the Kurdish National Congress of North America.

Most Kurds celebrate the Islamic holidays.

PALESTINIANS

There are only estimates of the number of Palestinian-Americans, and those estimates range from 100,000 to 400,000. Most people settle on 200,000 as a reasonable number. The difficulty in using estimates lies in the fact that in the last half century there hasn't actually been a country that Palestinian immigrants could call a country of origin. Because of the unusual Palestinian history, it is difficult to determine exactly when they first immigrated to the United States. Also, they came from many different countries in the Middle East, such as Jordan, Kuwait, Yemen and Israel.

The greatest wave of Palestinian immigration began after the Six Day War in 1967 and continued through at least the mid-1990s. Unlike the majority of Palestinian-Americans now, who are Muslim, many of the first wave that came were Christians, and while some came for political reasons the large majority came for economic reasons and educational opportunities. Initially, many of the early group settled in the Eastern United States but eventually moved to the Midwest, especially into and around Detroit, where they took industrial jobs. New York, New Jersey and Los Angeles also have substantial settlements of Palestinian-Americans. The more recent Palestinian immigrants to the U.S. have been more educated than their predecessors, often working as professionals.

While many Palestinians have made the transition to the new culture of the United States, others remain concerned about the lack of a Palestinian state. Many are characterized by some Americans as Arab rather than distinctively Palestinian, and some feel this is done to make them incompatible with other Americans.

HOLIDAYS AND CUSTOMS

The vast majority of Palestinian-Americans are Muslim, and Arabic is their language (since the seventh century).

They celebrate the holidays of **Islam**. Those who are Christian, of course, celebrate the holidays of that religion.

Sometimes, for special occasions, the men will wear the traditional *Kafiyyeh*, which is an elaborate turban or scarf.

In the U.S. many Palestinian marriage traditions have changed to conform to American law. They are encouraged to marry within their own ethnic group and are expected to respect their parents' wishes when choosing a spouse. The ceremony itself is a festive event, and celebrations last several days.[17]

TURKS

Because of the difficulty of translating Turkish into European languages and in various phonetic forms, it proved to be an unusually perplexing experience for everyone when a Turk had his initial encounter with U.S. immigration officials, according to *Turks in America* by Frank Ahmed.

Turkish-Americans who have studied their history in the U.S. have contended that when a Turk was asked his name, the immigration officials, who had little time or patience, would give the Turk any name he wished. The official needed a name, any name, for his records. Thus, feeling equally frustrated, more often than not the Turk accepted what the official gave him. The names Luleyman and Huseyin became Sam; Ahmed could become Ali. This initial exchange invariably gave the Turks new American-sounding names that stayed with them for their life in America.

The 1990 Census showed 86,000 Americans of Turkish ancestry. The assembly of Turkish-American Associations states that this is inaccurate and estimates this population to be 150,000 to 300,000.

The majority of the first group of immigrants who came from Turkey (pre-World War I, part of the Ottoman Empire) were Christians and Sephardic Jews, along with a large number of Muslims. These were Anatolian Turks, approximately 45,000 to 65,000 male Turks who entered the U.S. prior to World War I. No women came, just men to work temporarily.

Like many other immigrants of that time, a negative image of Turks was prevalent. The stereotype was one of primitive, bearded men who slew Christians and sacked churches.

These Anatolian Turks were the first to introduce the United States to the traditions and beliefs of Islam, providing yet another thread to the rich religious fabric of the United States. Their presence introduced an exotic Eastern culture to their new areas. Most migrated to New England, especially around cities of the north shore of Massachusetts and in the industrial North. These Anatolian Turks were long considered to be the most dependable element in Turkish society.

The largest number of Anatolians were from villages and towns in the thinly populated areas, such as Harput, Dersim, Capakcur and Rize.[18] Few in these Anatolian villages were literate, and reports of the success, adventure and wealth of Americans reached these villages by word of mouth.

According to U.S. immigration records, for the period 1900 to 1920 a total of 291,435 immigrants whose "Country of Last Residence" was Turkey entered the United States. This total included Turks, Kurds and ethnic minorities such as Armenians and Greeks. As stated earlier, approximately 45,000 to 65,000 were Muslim Turks, the majority of whom were motivated by a desire to find employment and to work long enough to enable them to return home rich by Anatolian standards. Their illusion of life in the United States and their ambition closely followed the pattern of European immigrants of that period. And, as mentioned earlier, these initial waves of immigrants were all male. As with many other groups, their cultural viewpoint was to emigrate, get settled and then bring their wives and families. Turkish women did not participate in any immigration until the conclusion of World War II. Many Americans believed that the Turks did not bring their wives because it was against their religion. Many of the men who came found work in the factories of New York, Detroit and Chicago. Others found jobs in the leather factories of New England, where workers were needed.

The Turkish immigrants' immediate and primary problem was the absence of a common language. Turkish, at that time for the United States Immigration Service, was a new language. Unlike immigrants who came prior to 1920, most of these Turks stayed briefly, the majority for only a decade but many for even shorter periods of time. Just before the Great Depression, the majority of Turkish immigrants collected their personal effects and what money they had saved and returned to their Anatolian villages.[19]

In the 1950s and 1960s, when Turkey was making a conscious effort to modernize, it began sending promising students to the United States for graduate studies. While some came with their families, most were single men and women. This signaled the arrival of Turkish women.

Turkish women who came at that time were prepared for life in the U.S. both professionally and by education prior to the 1960s. Up to that point no women had come for the purpose of education, they had come as wives, so it was a big turning point.

The most unique Turkish community in the United States today is located in Rochester, New York.[20] An executive of a large retail chain in New York City between 1955 and 1960 was planning to invite some Italian tailors to come to the United States to live and work in the Bond Stores of NYC's Rochester plant. One of his Turkish employees suggested he consider hiring Turkish tailors; he did and soon contracted with more than 200 Turkish tailors for their services in Rochester. For the first time, Turkish immigrants came as families. Unlike many of the European immigrants, including those of the 1950s, '60s and '70s, Turks did not come seeking religious freedom. They felt completely secure in their Islamic faith, and while many remained non-practicing Muslims, they were always mindful of their Islamic heritage.[21]

HOLIDAYS AND CUSTOMS

Turkish-Americans celebrate the **Islamic** holidays.

Turkish-American Day—April 24—Celebrated in New York City with a parade.

Youth and Sports Day—May19—Celebrated with games and athletic events.

Victory Day—August 20—Celebrates the Turks' victory over the Greeks in 1922.

Children's Day—April 23—This commemorates the founding of the Turkish Grand National Assembly in 1923, and it has been proclaimed as a day to honor children.

[1] Associated Press, September 30, 1990, Alixa Neff, Arab-American historian at the Smithsonian

[2] February 10, 1991

[3] Peter Appleborne, the *New York Times*, February 10

[4] Peter Appleborne, the *New York Times*, February 10

[5] according to Census data

[6] *USA TODAY,* February 6, 1991

[7] the *Washington Post,* July 22, 1994

[8] *We the People, Harvard Encyclopedia of Ethnic Groups*

[9] *Harvard Encyclopedia of Ethnic Groups*

[10] *Harvard Encyclopedia of Ethnic Groups*

[11] *We the People*

[12] January 3, 1996

[13] *We the People*

[14] *We the People*

[15] Mehrdad Izady

[16] Karl Meyer, the *Washington Post*, April, 1991

[17] Ken Kurson, *Gale's Encyclopedia*

[18] *Turks in America*, by Frank Ahmed

[19] *Turks in America* by Frank Ahmed

[20] *Turks in America*, by Frank Ahmed

[21] *Turks in America*, by Frank Ahmed

CHAPTER XII:
FROM CENTRAL EUROPE CAME AMERICANS OF AUSTRIAN,
CZECH, HUNGARIAN, SLOVAK AND SWISS ANCESTRY

The 1990 Census showed 950,000 people of Austrian ancestry in the United States.

Before 1860 very few immigrants came to the United States from Austria. Austrians, prior to World War I, were identified as part of the Austrian empire rather than an ethnic group, and the Austrian empire was vast and included Czechs, Slovaks, Ukrainians, Poles, Slovenians, Jews, as well as speakers of the German language.

In the early twentieth century, the area of origin for most Austrian immigrants was Burgenland, in eastern Austria—prior to 1921 it was a German-speaking region of the Hungarian empire. As is typical of most areas that sent migrants to the United States, it had a surplus of farm laborers. Over 70 percent of the migrants until 1930 came from Burgenland to Detroit, northern New Jersey and the Chicago area, according to *We the People*.[1] The Austrian immigrants of the late 1930s were different because they were primarily Austrian Jews who were fleeing the Nazis.

Most Austrian-Americans are Roman Catholic. In 1950 it was estimated that only 275,000 people in the United States were of this ancestry; in the past forty years those numbers have nearly quadrupled. The largest concentrations are now in the states of New York, California and Florida, according to the 1990 Census.

HOLIDAYS AND CUSTOMS

Most Austrian-American holidays center mainly around the seasons. For example, *Fasching* is an old winter custom that traditionally takes place in late February. It is a ceremony held in order to drive out the evil spirits of winter and prepare for spring.

Beyond such traditional holidays as Christmas, New Year's and Easter, Austrian-Americans cannot be said to celebrate many feast and seasonal holidays as a group. But those who came from or are ancestors of those from rural Austria (who are predominantly Catholic) observe **St. Leonard's Day** in November, **St. Nicholas Day** (December 6), **Corpus Christi** in June and harvest festivals (**OctoberFest**) in October.

The 1990 Census showed 1,300,000 Czechs in the United States: 52 percent in the Midwest, 22 percent in the South, 16 percent in the West, and 10 percent in the Northwest.

Czech ethnicity is based primarily on the ancestral or current use of the Czech language. Most Czechs arrived in the United States after 1850. They came as families, and very few returned to their homeland compared to other European immigrants. Once they arrived, a majority of the Czechs forsook their formal religious beliefs and organizations; they abandoned Roman Catholicism, and many joined the Protestant churches. A possible reason for their departure from the church is that in Czechoslovakia the Catholic Church was closely identified with the oppressive Hapsburg monarchy, according to Christine Molanari of the University of Chicago. And, by tradition, according to *We the People*, the Czechs inherited a rationality and freedom of thought, which prompted a lot of questioning about religion. Also, moving to the United States led many who moved to urban areas from rural areas to give up their religious practices.

The early Czech immigrants began as farmers with settlements in the upper Midwest. Those who migrated to cities preferred to work in factories and shops rather than outside in construction or railroading. In the early twentieth century, Czechs were the largest ethnic group working in the meatpacking industry, according to the *Harvard Encyclopedia of American Ethnic Groups*. And in New York City, 95 percent of the Czechs made cigars, and some later became skilled button makers.

Immigration to the United States increased after World War II, when the Soviets took over Czechoslovakia, because of communism and the loss of freedoms that Czechs encountered. By 1990, Chicago had twice as many Czechs as any other metropolitan area of the United States, according to Census data.

Czechs migrated also to Texas, in particular to Houston, which by 1980 had one of the largest Czech-ancestry populations in the United States. In the 1840s, Texas became home to the first group of immigrants from what is now Czechoslovakia. During the last half of the 1880s, more than 250 such communities sprang up in the four-county area between Dallas and Austin, and today Texas has the largest rural Czechoslovakian population in the United States, according to the *New York Times*.[2]

West, Texas, has a thriving Czech culture that started more than 150 years ago. Situated seventy-five miles south of Dallas and 120 miles north of Austin, West provides a fascinating alternative to the typical Texas icons of football and oil derricks.

West, Praha, Flatonia and many other towns have retained their Czech culture with a distinctive Texas twist. In many of the towns, Czech is widely spoken as a second language. It is not unusual to see men in cowboy boots and ten-gallon hats reading the state's largest Czech-language newspaper, or women greeting each other with a familiar "*dobry den*." Czechoslovakian signs identify items such as *Klobasa* (sausage) and *zeli* (sauerkraut).

Other foods that are familiar to Czechs are *kolaches*, which are soft, round buns filled with fruit jam, or *buchtas*, which are jelly-roll-style coffee cakes filled with fruits, nuts or sweet poppy seed pastry.[3] Czech-Americans have also introduced to Texans the sausage *klobasniki*, a kind of pig-in-a-blanket. Incidentally, a staple of Czechoslovak cuisine is pork.

Christmas Eve—Dinner on this night is served only after the first star in the sky is observed.

St. Sylvester Day—Celebrated on New Year's Eve in Czech neighborhood streets with song and dance.

Sprinkling Day—Celebrated the first Monday of Easter week, this tradition allows boys to run through the neighborhood spraying the girls with little homemade "Spritzers."

St. Joseph Day—March 19—A day honoring the Czech national heritage with religious services.

Rogation Day—The Monday, Tuesday and Wednesday before the Feast of Ascension. After Catholics go to church, the priest goes through the farm fields praying for a good harvest.

Taroky, a card game, is popular among Czech-Americans.

Czech-Americans at Christmastime put up the traditional "*putzes*," nativity scenes that encompass special lighting, music and narration.

WEDDING CUSTOMS

One of the Czech-American wedding customs is that the groom is not allowed to see the bride in her gown on her wedding day until 2:00 in the afternoon, when a sponsor presents her and her parents to him.

The 1990 Census showed 1,582,000 people of Hungarian ancestry in the United States.

The period of major immigration from Hungary began in the 1880s. Some immigrants did not speak Hungarian but were Slovaks and Germans. By 1924, immigration dropped sharply until after World War II and the Communist takeover of the country. Then, immediately after the 1956 uprising against the Communist regime, more than 200,000 Hungarians came to the United States. These people are referred to as the "Fifty-sixers."

The Hungarian immigrants were predominantly Roman Catholic, and the remaining groups were Greek Catholic, Protestant and Jewish.

Many of the early arrivals found work in the coal mines of Pennsylvania and in other heavy industries. They were very unlikely to be farmers because they were urban immigrants. People of Hungarian ancestry tended to live in New York, New Jersey, Ohio and Pennsylvania, and, by 1980, almost half (48 percent, according to *We the People*, which was based on 1980 Census data) continued to live in these areas.

HOLIDAYS AND CUSTOMS

According to *Gale's Encyclopedia of Multicultural America*,[4] there is no such thing as a specifically Hungarian-American holiday, perhaps because the attention of most unassimilated Hungarian-Americans is focused on the mother country. The holidays that Hungarians in the United States celebrate combine religious and patriotic elements. Patriotic, that is, toward their mother country.

March 15—**Revolution Day in 1848**—Marked by religious and patriotic festivities.

August 20—**St. Stephen's Day**— Marked by religious and patriotic festivities.

October 23—**Revolution of 1956**, which was the most significant anti-Soviet uprising of the postwar period.

The 1990 Census showed 1,882,000 people in the United States of Slovak ancestry.

Slovak immigration to the United States didn't start until the 1880s and the 1890s, and, in Census reports, many Slovaks were counted as Czechs because they had their origin in what was Czechoslovakia.

Most Slovaks came from industrial cities in their homeland and, like most other Eastern Europeans, were unskilled workers who found jobs in heavy industries in the United States. They also worked as anthracite miners and were part of the group of immigrant workers who displaced the English-speaking coal miners who were primarily Irish and Welsh around the first decade of the twentieth century. By 1980 some of the counties in what was the old anthracite mining area still had a substantial number of people of Slovak ancestry. Many came to earn money and, when they saved enough, would then return to their homeland to buy property.

The religion of the Slovaks was usually Roman Catholic, and their associations or "lodges" were formed around their ethnic life. Their values and beliefs were that of a rural people. In 1980, western Pennsylvania and the Cuyahoga County area of Ohio had the largest group of people of Slovak ancestry in the United States.

The Slovaks, representing one-third of former Czechoslovakia's 15.5 million people, have demanded and won the renaming and separation of the former Czecho-Slovakia, so that Slovakia is a separate and independent country.

The Slovaks, who came from the poorer eastern part of the country, have called for hyphenating the country's name to help earn more recognition for their people. The Slovaks have frequently complained that many foreigners fail to recognize them as a separate people who have their own republic.

HOLIDAYS AND CUSTOMS

For Slovaks, **Christmas**'s big celebration comes on Christmas Eve. First there is dinner, followed by church. After the day's fast, fish, not turkey, is the main course of choice. Traditionally, no meat or dairy products pass the lips of Slovaks on December 24. According to Christmas traditions of the Slovak-Americans, when the first star winks against a clear, darkened **Christmas Eve** sky, it marks the end of the day's fast, and the job of the children in the family is to find the "Star of Bethlehem" up above. Mom's job is to have the feast ready.

Many of the traditional beliefs of Slovaks are a blend of folklore and superstitions.[5]

WEDDING CUSTOMS

Many Slovak brides have reverted to their ethnic tradition of wearing national dress for their wedding. Traditionally in Slovakia a bride would have worn this dress not just at her wedding but on special days throughout her life. This use of ethnic costume in American weddings is experiencing a resurgence as many ethnic Americans gain a sense of pride in wearing the clothing of their heritage.

The 1990 Census counted 1,045,000 people of Swiss ancestry in the United States.

The Swiss first started to arrive in the United States in the eighteenth and nineteenth centuries. The Swiss were different from other immigrant groups because they included people that spoke different languages, such as German, French and Italian, with German-speaking Swiss being the largest group. The Swiss were predominantly Protestant in religion. The first settlements were in southeast Pennsylvania, and many of those were attracted by William Penn, a Quaker from England who founded Pennsylvania and who welcomed people of all faiths. Many had been converts to the Amish and Mennonite religions; later there were many converts to the Mormon faith. By 1990, California had more Swiss-Americans than any other state, according to Census data. Today, many Amish and Mennonites are of Swiss ethnic origin.

In 1845, Swiss immigrants flocked to a village called New Glarus in the southwestern part of Wisconsin. By the 1880s, the growth of a successful cheese-making industry prompted more old Glarusians to come over from Switzerland and settle.

Cultural ties with Switzerland remain strong, so the Swiss influence continues to permeate this picturesque village. The sights of the buildings, the flower boxes, the smell of the locally made cheeses and the taste of Swiss chocolate are sensual reminders of the old world traditions.

HOLIDAYS AND CUSTOMS

Yodeling—Yodeling began as a strange falsetto warble used by Alpine herdsmen to call herds of cows from pasture to meadow. It rose over the mountains and across the oceans, finding homes in places as remote as Appalachia, where it became part of American country music.

"Yodeling is happiness. It's when we are having a nice party with the cows in the high pastures," Yodeling Festival Vice President Gerry Hess told the *New York Times* in 1991. The men invariably yodeled with their hands in their pockets. The women, wearing high lace coifs, hide their hands under striped aprons, as if it were part of their dress code. Yodeling usually stems from male chorus singing. The themes all have to do with mountains: the cows in the pastures, the beginning of summer, the herdsmen's broken romances. Then comes the yodel: one or at most two powerful voices soar out of the group, leaping robustly from tenor to soprano in a wordless, improvised song.

The William Tell and Heidi Festivals are held in parts of Wisconsin.

The chalet is a house style of rural Swiss origin that is often used as housing at ski resorts.

[1] from the 1980 Census Report, an *Atlas of American Diversity*

[2] Sharon Voros, the *New York Times*, August 26, 1990

[3] Sharon Voros, the *New York Times*, August 26, 1990

[4] Steven Bela Vardy and Thomas Szendney of Duquesne University

[5] Christina Binkley, *Scranton Times*, December, 1992

CHAPTER XIII:

RELIGION AND ETHNICITY— BAHA'I, BUDDHISM, BYZANTINE CATHOLICISM, CHRISTIANITY, CHRISTIAN SCIENCE, CHURCH OF SCIENTOLOGY, EASTERN ORTHODOX CHURCH, HARE KRISHNA, HINDUISM, ISLAM, JEHOVAH'S WITNESSES, JUDAISM*, MORMONS**, ORTHODOX (THE TERM), PAGANS, WICCA, SEVENTH-DAY ADVENTISTS, SIKH***, ZOROASTRIANISM, RELIGIOUS SYMBOLS, RELIGION AND EDUCATION, RELIGION AND THE WORKPLACE

*   - *See page 81-87*
** - *See page 218-224*
*** - *See page 135-137*

Religious devotion and diversity are on the rise in the United States, and the combination of these trends is creating new challenges and new demands for employers and educational administrators and in particular human resource professionals. As a result, handling future requests for religious accommodation may require employers and educators as well as others to demonstrate greater sensitivity, tolerance and understanding of various religious beliefs.

The influx and growth of world religions in America has forced Americans to learn more about different faiths and practices. In some years, major Christian, Jewish and Muslim observances nearly coincide, offering us, particularly employers and educators, a rare opportunity for comparison and understanding.

Many of the religions that may seem "new" to Americans are very old, and their schedules of observances often are confusing. For example, unlike Christmas (a major Christian holiday) which is celebrated at a fixed time according to the solar-based Gregorian calendar introduced in 1582, some religious observances are based on ancient lunar calendars and fall at different times of the year.

Take the holy month of Ramadan, a 30-day period (described in the section on Islam) during which Muslims fast from sunrise to sunset. Because Islam's festival calendar is based on a lunar cycle, Ramadan begins about 11 days earlier each Muslim year.

This rotating schedule can be problematic for Americans used to a fixed-date holy day. Employers have trouble understanding when Muslim workers need time off, and school teachers and educational administrators have to be reminded why Muslim children may refuse to eat lunch or get a drink of water.

The same situation can occur for Buddhists. Their religious observances are even more difficult to predict because different schools of Buddhism follow different calendars.

The Jewish calendar is also based on a lunar cycle, but it has a built-in formula—similar to leap year—for adjusting time so that holidays fall during the same season. Passover, for example, is associated with spring. The high holy days of Rosh Hashanah and Yom Kippur are associated with the fall. And Hanukkah, not really a holiday but a popular family ritual, is always observed within a few weeks of Christmas.

Unfortunately, many corporate, educational and governmental institutions may not be prepared to accommodate the many forms that religious accommodation can take.

Americans have become an increasingly religious people. Since 1900, the nation's church membership has grown twice as fast as the population.

In addition, Americans appear to hold a high degree of religious devotion. According to Gallup's Princeton Religious Research Center, 90 percent of American adults say religion is either very important or fairly important in their lives; only 9 percent say religion is not very important.

Given the fervor and increasing diversity of America's religious beliefs, it is probably not surprising that charges of religious discrimination in the workplace have jumped 43 percent in the decade of the 1990's according to the Equal Employment Opportunity Commission.

Clearly, a respectful approach can go a long way toward dealing with religion in the workplace as well as educational institutions. Human resource professionals in all fields as well as educational administration should always show that they respect the beliefs of their employees and students and should avoid judging those beliefs. As a sign of respect, and to help understand the importance of any given request, it is important to become familiar with the fundamental tenets of several major religions.*

At times during this discussion on religion and ethnicity you may find the phrase "movable date or dates" to describe religious holidays of a particular group, meaning that the holiday is not fixed on the Gregorian calendar, with which Americans are most familiar. The dates do not move, but the calendars upon which they are fixed are not calculated the same way as the Gregorian calendar. Remember, the Gregorian calendar, while used in the U.S., mark's time passage only in a small portion of the world's religion and cultures. Islamic, Buddhist, Hindu, Chinese, Judaism and some African areas, for example, use other calendars.

Also notable is the fact that in many religions and cultures a month does not have to be thirty-one, thirty, or in February's case, twenty-eight or twenty-nine days - a month can mean as few as nineteen days. And some days do not start at midnight but rather at the sightings of new or full moons. Further, in many cultures and religions we are not in the twentieth or after the millennium in the twenty-first century; according to the Islamic calendar we are in the fifteenth century, in the Chinese calendar we are in the forty-seventh, in the Jewish calendar we are in the Fifty-eighth, and in the Byzantine calendar we are in the seventy-sixth.

The link between religion and ethnicity is intimate—so close, in fact, that it seems impossible at times to distinguish one from the other in considering either a person's or a group's identity. Immigrants to the United States brought their religion with them as part of their heritage, and religion has shaped immigrants' adjustment to a new world with new values and new patterns of behavior. Over the years, religion has served as a force to maintain, shape and erode ethnic identity.[1] It has served as a source of unity and division within ethnic groups and one of the foundations upon which good, and sometimes bad relations among different ethnic groups are fostered. This section provides a presentation of several religions and religious issues that may not be familiar to all Americans, many of whom know primarily about Christianity (Protestantism and Catholicism) and Judaism.

Where appropriate, discussions of religious beliefs that are strongly identified with certain ethnic groups are discussed in sections about those groups. Following the descriptions of various religions, you'll find a summary of issues concerning religion and education and religion and the workplace.

*   Patricia Digh

285

SOME IMPORTANT POINTS FOR YOU TO BE AWARE OF
CONCERNING RELIGIOUS HOLIDAYS:

(a.)   The dates given on calendars for Muslim Holy days are only approximate since the precise timing can only be fixed a few days before the actual event.

(b.)   All Jewish holy days commence at dusk.

(c.)   Some religious traditions contain such observances and restrictions on their holy days that children and adults may be unable to attend school or work if they wish to observe their religious traditions correctly.

(d.)   Sikhs and Buddhists are sometimes prepared to defer the celebration of significant feasts to the weekend closest to the actual event.

(e.)   Festivals and religious dates of some Asian festivals are subject to variation in both date and custom. This is understandable when one considers the vastness of the Indian sub-continent. Buddhist festivals and holidays in particular are difficult to generalize about since in different countries in which large Buddhist communities are to be found, different traditions and festivals are observed.

(f.)   Because the U.S. Congress (in 1980) decided that questions pertaining to religion could not be asked in the decennial censuses, no data (exact) can be provided on the Jewish population in the U.S.A.—However, Jews are an ethnic group, as well as a religious group, and clearly have a sense of shared identity as a special people.

The following alphabetical list of some major religions in the United States is an introduction to—not an exhaustive treatment of these religions.

Baha'i is a 150-year-old religion that teaches that all the great prophets represent the same divine spirit reaching out to humanity. Baha'i teaches that all religions are one, that there is only one God, and that the time has come for all humanity to unite and live in peace. The word Baha'i comes from the name of the founder of the faith—Baha'u'llah (the glory of God). Baha'i simply means "a follower."

The year 1992 marked 100 years since the death of the Baha'i prophet Baha'u'llah. There have been just two world congresses of the faith: one in London in 1963; the other in New York City in 1992. There are 5 million Baha'is in the world and 110,000 of them in the United States. In the United States there are approximately 7,000 localities where Baha'is reside. There are approximately 1,700 local Spiritual Assemblies, the Baha'is' democratically elected governing bodies. The Baha'is believe the world has finally come to embrace the religion's ideas of multiculturalism, equality of men and women, interdependence and what they have long called a New World Order. "All of humanity is waking up to these principles that were talked about more than 100 years ago," said Brad Bkornoy, a Baha'i spokesman.

The Baha'i faith is not widely known even among religious scholars, but it is nevertheless not generally regarded as a cult.

Iran is the land where Baha'u'llah was born and where the Baha'i people have long suffered persecutions at the hands of the country's Muslim majority. Their goal is to have salvation in the world and not in isolation. Baha'i makes few demands on the faithful. Sex outside of marriage and alcohol are prohibited. Members are encouraged to vote, but they are restrained from holding partisan political office since such roles can be divisive. Baha'is can, however, hold nonpartisan public offices, like judgeships. One of the United States' most famous Baha'is was musician Dizzy Gillespie.

In Baha'i there is no clergy. Decisions are made by the democratically elected bodies called Spiritual Assemblies. The Baha'i world headquarters is in Haifa, Israel, where Baha'u'llah is buried, but there is only a small community of 650 Baha'is in Israel. The greatest concentration of Baha'is is in India, where 2 million live. Other large concentrations of Baha'is are in Iran, Bolivia, Guyana and the Pacific Islands.

The only Baha'i temple in the United States is in Wilmette, Illinois. Elsewhere in the United States, Baha'is meet for prayer in small groups in adherents' homes. Services are held according to the Baha'i calendar, which is made up of nineteen months of nineteen days each. (Additional days are added to make the calendar consistent with the Western calendar.)

Baha'is reach out through periodic home gatherings they call Firesides. The Baha'i notion of "progressive revelation" contends that God sends messengers to earth in each era and that the prophecy of each builds on that of his predecessors.

Baha'u'llah is the most recent Baha'i prophet, but not necessarily the greatest. Each prophet is right for the time and place to which he is sent, according to Don Nossa, a Baha'i follower.

Although Baha'i teaches that all religions are true, when one becomes a Baha'i, he or she gives up any former faith and religious practices.

WHO IS THE BAB?

The Baha'i faith and its challenging ideas originated in Persia (Iran) in 1844. In that year, a young man who called himself the Bab (or "Gate") began to teach that God would soon "make manifest" a world teacher to unite men and women and usher in an age of peace. In 1863, Baha'u'llah announced to the remaining followers of the Bab (20,000 of them had been killed by the government) that he was the chosen manifestation of God for that age.

HOLIDAYS AND CUSTOMS

The Baha'i year consists of nineteen months of nineteen days each (i.e. 361 days), with the addition of four days (five in leap years) between the eighteenth and nineteenth months in order to adjust the calendar to the solar year. The Bab named the months after the attributes of God. The **Baha'i New Year**, like the ancient Persian New Year, is astronomically fixed, commencing at the March equinox (March 21), and the Baha'i era commences with the year of the Bab's declaration (1844 A.D.). The Baha'i day starts and ends at sunset, and consequently the date of the celebration of Baha'i feasts should be adjusted to conform to the Baha'i calendar. There are holy days on which Baha'is don't work, which include April 21 through May 2.

The following three days mark the anniversary of the declaration of Baha'u'llah: The first day of Ridvan, the ninth day of Ridvan, and the twelfth day of Ridvan.

May 23—The anniversary of the declaration of the Bab.

November 12—The anniversary of the birth of the Baha'u'llah.

October 20 —The anniversary of the birth of the Bab.

May 29—The anniversary of the ascension of Baha'u'llah.

July 9—The anniversary of the martyrdom of the Bab.

March 21—The Feast of Naw-Ruz.

According to Baha'i laws, work is forbidden on the **Nine Holy Days**. Believers who have independent businesses or shops should refrain from working on these days. Those who work for the government should, on religious grounds, make an effort to be excused from work; all believers, whoever their employers, should do likewise.[2]

SOME EXPLANATIONS OF THE HOLIDAYS:

The Nineteen-Day Feast—"The Nineteen-Day Feast was inaugurated by the Bab and ratified by Baha'u'llah in his Holy Book, *The Aqdas*, so that people may gather together and outwardly show fellowship and love, that the Divine mysteries may be disclosed. The object is concord, that through this fellowship hearts may become perfectly united, and reciprocity and mutual helpfulness be established...." (Abudu'l-Baha)

The Fast—The period of the fast is March 2 through March 20. "We have commanded you to pray and fast from the beginning of maturity (fifteen years); this is ordained by God, your Lord and the Lord of your forefathers.... The traveler, the ailing, those who are with child or giving such are not bound by the fast.... Abstain from food and drink, from sunrise to sundown, and beware lest desire deprive you of this grace that is appointed in the Book." (Azda)

Naw-Ruz— "The Naw-Ruz Feast (Baha'i New Year) should be held March 21 before sunset and has nothing to do with the Nineteen-Day Feast. The Nineteen-Day Feast is administrative in function, whereas the Naw-Ruz is the New Year, a feast of hospitality and rejoicing." (Shoghi Effendi)[3]

Feast of Ridvan—The period of Ridvan is April 21 through May 2, covering Baha'u'llah's Declaration in the Garden of Ridva outside Baghdad in 1863. He declared that he was the messenger of God who had been predicted by Bab.

Buddhism can be considered a religious practice or a non-religious discipline and set of ethical and moral values. Buddhism began some 525 years before Christ, when Siddhartha Gautama, the son of an Indian nobleman, found perfect enlightenment through rigorous physical and spiritual discipline. Buddhism is as much a system of philosophy, psychology and education as it is a religion. Buddhists believe in a multitude of gods but do not see such deities as Westerners view God.

There is no easy way to describe Buddhism. A religion—or a philosophy, depending on whom you talk to—that officially has been in existence for more than 2,500 years, Buddhism has more than 2,000 sects, each with its own set of rules—or no rules.

Unlike most religions, Buddhism teaches that the universe never begins or ends. "The cosmos we live in is only one of infinite number," states Frank Reynolds, a professor at the University of Chicago. "There definitely is an apocalyptic end to our world, by wind, fire or water." But there is no date attached to the destruction of the world, many Buddhists believe, and the universe endures.

Buddhism incorporates various doctrines. One Buddhist metaphor speaks of the afterlife as a passage into heaven or hell or another human existence. The individual's destiny is determined by karma, the effect of his deeds. This passage is sometimes represented as a judgment, presided over by a divine figure. There is no single judgment day in most Buddhist sects. Heavens and hells are usually temporary states until the individual is consigned to another rebirth. The goal is to escape suffering and attain Nirvana, a condition beyond being or nonbeing.

Some Buddhists believe that another Buddha named Maitreya, who is somewhat akin to the messiah, will come and establish an ideal society. "This will bring an easier access to Nirvana," states Professor Reynolds.

The sects have come about through various interpretations of the teaching of a man considered to be the historical Buddha, an Asian named Gautama who lived around 500 B.C. Or Siddhartha. Or Sakyamuni. Depending on whom you talk to.

"Because of the different languages that became connected with Buddhism, the references to the historical Buddha are different," according to the Dr. Ratanasara, the spiritual leader of the College of Buddhist Studies in Los Angeles. He says Gautama Buddha was born to wealthy parents and first lived a life of excess. When Gautama Buddha saw that his lifestyle did not bring him pleasure, he went to the other extreme, depriving himself of clothing, food and shelter in order to find true happiness. He didn't see any gain in suffering from either of his pursuits, so he took "the middle path;" he tried to live his life comfortably, but without too many material possessions. That way, there was no suffering.

Suffering became Gautama Buddha's focus and led him to derive the Four Noble Truths, his philosophy comprised of the ways to identify a person's suffering, to determine what is causing the suffering, to recognize that the suffering can be erased and to make a list of the ways to do the erasing.

"The Buddha found that, by following his own philosophy, he removed all of his own suffering. This is the fundamental basis for Buddhism: the cessation of suffering, which is caused by desire to find enlightenment," Ratanasara told Kyle Wagner of the *Naples Daily News (Florida)*.

"Buddha," then, is a term applied to anyone who has achieved enlightenment. This is not as simple as it sounds.

Depending on the type of Buddhism you follow, there are a myriad of steps, paths and ceremonies you might go through to attain the enlightened state, also known as "*nirvana*." Included in these steps is the Noble Eightfold Path, which is what Gautama Buddha derived from the Four Noble Truths to help students end their suffering.

The Eightfold Path, according to Dr. Ratanasara, first involves coming to harmonious understanding of suffering and possessing a strong desire to achieve an end to suffering. Once that aspect, referred to as *Prajna* (wisdom), has been attained, the second segment of the path, *Sila* (more integrity), may be attempted.

"The second portion of the Eightfold Path often is the most difficult," Ericson Proper, a Buddhist scholar who heads the Sakya Center for Buddhist Studies and Meditation in southwest Florida, told Wagner of the *Daily News*. "This is where you learn three things: how to speak in a clear manner that aids your path to enlightenment, how to conduct yourself in a manner that aids your path, and how to pursue your life, be it in work or private, to carry you into enlightenment."

The final three steps in the path are called *Samadhi* (concentration). Once at this level, Buddhists will attempt to put forth the proper actions toward enlightenment, will try to maintain the proper frame of mind, and will engage in what some call "perfect meditation."

"Meditation involves contemplating the direction given by the Buddha and applying it to everyday life," Proper said. It takes a conscious effort to meditate properly, and it involves dedication and discipline to achieve results.

There are two types of meditation: concentration (such as breathing techniques) and analytical. "Concentration is a way of calming oneself," Proper said. "Analytical offers the Buddhist a practical way to reflect on teachings and work through conflicts."

Dr. Ratanasara explains that chanting is a form of meditation; it offers a way to relieve the mind of negativity and to focus on more important things. A mantra, a formula of syllables, often is employed to offer something reflective to concentrate on.

Not all Buddhists chant; not all meditate. Some do neither; some do both. The differences among the sects appear to be a matter of interpretation, primarily between helping oneself and healing others.

"Theravada is the most literal interpretation of Buddha's teaching ever recorded," Proper said. Buddha conducted what is called the first Pali council soon after he created the path. He met with sixteen *Arhats* (a person who resides in a state of peace), and they formalized the Theravada (Way of the Elders) scriptures. After that peaceful session, according to Proper, the second Pali council was held, and that's where the trouble began.

"There was dissension among the *Arhats*," Proper said. This is where the Mahavana sect came about, along with its offshoots, such as Vairayana Zen.

The United States has had a hand in creating a few sects itself, as well as offering refuge for traditional orders.

"In Asia, countries are separate," said Ratanasara. "There is little chance for the sects to mix. It is almost impossible to determine how many Buddhists there are in America. We are estimating that there are 4 to 5 million practicing Buddhists in this country. We have 300 centers for study in Los Angeles." This may be an overestimate. In a nationwide poll, the City University of New York found only 1 million Buddhists. The most recent figures from the American Buddhist Congress, from 1992, put the worldwide Buddhist population at more than 665 million.

"Buddhism is not money-oriented. It does not worship any kind of idols. It worships life, and the people work toward making it peaceful for all," Ratanasara said. "Buddhism teaches that we must be satisfied with what we have inside ourselves."

Tibetan Buddhism is a sect in which the structure concentrates specifically on the suffering of the individual. It focuses on how to tame the mind and is geared toward promoting self-development and self-growth. To Tibetan Buddhists, "the Refuge" is where students go who formally indicate their desire to become Buddhists.

And, in Tibetan Buddhism, the female Tara is the activity of the Buddha. Tara also is the remover of obstacles: by removing poisons, she has power to heal people.

According to Aril Goodman, writing in the *New York Times*,[4] meditation is only one of the aspects of Tibetan Buddhism, which is considered particularly authentic because the sect was preserved and largely untouched by outside influences well into the twentieth century.

The Tibetan gods are not omnipotent, nor did they create the world. Rather, they are regarded as eternal forces of love and compassion.

Seen through Christian eyes, the Dalai Lama, who is the spiritual leader of Tibetan Buddhism, might be regarded as a living angel who is reincarnated in different human beings over time to lead people in both spiritual and temporal realms.

Buddhists have grown in number in the United States for two reasons. One is the influx of immigrants into the U.S. from Japan, China and Vietnam; the other is the adoption of Buddhism by Westerners, some of whom were encouraged by the example of Beat writers such as Jack Kerouac and Allen Ginsberg and composer John Cage.

In the 1950s and 1960s, Zen Buddhism, with its emphasis on silent meditation, was popular. In the 1970s and 1980s, Tibetan Buddhism took root and flourished outside its homeland.

In Thailand, a Buddhist monk is considered one of the country's best and brightest, a holy man whose virtue is needed to bring blessings on the people. He is referred to by his followers as "venerable," and, when he wanders the street, Thais offer him gifts.

In the United States, where there are about forty Thai Buddhist temples, a monk is a self-imposed captive, spending his days in prayer, study and instruction. He is afraid to wander the streets, where he might get lost and need to speak to an American.

But Thai monks, according to Norm Cohen of the *New York Times*, do not come to the United States to better their lives. The monks come because they are needed by the Thais in the U.S., and they generally keep to themselves. Typically, Thai monks in the United States rise at 5 a.m., chant and pray for two hours, then study holy books; in particular they read a forty-eight-volume set of books that can take a lifetime to learn.

The Thai Buddhist temples in the United States are often plain buildings. A Thai temple, unlike a church or synagogue, is not a place for communal prayer. There are no pews. A few chairs in an anteroom are set up for visitors, and on a wooden table visitors can leave money to support the monks.

According to Mettaysado Bhikkhu, a Thai Buddhist monk at Harvard Divinity School, Thais need to do good things for the monks in the hope of attracting good things to them. Monks are in a field of merit. It is an agricultural metaphor—if you plant one rice seed, you get a plant and perhaps 1,000 rice seeds. If people do good things for the monks, then it will bring good things for all the people, it is believed.

HOLIDAYS AND CUSTOMS

Theravada Sect—Ancestors from Burma, Cambodia, India, Laos, Thailand, Sri Lanka. All holidays are lunar days and vary in date.

Magha Puja—One of the holiest holidays; it marks the occasion when 1,250 of Buddha's disciples gathered spontaneously to hear him speak. The day falls on the full moon of the third lunar month, sometime toward the end of February. On this day Buddhists flock to the temple, observe the five precepts, listen to a sermon, serve food for monks and meditate or take part in other forms of meritorious activities. They also perform circumambulation, walking around a shrine or a Buddha image three times as a gesture of faith and respect in the Holy Triple Gem.

Versakha Puja—The most sacred of all Buddhist days, it celebrates the birth, death and enlightenment of the Buddha. It takes place on the full moon of the sixth lunar month. This is celebrated in very much the same way as the Magha, but on a larger scale and with more enthusiasm. This day is also known as Buddha Day, and it commemorates the three important events in the Buddha's life as mentioned.

Asalha Puja—This marks the beginning of Buddhist Lent and is the anniversary of Buddha's sermon to the first five disciples. The day is celebrated by Buddhists for three reasons: it is the day the Buddha delivered the First Discourse; it is the day the religion was established; and it is the day the order of Sangha came into existence and the Holy Gem became complete. It is also known as Sangha Day. It occurs on the full moon of the eighth lunar month.

Vassana—The beginning of the three-month period when monks stay in their temple to study and meditate. This takes place after the full moon of the eighth lunar month. Religious activities increase for both monks and laity.

Pavarana—This day celebrates the Buddha's return to earth after spending one Lent season preaching in Heaven. All the monks and lay followers assemble in halls in monasteries, where the lay followers take part in activities such as observing five of the eight precepts, listening to a sermon, and meditating. Various cultural programs may be observed and staged to educate and entertain people at this very merry occasion, which occurs the day of the full moon in the eleventh lunar month. This is also known as Lent-ending Day.

Kathina Day—This is the end of the three-month retreat by monks and is celebrated for a one-month period after Pavarana. It is often called the Kathina ceremony or, more popularly, the Robe Presentation Ceremony. At the ceremony monks in ancient India used to sew their clothes on. Now, it allows clothes to be presented to monks who have completed the three-month retreat.

<u>**Mahayana Sect**</u>—Ancestors from China, Japan, Tibet, Korea, Vietnam. All days are solar and dates are fixed.

Nirvana Day—February 15—Observes the passing of Sakyamuni, the original Buddha, into Nirvana. He obtained enlightenment and became a Buddha.

Buddha Day—April 8—This service commemorates the birth of Gautama in Lumbini Garden. Amida, the Buddha of Infinite Wisdom and Compassion, manifested himself among men in the person Gautama.

Bon—July 15—This day is an occasion for rejoicing in the enlightenment offered by the Buddha. It is often referred to as a "Gathering of Joy." Buddha had saved the life of the mother of Moggallana. The day is in remembrance of all those who have died.

Bodhi Day—December 8—This celebrates the enlightenment of Buddha.

SHINTO

An indigenous Japanese tradition that predated the advent of Buddhism, Taoism and Confucianism into Japanese society which occurred about 500 to 700 A.D., Shinto centers on the worship of Kami, spirits representing that which is sacred, pure and powerful. Kami can be mythological deities who created the world; natural features such as waterfalls, trees and boulders; or emperors or other powerful humans. The ancient religion has 2.8 million practitioners, and its shrines are popular attractions during seasonal festivals.

Byzantine Catholics are in union with Roman Catholics and as such recognize the Pope as the visible head of the Church. Both faiths have evolved since the establishment of the Catholic Church, with Roman Catholics in the Western world and Byzantine Catholics in the Near East and Eastern world. Consequently, the Byzantine rite has incorporated many of the various Eastern traditions and customs.

Among the most notable of these traditions and customs are icons, religious images that are meant to represent holy figures. And, as in the Eastern Orthodox churches, there is an impressive icon screen at the entrance to the sanctuary of a Byzantine Catholic church that represents a passage between heaven and earth. The figures on the icon are not meant to be realistic, but representative of people they portray. The Christ child does not look like an infant, but like a small human being. This represents the belief that Christ was a man from birth.

Again as in the Eastern Orthodox Church, the use of icons should not be equated with idolatry, the worship of a physical object as a god. Icons are meant to represent holy figures. By kissing an icon, the believer is expressing a love for a holy figure. It is no different than a person who holds a picture of a loved one close to his or her heart.

Similar to the Eastern Orthodox, the Byzantine rite also uses a three-barred cross. The top bar represents the inscription above Christ's head when he was crucified and the bottom slanted bar represents his foot rest. However, according to the symbolic meaning, the top bar represents St. Peter, the Apostle of the West, and the bottom bar represents St. Andrew, the Apostle of the East. The cross is considered to be a union between East and West.

The Divine Liturgy in the Byzantine Church is comparable to the Roman Catholic Mass. It is designed to appeal to all the senses. Icons are visually appealing. Incense represents the prayers rising to God. The Liturgy is sung or chanted, and Holy Communion of bread and wine is distributed with a spoon. Byzantine Catholics believe that, through consecration, communion becomes the body and blood of Christ.

As in other Eastern Rite ceremonies, the blessing of the Easter baskets is done according to Slavic custom.

Byzantine Catholics are also known in the United States as Greek Catholics, Eastern Rite Catholics, Rusin, Carpatho-Rusin or Carpatho-Ruthenian. Because the origin of Byzantine Catholics extended to the eastern part of the Roman Empire, the early centers of the faith were in Alexandria, Antioch, Jerusalem and Constantinople. Byzantine Catholics follow the Gregorian calendar and observe the same traditional holidays of the Western **Roman Catholic** Church. However, some special days are observed, such as the **Patronage of the Mother** on October 1, which is celebrated like May Day.

Even though the eastern rite of the Catholic Church or Byzantine Catholics are in union with Roman Catholics of the western church, a notable difference is that priests are allowed to marry and have children.

A religion based on the belief that Jesus, called the Christ, was the Messiah foretold by Jewish prophets. Modern scholarship paints a tortured early history of Christianity, depicting the years after Jesus's crucifixion by the Romans circa 30 as a time of power struggles and confused theology. It is possible to say and believe that such confusion persists in Christianity's different branches even as the world approaches the millennium—among them Roman Catholicism, Eastern Orthodoxy and Protestantism.

A Christian belief besides the affirmation of Jesus as the Messiah is the central conviction shared by Roman Catholics, Eastern Orthodox and Protestants—that Jesus is the son of God who offers believers forgiveness of sins and eternal life through his death and resurrection.

Many Christian customs are mentioned in chapters as they relate to various ethnic groups. Some of the Christian traditions are as follows:

Advent—Four Sundays before Christmas—This period starts the season preparing for Christmas and is one of the most joyful season of the year. Children sometimes receive advent calendars and families and churches display advent wreaths. The wreath is a display of green in a circle with four candles. Each Sunday of Advent a candle is lit.

Christmas—December 25—Commemorates the day that Jesus was born.

Shrove Tuesday/Carnival—the Tuesday before Ash Wednesday—This is the last day before Lent, the forty-day period of abstinence that ends with Easter. This day has inspired traditions and festivals all over the world. At one time, particularly in the Middle Ages, Lent meant a period of fast and abstinence that precluded the use of meat, butter and eggs. Therefore, on the day before Lent began, people used up all the butter and eggs in the kitchen. This included making pancakes and was especially prevalent in German homes. Since the day always fell on a Tuesday, the French called in Mardi Gras, or Fat Tuesday. In England it was known as Shrove Tuesday because people went to church to shrive, or confess, their sins. Also, since people considered it the last chance to have fun before the austerities of Lent, Mardi Gras also became the climax of days, weeks and sometimes months of festivities. The masked balls and costume parades have come to be known as Carnival. In Brazil, Carnival is the major holiday of the year. In Germany the days of Carnival are known as *Fastnacht*, or the "Eve of the Fast" are so enthusiastically celebrated that they are known as the fifth season. New Orleans celebrates with great parades, balls and festivities.

Ash Wednesday—the first day of Lent—Forty-six days before Easter, this is a period of abstinence that recalls Jesus' forty days in the wilderness. The ashes, which used to be showered over notorious sinners who came to church in sackcloth, became a symbol of penance for everyone. Today, Catholics and some other Christians still receive ashes, which are place on their forehead by a priest.

Palm Sunday—Sunday before Easter—This day commemorates Jesus' entry into Jerusalem. People greeted him by waving palm branches, and today many churches distribute blessed palms at the service.

Good Friday—Friday before Easter—This day commemorates the day Jesus was convicted of treason against the Roman Empire and crucified. Many people observe the day with solemn services or processions that reenact Jesus' walk to his death, carrying his own cross.

Easter—the Sunday following the first full moon after the Vernal Equinox in late March. May fall between March 22 and April 25—The most important day of the Christian year. It celebrates the resurrection of Jesus. That morning, according to the Gospel of St. Luke, visitors to Jesus' tomb found it empty. An angel of the Lord appeared and told them Jesus had risen. In the following days Jesus appeared several times to his disciples, who began to understand the full meaning of his death. Jesus had died for the sins of mankind, and his miraculous victory over death offered the promise of rebirth for everyone who believed in him. (Eastern Orthodox Easter only differs from this in that Easter must follow Passover.) The egg and the rabbit have become symbols for Easter because it was suggested that the word "Easter" came from "*Esotre,*" a goddess of spring and fertility whose symbol was a hare.

Ascension—Forty days after Easter—During the forty days after his resurrection, Jesus met several times with his Apostles, telling them to carry on his teachings. On the fortieth day he led them out to the Mount of Olives, where they watched as he ascended to Heaven.

Pentecost—Fifty days after Easter—The twelve Apostles gathered ten days after Jesus' ascension and the holy spirit descended on them. It appeared to them as though tongues of fire were sitting on each of them, and when they spoke, they were filled with the holy spirit. It is called Pentecost because it takes place fifty days after Easter. The day came to be considered the beginning of the Christian Church because it inspired the Apostles to begin their preaching of the Gospel.

Corpus Christi (Roman Catholic)—Eight weeks after Easter. In commemoration of Jesus' Last Supper with his disciples, Christians receive communion. Worshippers take bread and wine, consecrate it and eat it just as Jesus instructed his disciples, when he said that these things were his body and blood. Roman Catholic and Eastern Orthodox churches teach that Jesus is present in the bread and wine, and they celebrate this miracle on Corpus Christi.

All Saints' Day—Catholic and many Protestant churches celebrate this day to honor the saints.

All Souls' Day—The day after All Saints' Day when Catholics remember the dead. Many Catholics attend services and visit cemeteries to honor their ancestors

Reformation Sunday, or Reformation Day—The day commemorates the sixteenth-century movement in Western Europe that aimed at reforming some doctrines and practices of the Roman Catholic Church and resulted in the establishment of the Protestant Christian Churches. It is celebrated the Sunday before October 31.

In 1879 fifteen people living in the Boston area met together and voted to form an organization to be called The Church of Christ, Scientist. They were all students of Mary Baker Eddy, and it was on motion of Mrs. Eddy that they voted to "organize a church designed to commemorate the word and works of our master, which should reinstate primitive Christianity and its lost element of healing." That is the reason given for the church's coming into existence, according to the manual of the mother church authored by Mrs. Eddy.

Mary Baker Eddy, the founder of Christian Science, was born in New Hampshire in 1821 and grew up in a devout Congregational family. In 1866 she was healed of a severe injury, as she read the account of one of Jesus' healings in the New Testament. This led to her discovery of what she came to understand as the Science of Christianity. She saw her healing not as a miracle but completely in line with God's law, and for the next forty-five years she explored and taught Christian healing on exactly that basis. The manual of the mother church, which she wrote, is considered to be the constitution of the Christian Science movement.

The central authority of the mother church, based in Boston, is counterbalanced by the democratic self-government of the branch churches. The churches do not have ministers. Mrs. Eddy ordained the Bible and the book *Science and Health* to be the pastor of her church.

Christian Scientists are Christian and believers in Jesus Christ. Heaven and Hell are states of thought, not places. Christian Scientists do not believe in medical science, or what they call "*materia medica.*" They generally do not accept medical care for themselves, and many do not permit it for their children. They believe they can heal through prayer.

The questions most often asked about Christian Science deal with the matter of "healing." Healing as seen by them is an important proof of God's care for man, but it is only one element in the full salvation that is the goal of Christianity. A Christian Scientist relies on God instead of drugs for healing. The Christian Science method of healing is purely spiritual; it calls for a mental and moral change for finding one's true relationship to God. Consequently, it is thought that this doesn't mix well with medical treatment because such treatment is a system that looks into the body for causes and treats disease on a physical and chemical basis. The Church rejects "faith healing" as a description of its proceedings, claiming that its "scientific" methods are not reliant on miracles and are nothing less than a rediscovery of the methods of Jesus Christ himself.

A person known as a Christian Science practitioner is one who has given himself full-time to the public practice of Christian Science healing. The work is viewed as both a ministry and a profession. Since the practitioner also has to earn a living, his patients pay him as they would a doctor or psychiatrist. Practitioners are listed in an official church publication. On average they charge between $10 and $50 for treatment. In 1984 Allison Phanney Jr., then the chief editor of the Church's religious periodicals, wrote in the *Christian Science Sentinel* that "Christian Science," contrary to some recent misinterpretation, is not positive thinking, mind care or an alternative health care system.[5] The Christian Science belief is that one goes about healing through prayer and by turning completely to God for the answer to one's problem—whether that problem is a disease in the body or a discord in the family. Prayer in Christian Science means the desire to let God's will be done.

One of the church's best-known publications is the daily international newspaper the *Christian Science Monitor*. It reaches more than 120 countries throughout the world. About half of its subscribers are not Christian Scientists. Many of them are journalists and members of Congress and Parliament.

For Christian Scientists, Sunday church services consist of Bible reading, silent prayer and the Lord's Prayer, referred to as a lesson-sermon. Lessons are issued on a quarterly basis by the Mother Church (the Boston headquarters of the Church of Christian Science). The Bible lessons comprise the sermon. Each weekly Lesson-Sermon is made up of selections from the King James Version of the Bible and from the publication *Science and Health*, with a key to the Scriptures. Two readers both read aloud both passages. On Wednesdays, Christian Science churches hold public meetings, where, in addition to reading, people share experiences, testimonies of healing and remarks on Christian Science.

A peculiarity of the Christian Science Church is its prohibition of giving out membership figures, but the estimated total is 150,000 to 200,000 in the United States. There are more than 3,500 Christian Science churches, societies and college organizations in some fifty-one countries.

Christian Science is a native American species of religion, a distinct American contribution to the world's wide array of belief systems. "Christian Science at one moment seems respectable almost to the point of colorlessness, and at the next moment seems wildly unconventional, almost to the point of dangerousness," wrote Peter Steinfels, the religion writer of the *New York Times*.[6] He added: "A faith whose 'discoverer and founder' is always referred to as 'Mrs. Eddy' can never mask its genteel face." No doubt Mary Baker Eddy was at least partly the invalid Victorian author whose occasionally muddled metaphysical prose Mark Twain gleefully satirized.[7] She was also a rebel against Puritanism, yet one whose relentless pursuit of religious truth and organization of a new church demanded a good deal of Puritan iron.

Struggling to reconcile human suffering with her belief in loving and sovereign divinity, Mrs. Eddy concluded that the material world of the senses is not God's creation. It is instead a tragic misperception blocking access to spiritual reality. Mrs. Eddy's desire to restore bodily healing to a central place in Christianity, far from a doctrine of childish faith or positive thinking, was only part of a larger call to seek redemption from sinfulness and the illusion of material life through constant prayer and self-renunciation. Christian Science fosters a life of discipleship that other faiths can recognize immediately.

HOLIDAYS AND CUSTOMS

In general Christian Scientists celebrate **Christian** holidays. Incidentally, Christian Scientists do not smoke or drink.

The Church of Scientology was founded in Washington, D.C. by L. Ron Hubbard in 1952. Mr. Hubbard was also the director of the first organized church, from 1955 until 1959. By 1995 the organization had 2,000 "spiritual centers" in 107 countries. A spiritual center serves its local members as well as a center (in some cases) for ministerial training.

Mr. Hubbard developed a system called "dianetics" that remains the core of Scientology. It maintains that through years of counseling and study, a person moves through progressively difficult steps toward a condition called "clear"—the elimination of all painful memories and undesirable emotions.

For over four decades, critics and skeptics in the United States fought the Church of Scientology's claim of being a religion. In 1993, the Internal Revenue Service ruled that the church qualified as a religion for non-profit status.

In 1975, Mr. Hubbard was intent on finding a home base for his religion, which by that time had come under criticism in several countries. According to a report that appeared in the *New York Times* on December 1, 1997, the church paid $2.3 million in cash to buy a historic hotel building that was the symbolic heart of downtown Clearwater, Florida.

The report states that Scientology had come to Clearwater with a written plan to take control of the city. Confusion ensued and in 1982, the city commission passed an ordinance imposing stiff record-keeping and disclosure requirements on charitable and religious groups.

Scientology sued the city, and in 1993 a federal appeals court overturned the ordinance as unconstitutional. The city had passed the measure, the court said, with "an underlying objective to employ the tax laws to discriminate against Scientology, a purpose that is patently offensive to the First Amendment.

In the years after the Church of Scientology has tried to be seen as a good citizen of Clearwater and it is most visible in the downtown section of the city of 100,000.

Scientology describes itself as the only major new church to emerge in the twentieth century and boasts eight million followers worldwide by 1998, though critics put the number as far less. Though its main offices are in Los Angeles and Clearwater, the church maintains missions in many foreign countries, including Germany and Great Britain. Its founder, Mr. Hubbard, said people were immortal spirits who have lived through many lifetimes and accumulated traumatic memories that are obstacles to achieving their full potential.

Adherents believe those afflictions can be eliminated through a series of counseling courses known as auditing. Most of the courses involve detailed questioning about Scientology and the members' lives by church ministers who monitor responses with a crude lie detector they call an E-meter. The results after years of courses is an individual who is clear of problems.

Russian fur traders in Alaska first brought the Orthodox Church to North America. However, the tradition was spread mostly by immigrants arriving from Eastern Europe years later.

The Eastern Orthodox Church split with the Roman Catholic Church in 1054 A.D. Minor differences in theology and liturgy existed between Western and Eastern believers. But that didn't really cause the split. The main reasons were political differences between the Byzantine Empire in the East and the Holy Roman Empire in the West, as well as the issue of papal authority. The issue of papal authority continues to divide the two groups.

The two sides later reached a compromise and got back together in 1071. But bad feelings remained. Western crusaders severed the relationship forever by capturing Constantinople in 1204. After this, the Eastern Orthodox Church became the dominant church in Eastern Europe.

It arrived in Russia during the time of Peter the Great. The Russian Czar sent his scholars looking for religion, and they came back with the Eastern Orthodox variety of Christianity.

Believers in the Eastern Orthodox Church commemorate the crucifixion of Jesus Christ with a cross that differs from those used in other Christian denominations. It is a "triple cross," with three horizontal sections. The top bar represents the sign that proclaimed Jesus as the "King of the Jews." The middle section stands for the cross bar that bore the hands of Christ. The bottom section represents a foot rest. These foot rests were attached to crosses, and the bar is angled because the weight of Christ's body made the foot rest turn diagonally.

The head of the Russian Orthodox Church, called the Metropolitan, remains in Russia to this day. In 1970, American bishops received permission to govern themselves. The self-governing body was named the Orthodox Church in America. The Orthodox Church in America has 1 million members and is the second largest of Eastern Orthodox religions in the U.S. Since 1970 the Orthodox Church in America has completed mergers with Romanian, Bulgarian and Albanian Orthodox churches in the United States.

The services of the Eastern Orthodox Church are called divine liturgies. As part of the service the priest spreads incense through the church and upon the congregation. This incense reminds believers that when they are praying, their prayers will go up, like the incense does, into heaven.

Eastern Orthodox priests don't dwell on Hell, but they do believe one must attain salvation. In the Eastern Orthodox Church that means attending services faithfully, observing Church laws and praying for the forgiveness of sins.

The Orthodox Church observes many holy days, feast days and saint days. Everybody in the Orthodox Church venerates icons. Eastern Orthodox believers do not pray to icons, but rather the icons help them visualize when they pray. An icon is a painted portrait, usually of a saint, and is of special significance. The paintings are made by people who specialize solely in icon painting. An "icon screen" usually separates the nave in the church where parishioners sit and the altar table. The "royal doors," which open onto the altar, are two swinging doors in the middle of the screen. Only the priest can enter through these doors. The congregation usually stands through the entire traditional Orthodox service. Generally speaking, an icon is a presentation of a person important to Orthodox Christianity. Orthodox churches are usually filled with icons of biblical figures or saints.

To people unfamiliar with Orthodox thought, icons simply may seem to be religious pictures. Yet, as iconographers and Orthodox theologians are quick to point out, icons are much more than pictures. The primary function of the icon is theological, not decorative. They are often called "theology in color." The use of the icon by Orthodox Christians is virtually without parallel in contemporary Christianity, and the task of explaining its function is sometimes difficult. Orthodox Christians also like to describe icons as "windows to heaven," passages into the spiritual world. You don't worship an icon as if it were an idol. It becomes a channel of grace, like a mediator.

In the United States there are an estimated 5 million Orthodox Christians. These Orthodox believers are organizationally divided, although they share the same teachings and rituals and can worship in any Orthodox congregation. The Orthodox churches are ethnically based among Greeks, Serbians, Russians, Ukrainians, Copts, Bulgarians, Albanians, Syrians, Romanians and others. The immigrants in the United States set in place their own ethnic hierarchies, many of which are still governed from their countries of origin. During years of Communist control, some of the Eastern European countries led many of the denominations to split further into competing groups. Sometimes in one area there are overlapping bishops.

The largest Orthodox group in the United States is the Greek Orthodox Archdiocese of North and South America, with 2 million members.

The spiritual leader of the more than 250 million Eastern Orthodox Christians is based in Constantinople and is called Ecumenical Patriarch. He holds a position of spiritual primacy as first among equals of leaders of self-governing Orthodox churches in a score of nations. Unlike the Pope, the Ecumenical Patriarch does not have any direct authority over any of the churches, although they are all united in doctrine.

For the Orthodox Christians, Easter is the greatest holiday of the Liturgical Calendar. "Feast of feasts, holiday of holidays," Easter is the ultimate feast, the very essence of the Orthodox faith (as it has been referred to by some), so much so that for forty days after Easter Sunday the most common hymn, "Christ is Risen," is chanted in all services.

In the United States, Orthodox Christians generally follow the Julian Calendar. This difference marks the celebration of Christmas on January 7. A difference concerning the date of Easter arose between the East and the West as early as the second century. The date for Easter had been fixed (after much haggling) by the Council of Nicea in 325 A.D. It decreed that thereafter Easter should be celebrated on the Sunday immediately following the first full moon occurring after the Vernal Equinox (first day of Spring), but always after the Hebrew Passover, in order that consistency with the biblical sequence of events might be maintained. The Eastern Orthodox Churches have continued to adhere strictly to this formula, but the Easter of the Western churches is not necessarily preceded by Passover. (In the United States, the other Christian churches do not consider Passover in arriving at the date for Easter.)

Orthodox Christianity has been largely unaffected by Western philosophical, cultural and technological development, according to the dean of the Greek Orthodox Cathedral in New York City. Orthodoxy has a strong resistance to theological change; its emphasis on ritual and sacramental life and its hierarchical nature set it apart from most Protestant denominations. The dean further states that while this lack of changes has its negative aspects, to be sure, it also has very valuable advantages. Eastern Orthodoxy is uncompromisingly traditional. The question of ordaining women, for example, is still kept on the very edge of its collective consciousness. Peter Steinfels has written in his *New York Times* religion column that Eastern Orthodoxy often seems to exist in its own world, a self-sufficient alternative to secularism rather than an embattled foe.

Orthodox churches are noted for the beauty and elegance of their Byzantine architectures and often become focal points and landmarks within their respective communities.

Inspired by the Byzantine traditions of the Holy Orthodox churches from the 6th and 8th centuries, the main features that distinguish classic Byzantine style are a square on the ground level, a cross on the second and a dome on the third.

The entry point of the church, the narthex, usually provides an area of preparation for worship with its candle stand and icons. After perhaps making a donation, each visitor lights a candle in honor of Christ and memorializes an individual.

Icons of the Virgin Mary holding Christ and the saint for which the church was named also are prominently displayed. The visitor makes the sign of the cross and kisses one or more icons before proceeding into the nave.

In the nave or interior of the church, the floor symbolizes earth and the dome symbolizes heaven. The nave is adorned with icons that serve as examples to the faithful that they can attain heaven if they live according to the teachings of the church.

The sanctuary, separated from the nave by the ikonostasin, is always located on the east side of the church because Christ the Light of the World, will rise again in the east. The altar area of the Orthodox church represents Christ's tomb. As a usual practice, only clergy and male laymen go beyond the ikonostasion.

On Orthodox Sunday which has marked the beginning of Lent in the church since the year 843, children of varying sizes carry icons high above their heads, proceed through the church's aisles and face the congregation from the steps of the altar.

The tradition dates from the year 787 and the second Council of Nicea, which defended the doctrine concerning the veneration of images and relics. The veneration had been temporarily outlawed in 726 by Emperor Leo III, who earned the name of "Iconoclast."

Eastern churches split from the Roman Catholic Church in the year 1054. It's known as the Great Schism. Traditions and practices diverged from that point.

All the Orthodox churches are part of the Orthodox Church family with diverse, ethnic backgrounds. Most in the U.S. are not as ethnic as they once were because of intermarriage. Ethnic languages are used in some hymns but more and more English has recently been incorporated.

Other days, besides the traditional **Christian** holidays, that are celebrated by Eastern Orthodox Christians include:

New Year's Day—**St. Basil Day**

Epiphany—Twelve days after Christmas

First Day of Lent—Starts on the Monday before Ash Wednesday

Ascension Day—Forty days after Easter

Pentecost—Fifty days after Easter

Also, the days of various patron saints are celebrated in various countries and by different ethnic groups in the United States.

HARE KRISHNA

According to a report by the Religion News Service, the Hare Krishna sect is a modern offshoot of a sixteenth-century Hindu devotional movement. It traces its theology to the Bhagavad-Gita, a 5,000-year-old Sanskrit text, and worships the Hindu deity Lord Krishna as the "supreme personality of the Godhead."

Members of the International Society for Krishna Consciousness are supposed to refrain from eating meat, fish or eggs; gambling; having sex outside of heterosexual marriage or for any purpose other than procreation; and ingesting intoxicants and stimulants, including tobacco, coffee or tea. Devotees adopt a two-part spiritual name: "Dasa" for men and "Dasi" for women, denoting that they are servants of God, coupled with a Sanskrit word describing one of Krishna's many attributes. The sect teaches that adhering to its prohibitions enhances physical, mental and spiritual well-being. Hare Krishna devotees chant Lord Krishna's various names to achieve "Krishna consciousness" and to propagate love of God.

The Hare Krishna were established in the United States by A.C. Bhaktivedanta Swami, then 69, an Indian guru known to his followers as Srila Prabhupada. On July 11, 1966, Prabhupada registered the International Society for Krishna Consciousness (ISKCON) in New York state and the controversial, often-ridiculed Hare Krishna movement was officially launched.

The movement now claims an estimated 90,000 followers in the United States, of whom only about 800 live full time in the group's 45 American spiritual communities, called ashrams. At the movement's peak in the United States in the 1970s, about 10,000 devotees lived in American ashrams, but most now live and work in the secular world. Another significant shift is that where once the movement in the United States consisted almost entirely of American converts to Hinduism, about half of the people now worshiping in Krishna temples in this country are recent immigrants from India and Asia.

In recent years, the Krishna movement has experienced its biggest growth in Eastern Europe and in India, where it was once regarded with disdain by native Hindus. Internationally, there are now an estimated one million adherents to the Hare Krishna movement, known formally as *Iskcon,* or the *International Society for Krishna Consciousness.*

More than any other group, Hare Krishna epitomized 1960s enchantment with Eastern religions and became known—critics would say notorious—for its shaved-headed devotees who chanted on street corners and sold religious texts at airports.

Three decades later, devotees still chant in public and sell books. Both practices are integral to their belief that praying to the Hindu deity Krishna—whom they consider to be "the supreme personality" of God—is the world's best hope for individual enlightenment and societal salvation.

During the early years, devotees lived communally, worked for the movement and were supported by its then-considerable income, according to E. Burke Rochford Jr., a sociology and anthropology professor at Middlebury College in Vermont.

Professor Rochford has also authored a study concerning sexual and physical abuse of children in Krishna boarding schools, known as gurukulas, in India, where many American adherents sent their adolescent boys. The highest levels of abuse in American gurukulas were reported in Dallas, Seattle, and New Vrindaban, West Virginia. There have been several lawsuits arising from child abuse cases at Krishna schools in Alachua, Florida, and New Vrindaban.

The reasons for the abuse lay in the very culture and structure of the early Krishna movement, Mr. Rochford said in his article. The movement drew very young devotees, many in their late teens and early 20s. Those who were not successful proselytizing and collecting contributions on the street were put to work in the movement's boarding schools. There was no screening of teacher candidates, no training, little financial support, high turnover and often as many as 20 students per teacher, the article reported.

"The mentality of the time was that distributing the guru's books and engaging oneself in missionary activity was the most important service that one could be involved in," Mr. Rochford said in an interview. "People's status within the movement was very much based on their ability to be effective in those tasks. Family, the way we see present in most Christian traditions, was not valued in the same way. Sexuality and family were something for those that were spiritually weak."

Celibacy was the ideal, the article said. But to accommodate families, the movement's founder asked the Krishna temples in the United States to set up boarding schools modeled on the gurukulas. The goals was to immerse students in the spiritual life, which Swami Bhaktivedanta taught meant cutting the "ropes of affection" between parent and child, Mr. Rochford wrote.

Children were sent to the gurukulas as early as age 3 or 4 and visited with their parents as seldom as once a month, or even once a semester.

By 1996, however, Hare Krishna was a largely congregational movement of married lay followers, many of whom visit a Hare Krishna temple only on Sunday afternoons, if at all. Incidentally, women are beginning to assume leadership roles. About 1,000 devotees still live in Hare Krishna's two dozen American temple compounds, according to movement officials, while thousands more—there are no reliable figures on the current number of devotees—live in the larger community, earning their livings in a society that Hare Krishnas once rejected as spiritually empty and overly materialistic.

Its founder, Prabhupada, is said to have arrived in New York knowing no one and with just $7. By the time he died in 1977, his movement had spread across six continents, establishing temples and schools, Indian-style vegetarian restaurants and publishing companies. It sponsored street festivals on Hindu holidays and free-food programs on college campuses.

Prabhupada's followers were a mix of 1960s countercultural types. Some, according to Rochford, were serious spiritual seekers who found their religious yearnings unsatisfied by the faith of their upbringing. Far more were dropouts who were sometimes into drugs and the hippie scene.

HINDUISM

Hinduism is based on the Vedas, a collection of writings about 500 years old. The Vedas are not religious dogma but rather observances of the laws of nature, which never change.

The Hindus accept other religions and promote individual choice in religious practices, an attitude that has limited the need for overseeing religious organization. A Brahmin is a member of the Hindu priest caste that usually leads services at a Hindu funeral.

Those principles began coming under attack in the fifteenth century, when other nations, lured by India's various resources, began invading the country. The invaders constantly attacked and modified Hinduism, destroying the written Vedas, but Hinduism was memorized and passed from one generation to the next.

A lot of Hindu religious leaders rose in India to protect the Vedas philosophy, and sects developed around the teachings of the leader.

Asian Indians traditionally believe in astrology and consider certain days of the year more conducive to business dealing, purchases, etc. Yoga is also commonly practiced by Asian-Indian Americans.

One simple Hindu verse reads: "As the rainwater drop falls on the mountains or in the river or on the top of the roof of a house, ultimately all these drops join together and meet in an eternal ocean." The gist: We are all brothers.

In Hinduism, there are several cycles of time, hundreds of thousands of years long, and there are several doomsdays. The Sanskrit word for doomsday is *prahaya,* which means *dissolution.*

Eventually, the world is destroyed by fire and flood. Most Hindus affix no date to the end.

Hinduism has many sects, but generally there is no figure exactly like Jesus, the Messiah, though Hindus consider Jesus a Saint. "Many comparisons have been made between Christ and the Hindu deity, Krishna," says John S. Hawley, a professor at Barnard College. Many consider him an incarnation of the great god Vishnu. Krishna, said Mr. Hawley, is "a god of love who wishes to protect his devotees and to save the world from destruction.

Hinduism has many heavens and hells. One hell has trees with leaves of razor blades. But at the end of each doomsday cycle, the universe and all heavens and hells are destroyed.

There have been several ancient Hindu leaders—Buddha, Guru Govindsigh, Mahavir Swami, Lord Rama and Lord Krishna. The leader most associated with Hinduism is Mahatma Ghandi, who was also the great leader for independence in India in 1947.

Conflicts that arose in India between Hindus and Muslims have sometimes spilled over to the United States when members of each group migrated to the United States. Efforts to unite here, including United Days, have been started by several organizations in some locales, such as New York City.

There is in India and continues in the United States a widespread view of Islam as a kind of foreign religion, symbolized by the fact that a succession of Muslim conquerors over the centuries erected religious sites at the location of Hindu temples or shrines. Hopefully, like other immigrants who become more settled and assimilated here, these views tend to dissipate as children and grandchildren start attending American schools.

Hindus follow a special Hindu calendar and follow a lunar cycle, and the month starts around the middle of the Gregorian calendar. There is not a single month in the Hindu calendar that is devoid of religious festivals.

In the Dvaita denomination of classical Hinduism, which is one of three in classical Hinduism, it is believed that there is only one Supreme Being and that every soul is a unique spiritual entity. There was estimated in 1999 to be 100,000 Hindus in the United States as followers of the Dvaita school.

HOLIDAYS AND CUSTOMS

One of the Asian Indian-American holidays that is widely celebrated among the Asian Indian community in the United States is the **Festival of Lights** (sometimes referred to as Dassara and sometimes as Diwali). It marks the culmination of Ashwin, which lasts ten days in October or November. There is a time-honored belief that if any new venture or important undertaking is started on this day it is bound to succeed. So any undertaking, be it laying the foundation of a new building, opening a new shop or factory or even sending a child to school, is likely to start on these days.

Each year, Asian Indians in the United States celebrate their independence from Great Britain. Elaborate arrangements are made by several organizations to celebrate the anniversary of Indian **Independence Day** on August 15. In some states it is called **India Day** and celebrated often on the weekends. Religious and commercial groups join in the celebration, creating colorful parade floats. Food stalls are set up either along the parade route or at a gathering place for the celebration. Cultural programs that include music and dances are also held as part of the celebrations.

Another festival, sometimes celebrated in its mild form, is *Holi*, an annual rite of spring in India, symbolic of fertility and decoration and steeped in Hindu mythology. In its most innocent form, *Holi* (pronounced holy) is an occasion when families, friends and neighbors smear brightly colored liquid dye on each other, gaily sing and dance and celebrate the onset of summer and the harvest season. The origins of *Holi* have been obscured by time, but the festival has been associated with several gods of Hindu mythology, including Kama, the God of Pleasure.

There are many "deities" in Hinduism; three of them are Sanaswali, Lakshmi and Parvoli, or Dunga, who are believed to confer knowledge, prosperity and valor, respectively. There is also the God Rama, the hero of the epic Ramayana (the triumph of good over evil).

The Hindu temple in Lanham, Maryland, "The Sri Siva Vishnu Temple," a structure of over 12,000 square feet, is the largest of its type in North America. It is an example of the effort by Hindus to recreate the culture of their Indian homeland, some 10,000 miles away, for themselves and their children.

The temple experience is taken much more seriously in the United States than in other parts of the world because the temples are built the way they are in India. In England, for example, there are a lot of temples, and they're mostly in other buildings or converted churches. Although young Hindus in the United States don't spend much time in places of worship, temples remain a focus for Hindu communities in most U.S. cities.

As with other ethnic groups, Hindus are concerned about young people forgetting their culture and religion as their people assimilate into American culture. The temple at Lanham is one of such high profile that people think of it even when they're not looking to, a reminder of their heritage. Unlike churches or synagogues, Hindu temples have no fixed membership, and anyone, Hindu or not, is welcome to come in and pray at any time.

What follows is a brief description of the many other Hindu holidays and festivals that are celebrated by Asian Indians and by some other Southeast Asian immigrants from Sri Lanka and elsewhere. There are no fixed dates for these holidays and most are lunar holidays. Calculations are based on a formula dealing with the bright and waxing side of the moon.

Mahavir Jayanti—This festival is dedicated to Mahavir, the twenty-fourth Tirthankara (reincarnation) of the Jains who have a large following in Gujarat.

Buddha Purnima—This full moon day is celebrated as the day of birth, enlightenment and Mahaparinirvana, or salvation, of the Buddha.

Ratha Yatra—One of the greatest temple festivals of India, in Washington, D.C., profusely decorated chariot cars resembling a temple structure are drawn by thousands of pilgrims. Similar celebrations on a much smaller scale in other cities.

Teej—Teej is an important festival in Rajasthan and welcomes the monsoons. It is essentially a women's festival. The presiding deity is Goddess Parvati, who, in the form of a bride, leaves her parents' home for that of her husband. A procession of the goddess is taken out with a retinue of elephants, camels and dancers.

Naag Panchami—Celebrated to revere the Cobra (*Naag*) all over India, this day is dedicated to the thousand-headed mythical serpent called Sesha or *Anant*, which means infinite. Vishnu, the Hindu God of preservation, reclined on him in contemplation during the interval between dissolution of one aeon and the creation of another. For people from Rajasthan huge cloth effigies of the mythical serpent are displayed at colorful fairs.

Ganesh Chaturthi—Ganesh, the deity with an elephant head (son of Lord Shiva), is the god of good omen and is worshipped by most Hindus. The festival of Ganesh is celebrated with enthusiasm. Clay models of the deity, sometimes as tall as eight meters, are worshipped and taken out in a procession to the accompaniment of cymbals and drums and finally immersed in the sea.

Durga Puja—Durga Puja is mainly celebrated by those who came from Calcutta and the region of Bengal. The devotees don new clothes and entertain with music, dance and drama. On the last day, images of the warrior goddess are taken out in procession and immersed in the river or sea.

Dussehra/Ramlila—This is a joyous Indian festival that celebrates the victory of truth over evil.

Diwali/Laxmi Puja—The Festival of Lights—The gayest of all Indian festivals, Diwali marks the start of the Hindu New Year. Every city, town and village is turned into a fairyland with thousands of flickering oil lamps and electric lights or candles illuminating homes and public buildings.

Basanta Panchami—This festival is celebrated in honor of Goddess Saraswati, the goddess of knowledge.

Shivaratri—Celebrated by Hindus all over, Shivaratri is a solemn occasion devoted to the worship of the most powerful deity of the Hindu Pantheon—Shiva. It is purely a religious festival at which devotees spend the whole night singing his praises. Special celebrations are held at important Shiva temples.

Gangaur—This festival is held two weeks after Holi in honor of Parvati, the consort of Lord Shiva. In their invocation to Gauri, they ask for husbands like the one she has been blessed with. The festival, during which gaily attired young girls proceed to the temples, culminates in rejoicing with the arrival of Shiva to escort his bride Gauri (PaNati) home, sometimes accompanied by horses and elephants.

Vaisakhi—This is the Hindu Solar New Year's day observed virtually all over Northern India and Tamil Nadu. It is a religious festival when people bathe in rivers and go to temples to worship. The river Ganga is believed to have descended to the earth this day. For the Sikh community Vaisakhi is of special significance, as on this day in 1689 Guru Gobind Singh organized the Sikhs into the *"Khalsa,"* a military order who never shave their beards or touch tobacco and always carry weapons. In the Punjab, farmers start harvesting with great jubilation.

Ramanavami—Birthday of Lord Rama, the ninth reincarnation of the Lord Vishnu. This festival is celebrated all over India. The epic Ramayana is recited for days in the temples and homes of the devotees.

WEDDING CUSTOMS

Hindu weddings are usually arranged by parents or relatives. Advertisements or announcements of availability, and a dowry perhaps, are placed in various Asian Indian-American publications. There also is an increasing awareness of "Love Marriages," which are not arranged by parents. In the Hindu marriage ceremonies the newlyweds are required to share a plate of food.

Peter Steinfels, the religion editor of the *New York Times*, has written that American Muslims are a steadily growing group. With between 5 and 6 million Muslims in the United States, within a decade of the 1990s or so, they will outnumber Presbyterians and will eventually outnumber the nation's estimated 6 million Jews. Although still only a small fraction of the Christian population of more than 200 million, Muslims will be comparable in numbers to the larger Christian groups, such as Methodists or Lutherans.

The world of Islam is a world of peace and prayer and religious discipline. The word "Islam" means peace and submission to God.

Islam, Judaism and Christianity all grew from the same roots. While the world of Islam is divided into two main sects—the Sunni and Shiite—all Muslims consider themselves part of one family of believers. Muslim and "Moslem" are the same thing: a believer in the Islam religion, founded by the prophet Mohammed in Arabia in the seventh century.

Islam began in the seventh century when the great prophet Mohammed delivered the Koran, a book of knowledge, to the Arab people. While the Koran acknowledges Jesus Christ, it does not acknowledge the piety of the man worshipped by Christians as "God Incarnate." Islam does not have the complicated set of creeds and doctrines associated with Christianity. Its single and simple creed merely acknowledges the supremacy of God, the authority of Mohammed to reveal the Word of God and the call to prayer as spiritual peace.

The Bible, Islamic scholar Boyd Barrick states, is a book written by many authors about Jesus and the historical context of his life. The Koran, on the other hand, is "the" word of God, given by God directly to Mohammed.

All the world is God for Muslims, but man is separate and called to action by the Koran as conveyed to, and through, Mohammed.

While Jews and Christians have the Ten Commandments and Golden Rules, the call to action for Muslims is the five "pillars" of Islam: bearing witness of the faith; daily prayer; at least one pilgrimage to Mecca, where the Koran was revealed; fasting during days of the holy month of Ramadan; and giving a portion of one's wealth to the poor.

What is Islam? The word "Islam" comes from the three-letter Arabic root word "*sim*," which stands for peace. And, the way the Koran talks about it, Islam is the religion of peace. Islam means to surrender to God, to stop fighting God, to be at peace with him, to have a relationship of peace. Islam, in a sense, urges people to worship the same God that Christianity and Judaism address.

Many times Islam is identified by the crescent and a five-pointed star. Also, the color green is associated with Islam.

According to the American Muslim Council, in 1991, the ethnic background of Muslims living in the United States was:

African-American: 42.0 percent

South Asian: 24.4 percent

Arab: 12.4 percent

Other: 16.0 percent

African: 5.2 percent

Of the 5 to 6 million Muslims in the United States, a majority are immigrants from Asia, Africa and the Middle East. But there are also many American converts, both white and black. African-American converts are estimated to number 1 million, according to the American Muslim Council. Though Muslims are often associated with the Arabic world, that area accounts for only 25 percent of the Islamic world. Iran, for example, is not an Arabic nation.

Islam arrived in the United States along with immigrants from the Ottoman Empire at the turn of the twentieth century, but the Muslim population began to increase significantly only with the arrival of large numbers of students from Muslim countries in the 1960s. Islam is often confused with the Nation of Islam. The latter is actually a 10,000-member offshoot group, led by Louis Farrakhan, that promotes African-American consciousness.

Islam is expected to be the second-largest religion in the United States in the first decade of the twenty-first century. And Islam is said to be the fastest growing faith in the world.[8] Exact figures on the Muslim population in the United States are elusive because there is no official count.

Dawud Zwink, vice president of the Islamic Society in the United States, said many Americans have no idea that Muslims believe in one deity and one human family, and save for some dress and dietary laws and traditions, that they live pretty much the way their Jewish and Christian neighbors do.[9]

Muslim tradition forbids dating; marriages are arranged by parents, but children have the final say. Islamic law forbids drinking or serving alcohol. Muslim women must cover their hair in public. Many Muslim women use head scarves, which are called the "*hijab*," to cover their hair as an expression of religious conviction. Men and women usually don't shake hands and traditionally stand six feet apart. Muslims pray five times a day and gather on Fridays for congregational prayers. All Muslims must make a pilgrimage to Mecca in Saudi Arabia once in their lifetime.

Yvonne Haddad, a professor of Islamic history at the University of Massachusetts, has written about misconceptions of Muslims in the United States. "When we first came to this country, the stereotype of Islam or Muslims in America was camel jockeys, insignificant, on the margin of civilization. In the '70s, after the oil boycott, the stereotype became one of what I call the oil sheik—someone who's a threat to our way. And then, in the '80s, it became the terrorists."

Ben Wattenberg, a demographer, wrote in 1990[10] that the United States could at last be truly called a melting pot because, for the first time, it included a significant number of Muslims. But not all Muslims arrived in the U.S. that recently. In fact, there are Muslims who are fifth-generation immigrants in the United States. There are more than an estimated 2 million Arab-Christians in the United States. They sometimes get bashed with Muslims just because their last names are similar.

MYTHS ABOUT ISLAM AND MUSLIMS[11]

- Women aren't considered equal. According to the teachings of the Koran, God created man and woman of the same cell. They are supposed to be equal. They are equal in the eyes of God. The only distinction is in their marriage. Every unit must have a leader, and the man is seen as the leader. When a couple has to make a final decision in the Islamic social system, the husband makes it.
- Women can't drive. There is one country—Saudi Arabia—that doesn't allow women to drive. Muslim women drive all over the world except in Saudi Arabia.
- Muslims come from the Middle East. Arabs are just 25 percent of the Muslim population of the world. The majority of Muslims are not Arab. In fact, there are more Indonesian Muslims than Arab Muslims.
- The holy war. The word "*jihad*" has come to mean holy war in American terminology, but in Islam it has two meanings, or interpretations, including the lesser jihad and the higher jihad. The lesser jihad is holy war and the higher jihad, the more important, is the struggle of the self, the relationship with God and the struggle to resist the tendency toward evil.
- Fundamentalism. Fundamentalism is an American word. There is no Arabic word for fundamentalism. To the general public, the word has come to connote fanaticism. But Muslims do not follow their faith to extremes; they follow the laws of the Koran without interpretation.
- It is a general misconception that Islam wants women to wear a veil to cover their faces. Indeed, women are forbidden to cover their faces when they perform the *hajj*, or pilgrimage to Mecca, one of the holiest events in the Muslim religion. There, in the presence of the holy Kaaba, along with men from all over the world, the women are required to keep their faces uncovered. The veil is a regional and cultural tradition in some Muslim countries, and it has nothing to do with the Islam religion. Islam does require women to dress modestly in the presence of men who are not members of their immediate family. Part of this dress code is the *hijab*, which covers their hair with a scarf and looks somewhat like the head coverings of nuns, although it does not have to be white.

The idea of the veil comes from the Koran, which says women must hide their "adornments" from all but their husbands. This has led to the tradition of Muslim women wearing a whole range of scarves, veils and even masks when outside their homes.

Many Muslim women wear the "*hijab*" which covers the hair or most of it, but shows the face. Muslim women who have migrated from the Gulf states will sometimes wear a veil that hides the face and reveals just the eyes.

The wearing of the veil seems to cause as much fuss as any aspect of Islam, both in the Muslim world and outside. Westerners—and some Muslims—argue it is a way to subjugate women, but other Muslim women say it gives them a comfortable anonymity.

The place of worship for Muslims is the mosque. A mosque is a wonderfully simple building. It has a *mihrab* (a semicircular prayer niche in one wall), a *minbar* (a small elevated pulpit for the Imam), and the rest is pure, unencumbered space. Among the countries of the Islamic world, which spans from Morocco to Indonesia, there are, of course, a wide variety of mosque styles and traditions, but each is intended as a house of worship for Muslims of all sects and nations.

The observance of Ramadan, the ninth month of Islam's lunar calendar, is one of the pillars of the Islamic faith. For the entire month, no food or drink is taken during daylight. As a period of self-examination and abstention, it has some parallels to Yom Kippur, the Jewish day of atonement. The month of Ramadan begins with the sighting of the new moon in the appropriate month.

Ramadan is the month during which the Koran was revealed to the Prophet Mohammed. So during that month, every Muslim, male and female, is supposed to fast. The fast is an abstention from food, water and all the worldly desires in general, from dawn, which is two hours before sunrise, until sunset every day. The obligation to fast is to teach Muslims to pay charity to the poor and the needy, to teach them how to control themselves and to deny themselves. It is also a time of great joy, an occasion to appreciate one's blessings and to gather with other Muslims. Muslims break their fast and pray after sunset. Many eat again after midnight or awaken before dawn to eat another meal, the *sabur*. This, the holiest month, ends with a great, four-day feast, called "*Eid al-Fitr*," when the new moon is sighted.

During Ramadan, it is typical for Muslims to read the entire Koran, a chapter at a time during daily evening prayers

Muslims vow to refrain from all food, liquids, cigarettes and sex during daylight hours for the entire month. According to the Koran, the fast is to begin at the moment of daybreak when it is possible to tell a black thread from a white one and ends only when the fading light at dusk makes that distinction impossible.

Technically, the fast does not begin in a particular area until local Muslim authorities have seen the new moon. Because the Muslim calendar is eleven days shorter than the solar calendar, the month of fasting comes earlier each year. The day-long abstention from liquids works special hardship on the faithful when it occurs during the hot summer months.

Travelers, those who are ill, pregnant women and mothers who are breastfeeding may be excused, but they are expected to make up the days missed after the circumstances of the exemption are removed. Elderly or incurably ill persons may be excused from fasting, but are asked instead to give to the poor the equivalent of a day's rations for each fast day.

A person who inadvertently breaks most of the rules of the fast is expected to make up for it by observing an extra fast day after Ramadan, but one who breaks the restriction against sexual intercourse must atone by fasting for sixty days or feed sixty poor persons.

In many Muslim countries, during Ramadan, restaurants close throughout the day, governments and businesses trim working hours, children leave school early and people take daytime naps to stay awake for nighttime meals.

For the Muslim minority in the United States, Ramadan must be observed amid fast-food outlets, coffee breaks and nine-to-five workdays. Some find that the non-Muslim environment adds to the physical difficulty of keeping the month-long fast as well as to the spiritual rewards.

Many Muslim parents in the United States feel that one of the real difficulties with observing Ramadan is peer pressure faced by Muslim children, such as teenagers on athletic teams who want to be excused from fasting. In contrast to observance of Ramadan in Arab countries, where people can break their fast after sunset and then socialize until several hours past midnight, in the United States Muslims go to bed early in order to work the next day.

But Muslims in the United States are increasingly able to keep Ramadan as a community affair, by meeting nightly in mosques or Islamic centers for prayer and meals and extending these gatherings well into the night on weekends.

Another of the "pillars" of faith and a lifetime dream of every devout Muslim is making the long pilgrimage (the *hajj*) to pay homage at Islam's holiest shrine in Mecca. The trip is part of a tradition more than ten centuries old, practiced in Asia and Africa as well as the Arab world. Muslims from more than sixty countries participate in an elaborate series of rites upon reaching their destination.

In Mecca, the pilgrims circle the black stone Kaaba shrine at the Grand Mosque seven times. They make seven trips between the hills of Marwa and Safa to commemorate the search for water by Hagar, Abraham's wife, and drink from a sacred well, believed to have been provided by the archangel Gabriel. They pray from noon until sunset at the Plain of Arafat, where Mohammed gave his last sermon. In Mina, the pilgrims toss pebbles at three white pillars representing the devil, then sacrifice animals before circling the Kaaba[12] again seven times to complete the pilgrimage.

The *hajj* is performed at a place that is said to have been built about twenty-five centuries before the birth of Mohammed. Muslims believe that it was built by Abraham as he wandered in the Arabian Desert with Hagar at the time of the birth of his son Ishmail. These events mark the roots of the Islamic faith.

Besides Mecca, the nearby city of Medina is revered. It is held in high regard by Muslims because it was the first city converted to Islam by Mohammed.

The climax of the *hajj* (which lasts approximately thirty days each year) is the three-day Eid-al Adha feast honoring the willingness of Abraham to sacrifice his son Isaac at God's behest. Eid-al Adha is the Muslim festival of sacrifice. It is celebrated in the United States by Muslims first offering prayers at an Islamic center. After the prayers, they sacrifice sheep and other animals in commemoration of Abraham's actions. The meal is shared among family, friends and the poor.

"Abraham was ready to sacrifice what was closest to his heart, his son Ishmail," said Adam Hussain, a Muslim who lives in Rockville, Maryland.[13] "Renouncing the ego, we pray in congregation to Allah the God, and later symbolically sacrifice the animal instincts in each of us."

After the Eid prayer, men and women visit the homes of friends and relatives. Later they go home to perform the sacrifice. In the United States, where the sacrifice is not allowed in residential areas, Muslims pay butcher shops, known as *Halaals*, to purchase animals and prepare them according to tradition. The meat is divided into three parts—one goes to the poor, one to friends and relatives, and one to the family.

Eid-al Adha originates in a story familiar to Christians and Jews as well as Muslims: the Old Testament account of the willingness of the prophet Abraham—Ibrahim to Muslims—to sacrifice his first-born son, called Ishmail by Muslims, when God commanded. Moved by Abraham's obedience and sacrificial spirit, God provided a lamb for the sacrifice, and the boy's life was spared.

Commemoration of this event is the biggest feast of the year for Muslims. It puts sacrifice at the center of their lives. Part of the Eid-al Adha ritual is to have women sit behind men. "Americans think that's degradation, but it is really a sign of respect and modesty," Peggy Mohammed, of Washington D.C., told the *Washington Post* in 1990.

In terms of gift giving, Eid-Al-Adha is the Muslim equivalent of Christmas, with children receiving toys or gifts of money. American Muslims want the holiday to have a festival atmosphere and they want their children to be able to have fun and celebrate as people in other religions celebrate their holiday. Also to be proud of being Muslims in America.

The traditions of Islam require that everyone who can afford it sacrifice a lamb, or seven people together to sacrifice one cow. The idea is that God doesn't want human sacrifice. He wants a sacrifice of the human spirit. When you sacrifice the animal, it's to feed the people.

Muslim leaders have definite political and social goals, such as freeing school textbooks of anti-Islamic stereotypes, getting permission at school and work to observe Islamic holidays, having Muslim chaplains to assist in prisons and the armed forces, making food that meets Islam's dietary code more available and providing a drug-free, less sexually permissive environment for Muslim children, according to the Muslim Political Action Committee.

Many of these things have been achieved in communities with established Muslim populations such as Dearborn, Michigan, a city of 87,000, more than 20 percent of whom are believed to be Muslim.[14]

The American Muslim Council in Washington, D.C., which enlisted support from both immigrant and black American Muslim leaders, was founded in the early 1990s to politically mobilize Muslims.

Islam in the United States is divided between African-American Muslims, who may account for one-third of the total, and immigrants. It is a division reinforced by cultural and socioeconomic differences. Many of the Muslim immigrants from Pakistan, India and Egypt are physicians, engineers and businessmen who settled in suburbia and look forward to assimilating quickly into American society. Black Muslims, including some professionals, tend to be concentrated in or around inner cities.[15]

Immigrant Muslims are divided by nationality and ethnicity, by different forms of Islam and the generation gap between more assimilated immigrants and recent arrivals. They confront the same forces of assimilation and intermarriage that have affected the ranks of other religious groups. In Canada, for example, two out of three Muslim women are marrying men who were not previously Muslim (about half of the men convert). Islamic law forbids Muslim women to marry outside their religion. Muslim men, too, are forbidden to marry outside the faith.

As in other ethnic and religious groups, schooling is a major issue among American Muslims, both immigrants and African-Americans. In 1993 there were 165 full-time Muslim schools across the United States, although more than 90 percent of Muslim children remain in public schools.

The number of Islamic schools nationwide has jumped to 200 or more by 1998, says the Council of Islamic Schools in North America, an informal body that sponsors workshops for Muslim educators. But neither the council nor any other group keeps official track of new schools, and American Muslims say they think the national figures are higher.

Long a community of distinct and often introverted parts, American Muslims have begun a process familiar to many immigrant and ethnic groups. They are trying to reach beyond their internal origin and find a unified voice to defend and promote their interests in a multicultural society, so reports Swan Sacks in a *New York Times* story of October 1998.

Convinced that many Americans have a distorted view of Muslims and their Islamic religion, compounded by images in the movies and the media, they have created national organizations, lobbying groups, voter registration campaigns and outreach programs to explain Islam to their neighbors.

Those who help to create a school system see themselves as a integral part of this communal effort to define for themselves and for others what it means to be a Muslim in the United States.

The challenge for Islamic education is to create a spiritual educational experience that is also relevant in a secular society. It has been a process of trial and error, ad-libbing and self-discovery. Many schools get teaching materials from other countries.

Religious schools for American Muslims also have to contend with a widely diverse student body. Any one class might have children from Egyptian, Yemeni, Pakistani, Indian and African-American backgrounds. Souhair Ayach, a teacher of Islamic studies in New York, points out that having a mix of cultures requires her to constantly stress the difference between old country traditions and religion.

Like new immigrants, more established Muslims worry that their children may lose their religious identity or do poorly in public schools where their dress, holidays and religious taboos can make curiosities.

"Muslims are moving toward a system like the Catholic system," said Amina McCloud, who teaches Islamic studies at DePaul University in Chicago. "They are being forced by the increasing violence in the schools and the lack of academic focus, with people trying just to stay alive and avoid drugs."

The role of women is also changing among American Muslims. Many Muslims assert that Islam and its sacred text, the Koran, affirm the equality of women and that many restrictions on women in Islamic lands arise from local culture rather than from Islam itself. But there is no consensus as to where to draw the line between cultural custom and religious obligation. Changes in Islamic practice may come about as more women are educated "to read the Koran and know their rights," according to

Charles K. Alawan, chairman of the board of the Islamic Center of America in Dearborn, Michigan.

Building an Islamic community is many American cities can sometimes be a very difficult task for Muslims. It can become complicated. For example, it means finding a place to pray, either a mosque or a quiet place to spread one's prayer mat. It may mean difficulty in finding halal beef to obey Islamic dietary law.

For parents it means teaching and praying at home—and hoping the children aren't swept away by American culture.

And for everyone, it seems, it involves being ambassadors for the whole faith, knowing how it has been tarred in many American eyes.

As stated previously America is now home to a broad variety of Muslims: Turkish merchants, Egyptian technicians, Pakistani doctors, Indian broadcasters. Brought by economic or educational opportunity, or driven by war in their homelands, they come from places as diverse as the Caribbean, the Middle East and the Indian subcontinent.

However, there are community divisions, not everyone accepts everyone else. Just as Christian sects reject one another, some Islamic groups are said to be outside the pale. Examples of this are shown when some are followers of Karim Aga Khan of Paris, whom they regard as a direct descendant of Mohammad. Some who have settled in South Florida, known as Ahmadyya Muslims, believe Jesus was reincarnated in India in the nineteenth century. Most Muslims reject those beliefs.

Then, there is the Nation of Islam, founded on the belief that God appeared in the form of black prayer in Chicago in the 1930s and appointed Elijah Mohammad as his prophet.

As Muslims in America convert others, though, they worry about losing their own—to the huge, glittering and sometimes suffocating America culture. They worry that the music and luxuries and sex and alcohol will lure their friends and children away from the religion.

Whatever the difficulties, the Muslims insist they're here to stay. Not as immigrants or strangers. But as neighbors. As a Boca Raton, Florida, dentist says, "We live on the same land. We drink the same water. We're adding to the American culture."

HOLIDAYS AND CUSTOMS

Muslims calculate their year according to the phases of the moon. Following long-established customs, the beginning of a month is determined by witnesses observing the new moon. There is no regularity in predicting a given month in the Muslim calendar; there may be a difference of one or two days between previously predicted and actual celebrated holidays. They are:

Isra and **Miraj**—Commemorates the anniversary of the night journey of the Prophet and his ascension to Heaven.

Ramadan—Beginning of the month of fasting from sunrise to sunset.

Eid-al-Fitr—End of the month of fasting from sunrise to sunset.

Hajj—First day of the pilgrimage to Mecca.

Day of Arafat—Gathering of the pilgrims. Celebrated after *Hajj* to pray and meditate from noon to sunset on the plain of Arafat, outside the city of Mecca, where Mohammed gave his last sermon while preparing for completion of the *Hajj*.

Eid-al-Adha—Commemorates the Feast of the Sacrifice.

Muharram—The Muslim New Year. This marks the beginning of the *Hedjra* year. *Hedjra,* sometimes spelled Hijrah, was the time when the prophet Mohammed departed at midnight from Makkah to Madinab on July 16, 622 A.D., the day subsequently chosen to mark the first day of the Islamic era.

Eid-al-Maw'id—Commemorates the nativity and death of the Prophet Mohammed and his flight from Mecca to Medina.

WEDDING CUSTOMS

It is customary for a Muslim bride and groom, who have never met before the wedding, to view each other first in a mirror. The origin of this custom is in Muslims' native countries, where arranged marriages were commonplace and couples did not meet before their marriage. In the United States, although Muslim couples most likely have met before their nuptials, they often continue the tradition of viewing each other in the mirror before wedding ceremonies.

Jehovah's Witnesses, officially known as the Watchtower Bible and Tract Society, make up a Christian denomination that claims to have 4 million adherents worldwide. The denomination emphasizes biblical literalism and door-to-door evangelism. Founded in 1879, the Watchtower Society preaches that the world is in "the last days" and will soon be destroyed in a cataclysmic war.

A favorite statement from the group is: "The Bible is a language all its own and yet it can be spoken in all languages," Angelo Catanzano, the 1990 chairman of the group's convention, told the *New York Times*. The Witnesses believe in a rapidly approaching Armageddon, and only Jehovah's Witnesses can master the pure language, The Word of God.[16]

The movement has grown about 7 percent each year, and the aim of its annual convention and other activities is to spur growth. The Society is an evangelical Christian organization. They live like early Christians. Witnesses do not celebrate the usual Christian holidays, believing them to be of pagan origin and commercialized. The organization meets three times a week for regular religious and ethical discussions. The church does not recognize the authority of government, believing that the only true authority is that of God, whom they call Jehovah. Members are forbidden to smoke, but may drink alcohol in moderation and consume caffeine. They do not believe in the afterlife, but they do believe that one day there will be a rebirth on earth of all true believers in Jehovah.

A didactic faith that demands an unconditional obedience to God, the Jehovah's Witnesses Society is best known for tenacious door-to-door and street-corner missionary work. Organized around places of worship called Kingdom Halls, Jehovah's Witnesses canvass their neighborhoods with more thoroughness than Census-takers, knocking on doors to sell their magazines *Watchtower* and *Awake* and to aggressively prod outsiders into biblical discussions as a means of converting them.

Jehovah's Witnesses have attracted attention for their refusal to accept blood transfusions, saying that it goes against the teachings of the Bible, and for their refusal to pledge allegiance to the flag or to celebrate Christmas or birthdays. During World War II, according to Donatella Lorch in the *New York Times*,[17] Jehovah's Witnesses were tarred and feathered, castrated and burned out of their churches because they refused to salute the flag.

Though the Society says that it is politically neutral, its followers forbid abortion, condone the death penalty, consider suicide a sin but support the right to die. They are against premarital sex and birth control. Gay men and women cannot be baptized.

The religion's lack of official hierarchy and traditional worship ceremonies and the unwillingness of its leaders to talk about its finances have tinged it with a degree of secrecy. What serves as worship is sober instruction. The periodic conventions of the Jehovah's Witnesses are occasions for massive teaching sessions.

Jehovah's Witnesses believe that their faith prohibits them from celebrating birthdays. Many believe this not to be part of their worship and rather it stems from pagan teachings and the realm of magic.

ORTHODOX (THE TERM)

The term "Orthodox" is used by two groups of Christians and a segment within Judaism. In the United States a person identified as Orthodox may be a member of an Eastern Orthodox or Oriental Orthodox church, or an Orthodox Jew.

Eastern Orthodox refers to Christians who trace their heritage to the ancient patriarchates of Alexandria, Antioch, Constantinople and Jerusalem; to the newer patriarchates of *Bulgaria, *Russia, Georgia, Romania and Serbia, on to the autonomous churches of *Albania, the Americas, *Byelorussia (now called Belarus), Crete, Cyprus, Czechoslovakia, Finland, *Greece, Poland, Serbia or the *Ukraine. Starred churches are those found in the United States.

Oriental Orthodox refers to Christians who belong to the Armenian Orthodox Church, the Coptic Orthodox Church, the Ethiopian Orthodox Church, the Syrian Orthodox Church of Antioch and the Syrian Orthodox Church of India.

Orthodox Judaism encompasses those Jews who seek to observe the 613 laws and regulations established by Talmudic law, emphasizing the importance of *Halakhah*, the legal portion of the Talmud, and such later Jewish literature as the *Mishnah Torah* and the *Shulhan Arukh*. The expression "Orthodox Judaism" came into use in the late eighteenth century after the American and French Revolutions. It is now used to distinguish more traditional Jews from those who participate in the Reform or Conservative movements within Judaism.

PAGANS

Pagans are members of an eclectic modern religious movement that embraces varied beliefs, according to the Coalition for Pagan Religious Rights, a Maryland nonprofit corporation. The Coalition is an umbrella group for Witches, Druids, Mystic Christians, Shamans and other Pagans. Many have in common a reverence for nature, the use of myths and symbols from ancient faiths and a belief in male and female gods. Some Pagans float from one discipline to another. A Shaman is an intermediary between the natural and supernatural worlds. The Shaman uses magic to heal and to influence spiritual forces; they state that they see "through time." The Coalition states that Pagans share the same basic values as mainstream Americans. Some Pagans practice the "Law of Threefold," which holds that the good or bad one does is returned three times. Pagans want to make it clear that they do not worship Satan.

Wicca comes from the Old English word for "witch" and is used for numerous strains of Neo-Paganism, a nature religion that celebrates seasonal and life cycles using rituals from pre-Christian Europe. Like their ancient counterparts, modern pagans, including more than 100,000 in the United States and Canada, celebrate solstices and equinoxes and perform planting, fertility and harvest rituals. They also mark such rites of passage as birth, coming of age and death, combining ancient practices with those of contemporary tribal peoples and pagan beliefs with romantic themes drawn from science fiction and literary fantasy.

Their beliefs are a blend of pre-Christian paganism and New Age Earth worship. They have lunar assemblies every full moon and will wear hooded robes, chant to the lead of their chosen high priestess and dance around a fire well into the night.

On full moons and eight sacred holidays, witches gather to watch their high priestess lift her dagger over a ball of salt and honor the blessed earth. One such holiday is the spring rite ceremony.

Without a written guide like the bible, the many varieties of Wicca follow in common a version of the golden rule: "An ye harm none, do what ye will." Most Wiccans worship Mother Earth and Father Sky. They don't sacrifice animals or cast evil spells, as some would have you believe.

Most Wiccans prefer to conduct their rituals "Skyelad' - Their poetic word for naked. Then there are the Athames, the nine-inch daggers used at the high altar or sabbats.

Pentagrams are worn by Wiccas - they could be a ring or necklace etc. Also, Wiccas are pacifists.

SEVENTH-DAY ADVENTISTS

In 1990, the Seventh-day Adventist Church, a faith born and nurtured in the United States during the nineteenth century, came to terms with the stark fact that theirs is no longer strictly an American church. Its church members come from at least 184 nations. Paradoxically, Americans, who founded the church, no longer control it. Aside from the Catholic Church, the Adventists are now the most international church. With 6.2 million members worldwide, the Adventists have been remarkably successful in spreading their message. The church grew by about 40 percent from 1985 to 1990. Almost all the nations of the world have Adventist churches.

Founded in 1863 in Battle Creek, Michigan, the Adventist Church is based on the belief that these are the "last days" and that the end of the world is near. Out of the chaos of destruction, they believe, a new earth will emerge in which those redeemed by Christ will live eternally. Unlike some other apocalyptic groups, however, the Adventists do not set a date for the end of the world.

Adventists are very much concerned with matters of this world. They have put a great deal of emphasis on health care and have built a network of hospitals. Adventists do not drink alcohol or smoke tobacco.

Adventists give great authority to the laws outlined in the Old Testament. Invoking the Fourth Commandment, they observe Saturday rather than Sunday as the Christian Sabbath. Like some of those of the Jewish faith, they distinguish between "clean" and "unclean" meats as spelled out in Leviticus, observing a modified form of the kosher laws.

The Adventists' rate of growth is much higher abroad than in the United States. In 1989, for example, there were ninety conversions to the faith each day in North America (in both Canada and the United States), while there were 361 a day in East Africa. Today, only 12 percent of Adventists live in North America. About 30 percent live in Africa and 40 percent reside in Central and South America and the Caribbean. In recent years, Adventist President Reverend Robert S. Folkenberg told Eric Goldman of the *New York Times* that Adventists have had a much harder time winning adherents in "First World countries, where materialism and humanism predominate." Many blame this on the reluctance to ordain women, according to the *Times* article.

Despite lower growth rates in the U.S. than in other areas, interestingly, 80 percent of the annual budget of the church's world headquarters in Silver Spring, Maryland, comes from American donors.

The question of whether women should be fully ordained is hotly debated among Adventists, and both sides invoke the name of an early church leader, Ellen White, whose written accounts of visions of Heaven continue to shape the theology of the church. Church members who favor female ordination find it ironic and appalling that they can't ordain women when its leading founder is quoted more often than St. Peter or St. Paul. "But Mrs. White never accepted ordination," respond opponents of ordination such as Captain Herman Kibble, an Adventist minister in California. Reverend Mario Veloso, a church official based in Brazil, adds: "Instead, she followed the biblical pattern, in which only men were ordained for service by God."

ZOROASTRIANISM

Zoroastrianism was founded by the Iranian prophet Zarathustra (or Zoroaster, as the Greeks called him) around 1300 B.C. Zoroastrians "taught that the world has a beginning and an end forms the field of a cosmic battle between good and evil," between Ahura Mazda, the Lord of Wisdom, and Ahriman, who is wicked, so says James Russell, a professor at Harvard University. Zoroaster never specified a date for the world's end. But "he suggested it would end with the coming of a savior; and that the world would then be cleansed of death and wickedness and people would rise from the dead," according to Mr. Russell.

Zoroaster's followers later said the world would last 12,000 years; the final 6,000 years represents human history. "The process of apocalypse is played out over the final 3000 years of the human era with three saviors," says Mr. Russell. The final savior, and most important, is Astvat Ereta whose name means "righteousness embodied." Like Jesus, Astvat Ereta had a miraculous birth; his virgin mother was impregnated with Zoroaster's seed while bathing in a lake.

Although Zoroastrians have no concept of an eternal hell, they believe the wicked will be judged and punished in an ordeal of molten metal. Evil will be destroyed, and purified sinners will be renewed for eternity.

HELPFUL SYMBOLS TO IDENTIFY CERTAIN RELIGIONS IN THE UNITED STATES

Islam—An outside mosque will have a tower called a minaret inside of it. You might see the Islamic Book called the Qur'ans (Koran).

Judaism—Outside the synagogue or temple you might see the Star of David. Inside, you will see a curtain and behind it is an Ark. In the Ark is the Torah, written on scrolls.

Eastern Orthodox—Outside, the churches will have large tombs and a three-bar cross. Inside you will see icons or pictures of Jesus, Mary and the Saints.

Buddhism—Outside, Buddhist temples are built in many shapes and sizes. Some of the roofs might be curved up at the ends. Inside, you will see a statue of Buddha.

Hinduism—Outside, the temples or shrines appear quite plain. Inside you might see statues of some of the holy figures honored by Hindus in their worship.

RELIGION AND EDUCATION

The Supreme Court justices in 1963 wrote in their decision that ruled out school prayer that "one's education is not complete without a study of comparative religion or the history of religion and its relationship to the advancement of civilization." By acknowledging religion's importance while prohibiting its prevalence in public schooling, the justices hit on an issue that comes up often.

For educators and administrators in the American school system, the December holiday season has become a dilemma. To many parents and students, it seems Christmas is clashing with the increasing cultural diversity and awareness in the United States. "The public school system is a battleground during this time of the year," said Rabbi A. James Rudin, director of interreligious affairs for the American Jewish Committee in Washington, D.C. "I am very fearful that this December dilemma will become harder as America becomes more multiracial, multiethnic and multireligious." Thus Rudin sums up a serious issue generated by the different ethnic and religious holidays and customs that arise in a multicultural society such as the United States.

Those teachers and administrators who can remember school Christmas concerts of nothing but carols and hymns must be especially cautious. Many times the first season's greetings to arrive at school come from religious and civil liberties organizations that span the political spectrum. A blizzard of mailings arrive each fall summarizing different groups' interpretations of what the law permits.

Because the Supreme Court has never ruled on a case about holiday observances in public schools,[18] few absolutes are applicable. Legal authorities agree that schools can teach about religion but must not indoctrinate students in a particular faith. The Supreme Court ruled in 1989 that Christmas trees and Hanukah menorahs are secular symbols of the holiday season and that their public display does not violate the First Amendment.

A manger scene, for example, may be used during a lesson as a visual aid and so may a menorah, but teachers may not keep creches on view in their classroom or lead students in reciting a daily prayer over the Hanukkah candles. Legal authorities, according to the *Washington Post*,[19] have said that school-sponsored pageants reenacting Christ's birth or the Hanukkah miracle are problematic, too, because they could suggest that the school endorses a particular belief.

Like other governmental entities, schools cannot prevent individuals or student organizations from posting religious displays in spaces where other forms of expression are permitted. For example, a school cannot stop students from displaying a menorah in a display case.[20]

Although many schools and teachers have tried to present something about Christmas and Hanukkah in the past, more recently they have also found themselves facing the holiday season's recognition and celebration of Kwanzaa, an African-American celebration started in 1966. (See the section on African-Americans.) Further compounding the problem of accommodating different celebrations has been the increase in the student population of Muslims and Jehovah's Witnesses, whose faiths also have celebrations during the December holiday season.

Passions are quite intense as school boards in increasingly diverse communities across the country try to be sensitive to everyone. Some parents demand that a wide variety of other religious and ethnic holidays get equal time with Christmas, while others protest any diminution of Christmas.

Paradoxically, holiday observances in public schools, which now seem to be pulling schools and parents apart, were first devised at the turn of the century as a way to bring people together. "Schools went into the holiday business as a way of creating Americanizing rituals for new immigrants," wrote Leigh Eric Schmidt of Princeton University in his book *Consumer Rites: The Buying and Selling of American Holidays*. Professor Schmidt added that tampering with Christmas can be offensive to many people. "Not having 'Silent Night' and having a generic celebration with reindeer and Santa is deeply alienating to more tradition-minded Christians."

Some school systems have gone much further by having a four-holiday "Festival of Lights" curriculum for children in primary grades. In this, children learn about Christmas, Hanukkah, Kwanzaa and Diwali (the Hindu year-end holiday).

Since 1776 the United States has grown from a nation of relatively few religious and ethnic differences to one of countless religious and ethnic groups. This ever-growing pluralism challenges the public schools and the higher-education system to deal creatively and sensitively with students professing a variety of religions (or, as the case may be, no religion at all).

From 1970 on, the United States has absorbed a bulge in the immigrant populations from parts of the world that previously had not been as visible or had a smaller presence in U.S. schools. As the journalist Bill Moyers noted, "World religions that once seemed esoteric and remote are becoming our next-door neighbors."[21] Many of the immigrants are not of European, Western or even African ancestry and consequently have brought to the United States religions and religious customs not readily familiar or recognizable to Americans.

The surge of cultural diversity in America extends well beyond race and national origin. The New Jersey State Board of Education, for instance, officially recognized no fewer than fifty-seven different religious holidays in the 1999-2000 school year. The list does not include December 25, since all public schools are traditionally closed that day during the mainstream Christmas/New Year vacations. The New Jersey ruling means that children who observe any of those holidays for religious purposes may be legally excused from school and must be given full opportunity to make up tests, special assignments, and the like.

The world has never seen a nation as religiously diverse as the United States. With the impact of new immigrants, the United States becomes more diverse, and some astounding changes occur. For example, Muslims now outnumber Episcopalians and Buddhists are building shrines in the Bible Belt. Some of the assumptions made in the past twenty years that guided religious expression in public are being put to the test with much more effort than previously noticed.

The Supreme Court has ruled that students' First Amendment rights to free religious expression allow them to pray privately in schools, whether alone or in groups, to read Bibles or other religious literature; and to organize religious clubs.

Far too many times it has been drawn to the nation's attention that school administrators, teachers and other school officials have overzealously applied the notion of church-state separation, pointing out their lack of understanding of the First Amendment. President Bill Clinton, in an effort to remedy this situation, arranged for his administration to distribute to every school district in the country a written statement explaining what types of religious expressions are allowed. He assessed that the constitution "does not require children to leave their religion at the school house door." Too many Americans have felt their faith is threatened by the mechanisms that are designed to protect their faith. This comes from the misguided public perceptions rather than the Supreme Court decisions separating church and state. The president has stated that too many times school leaders, upon hearing about a court decision rejecting officially sanctioned public school prayer, wrongly assume they must root out even expressions of faith practiced by individuals and private groups. The statement to be issued by the Department of Education would be advisory, carrying no power of law. It is to be a neutral recital of current law, not an attempt to advocate new policies or push new Constitutional interpretations.

Instead of prayer in schools, the drive should be for religion in schools: as a subject to be taught. Today, it is amazing of the ignorance of college students about the world's religions. When Christian students are asked to describe the differences between Abraham and Moses, or Passover, Yom Kippur or Hanukkah, few know. And many Jewish students aren't any more informed about the basics of Christianity. Neither can offer anything more than a few words or mumbled syllables to questions about Hinduism, Islam or Buddhism. Atheists and Agnostics tend to dismiss belief as irrelevant, huffing that it's a waste of class time to be discussing superstitions. This does not mean that schools should devote an inappropriate amount of time to what, if it were a university, might be called comparative religious studies. Students should not be crammed with so much information about Christmas, Passover, Ramadan or Diwali that they are left with the impression that religion is an endless series of festivals.

Marguerite Kelly writing in her "family almanac" columns in newspapers throughout the United States has given excellent advice when presenting a holiday program in schools. She states: "A holiday program is best when all children feel that their religion and their culture is respected. If music is presented then, of course, there must be a balance of Christmas, Hanukkah and Kwanzaa songs, and if there are any Muslim children there should be some Islamic chanting, too."

Addressing all groups she continues by saying, "It's up to Christians to be sensitive to the loneliness and the isolation their faith can bring to others, especially at Christmas, just as it is up to Jews and Muslims to let Christians celebrate the birth of Jesus without making them feel guilty about it. Tolerance and empathy are the essential ingredients of a happy school and a happy society, and knowledge, especially the knowledge of other religions, makes us more tolerant and empathic than anything else."

The following reproduction of the Questions and Answers bulletin titled "Religion in the Public School Curriculum," cosponsored by fourteen educational and religious associations, offers explanations and options that schools have to deal with this matter.

RELIGION IN THE PUBLIC SCHOOL CURRICULUM - QUESTIONS AND ANSWERS

Growing numbers of people in the United States think it is important to teach about religion in the public schools. "Teaching about religion" includes consideration of the beliefs and practices of religions; the role of religion in history and contemporary society; and religious themes in music, art, and literature. But what is the appropriate place of religion in the public school curriculum? How does one approach such issues as textbook content, values education, creation science and religious holidays?

The following questions and answers are designed to assist school boards as they make decisions about the curriculum and educators as they teach about religion in ways that are constitutionally permissible, educationally sound and sensitive to the beliefs of students and parents.

Q. Is it constitutional to teach about religion in public schools?

A. Yes. In the 1960s school prayer cases (which ruled against state-sponsored school prayer and Bible reading), the U.S. Supreme Court indicated that public school education may include teaching about religion. In *Abington v. Schempp*, Associate Justice Tom Clark wrote for the Court:

It might well be said that one's education is not complete without a study of comparative religion or the history of religion and its relationship to the advancement of civilization. It certainly may be said that the Bible is worthy of study for its literary and historic qualities. Nothing we have said here indicates that such study of the Bible or of religion, when presented objectively as part of a secular program of education, may not be effected consistently with the First Amendment.

Q. What is meant by "teaching about religion" in the public school?

A. The following statements distinguish between teaching about religion in public schools and religious indoctrination:

* The school's approach to religion is *academic*, not *devotional*.

* The school may strive for student awareness of religions, but should not press for student *acceptance* of any one religion.

* The school may sponsor *study* about religion, but may not sponsor the *practice* of religion.

* The school may *expose* students to a diversity of religious views, but may not *impose* any particular view.

326

* The school may *educate* about all religions, but may not *promote* or *denigrate* any religion.

* The school may inform the student about various beliefs, but should not seek to conform him or her to any particular belief.[22]

Q. Why should study about religion be included in the public school curriculum?

A. Because religion plays a significant role in history and society, study about religion is essential to understanding both the nation and the world. Omission of facts about religion can give students the false impression that the religious life of humankind is insignificant or unimportant. Failure to understand even the basic symbols, practices and concepts of the various religions makes much of history, literature, art and contemporary life unintelligible.

Study about religion is also important if students are to value religious liberty, the first freedom guaranteed in the Bill of Rights. Moreover, knowledge of the roles of religion in the past and present promotes cross-cultural understanding essential to democracy and world peace.

Q. Where does study about religion belong in the curriculum?

A. Wherever it naturally arises. On the secondary level, the social studies, literature and the arts offer many opportunities for the inclusion of information about religions and their ideas and themes. On the elementary level, natural opportunities arise in discussions of the family and community life and in instruction about festivals and different cultures. Many educators believe that integrating study about religion into existing courses is an educationally sound way to acquaint students with the role of religion in history and society.

Religion also may be taught about in special courses or units. Some secondary schools, for example, offer such courses as world religions, the Bible as literature, and the religious literature of the West and of the East.

Q. Do current textbooks teach about religion?

A. Rarely. Recent textbook studies conclude that most widely used textbooks largely ignore the role of religion in history and society. For example, readers of high school U.S. history texts learn little or nothing about the great colonial revivals, the struggles of minority faiths, the religious motivations of immigrants, the contributions of religious groups to many social movements, major episodes of religious intolerance and many other significant events of history. Education without appropriate attention to major religious influences and themes is incomplete education.

Q. How does teaching about religion relate to the teaching of values?

A. Teaching about religion is not the same as teaching values. The former is objective, academic study; the latter involves the teaching of particular ethical viewpoints or standards of behavior.

There are basic moral values that are recognized by the population at large (e.g., honesty, integrity, justice, compassion). These values can be taught in classes through discussion, by example, and by carrying out school policies. However, teachers may not invoke religious authority.

Public schools may teach about the various religious and nonreligious perspectives concerning the many complex moral issues confronting society, but such perspectives must be presented without adopting, sponsoring or denigrating one view against another.

327

Q. Is it constitutional to teach the biblical account of creation in the public schools?

A. Some states have passed laws requiring that creationist theory based on the biblical account be taught in the science classroom. The courts have found these laws to be unconstitutional on the ground that they promote a particular religious view. The Supreme Court has acknowledged, however, that a variety of scientific theories about origins can be appropriately taught in the science classroom. In *Edwards v. Aguillard*, the Court states:

Teaching a variety of scientific theories about the origins of humankind to schoolchildren might be validly done with the clear secular intent of enhancing the effectiveness of science instruction.

Though science instruction may not endorse or promote religious doctrine, the account of creation found in various scriptures may be discussed in a religious studies class or in any course that considers religious explanations for the origin of life.

Q. How should religious holidays be treated in the classroom?

A. Carefully. Religious holidays offer excellent opportunities to teach about religions in the elementary and secondary classroom. Recognition of, and information about, such holidays should focus on the origin, history and generally agreed-upon meaning of the observances. If the approach is objective, neither advancing nor inhibiting religion, it can foster among students understanding and mutual respect within and beyond the local community.[23]

*Please see the addendum to this section on **page 387**

RELIGION AND THE WORKPLACE
PRESIDENTIAL GUIDELINES ON RELIGIOUS FREEDOM IN THE WORKPLACE

The federal government under President Clinton in August 1997 issued a 13-page "Guidelines on Religious Exercise and Religious Expression in the Federal Workplace," the guideline for federal departments and agencies "shall permit personal religious expression by federal employees to the greatest extent possible, consistent with requirements of law and interests in workplace efficiency." The president expressed hope that state governments and private employers will use the federal guidelines as models for the protection of religious liberties in their workplaces as well.

The guidelines distinguish between work time and personal time at the workplace and between private work areas and those of general public access.

They distinguish between an employee's freedom of expression and the more limited freedom of supervisors, whose religious expression in many contexts, because of their position of authority, might reasonably appear "as coercive, even if it was not intended as such."

They say agency regulations on workers' speech or actions for the sake of workplace efficiency must be applied "even-handedly and with restraint": If a nonreligious form of personal expression is permitted in a particular context, another expression cannot ordinarily be prohibited in the same context simply because it is religious.

328

Included in the guidelines are concrete examples of practices permitted or barred by the rules.

Under a rule on freedom of expression in one's private work area two examples are cited:

"An employee may keep a Bible or Koran on her private desk and read it during breaks.

"An agency may restrict all posters, or posters of a certain size, in private work areas, or require that such posters be displayed facing the employee, and not on common walls; but the employer typically cannot single out religious or anti-religious posters for harsher or preferential treatment."

The guidelines say display of religious items in places of public access may be restricted if it might be reasonably construed as representing "government endorsement of religion."

Even in workplaces open to the public, the guidelines say, "federal employees may wear personal religious jewelry absent special circumstances—such as safety concerns—that might require a ban on all similar nonreligious jewelry."

"In their private time employees may discuss religion with willing coworkers in public spaces to the same extent as they may discuss other subjects, so long as the public would reasonably understand the religious expression to be that of the employees acting in their personal capacity," the guidelines say.

They say that "employees are permitted to engage in religious expression directed at fellow employees" and may even invite or try to persuade fellow employees to attend their places of worship or join their religion.

"But employees must refrain from such expression when a fellow employee asks that it stop or otherwise demonstrates that it is unwelcome," the document adds.

It says supervisors, because of their power to hire, promote and fire, must operate under different rules.

It says, for example, that a supervisor can invite co-workers to a family-related religious event like a Confirmation, bar mitzvah or wedding, "but a supervisor should not say to an employee: 'I didn't see you in church this week. I expect to see you there this Sunday.'"

Clinton and members of the religious leaders' coalition that worked on the new guidelines compared them to the guidelines on religious access in public schools issued by the Clinton administration two years prior.

ACCOMMODATING TIME OFF AND DRESS

Providing alternate scheduling around religious holidays* is the most requested religious accommodation. What holidays you'll be asked to accommodate, and how you respond, depends partly on the demographics in your area - and the law in your state.

*See the World Calendar or the Ethnic Cultures of America Calendar published by Education Extension Systems.

In Michigan, for instance, proposed legislation says an employer can't penalize employees who elect not to work on a religous holiday. Employees must give at least one week of advance notice. They are entitled to time off from work, but employers are not required to pay them during their absence.

Possible solutions to scheduling around religious holidays include finding voluntary substitutes or trades, flexible scheduling job reassignments or lateral transfer.

Perhaps the most difficult situation arises when employees who cover for workers who are absent for religions reasons, according to Ronald A. Lindsay and Elizabeth H. Bach, attorneys with Seyfarth, Shaw, Fairweather & Geraldson in Washington, D.C., and authors of "Prohibiting Discrimination Based on Religion: An Employer's Obligation," an SHRM White Paper (availableat http://w.w.w.shrm.org/whitepapers).

The Equal Employment Opportunity Commission's guidelines instruct that infrequent or temporary payment of overtime or other premium wages will be treated as a *de minimis* cost to the employer. In other words, an employer cannot claim such an accommodation would result in "undue hardship," they wrote. However, regular payments of such wages, or payment when a large number of employees must take off on the same day, may be an undue hardship - especially if the business enterprise is small or operating costs are high.

Another concern is accommodating a religious employee's dress or personal appearance. "Head coverings, robes, beards, face paints, religious insignias and symbols and other outward tokens of faith may deviate not only from employer dress codes but also from co-workers' expectations," say Lindsay and Bach.

In these cases, ask yourself whether a workplace dress code is really justified by business necessity. In manufacturing plants where loose garments could be caught in heavy machinery, robes and long shirts would not have to be accommodated. But in an office environment, Lindsey and Bach report, employers have been sanctioned for forbidding religious dress or head coverings, long hair required by faith and religious insignias or tokens of faith.

If other employees object to a religious worker's manifestations of faith, document the nature of the problem and your attempts at resolution, say Lindsay and Bach. "Explore with the religious employee exactly what he or she feels is required by his or her religious beliefs," they say. "Confirm your conversations in writing." Then ask the employees who object to explain their objections in writing.

"If there does not appear to be any way to mediate the dispute, make sure you have some written record of the exact nature of the "disturbance" that resulted, e.g., loud discussions, inability to concentrate on work, etc.," they say, "Courts are unlikely to be sympathetic to an employer that ordered an employee not to display or wear an item of religious apparel if the employer has nothing to support its claim that the employee's actions interfered with business operations."

Having basic information on employees' religious beliefs can help you better understand requests for accommodation. But it is still up to employers to make a decision to accommodate or not.

When weighing options, make it clear to employees that they may express their religious views - provided that doing so does not impose on the religious beliefs of others.

Also make it clear that you will make reasonable efforts to accommodate employees' religious expression but that your primary concern is achieving business objectives. For example, safety should always take precedence. If religious items or apparel pose a serious risk of getting tangled in heavy machinery, they should be banned. If they do not pose a risk or cause other legitimate business risks, you should lean toward accommodation, if possible.

Accommodating for religious holidays may involve as little as posting a bulletin board notice asking for an employee to volunteer to switch shifts. Flexible arrival and departure times, flexible work breaks, granting optional or floating "personal days," exchanging lunchtime for early departure time and creating staggered work schedules may also be effective solutions.

Consultant Sondra Meyer Raile, PHR, a senior consultant with Boas Associates, an Overland Park, KS-based management consulting firm, suggests that HR professionals ask themselves three questions to determine their reponse to accommodation requests:

- Are there reasons, others than costs involved, for granting or denying an employee's request?
- Have you granted other employees' religious requests?
- Has the employee offered a possible compromise?

Asking and answering these questions can help you frame responses to accommodation requests that are fair, consistent and based on business reasons.

Issues involving religious discrimination can't be eliminated, but fair treatment and expressions of concern by employers can go a long way towards improving employee relations and minimizing the risk of claims of unfair treatment, says Raile.

Basically, a good-faith effort is a good place to start.

1 Pennsylvania Historical Society

2 Shogdi Effendi, U.S. Baha'i News

3 U.S. Baha'i News, October, 1950

4 1991

5 Caroline Fraser, Atlantic Monthly, April, 1995

6 March 13, 1989

7 Peter Steinfels, the New York Times, March 13, 1989

8 Islamic Society of North America and demographers, as reported in the September 13, 1990, New York Times by Karen DeWitt

9 The Islam Society of North America has headquarters in Plainfield, Indiana.

10 The First Universal Nation, the Free Press

11 according to Yvonne Haddad, professor of Islamic history at the University of Massachusetts

12 also spelled Ka'abah

13 1991 Islamic Center celebration

14 Peter Steinfels, the New York Times , May 7, 1993

15 Peter Steinfels

16 J.R. Brown, keynote speaker at annual convention

17 July 23, 1990

18 the New York Times, December 21, 1995

19 December 15, 1995

20 Post article

21 PBS program, 1994

22 This answer is based on guidelines originally published by the Public Education Religion Studies Center at Wright State University.

23 Religion in the Public School Curriculum: Questions and Answers is sponsored jointly by:

American Academy of Religion
Department of Religion
501 Hall of Languages
Syracuse University
Syracuse, NY 13244-1170

American Federation of Teachers
555 New Jersey Ave., NW
Washington, DC 20001

Americans United Research Foundation *
900 Silver Spring Ave.
Silver Spring, MD 20910

Association for Supervision and Curriculum Development *
125 N. West St.
Alexandria, VA 22314-2798

Baptist Joint Committee on Public Affairs
200 Maryland Ave., NE
Washington, DC 20002

Christian Legal Society
PO Box 1492
Merrifield, VA 22116

National Association of Evangelicals
1430 K St., NW
Washington, DC 20005

National Conference of Christians and Jews
71 5th Ave.
New York, NY 10003

National Council of Churches of Christ in the USA
475 Riverside Drive
New York, NY 10115

National Council on Religion and Public Education *
Southwest Missouri State University
901 S. National Ave.
Springfield, MO 65804

American Association of School Administrators *
1801 N. Moore St.
Arlington, VA 22209

National Council for the Social Studies *
3501 Newark St., NW
Washington, DC 20016

National Education Association
1201 16th St., NW
Washington, DC 20036

National School Board Association1
680 Duke St.
Alexandria, VA 22314

* These organizations have materials available for teaching about religion in the public school curriculum.

CHAPTER XIV:
SOME ETHNIC THINGS
YOU SHOULD KNOW

Pamela Nelson of the Balch Institute has written that American culture has clearly altered the traditional wedding customs of most immigrant groups. Change has occurred quickly or over generations. Some traditions have become unworkable; others have been forgotten, others have been rediscovered; still others have survived intact although their underlying significance has changed. Yet despite change ethnic weddings are becoming an increasingly popular way to celebrate one's ethnic heritage and have been shaped into a unique American form that combines American values and resources with ethnic culture and pride. Included in discussion of ethnic groups are statements concerning wedding traditions that endure.

***

EUROPEAN ANCESTRY

In 1980 two-thirds of Californians were whites of European ancestry. By 1990, according to the U.S. Census Bureau figures, this figure had fallen to 57 percent. It is expected that by the end of the 1990s this figure will fall to below 50 percent, making California the first state in which ethnic and racial minorities together will constitute the majority.[1]

***

ETHNIC RITUAL IN THE UNITED STATES

The importance of some public rituals among new and old ethnic groups in the United States is an example of its enduring potency. Gina Bria, an anthropologist and kinship specialist at The Institute of Family Development, a social science research group in New York City, states: "Ritual paces our lives, it tells us what next step to take. It is a social process that allows us to have a public identity. It helps people coalesce around a culture that is spreading out."

***

As it has for generations, the restaurant business remains a popular portal into the middle class for newcomers. From Irish pubs, to Korean barbecues, to Indian and South American restaurants, Greek restaurants, Colombian coffee shops, Pakistani and Korean delis and increasingly Arab- and Turkish-owned restaurants and stores as well as new Polish restaurants and Spanish and Egyptian food stores.[2]

***

MUSIC

In the United States, immigrants bring and have brought their music and mix it with what they find here; the growth of the Spanish-speaking population, in particular, supports many forms of music. Other local communities, from Creoles on the bayou to Irish immigrants, also concoct music that suits their needs, for a Saturday-night dance or, perhaps, a private moment of introspection. Whether they reach a broad audience is a matter of aesthetics, entrepreneurship and pure luck. These music styles are largely below the radar of mass pop public; they nevertheless command large and loyal audiences. Some of these styles are: *Tejano* - this style combines the accordion-driven polkas and *cumbias* of Mexican *conjunto* music with modern touches, including synthesizers and version of rock songs; its audience is young Mexican-Americans, reaching from the Southwest to California.

Old-Timey and Bluegrass - Old Timey harks back to Appalachian string-band music, emphasizing melody and clarity, while bluegrass is more flamboyantly virtuosic. Together, they support festivals and clubs.

Dancehall - Speedy, singsong rapping in a Jamaican patois, over a stark reggae beat. Dancehall has been spread throughout Caribbean enclaves in this country.

Salsa Romantica - Love songs in Spanish, with sumptuous arrangements and sometimes a hint of Caribbean rhythms.

Contemporary Christian - not a musical style but a message in music that resembles current mainstream styles including hard rock and hip-hop.

Tropical - A catch-all term for up-tempo Caribbean music, from Cuban rhumba to Puerto Rican bomba and plena to Dominican merengue and all their hybrids. Styles vary from Dominican *bachatas* (ballads) to West African *soukous*.

Banda - Rural Mexico reaches California in the music of *bandas*, rowdy brass bands that carry *oompah* music to new heights of exuberance. This is heard at block parties and on radio stations across Southern California.

Bhangra - a musical style that is a hybrid of North Indian music (particularly Punjabi drumming of long; sinuous vocal lines) with contemporary Western rhythms and strategies, from house music to reggae to rapping. This music reaches South Asian fans in England and the United States.

***

ETHNIC PRESS

In 1996 the Ethnic Press, operating in the shadow of mainstream newspapers, has quietly been building circulation and advertising revenue. So diverse are the papers—several hundred in at least forty languages—that their overall presence is hard to quantify because no one group or organization compiles data on the Ethnic Press. Plus, most of them are privately owned. However, if you look at any big city newsstand you will immediately see how vibrant a presence the Ethnic Press has. For example, there are over sixty newspapers covering the Vietnamese community. Further, the Ethnic Press represents an untapped source of revenue for corporations wanting to tap the ethnic markets. Census figures show that some ethnic groups are better educated and more affluent than the general population. While 62 percent of all Arab-Americans have spent some time in college, only 45 percent of all Americans have; 36 percent of all Asians in the United States have a bachelor's degree or higher, compared with 20.3 percent of the general population. The median annual household income of Arab-Americans was $39,500 based on 1990 Census figures ($44,696 for Asian Indians). The median household income for all Americans was $33,105.

The Ethnic Press in 1996 faced the traditional problems the immigrant press faced in the past. That is: upward mobility can pull part of the core of their circulation areas. For example, Andrea Mantineo, the editor of *American Oggi*, an Italian daily based in Westwood, New Jersey, states, "Forty years ago our readership was mainly in places like Little Italy in New York City. Now they have moved and spread out, and that makes it difficult for us to track them down." Papers such as *American Oggi* are constantly wrestling with ideas on how to attract members of the second or third generations, who may not speak the language of their parents or grandparents and whose ties to the old country are tenuous. Many have introduced sections in English or are going bilingual.

Many of the older publications aimed at Western European immigrants are losing readers, while Latino, Chinese, Vietnamese and Russian papers are making circulation gains.

Benjamin Franklin published in 1732 the first ethnic newspaper, the *Philadelphische Zeitung*, a German-language newspaper. Since then, ethnic papers have played an important role in helping immigrants adjust to the United States.

Barbara Straus Reed, professor of journalism at Rutgers University and author of a book on the history of the ethnic press, states: "With the help of ethnic newspapers, immigrants can find local institutions within their communities that will make the transition easier."[3]

***

ETHNIC BUSINESS NICHES

As in the past, immigrant groups tend to carve out niche businesses for themselves. In the years since 1960 the new immigrants have done the same. Some successful niche businesses serving the broad community carved out by recent immigrant groups in the United States:[4]

PALESTINIANS: Run many mom-and-pop grocery stores in San Francisco, Detroit and elsewhere.

KOREANS: Already successful with small markets in big cities, they are opening bigger stores and dispersing to the suburbs and beyond, especially in Southern California. Also, dry cleaning stores.

VIETNAMESE: Small store-front parlors for trimming and polishing fingernails, especially in the Los Angeles area.

BARBADIANS: Short-haul trucking, especially in Brooklyn and Queens.

CHALDEANS: Iraqi Christians, many of whom own many convenience/liquor stores in the Detroit and San Diego areas.

CHINESE: Started and remain at the center of the toy wholesale business in Los Angeles, and now employ many Vietnamese, Korean and Hispanic people.

CAMBODIANS AND VIETNAMESE: Doughnut shops, particularly scattered throughout Southern California. The suppliers to these shops are also Southeast Asians.

ASIAN INDIANS: Economy hotels, as discussed in the section describing them.

LATINOS: Construction and Landscaping

***

CENSUS CLASSIFICATION

This is how, in 1990, the government classified people by race and ethnic backgrounds for purposes of checking its own racial and ethnic composition:

"Asian or Pacific Islander"—"A person having origins in any of the original peoples of the Far East, Southeast Asia, the Indian subcontinent or the Pacific Islands. This... includes China, India, Japan, Korea, the Philippine Islands and Samoa."

"Black"—"A person having origins in any of the black racial groups of Africa."

"Native American"—"A person having origins in any of the original people of North American and who maintains cultural identification through community recognition or tribal affiliation. American Indians or Alaskan Natives are usually identified as Native Americans."

"White"—"A person having origins in any of the original people of Europe, North Africa or the Middle East."

"Hispanic"—"A person of Mexican, Puerto Rican, Cuban, Central or South American or Spanish culture or origin, regardless of race."

***

The United States has been a multicultural society from its earliest days. One of the first groups in the U.S. to know this was the American businessman because in a capitalistic society which had an ever-flowing immigration policy and with an ethnic diverse population, it lended itself to creating a method of advertising to selling its products.

***

ETHNIC IMAGES IN ADVERTISING

American businessmen in the early nineteenth century and into the twentieth century used ethnic images in a negative sense because their appeal was largely to an Anglo-American audience. However, as we grew as a country and society, ethnic groups started to complain to the advertisers and the negative images were softened. Today, ethnic images tend to be positive rather than negative. As the Balch Institute of Philadelphia has successfully pointed out in both its exhibitions and tests, ethnic image continues to be used to sell products in today's national market and unflattering stereotypes of older ethnic groups have been disappearing and replaced by more positive images.

"Ethnic marketing" has become a familiar phrase in the advertising lexicon. All too often, though, "ethnic" is used to mean Asian, Black or Hispanic. However, by the late 1990s more true ethnic marketing started to take place by ethnic groups such as Russians, Greeks and others.

Ethnic images have been used in advertising places in and on trade cards, magazines, posters, container packaging, songsheets, records, radio commercials, movie commercials, television commercials, etc.

TEACH YOUR CHILDREN

- Remember that children are always listening. When parents reveal prejudice, intentionally or unintentionally, it paves the way for their children to resort to prejudicial behavior directly patterned after remarks they have overheard.
- Never permit—or practice yourself—the use of expressions degrading to any member of the family or any human being.
- Provide experiences for the children to associate with people who look, speak or worship differently so they learn a natural way to appreciate differences and similarities among people.
- Provide accurate and forthright answers regarding differences such as skin color and religion.
- Teach children to be sympathetic, understanding and compassionate. Try in every way possible to help them to accept themselves and others. If children grow into emotional maturity, they will not need to use hostility and prejudice as a crutch for their own personality inadequacies. Part of this process of developing emotional comfort is becoming secure in their own groups—family, kin, church, school or child care. Then they will be less likely to feel threatened when they come in contact with people of other groups.[5]

[1] the *New York Times*, January 23, 1992

[2] the *New York Times,* January 27, 1995

[3] Sreenath Sreenivasan, the *New York Times*, July 22, 1996

[4] Paul M. Ong, professor of public policy at the University of California at Los Angeles, and Joel Kotkin, author of *Tribes* (1993), a study of the global ethnic Diaspora, the Chaldean Federation of America

[5] Ron L. Pitzer, family sociologist, University of Minnesota

CHAPTER XV:
SUMMARY

The United States is a nation to whose shores have come people from every continent, and history records their priceless contributions. From the beginning, the quality of life in the United States has been ennobled and enriched by the newcomers, and city and village streets have resounded with the music of many languages. It is a rich heritage, one to be nurtured, encouraged, cherished.[1]

From nearly every corner of the world individuals have streamed to America with a dream in search of fulfillment that eluded them and their families and ancestors in their beloved homelands.

In 1942 Franklin Delano Roosevelt uttered these inspiring words: "The principle on which this country was founded and by which it has always been governed is that Americanism is not, and never was, a matter of race and ancestry."[2]

America is enhanced by plurality. As Lawrence H. Fuchs wrote in *The American Kaleidoscope: Race, Ethnicity and the Civic Culture*, America is defined by both the *Pluribus* and the *Unum*; we are similar because we are different.

It does well for we as Americans to remember just what a diverse nation the United States is, and what Americans have accomplished in slightly over 200 years of history. The United States is a country that is a vibrant mix of cultures. Its people work side by side every day in factories, offices and governments, serving together in the armed forces and going to school together. Men and women of many races and cultures, for example, teach children in U.S. schools and share ideals and goals as they join in the common cause of educating the nation's future.

Sometimes we are too quick and prone to criticize our schools and teachers for some of the sociological ills that appear on our landscape. But we fail to acknowledge the tremendous good teachers have done to help Americans learn (at an early age) the respect for each other that is exemplified each day in the classrooms and on the playing fields of America.

It is true that our neighborhoods, schools and places change in their ethnic make-up. Older ethnic groups from Europe such as the English, Irish, Jewish, Polish, Italians, Germans and others are seeing their neighborhoods transformed by new Asian and Latino (Hispanic) immigrants—just as they themselves transformed the landscape when they arrived seventy-five to a hundred years ago.

Mark Shields, a well-known journalist, had it right when he wrote: "Every living American, with the exception of those whose ancestors were here to greet Columbus or were brought here against their will in chains, is the direct descendent of immigrants. The immigrant saga has profoundly influenced American politics and society. To leave family, friends and the familiar in order to strike out across the sea or the continent to a place you have never seen, to live among people you have never met, to speak a language you may have never heard, is an act of enormous courage. But to be an immigrant is also to be an optimist, to believe that somewhere I will be free to have a chance to make things better, if not immediately for myself, then for those who come after me."

The civil rights leader Jesse Jackson expanded upon Shields' remarks when he said, "America is like a quilt—many pieces, many colors, many sizes, and woven and held together by a common thread." It is that single thread of similarity that we should acknowledge. The quilt metaphor is a good one. Think about it: each patch adds a special nuance of color, texture, strength and utility to the combined fabric. Considering people, as opposed to a quilt, this means inherent in our diversity is a great potential, not the plague of prejudice. Our assets are the many differences we have among us. We must respect, cherish and appreciate (we most often do) each other's cultures, languages and thinking, and out of this comes a distinctive American culture, which is unlike all others in the world.

In the *Washington Post*, journalist Richard Cohen wrote, "Throughout Europe, it has been found that ethnic groups get along best by mail. For some reason, outside the United States and a few other countries, the storied pot does not melt, it explodes." Because America is made of many cultures, Americans have learned a particular and unique type of respect for one another. This produces behaviors like the one that keeps ancestors of Western countries shoeless in Japanese- or Asian-American homes; has Gentiles putting on yarmulkes at Jewish bar mitzvahs, sitting Shiva or other religious services; and has Jewish organizations manning Catholic hospitals on Christmas Day so the Gentile staff and volunteers can have the holiday at home with their families. We now celebrate some ethnic holidays that are not our own as if they were.

James H. Billington of the Smithsonian Institute wrote in the July/August 1995 issue of *Civilization* magazine:

> "As a historian, I see America itself increasingly becoming a world civilization—not just through the intertwining of national economies, but also through internal, demographic evolution. We have added a new wave of largely Asian and Latin American immigrants to our population of European, African and Native American ancestry.

> In the process, we are challenging ourselves to realize more fully an ideal inherent in our history: that democracy can work on a continental scale in a multiethnic and multireligious society—through collective dynamism that comes when freedom of opportunity is combined with the rule of law and open access to an ever increasing body of knowledge.

> America is a country that has always added without subtracting. And as we enter a time of increasing dependence on information, our historic investment in the life of the mind provides us with a common agenda in which the horizons of freedom can remain infinite despite growing limitations in the physical world."

Billington continues by pointing out what a great responsibility and duty teachers and others at all levels of the education community must understand. He states: "Many of our educators appear indifferent to ever contemptuous of their historical function of transmitting a basic understanding of our culture from one generation to the next. Instead of expanding and making more inclusive the idea of America, some academics would foster a balkanized America that assures there are no national traditions or shared values. Precisely because we embrace diversity, Americans have a special need to transmit to the young an understanding and respect for our durable constitutional system, our public institutions and our religious roots. The bridges we need to build to other cultures will not be solid unless they begin with foundations that are sunk deep in our own native ground."

University presidents should read and reread what Billington wrote and take it to heart with regards to their responsibilities. It is their responsibility to see that faculty members pass on these true culture forms and not have faculty members try to measure seventeenth-, eighteenth-, and nineteenth-century activities with twenty-first century information and values. It is insufficient for the university president to sit back and do nothing to correct misinformation while hiding behind "academic freedom."

In his book *Ethnic Identity: The Transformation of White America*, Richard D. Alba wrote the following: "Ethnicity, which had once been understood as exclusive—if you are Jewish you cannot be Irish Catholic—is now inclusive." His main discovery in researching the book (published in 1990) was the existence of a new group called "European Americans." It no longer matters where your ancestors came from in Europe. What matters is that your roots somewhere at some time were in Europe.

Alan Wolfe of the New School for Social Research points out if there really are "European Americans," then a fundamental change has taken place in the way white Americans think about their roots. They are emphasizing universality, not particularity. Ethnicity, then, which once implied difference, is increasingly suggesting sameness. The discovery of "European Americans" also means that whiteness is crucial to identity. (Please refer to the section on the term "African-American.")

Wolfe and Alba may be missing a point about why some Americans refer to themselves or others as European Americans. It may be because of the two, three, or four generations of intermarriage that has occurred in the United States. For example, it was estimated that in 1990 only 20 percent of white marriages had husbands and wives of the same ethnic background. About 50 percent of Jews marry outside their ethnic groups, and, according to Ben Wattenberg in *The First Universal Nation*, about 80 percent of Polish-Italian-Irish-Americans now marry outside their ethnic group. Here I'd like to point out my own family's situation.

As of the writing of this book, my wife and I have four grandchildren. Because we are from different ethnic backgrounds, both of our daughters were of a mixed ethnic background. They married men who are of different backgrounds, as well. Thus, their children have an even more diverse ethnic makeup:

Jonathon, Jason and Jackson Hollawell are:		And Katie Keller is	
3/10 English	30.0 %	3/8 Pennsylvania Dutch	37.5 %
1/4 Italian	25 %	1/4 Italian	25 %
1/4 Polish	25 %	3/16 German	18.6 %
1/12 Welsh	12.5 %	1/12 English	8.4 %
1/16 German	6.3 %	1/12 Welsh	8.4 %
Other	2 %	Other	2 %

Yet there doesn't seem to be any white European traditions or customs in the same sense that ethnic traditions, holidays or customs are observed. Again, using the above example, these children take part in particular ethnic celebrations. Whether those traditions are carried beyond their generation remains to be seen.

Lois Pierce, ethnic diversity director of the Association of Bridal Consultants, gives this statement some credibility when she states: "The culture in American society is changing. People are marrying now for the person rather than the ethnic type. This makes it more interesting and unique to learn about other cultures and to teach other people about the culture itself."

MULTI-RACIAL AMERICA

No book concerning ethnic cultures can be complete without discussing some of the changes taking place in our country with reference to children of mixed racial marriages. Many prominent social scientists, newspaper columnists, sociologists and demographers have studied and commented on this matter. In order to properly understand this group of Americans and in order to relate pertinent information to you, I have studied the writings of Nathan Glazer, Amitai Etzioni, Stanley Crouch, Morton Kondracke, Ben Wattenberg, Orlando Patterson, James Glassman, Michael Fletcher, George Will and others.

In the early 1990s the U.S. Office of Management and Budget along with the U.S. Census Bureau was confronted with a proposal to add a new category "multiracial" to its racial classifications of White, Black, Native American, Aleut and Eskimo, Asian and Pacific Islanders, and others.

Legislation was introduced in Congress to require such a check off in the 2000 census. Many referred to this as the "Tiger Woods Bill." Woods, a sensational young golfer in the 1990s considers himself multiracial. He states, "Growing up, I came up with this name: 'Cablinasian'"—since his heritage is one-eighth Caucasian, one-fourth Black, one-eighth American Indian, one-fourth Chinese and one-fourth Thai.

Between 1960 and 1998 the number of interracial couples in the United States has increased more than tenfold to 1.6 million, including marriages involving Hispanics. Such unions accounted for about 4 percent of U.S. marriages, a share that is expected to mushroom in future years. Because of this there was powerful evidence that many Americans were jettisoning old prejudices as never before. The number of children from interracial marriages jumped to 2.3 million by mid-1998.

Not only are interracial unions complicating predictions about the future racial makeup of the nation, they are calling into question widely understood concepts of race. Remember that it wasn't until 1967 that the U.S. Supreme Court ruled anti-miscegenation laws unconstitutional, wiping those statutes off the books in Virginia and 15 other states.

By the end of 1998, almost one-third of U.S. born Hispanics ages 25 to 34 were married to non-Hispanic whites. In addition, 36 percent of young Asian Pacific American men born in the United States marry white women, and 45 percent of U.S. born Asian Pacific American women took white husbands. The vast majority of American Indians also marry whites.

The high rates of interracial marriage and evolving notions of race forced the federal government to rethink the types of categories and classifications it will use in the 2000 census. One group for which interracial marriage (while increasing) remained far lower than those of other racial minorities was African-Americans. The only figures available concerning the rate of white-black marriages was from the 1960 to 1990 census. They showed the figures tripled from 1.7 percent to 6 percent of all marriages of African-Americans. To many African-Americans, say researchers who have studied the issue, to marry a white is to betray their race, an attitude that is less prevalent among Asian-Americans and Hispanics. A reason for this is that these two groups came from societies where interracial marriage was more common.

This whole matter caused a huge controversy and brought up the issue of why the census has gotten so deeply into trying to define racial classifications. Mixed race Americans and their parents did not like the category of "other" which was used in the 1990 census, because it never has been fully recognized as an independent grouping. So, the question why not introduce a new "multiracial" category?

This very idea infuriated some leaders of the African-American community, arguing that it reflects a drive to undermine black solidarity. Fears were expressed that in cities where blacks now hold majorities, the new category will divide them and undermine their dominance. Also, African-American leaders objected to the new multiracial category because race data is used to enforce civil rights legislation in many fields. Liberal groups opposed it because they feared it would dilute their political power.

After a three-year struggle with the question of how best to describe this segment of Americans, a federal task force came up with a novel answer: Let the population describe itself. People in the multiracial group will now be allowed to identify themselves by as many of the five official racial categories as they see fit. This was deemed preferable than the alternative of checking "other."

In summary, race and ethnicity are not fixed, easily definable scientific categories. And Americans need not go beyond their own borders to see this. We easily forget that as late as the beginning of World

War II, Jews in the United States were considered a separate "race" by many Christian Americans.

Irish-Americans can tell a similar story about their ancestors. Until the early decades of the twentieth century, the Irish-Catholic "race" was stereotyped in Britain and the U.S. as subhuman, lazy and violent in both scientific and popular writings. The Irish, like the Italians—another group previously considered "nonwhite"—had to struggle hard for their reclassification into the white "race."

Distinguishing between race and ethnicity is an ingrained part of Americans' racial ideology.

Stanley Crouch, writing in the *New York Times Magazine,* September 29, 1996, stated the following: "I am fairly sure that race, as we are currently obsessed with will cease to mean as much 100 years from today. The reasons are basic—some technological, others culture."

In the future, definition by racial, ethnic and sexual groups will most probably have ceased to be the foundation of special interest power. Ten decades up the road, few people will take seriously, accept or submit to any forms of segregation that are marching under the intellectually ragged flag of diversity. The idea that your background will determine your occupation, taste, romantic preference or any other thing will dissolve in favor of your perceived identity, as defined by your class, livelihood, and cultural preferences. Americans of the future will find themselves surrounded in every direction by people who are part Asian, part Latin, part African, part European, and part American Indian.

John Silber, president of Boston University, has pointed out and stressed (when discussing language) that in no other nation do so many people, spread over so large an area, speak the same language as in the United States. This nation, which Lincoln said is dedicated to a proposition, is a creedal nation, founded on shared affirmation, not on ethnicity. Here, Silber said, ethnicity is a "private matter." Various ethnic groups celebrate their saints and other sources of communal pride. Such private and voluntary undertakings are splendid. However, the government properly recognizes only Americans, not ethnic groups.[3]

No other country can come close to claiming the diversity with which the United States interacts with the world. In a sense Americans are so diverse that we look like the world. Or, to put it another way, the world is coming to look like us.

We have experienced no historically unprecedented difficulties in assimilating the largely non-European immigrants of the last quarter of the twentieth century into American society. They (Asian Latin American immigrants) are, on the whole, doing what previous waves of new Americans have done—they are finding their way, regardless of the continent from which they came.

Sociologists have long observed that a major reason the United States experiences few confrontations along lines of class is that people in this country believe they can move from one economic stratum to another—and regularly do so. For instance, workers become foremen, and foremen become small businessmen, who are considered middle class. There are no sharp class demarcation lines here, based on heredity, as there are in Britain.

Americans are not perfect. We're not even as good as we can get—yet. In 1999 we had some racial and ethnic problems we still had to solve. Some of these problems were new ones: as stated elsewhere in this book, in the fifty years before 1965, about 11 million immigrants came to the United States, and about 75 percent of them were of white European ancestry. Between 1965 and 1991 about 14 million immigrants entered the U.S.—27 percent more people in half the time, and about 85 percent of these were not of white European ancestry. Hence, there are new racial and ethnic problems to solve. We won't learn to solve these issues unless (as we did before) we take time to simply learn about each other. But we've come a long way in the 225 years since Thomas Jefferson penned the immortal words of the nation's most precious document.

Besides sharing in the nation's triumphs, Americans have endured many difficulties, wars, depressions, recessions and tragedies. Yet enduring doesn't mean agreeing all the time. We have had our share of disagreements. But isn't that part of what the United States is all about? The right to disagree. And more important, to be ourselves.

As we have now arrived at the next millennium, and Americans look forward to it, it is also useful to look back at the past century to try to better understand where we are versus where we were as the country approached the twentieth century with reference to certain ethnic groups. I haven't tried to compare all groups because many had yet to start their great migration until after the twentieth century was well started. African-Americans, certain white ethnic groups here at the time and Asian-Americans are all very different today from what they were in 1899.

As the United States entered the twentieth century, half of the African-American population of this country could not read or write. Most Chinese-Americans lived in crime-ridden Chinatowns. Most of the Irish were unskilled laborers. Most Jews were poor. Most Italians hadn't arrived yet.

All of these groups—and others—rose because of tremendous efforts that they made to improve themselves. It was not just that other people's "perceptions" of them changed. Reality changed.

Thomas Sowell, a Stanford University professor who has studied and written about America's racial and ethnic groups, states: "In reality, Blacks were advancing long before the civil rights demonstrations of the 1950s and 1960s and long before anyone even heard of 'Affirmative Action.'" He continues: "Asian-Americans do not have any famous leaders or any videotaped demonstrations and historic speeches that can be replayed endlessly on television to create the illusion that their advancement came from moral melodrama and political deliverance. The story of their advancement over the past hundred years is largely the story of thousands of little-noticed individual struggles to get better education, to save their money and to do all the many undramatic internal improvements that pay off in the long run.

"The role of the Catholic Church during generations of struggle in the Irish-American community, as well as in many other forms of self-improvement, was a crucial part of the story of the rise of that community and the eventual disappearance of signs that read, 'No Irish Need Apply.'"

The immigrant Jews of a century ago had many things to overcome besides anti-Semitism. Even the existing German-Jewish community in America was visibly ashamed of these newcomers from Eastern Europe and constantly preached to them the virtues of better behavior.

One of the most remarkable stories about African-American self-improvement is the history of all black Dunbar High School in Washington, DC, which had an outstanding record of academic achievement from the 1870s to the 1950s.

Sowell ends up by saying, if we want to know what is likely to work in the future with new immigrant groups, we need to look at what has worked in the past.

It is worth repeating something that I stated on the first page of the acknowledgments section of the book: I have tried to be accurate and fair in interpreting and recording the data I obtained for each ethnic group. However, sometimes the data available precluded me from writing to the same extent about all ethnic groups. The information that may not be included concerns primarily customs and holidays of a particular ethnic group. Therefore if you discover something of this nature that is missing I would be most grateful if you would write to me and detail this information so I can include it in future revised editions.

Please send it to:
Educational Extension Systems
c/o P.R. Fischetti
PO Box 472
Waynesboro, PA 17268

[1] Joint National Committee on Languages and Council for International Studies.

[2] Lawrence H. Fuchs

[3] George Will

INDEX

A

D

F

G

H

Halaals, 315
Halakhah, 320
Haman, 84
hamantaschen, 84
Hamilton, Alexander, 16
Hammond, Ruth, 118
Hampartzoom, 263
Hancock, Ian, 34, 80
Hangawi-Nai, 131
Han-ka-wee, 131
Hans Christian Anderson Day, 51
Hanukkah, 83-84, 284
    in public schools, 323-324
haole, 106
Hare Krishna
    alleged child abuse in, 305
    followers in U.S., 304, 306
    international followers, 305, 306
    origins of, 304
    tenets of, 304
Hargobind, Guru, 134
Harlem Day, 237
Harmohindar Singh, 136
Harmonites, 225
haroseth, 85
Harper's Ferry, 231
Harvard Encyclopedia of American Ethnic Groups,
9, 10, 16, 39, 215, 268, 277
Hasidic Jews, *see* Jews, Hasidic
Hasidim, *see* Jews, Hasidic
Hawaii
    American Pacific Islanders in, 105
    Chinese in, 112
    Filipinos in, 106, 115
    Japanese in, 123
    Portuguese in, 73
    Puerto Ricans in, 171
    racial harmony in, 106
Hawaiians, 105
    holidays and customs of, 106-107
    native, 106
Hawley, John S., 306
headship veil, 216
Heaton, Tim, 221
Hedjra, 318
Hee Haw, 209

Heidi Festival, 281
Height, Dorothy, 234
Hess, Gerry
hex signs, 226
Hickey, James Cardinal, 19
Hidden in Plain View; A Secret Story of Quilts and
    the Underground Railway, 241
Hidjra, *see* Hedjra
Highlanders, 45
Highland Games, 44, 46
Higman, J. 81
hijab, 268, 311, 312-313
Hinckley, Gordon, 219, 220
Hindu calendar, *see* calendars
Hinduism
    among Jains, 120
    Asian Indian, 139, 140
    conflict with Muslims, 307
    deities of, 308
    Dvaita school of, 307
    holidays and customs of, 307-309
    in the U.S., 308
    leaders of, 306
    symbols of, 323
    tenets of, 306-307
    wedding customs of, 309
Hispanic Business Magazine, 158
Hispanic Day, 170
Hispanic Heritage Month, 154
Hispanic Policy Development Project, 152
Hispanics, 339. *See also* Latinos
    business ownership of, 156-157
    derogatory connotation of term, 154
    diversity among, 153, 154, 155
    ethnic population statistics for, 153
    friction among, 155
    interracial marriages of, 347
    meanings of term, 155
    numbers in U.S., 152
    religions of, 152, 154
History of Ellis Island, 9
The History of Us for Children Ages 8 to 13, 190
Hitler, Adolf, 11
Hmong
    difficulty adapting to U.S., 117, 118
    holidays and customs of, 118

J

K

M

P

Paca, William, 71
Paczki Day, 93
padrone system
    among Greeks, 67
    among Italians, 69
pagans. *See also* Wicca
    tenets of, 320
Pahiyas Festival, 121
Pakistan Day Festival, 134
Pakistanis
    holidays and customs of, 134
    numbers in U.S., 134
    occupations of, 134, 139
    religions of, 134
Palaians, 105
Palestinians
    holidays and customs of, 271
    numbers in U.S., 271
    occupations of, 338
    religions of, 271
    wedding customs of, 272
Palm Sunday, 296
Panamanians
    holidays and customs of, 170
    numbers in U.S., 170
    religions of, 170
The Pariah Syndrome, 80
Parks, Rosa, 238
Paryushana Parva, 121
Passover, 85, 284
Patronage of the Mother, 295
Patterson, Orlando, 346
Pavarana, 293-294
Pawnee, 200
Pehum Ben, 111
penas, 246
Penn, William, 201, 217, 281
Pennsylvania. *See also* Philadelphia; Pittsburg
    Amish in, 201
    Arab-Americans in, 259
    Brethren, in, 216
    Croats in, 63
    Germans in, 32
    Hungarians in, 279

    Irish in, 42
    Italians in, 69
    Lithuanians in, 90
    Mennonites in, 215
    Moravians in, 217
    Poles in, 92
    Portuguese in, 73
    Puerto Ricans in, 171
    Russians in, 95
    Scotch-Irish in, 44
    Serbs in, 64
    Sikhs in, 135
    Slovaks in, 280
    Slovenes in, 66
    Swedes in, 55
    Swiss in, 281
    Ukranians in, 96
    Welsh in, 47
    Yugoslavians in, 62
Pennsylvania Dutch. *See also* Amish; Germans;
    Mennonites
    dialects of, 225
    holidays and customs of, 226
    numbers in U.S., 225
    origins of, 225
    religions of, 225
pentagram, 321
Pentateuch, 84
Pentecost, 297, 304
Pentecostals
    African-American, 233, 234
Perea, Juan F., 23
Persia, 84
Peruvian Independence Day, 253
Peruvians
    holidays and customs of, 253
    numbers in U.S., 253
    occupations of, 253
    reasons for immigration of, 253
    religions of, 253
Peters, Jacquelyn C., 241
peyotism, 11, 198. *See also* Native American
Church
Phanney, Allison Jr., 298
Philadelphia. *See also* Pennsylvania
    African-Americans in, 230

Q

R

S

U

Y

On December 18, 1999, President William J. Clinton issued new guidelines clarifying how public schools can work with religious group without violating the constitutional separation of church and state. He stressed the importance of faith to a well-rounded education. "Common sense says that faith and faith-based organizations from all religious backgrounds can play an important role in helping children to reach their fullest potential. Our new guidelines will help them work together on common ground to meet constitutional muster, to avoid making students uncomfortable because they come from different religious traditions, while helping students make the most of their God-given talents," the president said.

Overall, the guidelines expand on a list of do's and don'ts published in 1995. The president emphasized a new element: encouraging schools to actively invite churches and religious organizations to partner with them in a wide array of programs during and after school, including school safety, student literacy, and discipline.

"Finding the proper place for faith in our schools is a complex and emotional matter for many Americans. But I never believed the Constitution required our schools to be religion-free zones, or that our children must check their faith at the schoolhouse door." Clinton mentioned, for example, that students have the right to pray privately, the right to say grace, the right to read the Bible, the right to meet in religious groups on school grounds, and the right to use school facilities just like any other groups do, without saying what they don't have the right to do.

The revised education guidelines say that students have the rights to express their religious beliefs in homework artwork, "free of discrimination based on the religious content of their submissions."

In describing the new partnerships, the guidelines emphasize that "it is not appropriate for members of faith communities to use their involvement in public schools as an occasion to encourage participation in religious activity.

They warn religious crisis counselors not to proselytize while students are emotionally sensitive. They tell schools not to hang religious symbols in classrooms, and not to condition grades on participation in religious activity.

Most important, they tell schools not to limit participation in programs to religious groups but make them equally accessible to secular organizations.

"School officials may not endorse or favor religious activity or doctrine, coerce participation in religious activity, or seek to impose their religious beliefs on impressionable children." So wrote Education Secretary Dick Riley in his report to the school principals.

The guidance given to more than 100,00 schools about forming partnerships with religious groups includes:

- Ensuring all activities and programs provided by the groups are "purely secular."

- Selecting student participants without regard to their religion.

- Telling volunteers not to pray with students or preach about faith.

- Recommending that schools put a partnership agreement in wiring and make sure any space used for teaching is free of religious symbols.

It should be noted that the proper role of faith in schools continues to be widely debated. Still, new areas of cooperation between religious groups and civil libertarians, especially in schools, have emerged during the decade of the 1990s.

Note: This information was compiled from news reports by the *Associated Press* and the *Washington Post*.

DATE DUE

DEC 1 9 2005		
NOV 0 5 2002		
APR 0 6 2003	JUN 2 5 2008	
JUN 2 2 2003		
JUN 2 6 2005		
MAR 2 9 2006		
APR 0 4 2006		
DEC 1 4 2006		
APR 1 6 2007		
JUN 2 5 2008		

Demco, Inc. 38-293

WITHDRAWN